D0800848

AVATARS!

Exploring and Building
Virtual Worlds
on the Internet

Bruce Damer

POCKET IN BACK OF BOOK
CONTAINS ___1___ COMPUTER DISK(S)

CD-ROM

 Peachpit Press

Avatars!
Exploring and Building Virtual Worlds on the Internet
Bruce Damer

Peachpit Press
1249 Eighth Street
Berkeley, CA 94710
510/524-2178
800-283-9444
510/524-2221 (fax)

Find us on the World Wide Web at:
http://www.peachpit.com

Find the *Avatars!* Web site at:
http://www.digitalspace.com/avatars

Peachpit Press is a division of Addison Wesley Longman

Editor: Jeremy Judson
Copyeditor: Jackie Dove
Interior design: Richard Walker
Production: Richard Walker, Kate Reber
Cover illustration: Steve DiPaola, Ali Ebtekar, Stasia McGehee

4-2-98

ISBN 0-201-68840-9

9 8 7 6 5 4 3 2 1

Dedication

This book is dedicated to my parents, Enid and Warren Damer

and

to the loving memory of my sister, Renee Williams

Acknowledgments

I would like to extend my heartfelt thanks to the following people and companies for their help in making this book possible. Many of these people built avatar cyberspace for the rest of us to enjoy, while others were pioneering users who showed us how to live in a virtual world.

I would like to personally thank **Mark Pesce** for being an inspiration in how to stay creative and stay free. A big hug for **Wendy Sue Noah** for days spent driving from San Francisco to Boulder Creek to beta test chapters with the virtual worlds. **Allan Lundell, Sun McNamee,** members of the cybertribe, and **Ranger John Turner and family**, are all kind neighbors and kept me fed and in contact with humanity during some very isolated times. Lastly, I could not have lived without the whole Boulder Creek community and its redwoods keeping life safe, clean, wet, and green.

Thanks to the world makers

I would like to gratefully acknowledge the support of the people and the companies whose virtual world software is featured in the book and included on the CD-ROM:

Dave Gobel, Dave Leahy, Wolf Schmidt, Ron Britvich, Russell Freeland, Cole Larson, Maclen Marvit, Andrea Gallagher, Danny Viescas, Misty West, Leif Bennett and **Rob Schmultz** all formerly of *Worlds Incorporated* for bringing us the first wave of avatar cyberspace. **Konstantin Guericke, Dawn Drake, Dia Cheney, Bob Rockwell, Walter Schwartz, Rob Rothfarb,** and the whole team from *Black Sun Interactive*. **Cliff Figallo,** who was working at *Virtual Places/GNNe* (he is now an independent consultant) for giving me a great history of the WELL and his past community experiences. I would also like to thank **Udi Shapiro** and **Mike Yudin** of the *Ubique* and *Virtual Places* teams who work with *America Online*. **Reid Hoffman, Tony Christopher, Judith Rubin, Tammy Sims, Greg Oberfield,** and the whole WorldsAway team at *Fujitsu Software Corporation*. **Katherine Bretz,** also of *Fujitsu,* for her community building efforts in the avatar realm. **Skuli Mogensen, Rick Denny, Andrew de Vries, Gudjon Mar Gudjonsson, Sigurdur Olafsson,** and the whole team at *OZ Interactive*. **Scott Lewis, Jim Larson, Rocky Harris,** and the whole *Intel* team for their support of Moondo and Moondo II. **Linda Stone, David Kerlander, Manny Vellon,** and the whole *Microsoft* team for their careful review of the Comic Chat chapter and for hosting me so warmly at Microsoft and touring me through V-Chat. **Steve DiPaola, Kevin George, John Wentworth, Stasia McGehee, Orca Starbuck, Eric Budin, Drew Lanham, J.M. Valera, J.R. Manes,** and the whole *Onlive Technologies* team for their help on Traveler. **Jim Bumgardner, Mark Jeffrey, John Throckmorton, Sean Calhoon,** and all of *The Palace* teams from Hillsboro Oregon and Burbank California. **Janet McAndless** and the team at *Sony Pictures ImageWorks* for meeting me in Sony

Community Place Browser **Randy Farmer, Chip Morningstar, Benita Kenn, Matthew Burgess,** and everyone working on the Microcosm project for *Electric Communities.* **Dan Greening** and **Glenn Crocker** of *Chaco Communications* for their work on Pueblo. **Kayla Block** and the team at *Sensemedia* for bringing us ChibaMOO-The Sprawl **Merilee Kern** and **Mike Hilgenberg** of IDS, for their support on the section on V-Realm. **Tim Takeuchi** and his team at *NTT Software,* for their help in bringing me up to speed inside InterSpace. **Linda Lubken** of *Sierra Online* for supporting our coverage of The Realm in Gaming Worlds. **Mike Sellers,** formerly of *3DO,* for introducing me to Meridian 59.

Thanks to the studios, artists, and tool makers

The creative community that designs worlds, avatars, and tools are an integral part of this community and provided essential support and content for this book.

Saul Kato of *Sven Technologies,* for his excellent work in Avatar Maker (find it on the CD-ROM!) The great folks at *ParaGraph International,* including **Gregory Slayton, John Poluektov,** and **Leonid Kitainik,** for providing Internet Space Builder, a first class world builder created by their team in Moscow (on the CD-ROM, too!). **Todd Goldenbaum** (now independent), **John Shiple, Mark Meadows, Lisa Goldman, Gever Tulley, James Waldrop,** and the whole team at *Construct Internet Design,* for showing what a great VRML studio can be. **Tim Riley** and **Patrick Mahoney** of *dFORM Internet Design,* for believing in the Biota mission. **Peter Hughes** (now independent), **Eric Chen,** and **John Sculley** of *Live Picture/Realspace,* for developing the technologies to make us suspend our disbelief in avatars and their worlds. **C. Scott Young, Barrett Fox, Frank Revi,** and **Eli Sagiv,** for being there and being creative. **Paul Godwin** and **Phil Harrington,** for creating the *Voce* experience and showing the world new magic in sound, music, and voice through avatar cyberspace. **Fabrice Florin** of *Zenda Studios,* for innovating game play to enliven social worlds and for a great interview in the Palace. **Michael Powers** of *Insideout* for encouragement, teamwork on courses and conferences, and for agreeing to cross reference each other's books.

Appreciation to the students, researchers, and philosophers of virtual worlds

Those who study, ponder, test, present, decompose, and wax poetic about virtual worlds have been key in moving forward my understanding of the almost infinite size of this new medium. **Derrick DeKerckkhove** of the *Marshall McLuhan* program of the *University of Toronto,* for helping spread the medium and the message of avatars around the global village. **Patrice Arnera, Eric, Phillipe, Maurice,** and the other students of *Sophia-Antipolis University* in France, for providing five wonderful days in Florence Italy building virtual universities. **Mark "Spoonman" Petrakis,** for showing how all of this is just a big theater of the virtual. **Jonathan Grudin, Kate Ehrlich, Arnold Smith, Peter Polson,**

Jim Larson, Steve Poltrock, Noi Sukaviriya, Matt Belge, Richard Anderson, Greg Panos, Amy Bruckman, Steve Benford, and Judith Donath, for introducing and debating over avatars to the *Computer Human Interface, Cooperative Work* and *SIGGRAPH* communities. Paul Rankin and Patricia Griffin of *Philips Research*, for their continuing support of research on avatar virtual communities.

Thanks for getting me started in this industry

I wouldn't have gotten this far without the following folks:

Mark Conway and Reed Riner for introducing me to *SolSys Sim* and showing me that this would be the "next great thing" on the Internet. Jim Funaro, Reed Riner, Joel Hagen, and all the others who put *CONTACT* together over the past 15 years and made the *Contact Consortium* possible. Thanks Larry Niven for putting the final stimulus on the conception of virtual worlds back in March 1995. Terrell Hoffman and Chris Kekenes, who helped get the *Contact Consortium* going as a forum for avatar virtual worlds. The core members of the *Contact Consortium,* including Lynn Macias, for helping us put on a great Earth to Avatars 96, Nancy and Roger Zuidema, for being there through thick and thin, Wendy Sue Noah, for her positive energy and community building, and Stuart Gold, for his tireless work on TheU Virtual University and architecture competition.

Thanks to the book production team

Utmost appreciation to the patient and courageous team at *Peachpit Press* for pressing forward with what was obviously a risky new book project and a very difficult challenge (to keep up with the worlds!). Along with Peachpit, there were many other people "on the project" who deserve mention here.

I would like to especially thank my editor, Jeremy Judson, for his flexibility and creative input into this work; Peter Gordon of Addison Wesley Longman, for introducing me to Ted Nace—then publisher—and helping me to sell this first-ever book on avatars; Jackie Dove, our patient copyeditor; Nancy Ruenzel, the new publisher at Peachpit, for supporting this venture right away; Hannah Latham, Gary-Paul Prince, and the whole marketing team; Kate Reber, for technical support; Mimi Heft and Richard Walker for great interior design concepts; Victor Gavenda, who built the CD-ROM interface; and Roslyn Bullas for getting all the agreements signed. Warmest thanks to Roger Zuidema and Steven Hanly for their work on the interior art, CD-ROM, and Web site art. Thanks to my agent at *Waterside Productions,* David Fugate, for helping negotiate for this book, and Bill Gladstone, for getting it in front of the whole computer publishing industry. Greatest appreciation to Rusel DeMaria and Alex Utterman for educating me on the fascinating world of computer games, helping me to find an agent, providing advice in writing this book, and for throwing great summertime parties. Kudos to **Nick Herbert** for advice about selling a book, and both writing and procrastination in the writing process. **Darek Milewski** for encouraging me to write the book in the first place. Gratis to **Steven Lambert** and **Gail Nelson** for hosting me on my visit to Microsoft and helping me understand the computer book industry. Hey, **Steve Weiss** at *New Riders,* thank you for just saying, "this book has to be written, go for it, Bruce."

Of course, deep appreciation to all my family in Canada, including my parents **Enid and Warren Damer,** and my many siblings, notably my brother **Eric** who gave the Web draft a quick read and encouragement.

Thanks to you who agreed to appear in the book

The brave souls who agreed to take a visible role in this book, include:

Mark Pesce, Clifford Stoll, Rob van der Haar, Reed Riner, Wendy Sue Noah, Laurel, Tazunu Inoue, The Kindrick family, The Chicago Five: David and Debbie Maloney, Bill DeVercelly, Jody Christensen, Jeff Wilson, Pam Miller, Larry Kay, Pat Paquette, Rick Noll, Graham Evans, SeaJay (Charles Langley), Coyote, and **Nabih Saliba (a.k.a. Gekko).**

May your avatars live long and prosper!

Thanks to all you people out there in the industry who pitched in

The following community of talented people all made their contribution to your author's learning curve and helped make this book a true log of the development of this new medium:

Dave Marvit (*Starbright* project); **Bruce Blumberg, Pattie Maes** (*M.I.T. Media Lab*); **Matthew Burgess, Bill Welty; Scott McLaine** (*3rd Dimension Technologies*);

Mark Rudolph, Dave Story Rob Meyers, Susan Lynn Kropf, Kevin Hartz, Dave Frerichs (*Silicon Graphics*); **Tarik Thami, Michael Powers, Celia Pierce** (coursework at *San Francisco State*); **Charanjit Sidhu** (*British Telecom Research Laboratories*); **Sandy Stone** (*U.T. Austin*); **Sherry Turkle** (*Harvard*); **Nicole Kidd; Keith Wescourt, Barbara Hayes-Roth** (*Extempo*); **Axel Roselius, Kevin Rattai, Brian Williams; David Traub; Michael Gosney, Bob Gelman, Julia Gilden, Nancy Levidow; Karen Marcelo, Tony Parisi** (*Intervista*); **Charles Ostman; Timothy Childs, Linda Jacobson, Peter Rothman** (*VeRGe*); **Mitra, Abbott Brush, Bernie Roehl, Kirk Parsons, Moses Ma, Ioannis Paniaras, Sang Mah; Frank Schwatz, Kitty Wells; Bonnie Nardi** (*Apple Computer*); **Gail Williams** (*the WELL*); **Steve Poltrock, Rick Wojcik** (*Boeing*); **Rick Hopkins** (*Nortel*); **Lisa Neal** (*EDS*); **Tom Kouloupolous** (*Delphi Consulting Group*); **Lewis Henderson** (*William Morris Agency*); **Avram Miller** (*Intel*); and **Doug Engelbart.**

Thank you fellow writers

I would like to thank print journalists **John Moran,** writing for the *Hartford Courant*; **Natasha Wancek,** writing for the *San Jose Mercury News*; **Leslie Miller,** writing for *USA Today*; **David Bank,** writing for the *Wall Street Journal*; **Alex Lash,** writing for *24 Hours in Cyberspace* and *C\Net*; and **David Pescovitz,** writing for the *L.A. Times*. Special journalistic thanks goes to **Sue Wilcox** for nonstop encouragement and for promoting both me and the book, whether I deserved it or not! See Sue's upcoming book (some time in 1998) on the subject of avatars. I would also like to thank **Adrian Scott** and **John Gluck** of *VRMLSite* for giving avatars a webzine presence.

Thanks to you citizens of Avatar Cyberspace

I could not have written a line of this book without the hundreds of users who helped me in-world and told their own stories which I have tried to faithfully reproduce. The following is a very short list of people whose avatars I would like to thank:

Active Worlds and AlphaWorld—**Protagonist, Da8id, Dataman, NetGuy, North, Black Thorne, DrumGod, UserX, Laurel, Spark4Love, Stephen Lankton, ToonSmith**, the bride and groom **Janka and Tomasi, Moria, Paul Klee,** the **DigiGardener Multivar, luna (Susan Mackey), (Rauno Eskelinen)**, and special thanks to **Johanna Silverthorne** for her help as lady of the lands in Sherwood Forest Towne.

Worlds Chat—**CyberHouse1, Katt, Blue Bears**, and **Guest 420**.

WorldsAway—**Stayce Jaye, Duckolyte Jim, Daira, Cinnamon Cupc@ke, Duckolytes**.

The Palace—**TurboDog (Mark Herman II)**, Nathan Wagoner, John Suler, and **mr. rotten**.

Comic Chat—**Bill_Gates, Superman**, and **Joanne Ascunsion**.

And thanks to the many, many other people who have helped in immeasurable ways on this book project. And last, but certainly not least, to **Alex,** the big black cat, who slept through the writing of this book!

More on the community members

Many of the people mentioned here presented at the 1996 Earth to Avatars conference. The conference is described on the Web at http://www.ccon.org/events/conf96.html and their individual biographies and vision are at http://www.ccon.org/events/bios.html. You can also find more contact information about the companies mentioned here on the book companion Web site.

Table of Contents

Introduction

"As Hiro approaches the Street, he sees two young couples, probably using their parents' computers for a double date in the Metaverse, climbing down out of Port Zero, which is the local port of entry and monorail stop. He is not seeing real people, of course. This is all a part of the moving illustration drawn by his computer according to the specifications coming down the fiber-optic cable. The people are pieces of software called avatars."

—Neal Stephenson, *Snow Crash*

Welcome to a New World

Just like me, you probably spent your first few hours on the Internet "visiting" sites on the World Wide Web. Apart from being a very useful source of information, the Web is really just a big pile of documents, and a pretty lonely place. Web surfing is like going to someone's house only to find that it is just a billboard and there is nobody home. As was once said about the Internet: "there is no *there* there." All of that is now changing; the Internet is about to become a place for people, and it will be the biggest place in the world. With your copy of *Avatars!*, you have booked a trip to cyberspace with a human face. You will be getting a glimpse at what might become a whole new way we will communicate, learn, play, and work together in the 21st Century.

Avatars talking in the Utopia Gateway using Onlive Traveler.

In the back of the book you will find a CD-ROM. On the disc is a collection of software which will change the way you see and use the Internet. Each software program is a doorway into a virtual world. Some virtual worlds contain large three-dimensional cities, others are space stations, marketplaces, stages, and weird places that don't look like anything in the real world. The best part about these virtual worlds is that when you visit them, you are not alone! Hundreds or even thousands of people are there with you, exploring, communicating, and creating. Every one of these people has chosen a digital body you can see, a kind of virtual persona called an *avatar*.

Avatar is a very old word from the Sanskrit language which roughly translates to "God's appearance on Earth." The quotation at the beginning of this introduction is from Neal Stephenson's 1992 hit novel, *Snow Crash*, one of the first books to popularize the idea of avatars. I don't think Neal or any of us could have predicted that avatar virtual worlds would appear on the Internet only three years later.

People seen on the Internet!

When you don your avatar and join thousands of other people who are trying out life in virtual worlds, you are joining in a great new experiment in human contact. As you will see in the following pages, this contact goes far beyond simple chat to become a *whole new way of being with people*.

This book is your guide to life as an avatar in virtual worlds. First, we will start out with a *Grand Tour* through some of the most fascinating virtual worlds on the Internet. For each world, I will help you to install the special software it needs, give you lessons on how to move around and talk with people, and clue you in to the hot activities in the world. But there is much, much more. In this book you will find tools and guides to building your own world and designing your own avatar, good etiquette and manners in avatar life, a glossary of new lingo heard on the digital street, and a directory of people and projects finding new things to do in avatar cyberspace.

In the adventure that follows, you will become a true "cybernaut" and embark on multiple missions of discovery into digital space. If you want to know a little bit more about avatar cyberspace, this book, and some of my thoughts on where this is going, read on. If you want to get started, skip right to "The Grand Tour of Worlds."

Welcome to a whole new world!

Where is All this Going?

This new medium raises so many questions. While writing this book I was struck by how almost everyone seems to have a strong opinion about avatars and the people who use them. I have presented live demonstrations of avatar virtual worlds all over this real rock Earth and always get a crowd of people coming up afterwards. Some say "let me try that!," a few demand "why are we doing this?," some ponder "wow, what could this become?," while others have told me they were downright disturbed by what they saw! My hasty answers are usually something like "it's too new to know where this is going," or "try it out and see for yourself," or "yes, it is scary, but so was the telephone to many people."

There is something exciting about such a large unknown, and to be around at the birth of a new medium. The first radio programs tried to be like lectures or live theater, the first television tried to be like radio or newsreels. So it is probably futile to try to predict what virtual worlds will eventually become. There is one big difference between radio, the movies, TV, and this new medium: avatar cyberspace is constantly created and recreated by the people who use it. Every company that has produced and hosted a virtual world has expressed to me their amazement about what ordinary users manage to do in the world and how they change it. In a successful virtual world, the citizens are in the driver's seat. This is not a revolution that comes out of university labs or large companies, it is being made by ordinary people at home.

Is this for real?

You might be saying to yourself: this is not "real" life, and playing around online with other people is not a "real" form of community in a "real" place. The last time you lost yourself in a good film or book, did you feel the power of the reality the story created inside your mind? Have you ever recovered from an illness only to find that your "reality" had somehow changed? I find when I am driving, especially on a fast highway, that my sense of the world becomes very different. Our sense of reality is a creation of our conscious minds in the particular circumstances we find ourselves. One of the great talents of the Human species seems to be our ability to accept and digest new realities. Virtual worlds on the Internet are yet another way for us to experience a flavor of reality.

Yes, but it isn't a virtual reality!

One of the reasons I and many other people refer to this new medium as *virtual worlds* and not *virtual reality* is that the worlds we visit are virtual (they exist nowhere else but in cyberspace and in our minds) but we go there to meet and interact with *real* people. There is nothing *virtual* about the *reality* of your interactions and relationships with other people in these spaces. You can feel just as thrilled, offended, titillated, intrigued, or bewildered by your remote conversations in an avatar community as you do on the telephone.

Virtual reality conjures up images of people thrashing around in those funny helmets and body suits. Virtual worlds run on ordinary computers without any exotic hardware and tie into the Internet through a regular phone line. Many of the virtual worlds are not even three-dimensional, a hallmark of virtual reality. People visit virtual worlds for the other people, not just to be immersed in fantastic landscapes. Some of the most engaging conversations and activities I have experienced took place on pretty boring two-dimensional landscapes.

Hey, I know a community when I feel it!

Would you agree that avatars represent yet another experience of reality? And would you also agree that the people using these worlds are part of bona fide communities?

Back in the late 1980s, one of the first experiments in "virtual community" was under-way in an on-line text chat and conferencing system called the WELL. At this time, the WELL was under attack, one of its members who was systematically harassing (through text messages and by telephone) many other participants. A definitive moment for the WELL came at a point during the months of dialogue on how to deal with the crisis created by this one member when other members began saying that she was destroying their "community." The hard pressed operators of the WELL (one of them was Cliff Figallo, who went on to run the community in Virtual Places) read these message and remarked to themselves that the members were calling it a community! The WELL survived that test and was strengthened into a real community of people who began to meet frequently.

Like the WELL, many people using avatar virtual worlds describe the people in their world (or often just a certain group) as a community. In addition, avatar users often get together in person, wherever this can be arranged. New friendships, marriages, and long histories of personal experience can develop through the medium of avatar cyberspace. Strong relationships rarely stay just in cyberspace. I was flying through the AlphaWorld cityscape one day looking at the buildings people had put up. I was trying to recruit builders for a virtual town and spied a building that told me its creator really knew what he was doing. I landed on the street right next to the mailbox the person had placed to allow people to send him e-mail. What I did not know when I clicked on that box to send mail to Mr. San Marco was that I would be initiating a friendship with a London architect and software engineer, Stuart Gold and his wife Danielle. Within a few months I was on a plane to London. Within six months, he and Danielle were on a plane to San Francisco to attend a conference I organized in San Francisco called Earth to Avatars where they felt very much a part of the "avatars community."

Avatar worlds seem to have great power to develop a new web of human relationships, many tenuous or temporary, some strong and likely to last a lifetime. In an era where we have less in common with our neighbors than our long distance telephone or e-mail relationships, avatar cyberspace may be an important binding force that allows us to build stronger personal communities. Using avatar worlds, I often find myself saying to someone by telephone or e-mail who is separated by a continent, "hey, lets meet in a world and I will show you what I have been up to." I use avatar worlds to build new friendships, to strengthen the ones I have, and build up my own personal community.

So are all those people milling around as avatars a real community? Building and maintaining a community takes a lot of work, as the members of the WELL discovered, regardless of whether it uses cyberspace as the primary medium of contact. In avatar cyberspace, just as in the WELL, after all this work is done and a few tough tests have been survived, you can sometimes hear people exclaim "we made it, we are a community, we can *feel* it." If you want a good taste of avatar community to come, see the story of the Chicago Five in the "Black Sun Passport" chapter.

So, really, where is this going?

When I am asked this question, I whip out a beautiful big color print of the following figure and exclaim "outwards to infinity!" People zero in on the print and say something like "I think I know what this is, but . . . ." With bated breath I reply "it is a three-dimensional city in the Internet built by and inhabited by some 170,000 people and you are looking at a satellite view of only 8% of it." If their eyes don't immediately glaze over, I continue . . . "and you can sit on your PC at home and fly over all 4,000 square miles of it and wave to people (avatars) down below and build something yourself; have you read *Snow Crash*?" At this point, people think you are certifiable to the local funny farm or just stand there saying "I didn't know this was happening in the Net . . . ."

I go on to tell them about the baby who sucked and screamed his way into avatar cyberspace on his own (see the "Onlive Traveler" chapter), about dancing up a storm with people in Iceland in a discotheque aboard a space station (see the "OZ Virtual" chapter), about crime and theft of valuables in a private avatar apartment (see the "WorldsAway" chapter), and the weirdest thing of all, the emergence of robot avatars and artificial life growing and evolving in virtual worlds (see the "Life in Digital Space" chapter).

Imagine virtual worlds beyond the year 2000

In short, there is no short answer to the question of where this is going. The explosion of human creativity that occurred in a mere 18 months in AlphaWorld is a

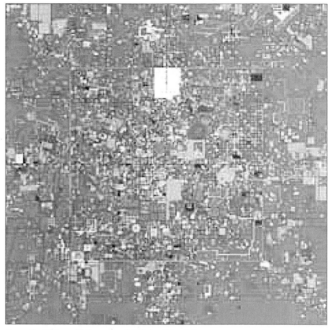

A satellite picture of AlphaWorld.

portent of things to come. The surface area of virtual worlds (if an avatar's height is taken as a unit of measure) will probably exceed the surface area of the Earth within a couple of years. This vast digital space will be shot through with all that can issue from the human hand, mind, and soul. Take yourself into the virtual worlds of the early 21st Century where you might be traveling into fantastic landscapes housing utopian community experiments which rise and fall over periods of days; visiting soundscapes where you can fly in a symphonic avatar flock leaving contrails of music, entering pulsating visualizer machines where avatars follow light through translucent ducts; or boarding a thousand starship *Enterprises* hosting simultaneous and unique missions with eager Trekkie fans playing in the roles of crew members.

Will we all be assimilated?

Will we be lost in digital space? Will our personal contact with friends, family, and neighbors drain away as our brains *borg to binary?* Throughout the book in sections called "Digi's Diary" (found at the end of most chapters), I will consider some of these controversial questions. If you want to hear the opinions of some other thoughtful people, including **Mark Pesce** and **Clifford Stoll**, turn to "Philosophers of Avatar Cyberspace," in Appendix A.

Where Did All this Come From?

Virtual worlds are the children of two humble parent technologies: the text-based virtual community and the computer game. They are vibrant communities of interest have been built up around simple text messaging. The WELL, described earlier in this section, is just one example. Other virtual communities employ text systems called MUDs (Multi User Domains), IRC (Internet Relay Chat), and chat rooms in on-line services. Early experiments to put a graphical interface on text-based virtual communities started back in the mid 1980s with Habitat. See "Predecessors to Avatar Cyberspace," in Appendix A for a description of Habitat, a brief early history of virtual community and projects such as the WELL, SolSys Sim, and de Digitale Stad.

The other parent of virtual worlds is the computer game, designed to run efficiently and look good on minimal computer hardware. The speed of 3D games like *Doom* and *Descent*, a long line of trigger-finger-fast two-dimensional gaming worlds, and the beauty and ambiance of CD-ROM games like *Myst* were provided proof that a home computer could deliver a compelling virtual world. With the Spring 1995 launch of Worlds Chat, it all came together: a fast 3D space station world full of special effects hosting hundreds of real Internet users dressed up as avatars and having a great time chatting and chasing each other around.

Cool worlds for the rest of us

Contrary to what you might think, virtual worlds inherited almost nothing from more exotic technologies like immersive virtual reality, artificial intelligence, and high bandwidth multimedia streaming. These high flying technologies cannot run on ordinary personal computers with 28.8K bps modem Internet connections, which is where virtual worlds make their home. Most of us have not even seen or experienced these exotic technologies except through TV shows or pictures in magazines. Virtual worlds, however, can be visited through most of the computers sitting on our desktops.

Kudos to the world builders

The accomplishment of the people who made and host virtual worlds is anything but humble. Within two years of their introduction, home users had built more three-dimensional virtual space than all the laboratory and university virtual reality environments combined. In 1996, through ordinary modems, users were experiencing better networked voice audio (coming from 3D lip synchronizing avatars) than I had ever seen or heard inside a company or university research group. Virtual world servers have been hosting thousands of users at the same time and managing crowds of avatars in conversation (and a large 3D world to boot) baffling network experts. It all comes down to good design, efficient use of resources, and the increasing power of home computers to render complex worlds and use the network only to get avatar positions, stream conversation, and make small updates to the world. If anything could characterize the design of virtual worlds, it is the philosophy *think globally but cache locally*. Virtual worlds connect to the whole Internet, but use the power of your computer to make the world compelling.

Who brought us these worlds?

Multi-user virtual worlds have been built and hosted by a variety of companies, large and small. Research divisions of large organizations such as Microsoft, Intel, Fujitsu, Sony, Nippon Telegraph and Telephone as well as small startups like Worlds Incorporated, Black Sun Interactive, Ubique, OZ Interactive, Onlive Technologies, and The Palace. Eventually, tools to build and host avatar worlds will become so commonplace and easy to use that you will be able to host your own *homeworld* almost as easily as you can have your own *homepage* on the World Wide Web. I would like to take this opportunity to applaud the individuals and companies who have made this all possible and invite you to visit their homepages or contact them. For a listing of most of these companies and other people and organizations in the young avatar industry, see "A Directory of Companies, Organizations, Projects, and Conferences," on the book companion Web site.

Conventions Used in this Book

Every chapter in this book is broken down into standard departmental topics, such "Installation" and "Digi's Diary." To highlight these areas, I indicate where they appear within a chapter by using the following icons:

Installing

First Steps

Meet the Natives

Hot Spots

Digi's Diary

Help

Sidebar

You'll also find background information, anecdotes, and help in sidebars like this one, which are intended to enrich a discussion or indicate non-essential areas that you might want to skip and go back to later.

How this Book Was Made

This book was a great personal challenge for me. Not only was it the first book I have written, but the virtual worlds are a constantly moving target. Avatars are powered by a completely new breed of software. It is software that changes constantly. Some worlds update themselves every time you log on, so by the time you read this book, the software described in each chapter may have changed. I felt like the workmen who upon finishing painting the Golden Gate bridge have to then go back to the beginning and start again. Often when I finished a chapter I had to immediately go back to the beginning to start revising it. This constant change is why when we were planning the book, we decided to make a really great companion Web site to keep the readers up to date with changes in their software as well as events in the worlds. You can visit that Web site at **http://www.digitalspace.com/avatars**.

Hey, that software is inhabited!

Another feature of virtual world software is that it is *inhabited* by its users and developers. It is very handy to be able to meet the developers in-avatar inside their own worlds. I have done this many times to get help with the software and ask questions for the book. One problem is that there are users there also, thousands of them, and they are often *changing the world*. This means that places I visited to take screen shots are often completely changed or gone the next day. On the upside, I interviewed hundreds of people in-world and was able to convince some of them to send me text and pictures describing their experiences in avatar life. You can read many of these stories in the chapters on the worlds. These personal interest stories really spice up the book and bring it down to Earth. I guess I became one of the world's first virtual journalists!

I once asked Ron Britvich, the creator of AlphaWorld (now called Active Worlds) what was the most memorable thing that happened to him inside his world. He said that it was when he first came into his world, only a few days old (and not even linked into the Internet), and was approached by some other users in-avatar. They said to him: "hey, come with us and see what we did." Ron was astonished. He had expected to be User Number One (he was beaten there by four people, actually) and he never expected what he saw. These users, without any help files or much of an interface, had figured out how to build with the few parts lying around, and had put together, piece by piece, a castle. This really set the stage for what was to happen later. In just over one year, citizens of AlphaWorld had placed down over ten million objects!

No paper changed hands!

I and my publisher realized that this book was going to be large, complex, and have to be done with a lot of help from users and the creators of the virtual worlds. I built a huge Web site that contained the full contents of each chapter in HTML (with images and good formatting). As each chapter was finished, we pointed each company or community of users to it for review. I would often get feedback within hours and could turn around and update the pages within minutes. All copy editing and delivery of the images was done by the Peachpit staff simply clicking on links. We could update and deliver an image in minutes for everyone to see. Not a scrap of paper was used in the production of the book (although we produced paper galleys for review).

And why not a world?

When planning the book, we thought: well, if it has a CD-ROM and a Web site, it might as well have a world! By the time you read this, we should have some sort of Book World up and running. We will post information about how to get there on the companion book Web site at **http://www.digitalspace.com/avatars**. Who knows, you might even see me there in my avatar, DigiGardener, signing books.

What this Book is Not About

This book is not a comprehensive technical guide to avatar design, virtual world server and client architectures, world building with VRML (Virtual Reality Modeling Language), or any other technology. There are plenty of books on those subjects. Rather, it is a personal avatar starter kit, designed to serve as your travel guide as you become a citizen of many different kinds of virtual worlds on the Internet. We have some great tools on the CD-ROM for world building and avatar design and real cyberspace technical gurus will find some great stuff in this book. Frankly, what I find makes these worlds so fascinating is not how they are built, but what ordinary people *do in there*. This is why I designed the book for you, the general user of the Internet, whoever and wherever you are, for it is you who make these worlds worth visiting.

Welcome to the new worlds of avatar cyberspace!

Black
Sun

The
Palace

Grand Tour

of
Worlds

Worlds
Chat

Comic
Chat

Brave
New Worlds

Active

Life in D

Your Guide to
Grand Tour of Worlds

"Hiro is approaching the Street. It is the Broadway, the Champs Elysees of the Metaverse. It is the brilliantly lit boulevard that can be seen, miniaturized and backward, reflected in the lenses of his goggles. It does not really exist. But right now, millions of people are walking up and down it."

—Neal Stephenson, *Snow Crash*

Introduction: Preparing for the Tour

Neal Stephenson wrote this passage in his hit 1992 novel *Snow Crash*, long before there were any avatars actually walking around in the Internet. Back then, people were starting to experiment with something called virtual reality, where you put on an immersive headset (or goggles, as Stephenson described it) and "jacked in" to alternate universes beamed into your eyes.

It is hard to believe that only three years later, in the spring of 1995, Worlds Chat, the very first three-dimensional virtual world appeared on the Internet, complete with avatars moving around and talking in a simulated space station. With Worlds Chat and the other virtual worlds you don't need goggles; the world appears inside a window on your computer. Since Worlds Chat, there has been an explosion of virtual worlds on the Internet with hundreds of thousands of people discovering what it is like to be an avatar in cyberspace. Stephenson's huge Metaverse virtual world with its millions of inhabitants jacking in with goggles is not here yet, but you can experience something like it on your computer today.

It has been a thrill to write this book, but even more thrilling to be able to spend so much time exploring and building virtual worlds on the Internet. Living as an avatar over the past year I have met thousands of people from all over the world, attended virtual weddings and parties, built a three-dimensional town with 60 other people, gone skiing with avatar friends, and much, much more. I have met many of the people in person whom I met first in virtual worlds. I can truly say that my experiences in avatar cyberspace has changed my life in the real world.

So it is a great pleasure to invite you today to explore these worlds with me. I look forward to being your tour guide and I hope you enjoy the ride and find a whole new way to be with people and express yourself creatively in this new medium. Don't worry about being hunted by monsters in these virtual worlds. For the most part, they are not games, but places to meet, communicate, and create. Without further adieu, let us get started.

For my avatar, I chose the same name in every virtual world: DigiGardener. This name expresses my desire to be a kind of digital Johnny Appleseed, who ventures out to sow seeds all across the new frontier of cyberspace. DigiGardener is now a seasoned traveler, qualified to be captain of his own ship, the HMS Avatar. Captain Digi invites you aboard his sturdy cybernautic craft. He will take you on a grand tour of the avatar cosmos. In each chapter, you can read Digi's personal diary entries for some thought-provoking ideas and challenging questions.

Your keys to avatar cyberspace: The Book CD-ROM and Companion Web Site

To make it easier for you to tour the virtual worlds, I have provided a CD-ROM with this book. It is packed with free virtual world software, artwork, and of course, avatars. This will save you the time and trouble of downloading a whole lot of software from the Internet. See "The Book CD-ROM" chapter for instructions on how to use the CD-ROM. Individual instructions for installing each piece of virtual world software and tools can be found in the chapters for that world.

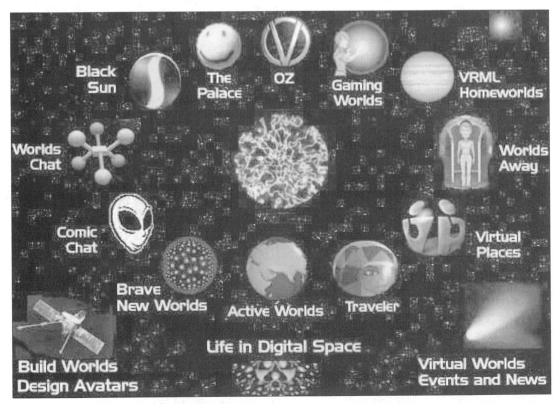

A map to the Virtual World Cosmos.

Access to most of these worlds are free of charge or offer some level of free trial access, but you have to have a connection to the Internet or an on-line service, which will cost something. I've tried to cover most of the worlds, but new ones are being created all the time. Chances are if you don't find it in this book or on the CD-ROM, you will find it on the Companion Web site at **http://www.digitalspace.com/avatars**. Because some of the virtual worlds may have been updated with new features, you may have to download new versions. You can also do this using the book Web site.

Destinations in Digital Space

Fearless rookie cybernaut, Captain DigiGardener (that's me!) says, "all aboard!" It is time to board our intrepid Internet space cruiser, the good ship Avatar. We will fire up its digital drives and head for orbit on a journey to the farthest reaches of digital space. You will be leaving the normal world of Web pages, e-mail, and text chat far behind. You will become a true cybernaut, exploring many strange new worlds, fraternizing with the locals, building bases on virtual planets, and having more fun than you ever thought possible on the Internet!

All you have to do now is look over all the possible destinations and then choose your own tour package and the Captain and crew of the good ship Avatar will take you on any trip you want. Let's take a look at some of the worlds awaiting you . . .

Captain Digi says, "all aboard!"

Your guide to the Solar System of Worlds

Worlds Chat Space Station
First Stop in Digital Space

The first stop of your journey into digital space will be the orbiting Worlds Chat Space Station. This is the first waystation you come upon before you venture out into the far reaches of the virtual solar system. In Worlds Chat you will get your space legs, learn how to navigate in three dimensions, and chat with the locals. When you graduate from this space academy, you will be ready for your first interplanetary hop.

The Palace
Chat Cosmos

On your way out into the virtual solar system, you will encounter an asteroid belt of tiny worlds. This is The Palace, a constellation of thousands of chat worldlets with their populations of wafer-thin avatars. Here you will learn how to navigate and communicate in a two-dimensional world, how to throw a snowball in cyberspace, and how to design your own avatar!

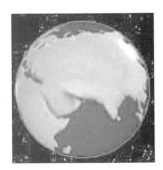

AlphaWorld and Active Worlds
Green Planet

You will make first planetfall at AlphaWorld, a huge green planet covered by a sprawling city built by some of its 200,000 citizens. In AlphaWorld and other Active Worlds you will learn about street life in a large three-dimensional virtual city, how to build your own digital homestead, get married, and even go skiing in cyberspace!

WorldsAway
In This Dream, You Can Fly

On your next rendezvous, you will be caught up in a dreamlike state and our good ship Avatar will enter a mysterious zone, the WorldsAway Dreamscape. Here avatars mill around in a community with a carnival atmosphere. In WorldsAway you will learn how to buy and sell a whole new body, run a Bingo racket, and rent an apartment of your own.

Onlive Traveler
Mystic Voyages Through Sound

Next you will be called onward to a glowing world of a thousand voices. Onlive Traveler is a place where avatars in giant three-dimensional heads talk in their own voices. Here you will learn how to sing in cyberspace, use the Internet to talk to friends and family across the world, and even visit an avatar football sportplex!

Virtual Places
Grand Central Station of the Web Universe

Piloting the good ship Avatar we will pass into a continuum of two alternate universes, where the Web and avatars meet. In Virtual Places every Web page turns into a virtual world. You will take your first virtual driving lesson and pilot a big yellow bus full of avatars on a grand trip around the Web. Here you will also learn how to make your own avatar and furnish your place in a town of avatar apartments.

Black Sun Passport
Through the Star Gate

Our cybernautic craft will drift through timeless digital realms toward the invisible attraction of the Black Sun. The Black Sun is a star gate into a whole universe of worlds. In the power of Passport (the vehicle carrying us through this gate), you will get lost in a maze of three-dimensional landscapes, and learn how to build your own world.

Comic Chat
Comic Colony

Time for shore leave for the crew of Avatars and we will all head for some comic relief in Comic Chat. In Comic Chat you will be cast as an actor in a living comic strip and play a part in a live comedy theater. You will meet famous personalities, including a Bill Gates impersonator who is pretty convincing (at least for your gullible captain Digi!).

OZ Virtual
Journey to the Dark Star

By this time, the cybercraft Avatar will be in need of a refit so we will head for the dark star of OZ, a cluster of deep space stations. On board OZ you will cruise through one of the coolest places in the virtual universe. Learning to dance in digital discos and experiencing walls of sound and music will be just part of your experience on the OZ stations.

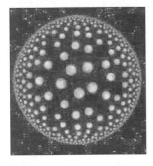

Brave New Worlds

Is this the end of our mission? Not yet! New virtual worlds are being born all the time. As avatar cyberspace spreads across the Internet, you will find worlds for every interest, culture, language, and purpose. We will take a glimpse into these brave new worlds and beyond into the future of *digital* space.

Gaming Worlds
Avatars at Play

Virtual worlds are not the only place you can find avatars. We will visit some multi-player gaming worlds where avatars are starting to show up and where you can socialize as well as do battle with dragons or other human inhabitants. You will get a preview of some of these worlds and learn how to get into the game!

Life in Digital Space
Bots, Biota, and Virtual Pets

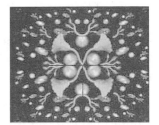

What is an adventure into the unknown without meeting something truly alien? How about E.T. in cyberspace? Well, Biota comes pretty close! You will learn about the weird world of daemons, agents, bots, biots and virtual pets and try your hand at planting a seed or hatching an egg in cyberspace!

Build Your Own World, Design Your Own Avatar

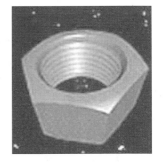

The digital drive on the good ship Avatar will just about be out of juice by now, so we will head home. After all the worlds we will have seen, you might want to take up the trade of world builder and craft a few of your own. You may also want to learn how to design avatars and open a cyberspace body shop. In this chapter, I will introduce you to the tools that will give you an apprentice certificate in world building and avatar designing.

The Tour Packages

Now that you have had a chance to look over the destinations in the travel brochure, you are well equipped to choose your tour package. You can choose the trip that best suits you from the following roster, make up your own itinerary, or do it all and take the Grand Tour of Worlds.

Bon Voyage!

Captain DigiGardener

Are you driving a Macintosh or Windows PC?

The following guidelines should help you decide which worlds you can visit. More specific descriptions of the computer you must have can be found at the beginning of each chapter.

PLATFORM	WORLD SUPPORTED
If you have a Macintosh you can use:	The Palace
(note many of the Brave New Worlds and Gaming Worlds run on both Macintosh and PC platforms)	Virtual Places
	WorldsAway

Note that there may be Macintosh versions of new worlds coming out, so keep an eye on the Avatars Book Web Site at **http://www.digitalspace.com/avatars**.

PLATFORM	WORLD SUPPORTED
If you have a Windows 3.1 PC* you can use:	Worlds Chat
(note many of the Brave New Worlds and Gaming Worlds run on both Macintosh and PC platforms)	The Palace
	Virtual Places
	WorldsAway

PLATFORM	WORLD SUPPORTED
If you have a Windows 95 PC* you can use:	Worlds Chat
(note many of the Brave New Worlds and Gaming Worlds run on both Macintosh and PC platforms)	AlphaWorld and Active Worlds
	The Palace
	WorldsAway
	Virtual Places
	Onlive Traveler
	Black Sun Passport
	Comic Chat
	OZ Virtual

*Note that most of the worlds software that runs under Windows 3.1 and Windows 95 will run under Windows NT and the upcoming Windows 98, but you should check the installation guidelines for each application. Note also that Windows emulation systems on the Macintosh, OS/2, or Unix/X-Windows may be able to run some of this software.

The Tours

Novice or young user tour

Just getting your Internet legs? If so, easy does it and try this itinerary. For starters try chatting up a storm and exploring "The Palace," and for a little comic humor visit "Comic Chat" and then when you are ready for a little more dimension (third, that is), try boarding the "Worlds Chat Space Station."

Social butterfly tour

Lets talk! Hooked on daytime soaps or talk radio? Addicted to chat rooms in your on-line service? Feed your rumor mill with this tour package. Start off with "The Palace," and then move on to "Virtual Places" which runs both on America Online and the Internet. If you are a CompuServe subscriber or have an Internet connection, try "WorldsAway." If you are ready for chat in three dimensions, check out "Worlds Chat." Step up to the ultimate in talk on the Internet with "Onlive Traveler" where you can use your own voice to speak with others in a great 3D virtual world.

Pro gamer tour

Looking for cool new spaces on the Internet? Grab your board, run down to the virtual surf and catch this ride! If you want fast 3D chat, start with "Worlds Chat." This will get your 3D legs in shape as you careen around in the space station. Find your voice, recruit a team, and play avatar football in "Onlive Traveler," then roll on through to the spacey VRML world, "OZ Virtual." Remember, you can't kill other people in social avatar worlds, but if you still have an itch to shoot, check out the avatar arcade of "Gaming Worlds." There are new gaming worlds coming out all the time, so keep an eye on the Gaming Worlds page on the *Avatars!* Companion Web site at **http://www.digitalspace.com/avatars**.

Wheeler dealer's paradise tour

If buying low and selling high is where you get your thrills, then "WorldsAway" is for you. Buy and sell objects, earn credits, gamble on bingo, and rent your own apartments. You should also check out the "Gaming Worlds" where swords and sorcery are available, for a price! If becoming a land baron is your dream, step into "AlphaWorld and Active Worlds" and develop suburbs and strip malls for hungry new avatar consumers.

Working vacation for the world builder tour

Intent on building the greatest homeworld of your imagination for all to see on the Internet? Spending all day and night coding 3D scenes, modeling behavior, or painting pixels? Then try the World Builder's Special. Start out with "AlphaWorld and Active Worlds" where you can easily put together pieces and build an entire virtual city. Move on to the VRML homeworlds of "Black Sun Passport" and the Sony Community Place Browser in "Brave New Worlds" where you can learn how to connect to your own custom homeworld and watch the avatars stream in! Marvel at the beautiful VRML, sculpted sound and music, and the craftsmanship of avatars and their gestures in "OZ Virtual." Finish with a visit to the "Build Your Own World, Design Your Own Avatar" chapter where you'll get a hands-on look at the master builder's workshop complete with real professionals' tools.

Beta tester fanatic's heaven tour

Many of these worlds are in some form of beta, but if you really want the thrill of first cut software on your hard disk, try "Brave New Worlds." There are new worlds coming out all the time, so keep an eye on the Brave New Worlds page on the *Avatars!* Book Web site at **http://www.digitalspace.com/avatars**.

Digital anthropologist cyberspace research tour

Get those notebooks out and questions ready to interview the natives. Start out with a little bookwork by taking the tutorial on the companion Web site, and then learn the language of avatar culture from the "Glossary of Terms." Next, step into inhabited cyberspace with field work in the highly developed community of "WorldsAway." Research how people identify strongly with the spaces they have built in "AlphaWorld and Active Worlds" and "Black Sun Passport." Conduct interviews in the voice enabled worlds of "Onlive Traveler." For further research and background on the medium, see the "Bibliography of Recommended Reading" and "Appendix A: Projects, Groups, Events, and Philosophers in Avatar Cyberspace." And lastly, watch for new developments in the medium posted on the *Avatars!* Book Web site at **http://www.digitalspace.com/avatars**.

The digital Darwin tour

For believers in artificial life and robots ruling the world, look no farther than "Life in Digital Space." Work deep into the night on your own digital organics, but please don't let your Frankensteins escape onto the Internet!

The Grand Tour: If you want it all!

Don't want to miss a thing? For true cybernauts, we have designed the grand tour! Join us on a ride through the whole solar system of virtual worlds. We will not miss a single planet, space station, or asteroid on our route! When you are done, you will be the toast of parties in the digital universe, a key operator in the coin of the virtual realm, and a top apprentice builder ready to construct worlds to suit! Just follow the whole itinerary in "Destinations in Digital Space" and check your Avatars! Book Web site at **http://www.digitalspace.com/avatars** for any new worlds to explore.

A Road Map to the Rest of Avatars!

When you have returned from your first tour of duty in virtual worlds, you will find that the digital space academy has plenty more to offer. Arm yourself with new knowledge by visiting other parts of your Avatars book. I have provided chapters and appendices to meet all your needs.

The Companion Web Site
Enter the Avatar Teleport

This chapter will introduce you to the Companion Web site for this book. This Web site is called "The Avatar Teleport" and is one of the most useful tools for explorers of virtual worlds. The Teleport provides live links to world providers' Web sites, citizen home pages, and events and news about avatar cyberspace. In addition, *Avatars!* will assist you if you are a researcher or educator using the book in the lab or classroom (see "Advanced Course at Avatar University," on the companion Web site). Lastly, there are new worlds and tools and links to worlds constructed for you, which make the Avatar Teleport (**http://www.digitalspace.com/avatars**) worth revisiting frequently.

The Book CD-ROM
Your Key to Avatar Cyberspace

In this chapter, I step you through installing a virtual world and other software from the Book CD-ROM. I will also provide you with a map of the files and folders on the CD-ROM, which will also include the full HTML version of this book and other special materials.

Bibliography of Recommended Reading

This bibliography will give you a kind of Avatars 101 reading list on where this technology all came from and where it all may be going. There are not many books on avatars (the one you are holding now is one of the first) so titles from this list should be quite thought provoking!

Glossary of Terms

With a new medium comes a whole new language. Actually, each virtual world has developed a few unique terms of its own. The Glossary is a compendium of all the new words (at least in English) I have heard spoken while in virtual worlds.

Appendix A:

Projects, Groups, Events, Philosophers, News, and Predecessors in Avatar Cyberspace

This appendix lists some of the most interesting projects, groups, events, and people in avatar cyberspace, with a couple of fascinating interviews. Copious links to Web sites are given where you can find further information. I hope that you follow up with some of these links and get more involved in the avatar community.

Appendix B:

General Questions and Answers

Got a general question about virtual worlds? Does something seem wrong with a virtual world or your computer system since you installed it? This appendix will give you some plain-English answers. Note that almost every virtual world also has a FAQ (Frequently Asked Questions) section on the companion Web site to this book.

Worlds Chat
Space Station

FIRST STOP IN DIGITAL SPACE

The good ship *Avatar* has made it into orbit with captain DigiGardener (that's me), the crew, and you, honored passenger. A great space station, our first stop on the way to the worlds of avatar cyberspace, is coming up on the ship's view screen. Our mission of exploration into digital space requires only an open mind and virtually unlimited curiosity. We will meet all sorts of people along the way. The natives of the virtual worlds we will encounter will be as diverse and fascinating (or as dull and offensive) as any group of people anywhere. It is your virtual theater, so strut onto the stage and find your audience!

What do you need for the trip? Pack your computer, modem, some free hard disk space, an adventuresome spirit, a little sack of patience, and plenty to say.

Your Guide to Worlds Chat Space Station

WORLD GUIDE

WORLD SKILL LEVEL	Beginner
BUILDING CAPABILITY	No
SYSTEM REQUIREMENTS	Windows 3.1, Windows 95
AVATAR CREATION CAPABILITY	Yes, but for experts only
DEPTH	3D
SOUND SUPPORT	Music, sound effects

MINIMUM MACHINE

OPERATING SYSTEM	Windows 3.1
COMPUTER	486DX 66 MHz PC; 256-color VGA monitor
RESOURCES	8MB RAM; 6MB free disk space (24MB for Gold version); 16-bit sound card optional for music and sound effects
CONNECTION	SLIP/PPP dial-up to the Internet at 14.4 kbps

Worlds Chat Space Station: First Stop for Cybernauts

The good ship *Avatar* is in orbit and racing toward our first stop, the Worlds Chat Space Station. Worlds Chat was one of the first virtual worlds launched on the Internet, back in the spring of 1995. And unlike President John F. Kennedy's Apollo project, which won the race to the moon, but left no base to go back to, Worlds Chat has given us a great waystation, or stopover point, on the way into the digital solar system.

In the past, surfing the World Wide Web, sending e-mail, or chatting with text were the only experiences you could have in cyberspace. With Worlds Chat, you

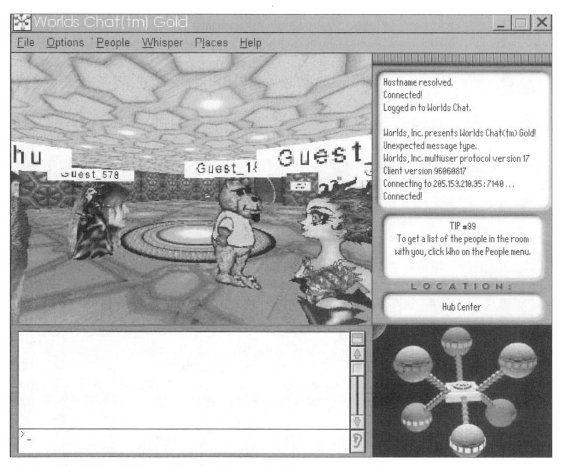

The bustling hub of the Worlds Chat Space Station.

can explore a three-dimensional virtual world full of people who represent themselves in digital costumes called *avatars*. This is what I like to call, "the new avatar cyberspace," for it is truly a new frontier. With the coming of avatar cyberspace, the Internet is changing from an interface into a place. People are communicating and creating new types of communities, based not on the towns in which they live, but on the interests and beliefs they share. Sometimes I like to say that they are creating a new life in *digital space*. Many people question whether digital space is a real place, and whether this is a real life. But then, revolutionary inventions are always questioned and criticized in the beginning. Over 100 years ago, a businessman was reported to have commanded a visitor to his office to remove a certain "toy" from his office. That unfortunate visitor was Thomas Edison; the "toy" was a telephone.

Worlds Chat and other virtual worlds offer a whole new way of being with other people. The virtual world may be as important to the twenty-first century as the telephone was to the twentieth. Worlds Chat is a kind of space academy where you will learn the basic skills of this new medium and begin your life as an avatar in digital space.

Installing Worlds Chat

Installing

What do I need to get to Worlds Chat?

To visit Worlds Chat, you must have a PC, though it does not have to be a very powerful PC. As shown in the minimum machine table at the beginning of this chapter, all you need is a 486, 66 MHz PC running Windows 3.1 and a direct connection to the Internet. You can't use Worlds Chat through on-line services like America Online, CompuServe, or Prodigy unless they support direct Internet access through the 32-bit Winsock (the software that Windows uses to communicate with the Internet). For example, you can use Worlds Chat through the Microsoft Network or CompuServe 3.0, as they do provide this service. You may be able to configure your on-line service to run Worlds Chat. See, "Setting up your on-line service to connect directly with the Internet," in Appendix B. If you have further problems, contact your on-line service for help.

You have to be directly connected to the Internet by a dial-up SLIP or PPP with a 14.4 kbps connection. If you are at work, or a place where you have a PC on the Internet full-time (such as a university or college), you can also use Worlds Chat. Connecting from work might require you to check on your *firewall* restrictions; see the section, "Firewalls and Proxies," in Appendix B for more information.

Getting started and a few disclaimers

Worlds Chat is easy to install and very easy to use. Using the step-by-step guide in this chapter, you will explore a three-dimensional virtual world and experience your first social interactions in digital space. Worlds Chat comes in two versions: demo and gold. The demo version is free, and provides you with much of the experience of 3D chat in a virtual world. The gold version must be purchased on a separate CD-ROM. You can install the Worlds Chat demo version either from the CD in this book, or by downloading it from the Internet. Doing this is easier than you might think, and once the download is complete, you will be living the life of an avatar in no time.

A big plus is that the Worlds Chat demo version is free to use (you have to accept the terms of a free license during installation). You are not charged for the time you spend exploring and chatting in Worlds Chat, but you could be charged for the hours you use from your Internet service provider (ISP). Check with your ISP on its monthly free hours and rates.

The version of Worlds Chat you will find on your *Avatars!* CD is the one described in this chapter. However, Worlds Chat may have evolved since this chapter was written, so when you log on, you may be asked to upgrade to a new version. If you download an upgrade from the Internet, or a whole new version of Worlds Chat, it may look somewhat different from what I have described. To download an upgrade, or a completely new version of Worlds Chat from the Internet, follow the instructions in the section, "Installing or upgrading Worlds Chat from the Internet," later in this chapter.

Help

Virtually up-to-date

As a special service for readers of *Avatars!*, I have a home page on the World Wide Web devoted to keeping you up-to-date on your favorite worlds. Find news about software updates, social events held within these virtual worlds, and brand new worlds you might want to try at http://www.digitalspace.com/avatars. Bookmark it!

Worlds Chat may be changing homes

At the time I was finishing this chapter, Worlds Inc. informed me that it was looking for a new company to host both Worlds Chat and Active Worlds (including AlphaWorld). The company assured me that both Worlds Chat and Active Worlds would continue to operate online, and that they expected the new hosts to continue developing them. By the time you read this book, both Worlds Chat and Active Worlds may have already moved. Please see the Worlds Inc. home page at **http://www.worlds.net**, or your *Avatars!* book home page at **http://www.digitalspace .com/avatars**, for news about both Worlds Chat and Active Worlds.

If you have questions or problems

If you have questions or problems installing or running Worlds Chat, consult, "Frequently Asked Questions," on the companion Web site to this book. If this does not help you, check the Worlds Inc. home page at **http://www.worlds.net**, and its special Frequently Asked Questions page at **http://www.worlds.net/support/wcg-faqs.html**, for help on common problems. Worlds also maintains a forum for technical issues and pointers to newsgroups at **http://www.worlds.net/support/wcg-forum.html**. To contact the Worlds Inc. Worlds Chat team directly with your suggestions, bug reports, or comments, fill out the feedback form at **http://www.worlds.net/feedback.html**.

Another good source for information on how to use Worlds Chat is the on-line help file. Just press F1 while using Worlds Chat, and use the table of contents or index to find the topic you are looking for.

I appreciate your feedback on *Avatars!*, but I don't have the resources to provide technical support. We would be happy to hear about your experiences with Worlds Chat. Contact us through the *Avatars!* book Web site at **http://www.digitalspace.com/avatars**.

Macintosh, UNIX, and OS/2 versions, and running under Windows NT

At this writing, there are no native versions of Worlds Chat for the Macintosh, UNIX, or OS/2 platforms. Check the Worlds Inc. and *Avatars!* book Web pages for updates on new versions which might support these platforms. You also may be able to run Worlds Chat using a Windows emulation system on non-Windows platforms. Worlds Chat may run under Windows NT, but Worlds reports that you may also experience problems. Check the Worlds Inc. Web site for assistance with operation under Windows NT.

Bear with me through the following step-by-step instructions, and soon you will be experiencing life as an avatar in digital space!

Do you have a previous version of Worlds Chat installed?

If you have previously installed Worlds Chat, it may be wise to delete it before installing the version from the CD. Our version is demo version 1.1c. If your version of Worlds Chat is more recent, or you have the gold version for registered users, you may want to stick with it. The installation program will probably give you the option of deinstalling your old Worlds Chat software, but there are ways you can do this yourself in advance.

To remove a program in Windows 95: Open the control panel, double-click on the Add/Remove Programs icon, scroll down to Worlds Chat, highlight it, and click on the Add/Remove button to delete it from the system. You can also delete the Worlds Chat folder (usually C:\worlds\chatdemo or C:\worlds\chat). If you are running Windows 3.1, deleting the folder might be your best option.

Installing Worlds Chat from the Avatars! CD

If you have a CD-ROM drive on your PC, you can install the Worlds Chat 1.1c demo version directly from there. If you don't have a CD-ROM drive, skip to the section, "Installing or upgrading Worlds Chat from the Internet." In "The Book CD-ROM" chapter, I provide a step-by-step example of how to install from the CD-ROM. I suggest you refer to this chapter. Once the installation program on your CD-ROM has started, then you can return to this chapter and refer to the section, "Running the installation."

Installing or upgrading Worlds Chat from the Internet

If you want the very latest version of Worlds Chat, or were informed that you had to upgrade the version found on your *Avatars!* CD, then you must download it from the Internet. If you haven't done this before, don't panic; it is easier than you might think! Just follow these steps:

❶ Connect to the Internet (dial up with your modem or make sure your Internet connection is active).

❷ Launch your Web browser, such as Netscape Navigator or Microsoft Internet Explorer. At the top of the browser window, you will see a text box called Location, where you can enter text.

❸ Click in the Location box, delete the text inside, type in **http://www.worlds.net**, and press Enter. After a few moments, the home page for Worlds Inc. should appear. If nothing comes up for a long time, check to see that you are online.

❹ If the Worlds Inc. page is not available for some reason, try entering the location for the *Avatars!* home page (**http://www.digitalspace.com/avatars**). This page may contain more up-to-date links for Worlds Inc. and Worlds Chat.

   1. Once you are in the Worlds Inc. home page, follow the instructions for downloading or upgrading Worlds Chat. At one point, you will click on a

Worlds Chat Gold System Requirements

The Worlds Chat 1.0 Demo is 4.73 MB and will take approximately 30 minutes to download using a 28.8 modem. **Installation instructions and information for the Worlds Chat 1.0 Demo are available** here.

Download Worlds Chat 1.0 Demo from Worlds

Please note, if the above site is busy, the Worlds Chat 1.0 Demo is also available from TUCOWS mirrors, in their Text Chat section. If you are overseas, you may actually get faster results using a mirror close to you. Use one of the links below to download the Worlds Chat 1.0 Demo from TUCOWS mirror:

- British Columbia
- Chile
- Kuwait
- Netherlands
- Russia

link and be prompted for a place to save a file. Note that if you are not in the United States, you may want to select a location closer to you from which to download. The shorter the distance those Internet packets have to travel, the faster you will receive the file. The figure to the left shows some mirror locations available for downloading.

Step 1: Find and click on the link to download the Worlds Chat demo software.

2. A few seconds after clicking on the link, you will be presented with a dialogue box similar to the one in the figure to the right; click Save File (Netscape) or Save As (Internet Explorer) to download the file to disk (or you can save it on your desktop if you are running Windows 95). This is the file that you must download.

Step 2: Ask the browser to save the file.

3. Next you will be prompted to choose a folder in which to save the downloaded file. Note where you saved the file, and the name of the file (in this example, wcd10.exe). You can use the folder that the Web browser suggests, or move back up and select another. I put all downloaded files in a folder which I call \download.

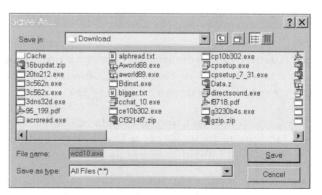

Step 3: Choose a folder in which to store the downloaded file. Don't forget where you put it!

4. Wait patiently; this download is large (5MB or more) and may take between 40 minutes and well over an hour, depending on the connection speed. You can do other work, but be careful not to interfere with the connection. Try not to do more work on the Internet while the download is progressing, and if you are using your regular telephone line for the modem, don't make calls. You may want to turn off any call-waiting feature you may have because if someone calls, this could interrupt your download. You can be more confident of doing work at the same time as the download is progressing if you are running Windows 95 (it has a wonderful feature called *multitasking*, which means you can safely do more than one thing on the computer at once).

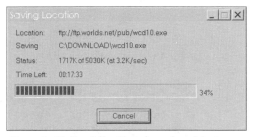

Step 4: Wait while the download is in progress...please be patient!

5. After the download is finished, you must open the folder where the file is located, and double-click on the file to start the installation. To do this:

1. Open the My Computer icon on your desktop.

2. Open the MS-DOS C: icon representing your hard disk.

3. Open the folder where you saved the file (in C:\download, as shown in the adjacent figure).

Step 5: Find the file you downloaded.

Running the installation

Whether you are running the installation from the CD using your Web browser, from the CD file you directly copied, or from the file you downloaded from the Internet, use this section to guide you through the installation. Note that if you downloaded Worlds Chat from the Internet, the installation process may have changed. If this has happened, refer to instructions on the Worlds Inc. Web site.

❶ After the software has been downloaded, close the browser and go to the directory (or desktop) location where you saved the file. Double-click on that file (it may be named wcd11c.exe, if it came from your book CD) to launch the WinZip self-extractor application (see the following figure).

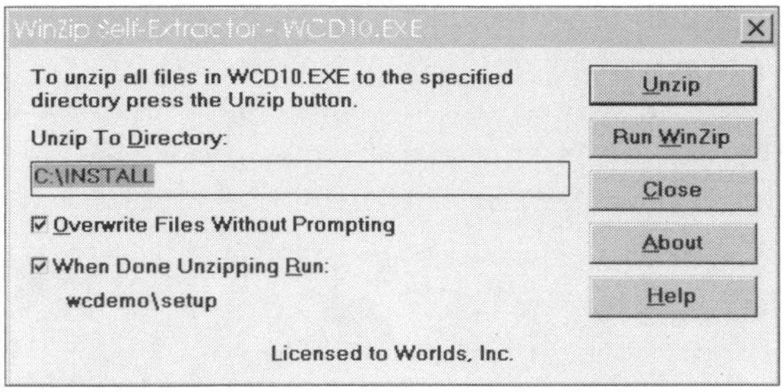
WinZip Self-Extractor - WCD10.EXE
To unzip all files in WCD10.EXE to the specified directory press the Unzip button.
Unzip To Directory:
C:\INSTALL
Overwrite Files Without Prompting
When Done Unzipping Run:
wcdemo\setup
Licensed to Worlds, Inc.
Unzip
Run WinZip
Close
About
Help

Step 1: Unzip the file with the WinZip self-extractor.

Make sure that the settings, Overwrite Files Without Prompting, and When Done Unzipping Run: wcdemo\setup, are checked. Also note the Unzip To Directory path, as you will have to clean up files there later. I recommend that you set the Unzip To Directory path to a temporary directory like C:\temp or C:\install. I copy programs I download from C:\download to my C:\temp directory before installing them. This keeps the downloaded programs in C:\download separate from all of the temporary files created in C:\temp when I install. After a successful installation, I delete all of the files in C:\temp. This may seem like a lot of steps, but PCs are like cars before 1910; you have to be your own mechanic to own one.

It is a good idea to close other programs before you continue with the installation. In Windows 95, you can do this by clicking on the running application icons on the task bar, and then closing them. In Windows 95 and Windows 3.1, you can use Alt+Tab to access other running applications, even when the installer is waiting for your input, and you cannot see the task bar. Simply hold down Alt while pressing Tab, and select the icon representing the running application. You can leave the Internet connection running. When you are ready, press the Unzip button.

❷ In 20 to 30 seconds, the files will be unzipped. Click OK and wait another 10 seconds or so for the Worlds Chat installation program to run. You will be presented with a license agreement; click Accept, and you will be presented with the installation options dialogue (see the adjacent figure). I recommend that you select Express Setup. If you already have Worlds Chat installed, choose Deinstall current installation. In this case, your old version will be removed, and you'll have to restart the installation.

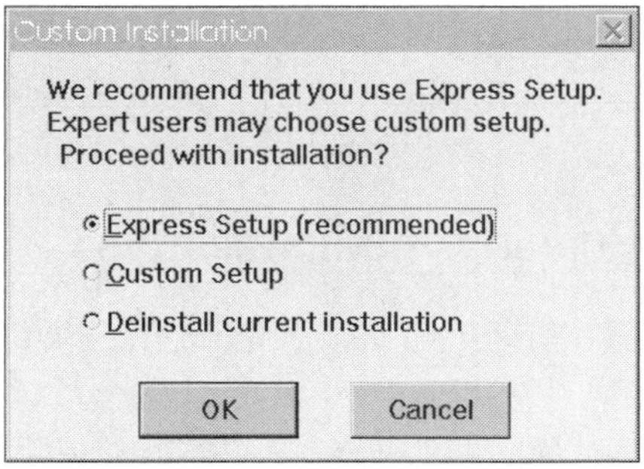
Custom Installation
We recommend that you use Express Setup.
Expert users may choose custom setup.
Proceed with installation?
Express Setup (recommended)
Custom Setup
Deinstall current installation
OK
Cancel

Step 2: Run the Worlds Chat installation program.

❸ If you are running a monitor with more (or less) than the 256 colors shown, the Worlds Chat installation program will warn you (as shown in the following figure). You can still go ahead and install Worlds Chat. It will run in more than

256 colors, but some things may not show up well. For optimum performance, you should set your screen to 256 colors. Also, the Worlds Chat window is optimized to run on a VGA (640 by 480) resolution. It runs just fine on screens of up to 1,280 by 1,024, but the window will look a little small. When I demonstrate Worlds Chat to larger audiences, I do it at VGA resolution. Please see, "Changing your screen colors or resolution," in Appendix B for more information on changing screen colors or resolution.

Step 3: A warning about your monitor display mode.

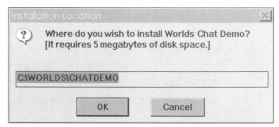

Step 4: The installer asks to verify the location.

❹ The installer setup program will run Install Worlds Chat and prompt you for the default folder. As the preceding figure shows, that default is C:\worlds\chatdemo. I recommend that you use the default folder (directory path) you are given.

The two following figures illustrate what you should see as Worlds Chat installs and completes a successful installation. This should take only a minute or two. You may be prompted to install a *WinG* graphics driver. I recommend installing it. WinG is a special graphics system for Windows 3.1; installing it should not cause problems.

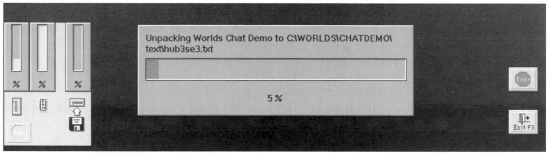

Worlds Chat is installing.

Confirm that the install is complete.

Avatars!

❺ After the installation is complete, you should see a window similar to the one in the adjacent figure. With your right mouse button held down, drag and drop the Worlds Chat 1.1c demo shortcut onto your Windows 95 desktop and select, Create Shortcut(s) Here. If you do not want to put a shortcut on your Windows 95 desktop, you can find

Step 5: Create a shortcut to Worlds Chat from the window displayed after installation.

Worlds Chat in your Start ➪ Programs ➪ Worlds folder under the Start menu. You can close program manager. In Windows 3.1, you should see a program group called Worlds, which should contain an icon called Worlds Chat 1.1c demo.

❻ You will have to reboot your computer to start Worlds Chat. If you were prompted to change your screen colors to 256, do this now before rebooting. To reboot in Windows 95, click on the Start button, select Shut down, and then Restart the computer. In Windows 3.1, exit Windows (if you can), and then turn the computer off and back on again, or press the reset button.

After the computer restarts, I recommend that you do the following cleanup of files before you start getting absorbed in Worlds Chat. After this, you will be ready to get started.

Cleaning up after installation

If you copied the Worlds Chat installation file onto your desktop, into a folder, or downloaded it from the Internet, you can delete it after the installation is complete. It should have a name like wcd11c.exe. You can keep the original installer around just in case you have to reinstall Worlds Chat. Of course, you have the CD with the original installers there, so you do not need to take up valuable hard disk space (5MB just for the Worlds Chat installer).

You will also have to delete the files you unzipped into your Unzip To Directory (see Step 1 in the section, "Running the installation"). You can find the directory (which might have been called C:\install or C:\temp) by opening My Computer and the MS-DOS C: hard disk. Find the folder named wcdemo and delete this folder and all of its contents. After the installation is complete, you do not need to keep these files. Be careful not to delete the Worlds Chat application folder (\worlds\chat demo).

The readme files

There will be files called readme.txt or Worlds Chat 1.1c demo release notes placed in your Start Menu folder or Program Group folder. If you open these files, you will find general information about this release of Worlds Chat.

Orbital Rendezvous: Stepping Aboard Worlds Chat

Before you start Worlds Chat, you should connect to the Internet (dial up with your modem or make sure your Internet connection is active). If your Web browser can bring up a Web page, then your Internet connection is probably active.

If you are running Windows 3.1, go to the program manager, open the Worlds program group, and double-click the Worlds Chat 1.1c demo icon to begin. Worlds Chat installs a special graphics library called WinG for Windows 3.1. If this is the first time you are running Worlds Chat with WinG; you'll see the "red worms" of the WinG self-test program. This is WinG setting itself up. You will only see this once—the first time you set up WinG for Worlds Chat on Windows 3.1.

In Windows 95, click the Start button, select Programs ➪ Worlds ➪ Worlds Chat 1.1c demo. You can also start Worlds Chat by double-clicking on the shortcut on your desktop (if you put one there). After 10 or 20 seconds, Worlds Chat will launch and present you with the startup screen. If you experience problems at this point, see the "Worlds Chat FAQ," on the companion Web site for this book.

Docking in the Worlds Chat Space Station

Before arriving at the docking port, you have to choose your avatar first, so stop in at the avatar gallery and take a look around. You should see the avatar gallery on your screen (see the following figure). Once you choose an avatar, you can enter the Worlds Chat Space Station.

Whoa, the floor is moving!

When Worlds Chat lands you into the gallery, you will soon find that when you slide your mouse forward and back, you *move* smoothly through the space. The mouse is tied to motion. If you move the mouse left or right, you will turn. Repeatedly lifting the mouse up, setting it back down, and pushing it away from you will move you forward; this is called "mousing" or "pucking it" (like pushing a hockey puck around). You can move backward with the opposite motion.

You may be surprised at how smoothly the scene changes around you. Unless you have played games like *Doom* or *Descent*, this kind of experience can be truly breathtaking for the first-time visitor. Before the power of PCs and the speed of computer games combined to make virtual worlds possible, you would have had to know someone with a very expensive virtual reality computer to try this.

Step into the gallery to choose your avatar.

So, let's get back to the fun. Turn to your immediate left and travel along the wall of portraits toward the corner window. Looking through the window, you will see a multipod space station (as the adjacent figure shows). That is the Worlds Chat station out there on the Internet. There may be up to 1,000 people on board at the same time. Getting excited? I sure was the first time I visited here. Let's choose an avatar and get connected!

Look out at the space station.

Click your mouse. You should see a green walking man symbol appear at the bottom right-hand corner of the view window. This indicates that the mouse is no longer tied to your motion. You can use the mouse to select an avatar or menu items. Just click on the green walking man to start moving again with the mouse. Relax, you'll get the hang of it. If you move the mouse too fast or too far, it can go outside of the Worlds Chat window and you will stop moving, so be careful to take small steps.

The green walking man symbol.

Pucking along with the mouse can get tiring, and it is not a very precise way to move (joystick support would be good). A good alternate way to move is by using the arrow keys on your keyboard. If your arrow keys are only on the number pad (they also have numbers on them), make sure your Num Lock key is off (a light may go off when you press it) so that your arrows can control direction. Many keyboards have separate arrow keys, and it is better to use these. The following table shows the keys and how they move you. You will find after awhile (unless you are already an avid gamer), that you can roll your fingers from one arrow key to another, and even hold two down at once (say, forward and right), to make smooth turns. You certainly don't have to just move forward then left in separate steps. Good computer games have given us this turbo-control to fly through virtual spaces . . . bravo!

Arrow keys and how they move you	
KEY	**ACTION**
↑	Move forward
↓	Move backward
←	Turn to your left
→	Turn to your right

Click on the green walking man and switch to the keyboard to try this out. While you are at it, take a look at the portraits on the walls of the gallery. This is not just some digital museum; you are looking at avatar body styles. Stop, click your mouse to get it back, and then you can click on any of these avatar choices.

Personally, I prefer the penguin. Maybe it is just that I have always wanted to own a tuxedo! When you pick an avatar, it emerges from the portrait and spins before you. If you like the look of it, you can opt to be embodied by it, or go back to the gallery to look for another. Don't worry, avatars won't be offended if you don't choose them. If you like, you can enter Worlds Chat as a different avatar every time you go in. When you re-enter Worlds Chat, you will still have your last avatar choice. You can always return to the gallery and change your selection.

Once you have chosen your avatar, you are on the verge of boarding the space station (you can enter as a guest or as a registered user). I will tell you more about the benefits of being a registered user in the section, "Going Gold: The Good Life as a Registered User." For now we will enter as a guest; just press Enter Worlds Chat.

You should see messages in the window as your Worlds Chat software tries to connect to the server at Worlds Inc. If you cannot connect, it could be because of the following reasons:

- Your Internet connection is not working from your PC, or you forgot to dial in (or you timed out and disconnected). Test your connection to the Internet or reconnect and try again (you will have to close and restart Worlds Chat).

- Worlds Chat's server is not working or is overloaded at the moment. Try again in a few minutes (or even the next day).

- The Internet is just too busy, and it is taking too long to reach the server. Try again in a few minutes (or in an hour or two).

Single-user mode . . . alone and lost in space!

If you cannot connect to the Worlds Chat server, you will be given the option of going into the station in single-user mode. If you click on Y for yes, you can enter and explore the station on your own. You can use single-user mode to practice your navigation skills and explore the station, although you will see no other users there. If you do not want to go into the station in single-user mode, click on N and try again later.

Sound and music in Worlds Chat

Under the Options menu, you can turn sound and music on or off. If your computer does not have a 16-bit sound card capable of playing WAV files (such as the SoundBlaster 16), then you should turn sound and music off. Do this by checking the Sound and Music items off from the Options menu. You can also press F2 and F3 to turn sound and music on and off.

Note that if you have no sound cards, Worlds Chat may crash if you attempt to log on with sound or music turned on. The avatar gallery has no sound or music, so you have a chance to adjust these settings before entering Worlds Chat.

Your time in paradise is limited

Worlds Chat demo users (the version on the CD in this book) have a time limit for each session. You will hear beeps, see text warnings, and the Worlds Chat screen will start to go white when you are close to being timed out. Just log back in to start the timer again. Becoming a registered user (see "Going Gold: The Good Life as a Registered User," later in this chapter) will allow you to stay on as long as you want.

Your Worlds Chat demo version may have an expiration date. Check the readme.txt file in the \worlds\chatdemo directory for the exact date. Users of expired Worlds Chat demo will not be able to log in to Worlds Chat's server, and may see a message that they must download a new version of Worlds Chat from the Internet. If this happens to you, see "Installing or upgrading Worlds Chat from the Internet," earlier in this chapter, for instructions on how to get a new version of Worlds Chat.

Beam me in, Scotty!

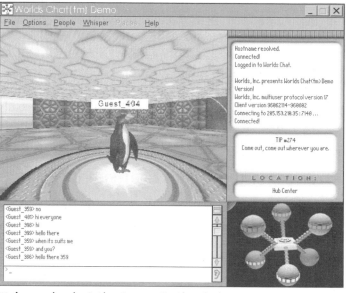

We are in! The *transporter* has teleported us right into the hub, in the heart of the Worlds Chat Space Station. The penguin you see in the adjacent figure is what I look like to other avatars. In Worlds Chat, you are in *first person* view, that is, you see the world through your own eyes. There is no way to see yourself except through the mirror on board the station. You can have someone take a screen capture of you and send it, which is done quite often.

We've arrived at the Space Station hub.

The following figure shows the *teleport* Ground Zero. Ground Zero is the point at which everyone enters a virtual world. It is a good idea to move off the Ground Zero point right after you come in to avoid being landed on by the next person's avatar. Watching the Ground Zero in Worlds Chat, you can see people materializing as they teleport into the hub. A blue flash announces the arrival or departure of an avatar. If you have sound activated (and have a 16-bit sound card and speakers), sounds accompany the blue flash, which makes for a dramatic and fun effect.

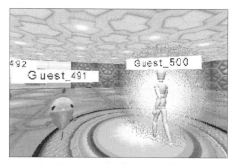

The new guest ("Guest_500") who has just teleported in is dressed as a crash dummy avatar. This is the default avatar, also called a *dummy-tar*, meaning that Worlds Chat has not yet been told by the server which avatar this person really chose. If you wait a few seconds,

New avatars materialize in the hub.

Guest_500 may change from the dummy avatar into their real choice. If you see a lot of dummy avatars running around who don't change, this means they are using an avatar which your version of Worlds Chat cannot show. This may also mean that they are registered users with special avatars, or are using avatars from a third-party source.

Hey, you want to buy an avatar?

There is an active market in custom-designed avatars. The most popular avatar repository can be found at Sting's Place on the Web at **http://sting.yrams.nl/**. This site contains instructions on how to create a custom avatar, and how to download a prebuilt custom avatar and include it in your Worlds Chat. I will not cover this topic, as it is not a feature built into Worlds Chat. But it is a kick just to watch people arriving in their costumes at the digital masquerade. Some users come in the fancy avatars available only to registered users. If you are really interested in customizing your own avatar, there are more juicy details in "Creating Your Own Avatar and Other Activities," later in this chapter.

More on the Worlds Chat interface

Take a look at your Worlds Chat software. You will notice that in the lower right-hand corner there is a three-dimensional map of the space station. The glowing section in the center is the hub, which glows because you are there. You can move your mouse (click to get it back, and to get the green walking man) over to this map and click on any part of the station you want to visit, and this will teleport you to that spot in a flash. Let's not go there yet, as we will try to find someone to take us on a walking tour. You see a lot more by touring around on foot.

Let's Chat!

On the lower right, there is a chat area. At the very bottom of this area is a chat entry field. If you type in a message, and then press Enter, you will send your words (next to your avatar badge name) into the general chat. You will see your words appear in the chat box above the entry area with your given name labeling your chat. Other people will be chatting this way. You can see all the chat from people within a distinct area of the station, such as the hub. Note that you will see the chat from only the six nearest avatars. If you want to have a private conversation with someone, you can move away from other avatars or use the whisper feature (described later in this chapter). A last point: Worlds Chat sometimes can be a bit slow at picking up the text you type, so sometimes you can make spelling mistakes. If you make a small mistake, don't worry; spelling does not have to be perfect!

It is best to try and get in front of someone's avatar before trying to chat with them. Use their name to get their attention (they should see you, unless they are not at their computer). You could say something like, "Hey Guest 222, I like your funky Ken Doll avatar!"

Social etiquette in digital space: It isn't any different there

Be careful to check the chat box to make sure that the person you want to chat with is not already deep in conversation with someone else. Rules of social etiquette and politeness apply here as they do in the real world. Remember, treat others as you would have them treat you. You must be extra careful not to offend because you know even less about the people (their opinions, culture, or even language) you are talking to.

English is not the only language of humanity!

If you encounter someone using a language other than English, respect them. If you know that language, or even just a few words, it would be polite to use their language. Do not assume automatically that they know English. Nine out of ten people on the planet do not speak English as their first language. English is the lingua franca of computers and on the Internet, but why not let virtual worlds be enriched by the many cultures and languages of humanity? I have encountered Koreans chatting by keying in versions of Korean characters using the western alphabet. This was tedious, but seemed to serve them (they could not use their own Chinese-style pictographic characters). Instead they used made-up English words that sounded like Korean characters. This is completely indecipherable except to experts in the technique, so I just left them in peace. I have yet to see Navajo spoken in there, but any day now . . . ?

Body language

As previously mentioned, when moving around you can pass through doors, but not walls. You will bump into walls and slide along them. However, you *will* pass through other avatars. This was a practical design decision made by the builders of Worlds Chat, but it poses some interesting social challenges. One obvious rule of avatar body language is, *don't block someone else's view if they are trying to have a conversation.* The adjacent figure shows a problem I had in trying to talk to my friend, Blue Bear. A general rule of thumb says that it is OK to pass through someone's avatar if you do it by accident (and apologize), or do it quickly, and don't linger in another's space. In other virtual worlds,

Hey! Please don't block my conversation!

avatar bodies make contact and bump each other, which provides for some interesting social dynamics. Note also that if you get very close to another avatar, it turns toward you. This is an automatic reaction of the Worlds Chat software; the person running the avatar did not actually turn.

Come closer: You can whisper to another person or group

There are a few more options for chatting. You can chat with a specific person by whispering. Note that whispering can be used like a walkie talkie because it works anywhere throughout the station. You can send a message to someone using whisper, even though you might be in different rooms where you could not normally see each other's chat. This can be done in the following ways:

- Click with the left mouse button on someone's avatar and select Whisper to, as shown in the following figure. After this, what you type will go just to that person. It will appear in the chat box with everyone else's chat, but will have the symbols {their name: your name} before your words.

- Press F7 before you type, and that will let you whisper again to that same person.

- You may also want to whisper to a group. In the figure, you will notice the Group Member option. If you click on a person's avatar, and add them to your group, then all whispers will be directed at that member, and to every other member you have included in that group. This is a convenient way to set up a discussion with a chosen set of people. Remember, whispers to the group will work throughout the space station, even if you are in different rooms. Private conversations can also be held in rooms where you are the only person around, but to guarantee privacy, set up a group!

Left-click on an avatar to get the Member Options pop-up menu.

Muting someone: When you just cannot stand it anymore

If you have simply lost patience with someone, you can click on their avatar and select Mute. This means that you will not see any text they enter. Use Mute only in extreme cases, as ignoring someone in this way is a form of rudeness in the real world. The muted person will still be able to see what you say, unless they choose to mute you in return. Note that the muted person will not know that they have been muted.

Anonymity

In Worlds Chat you are anonymous, that is, no one knows who you really are or knows your e-mail address. Anonymity can make obnoxious users less responsible, or shy users more outgoing. Anonymity is an important issue for people who create and use virtual worlds.

Big type and good chatiquette

If you are having trouble reading the chat, or are using a demo of Worlds Chat, you might want to select Options ⇨ Font to change to bigger characters. If you are really studying the chat, you will notice that it is not just all gibberish, but it has its own conventions and structure. I will go into greater detail about this in this section and throughout the book.

You can also get the big picture by pressing the small button at the upper right-hand corner of the chat box (see following figure). This will maximize the chat area so you can read more chat at one time. You can scroll down this window to read the last few minutes of chat. Press the small button again to minimize the chat window again. As you can see in the following figure, the chat contains some interesting features, some of which illustrate good and bad chat etiquette (chatiquette):

- People use abbreviations such as, "i could show u." The use of lowercase letters can be a real time-saver, although it can be considered bad manners to type some-one's name without capitalizing the first letter.

- People type in UPPERCASE when they want emphasis; this is called shouting, and can be considered rude if overused.

- People use special letter combinations, such as LOL, which means Laughing Out Loud. These are derived from the pure text chat and *MUD* environments, and can be cryptic. See the glossary at the back of this book for a guide to these expressions. The use of *emoticons* (special combinations of characters like :) to mean a smile, or ;) to mean a wink) is very common, and a good practice.

- In real life (RL), people say proper good-byes. This can be a problem in cyberspace because sometimes conversation is broken off without a

<Guest_449> well its a pity but i have to go now as i am expecting a call.. it was nice to hear from you
<Guest_491> and the spacewalks...terrific!
<DigiGardener> where is that, above the hub?
<DigiGardener> how do u spacewalk?
<Tweety Bird> than I can say to you HEY DUHHHHHHHHH
<Guest_491> in the upper deck...i could show u
<Temptrest> hahahahahahhaha...that's me!!!lol
<DigiGardener> please do!
<Tweety Bird> LOL LOL LOL LOL ROFL HAAHAHAHAHAHAHAAHAH
<Temptrest> hahahaha

Maximize the chat window by enlarging the font.

good-bye. You can be talking with someone, and suddenly they teleport out of your sight. Sometimes someone's avatar stays in front of you, but they stop talking. This could be due to problems they are having with their software or connection, or maybe they just had to step away for a second or two (nature does call, occasionally). Just ask if they are still there, and see if they answer. Patience is a true virtue in virtual worlds.

Who is out there to talk to?

Use the People menu to find out about the other people in Worlds Chat.

If you are in an area, and wonder about all the other people there, just select the People menu and pick the Who list (for a sample Who list, see the figure on the right). The People menu will also show you who is in your whisper group and who you have muted out.

Who List
Guest_491
Susie-Q
Dandy Don
Slip
seal
Reno Jim

A Who list accessed from the People menu.

Just who am I talking to?

You might have noticed that avatars are walking around with big signs over their heads. These are called *badges*, and they let you distinguish between avatars. There are only a limited number of avatar choices, so badges are essential. Have you ever been to a conference of identical twins? There would certainly be name tags there! My registered user name is, as always, DigiGardener, the digital gardener, sowing seeds in cyberspace. To have your own choice of name, you must become a registered user and purchase the gold edition CD of Worlds Chat from Worlds Inc. See the company Web page at **http://www.worlds.net** for details.

Badges help to identify twin avatars.

Got a question? Ask a local

Often, the best way to learn about a world like Worlds Chat (other than buying this book!) is to ask someone in the world for help. This is the first time in history that graphical software has been inhabited by people, and it is your opportunity to really become a pro. Sometimes, there are people who have used a virtual world (and the same avatar or badge name) for a very long time. These users are often called *veterans* or *ancients*. Someone who has used Worlds Chat for a few hours a week over a month could easily become known as an ancient. If ours is an accelerated culture, then virtual worlds are the most turbo-charged communities! The shapes of rooms, choices of avatars, and mix of people can change overnight (or over a few minutes). If you revisit a world you looked at a few months ago, you might be amazed at the changes.

Stepping out: How to get out of this world

Getting out of Worlds Chat is easy, just select File ⇨ Exit. Don't forget to disconnect from the Internet; you don't want to run up bills if you are paying for connection services by the hour.

Have Avatar, Will Travel: Touring the Space Station

Meet the Natives

Worlds Chat is not quite as big as the station in *Deep Space Nine,* or the movie, *2001, A Space Odyssey,* but you can get seriously lost here. You may have to ask around a few times, but chances are you will find another avatar who will be happy to help you get around. In Worlds Chat, you cannot do much more than chat or explore, so giving or receiving a guided tour is one of the biggest activities here. I was lucky this time; the first person I ran into, Guest 420 who I nicknamed Blue Bear, and who turned out to be a student from South Carolina, was happy to show me around. I hadn't been in Worlds Chat for months, and there was much more there.

Blue Bear took me out of the hub through the sliding door (just crash your avatar against doors and they usually open) and down the hall, as you can see in the following figures. I could hear the throbbing sounds of the space station machinery running (make sure your sound and music are on by clicking on the Options menu). Looking out of the window in the hallways, I could see the pods of the space station stretching out into the deep, starry void. Other cybernauts were careening down the hallways around the hub. Blue Bear then raced me to the door of the nearest escalator, which opened and sucked him in (see the following fig-

Following my tour guide out of the hub.

ure). I paused for a moment, and then raced through, joining a Goldilocks avatar on the way up the escalator. Arriving in the pod, I found Blue Bear and others engaged in conversation.

I noticed a shimmering doorway and asked Blue Bear, "what's that?" He and I both tried to enter, but were bounced back and given the message, "Access to this area requires an upgrade to Worlds Chat 1.0 Gold," and given the Web site of Worlds Inc. to order it. "Drat!" I said, but thought that it was very good marketing. Worlds Chat and the other virtual worlds are often supplied free to users, so the companies who

Going through the sliding door into an escalator can be scary!

Sailing up the escalator with Goldilocks.

Trying to get through a shimmering doorway.

put the work into creating and running them have to entice us to buy their gold versions to make a living. Please see the section, "Going Gold, the Good Life as a Registered User," later in the chapter.

Gullible's Travels continued

Thanking Blue Bear, I set off to explore on my own. Going back down the escalator from the pod, I discovered another doorway in the hallways around the hub.

This turned out to be an elevator called, "Water Lift." I got in and pushed what seemed to be the down button. Sure enough, I went down and emerged into tunnels in the engineering deck below the hub. I explored these mysterious areas for a while and struck up some conversations. This area reminded me of a ship in the *Alien* movies, and I was constantly watching out for horrible space monsters or eggs. Someone suggested that I try the observation deck above the hub, and showed me how to click directly on the map and teleport there (see following figure). I could not find the elevator anyway, so this was my only way out.

Exploring the tunnels in the engineering deck under the hub.

Click on the map to teleport up to the observation deck.

After wandering around for a while, I found the observation dome, and what a sight! I knew that I would want to return to this area, so I created a placemark for it (see the following figure). A placemark is like a bookmark in Web browsers; if you click on it, you will be taken back to exactly the same spot in a virtual world. Note that placemarks are only available to registered users of the gold version of Worlds Chat.

Creating a placemark for the observation deck.

The observation deck had a strange feature—a force field which would not let me pass. Another odd thing was that other avatars were floating off in deep space near the observation deck, so I asked how they could spacewalk in this way, and I was told that they simply jumped off the station.

I came upon a couple of avatars attempting to spacewalk. I got in line and tried my best to run at the railings, but just could not do it. Perhaps you will have better luck. It is good that there are some tricks on board that require skill to master, as this adds to the appeal of Worlds Chat. There may be other tricks yet to be discovered.

How do these people spacewalk?

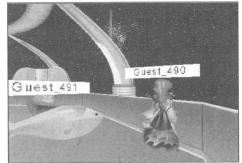

Avatars attempt to jump off the station and spacewalk.

Worlds Chat Tips and What to do About Those Nasty Avapunks

Dangers on board

Worlds Chat, like any open social setting on the Internet or in real life, can fall prey to people with bad intentions. You can encounter people who use coarse or offensive language, or who SHOUT (typing in uppercase), but they are almost always the exception. What is the best way to handle these avapunks? It is a good rule of thumb to ask them politely to stop, and to walk away if they don't. If they follow you, try to lose them in the hallways of Worlds Chat. If they keep after you, and it really both-ers you, exit Worlds Chat and come back later. Chances are you will not see the same abuser more than once.

Community to the rescue

I have seen time and time again how the community of avatars acts to stop what they see as unacceptable behavior. Avatars will crowd around a misbehaving member and ask that person to stop what they are doing.

In the early days of Worlds Chat, in May 1995, I was in the hub with an avatar which was simply not moving or communicating. People gathered their avatars around her, some saying, "I think she's a bot (a robot)," while others disagreed. In truth, this person could have been away from her computer or perhaps Worlds Chat had crashed and left her avatar hanging. Suddenly an aggressive avatar rushed over and started to pass back and forth through the disabled avatar. In Worlds Chat, you can pass through other people's avatars. This is not considered rude if you do it by accident or quickly, making sure you are not blocking a con-versation. However, this kind of avatar abuse (also called *avabuse* or *avattacking*) was different. Seeing this, the other users became very defensive, saying, "Hey you, you can't do that; that avatar belongs to a person; stop!" It was a fascinating insight . . . if an object is associated with, or somehow embodies a person in our minds, we treat it differently.

Don't worry, no one can kill your avatar (this is not *Doom*), and you cannot be excluded from Worlds Chat by anyone.

Harassment in Worlds Chat (or, when chat turns ugly)

Terry-NZ, a Worlds Chat expert citizen, recently contributed the following piece on harassment in Worlds Chat. You can find it at Sting's Place on the Web at **http://sting.yrams.nl/harass.html**. I have modified it slightly for length and accuracy to the current version of Worlds Chat.

"As those of us who live there (well, spend most of our waking hours there) know, Worlds Chat is a great place to socialize. Chatting can take many forms, ranging from humorous social banter to deep philosophical discussions. Intimate relationships can even develop, from a one-night stand of cybersex (wow!), to more serious and long-standing affairs.

"Being an anonymous forum, Worlds Chat provides an opportunity to take on an alter ego, and perhaps try things which the constraints of the real world would not allow. However, like the real world, there are certain patterns of behavior which are clearly anti-social and unacceptable. While such activities are uncommon at present, occasionally a small minority can inflict its ugly brand of humor on other users. It's possible that if these forms of behavior become common in chat, then many people may simply stop visiting. In a worst-case scenario Worlds Chat could become like some of the darker areas of the world's major cities . . . a hostile environment, visited only by roaming gangs of cyberpunks.

Cyberspace is often thought of as an equalizer, giving the powerful and the weak an equal voice. Some virtual worlds, like chat rooms, have moderators who can identify users who they feel are not meeting the community standards. Moderators can identify those users by their e-mail addresses or registration numbers, and can throw them off the chat channels. Worlds Chat is unmoderated, and contains none of these mechanisms; so here, it is all up to the community.

From time to time, any of us may experience an unpleasant time in Worlds Chat for a number of reasons. It could occur if you reject a proposal for cybersex (especially if you are female), and the rejected party takes exception to the refusal. It could occur if you have won an argument, or if you've asked someone to stop acting like a jerk. It could happen simply because you are female (or at least have a female avatar)."

Terry's harassment guidelines are outlined in the following section.

Forms of harassment

Harassment seems to take three forms. These are listed in order of increasing seriousness.

1. Abuse

   Aggressive, obscene whispers, perhaps combined with the continual presence of the offender's avatar . . . usually right in front of your face! As you can't kick them in the you-know-where, the best policy may be to ignore them until they go away. They will soon tire of the game.

2. Shutting down your system

   This can occur if the offender whispers many single letters or words to you repeatedly, in rapid succession. It certainly prevents you from talking to others, and if you have a minimum system (8MB), may even shut you down completely. A very vicious form of this can involve two people, where one sends the whispers while the other publicly denigrates you. Of course, you are unable to refute what is being said.

The best solution is to use the mute function to turn off the offender's words, and whisper to your friends about what happened. Let the offenders have it publicly before they can shut you up again. With any luck, your friends will support you in this.

3. Impersonation

This can be one of the most vindictive and malicious acts in Worlds Chat. Here, the offender takes your name and avatar, and visits people you know, gossiping and generally causing trouble. Often it's obvious to your friends that it's definitely not you, but sometimes the offender can be very subtle. They may even accuse their victim of harassment just to watch the fun. Having your own custom avatar may not be any guarantee of security, either. It should be easy enough to take a screen shot of someone's avatar, and construct an identical one, which the offender then could use.

Reducing the risk

Nothing can be done to stop people from masquerading as you if they want to, but there are some ways to lessen the risk.

- If you have had an unsavory experience with someone, don't tell a new stranger too much about yourself until you get to know them reasonably well. It may be the offender collecting information to use against you later.

- If you think you might be talking to someone masquerading as a friend, test them with a few questions based on what you know about them. For example, if you know your friend has no kids you could say, "How's the baby?" If you get the reply, "fine, thanks," then you're talking to an impostor!

- Whisper any personal details to people. Don't make them public; you don't know who might be listening.

- If you know someone has been deliberately impersonating you, tell your friends, and put it on Sting's message board or any other public mailing list or newsgroup about Worlds Chat.

Of course, people may use your avatar and name quite innocently, especially if the latter is a common name. For example, having a female avatar with a name like Rebecca is hardly going to be unique.

Worlds Chat is a free, anonymous, unmoderated venue. This is both its strength and weakness. It means we must all be responsible for moderating our own behavior and any anti-social behavior in others. In this way, we'll all enjoy the party!

Going Gold: The Good Life as a Registered User

You can become a registered user of Worlds Chat. To do this, see the details on the Worlds Inc. Web site at **http://www.worlds.net**. If you order a gold membership, you will be sent a Worlds Chat Gold CD with a special version of Worlds Chat, which you can install to replace your old demo version (see the following table for a comparison of the Worlds Chat Gold and Worlds Chat Demo features). The key benefits are the following:

- You will be able to go through the shimmering farcaster doors into six new outer worlds with over 600 rooms to explore.

- You can choose from over 40 avatars in the gallery, and select your own name (no more Guest 999).

- You can include your own custom avatar, or select one from links to several avatar archives on the Web (other users must have demo version 1.1c to see your custom avatar).

- You will be able to sample over 24MB of art, music, and sound effects.

- You can use Worlds Chat as long as you want, and will not be timed out (as you are in the demo version).

- Up to three members of your household can have their own separate identities in Worlds Chat Gold.

A glimpse through those shimmering farcaster doors

What awaits you through those shimmering doors (known as *farcasters*) as a registered user? I will take you on a brief tour to give you an idea.

First stop: the gorgeous Garden of Eden. This area features a labyrinth of separate gardens, each with its own theme. There is the flower garden, the Zen-style tranquillity garden, the breezy poplar grove, and the Koi pond, featuring a cat that meows.

Don't forget to explore the Hall of Sadness for a more somber mood, and the Gothic area, where you will find a multilevel castle.

One of the most magical spaces is Skyworld, which you can reach through the airdoor. Catwalks take you over dizzying heights between the mysterious obelisk monolith and a maze in the sky.

Features of Worlds Chat Gold and Worlds Chat Demo

TOPIC	WORLDS CHAT GOLD 1.1	WORLDS CHAT DEMONSTRATION VERSION 1.1C
User names	New in version 1.1. Can establish up to three user names per serial number.	Temporary visitor registered as Guest
Passwords	Password protection lets visitors have permanent identity	Can only use guest names, which are different each time
Avatars	40 avatars to choose from	15 avatars to choose from
Custom avatars	Lets visitors use custom avatars	No custom avatar support
Worlds	Space station and six worlds in which to travel	Travel limited to space station
Rooms	800 rooms to visit	50 rooms to visit
Art and sound	24MB of art, music, and sound effects	4MB of art
Session length	Unlimited session length	Timed sessions—visitors may be logged off after a time limit
Simultaneous users	Unlimited number of gold users	Number of Guest users may be limited by the server
Placemarking	Placemarking feature lets you make your own shortcuts and navigate easily between Worlds and rooms	No placemarking features
Price	$32.95 (SRP) plus $5.00 shipping and handling	Free download from Worlds Inc. Web site

If you are a fan of Frank Herbert's *Dune,* you will like the Desert Planet and the Ziggurat. Haunting music and distant flying creatures give this world a surreal feel.

Our last stop is Asteroid 1541, a party zone. There is a room here with a mirror so you can powder your nose or straighten your avatar before going into the soiree with the digerati. A strange feature of this mirror is that you can only see yourself, and no one else's reflections!

Eve (Cyberhouse1, actually) is in the Garden of Eden.

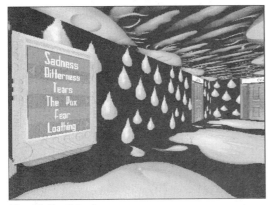

The Hall of Sadness.

A dramatic view of the catwalks in Skyworld through the airdoor.

Well, it's all about chat, and maybe romance too? I caught two avatars kissing in Worlds Chat (see figure on the right), and thought for a moment: true virtual love! But no, it was only an illusion! I just caught the avatars at a strange angle. But you never know . . . For more images of Worlds Chat and Worlds Chat Gold, see the color section in the center of the book.

See yourself in the mirror in Asteroid 1541.

True love in Worlds Chat? No, only an illusion.

Creating Your Own Avatar and Other Activities

When I was writing this book, it was possible to create your own avatar in Worlds Chat, albeit a bit difficult. But hey, it is possible! Some Worlds Chat citizens make custom avatars, or use big avatar clearinghouses where people can choose a new avatar. Some of these avatars are copies of well-known personalities or cartoon characters (otherwise known as trademark violations, or *avamarks*), so if you are moonwalking around as Michael Jackson, and some blue-suited lawyer avatars start chasing you, you can't say you weren't warned. But seriously, picking out a personal original avatar is fun. I recommend that you start by paying a visit to Sting's Place (a Web site listed in the section, "Hot Spots: Web Sites by Worlds Chat Users") where you can follow all the steps to get your own avatar. There are several other Web sites with custom avatars and instructions on how to make them, later in this chapter.

Join a Worlds Chat citizen group

One thing to do in Worlds Chat is to join one of the many unofficial citizen groups. The OPUS is an informal group of all-penguin avatars in Worlds Chat. Look for penguins, and ask if they belong to OPUS. They hold big, all black-tie affairs in the Rave Room.

Step on a crack and step off the station

If you manage to hit door hinges by the entrances to escalators just right, you can get off the station. Floating in space, you can see people walking around in the hallways (and asking how you did it). They will see you as a tiny avatar in the distance, sometimes showing through walls. You can come back in by passing through the walls, although you still might be perceived as small. There are a number of places around the station from which you can jump (I saw some people earlier who were trying to jump off an outside platform). Ask someone, and they might be able to tell you how to do it.

Hot Spots: Web Sites by Worlds Chat Users

Hot Spots

Sometimes all a wannabe-avatar needs is a little inspiration. Check out what others have done at the Web pages described below.

Note that some of the Web page links in the following table may have changed, or the Web pages may have been discontinued. Consult your *Avatars!* book home page at **http://www.digitalspace.com/avatars** for a more up-to-date list of links.

Official pages

Worlds, Inc.
http://www.worlds.net

Sting's Place
http://sting.yrams.nl
A pioneering Worlds Chat Web site full of custom avatars and instructions on how to integrate them into Worlds Chat. Sting hosts forums and gives oodles of helpful tips, especially for avatars who don't see eye to eye. Sting and his avatar clearinghouse hail from the Netherlands.

Eric Schuler's Page
http://www.preferred.com/~eschuler/wc.htm
Pretty wild avatars.

Y7ALANZO's Page
http://people.tais.com/~y7alanzo/
Avatars as creative as they get.

Beach Girl's Page
http://www.primenet.com/~roessler/Beach/av_01.htm
Avatars with a feminine touch.

Unofficial pages

Worlds Chat Community Headquarters
http://members.tripod.com/~wcc/

Predawnia Universe
http://www.predawnia.com/
A cornucopia of resources for Worlds Chat.

The World Wide Chatter's Guild
http://www.geocities.com/TimesSquare/1809/

European Worlds Chat Guild
http://www.op.se/hall/silke/ewcg/
A Worlds Chat site from Sweden.

Odin's, The Worlds Chat Avatar Grade Book
http://www.ptw.com/~chuckr/worlds/intro.htm

Beach Girl's Worlds Chat Links
http://www.primenet.com/~roessler/Beach/WChat.htm

Avatar's World Chat Pics, the End of the World
http://www.geocities.com/TheTropics/2467/
Documents when the old Worlds Chat was destroyed to make way for a new
version. End-of-the-World party coverage can also be found.

The Doctor, Worlds Chat Hall of Shame
http://www.ozemail.com.au/~willp/

Worlds Chat gossip lines

The Worlds Chat Tribe 2
http://www.predawnia.com/tribe2/index.html
Supports a Powwow conference about Worlds Chat.

Katt's Litter Box
http://www.geocities.com/~katt
A little Worlds Chat scandal sheet that contains interviews of famous Worlds
Chat citizens, such as Sting, CRUZIN BIKER, and Jefe.

Tilly Tells All: Goldgossip's Home Page
http://www.geocities.com/TimesSquare/1974/
A place where you can get all the latest gab on Worlds Chat citizenry.

A Brief History of Worlds Chat

Beginning in April 1995, Worlds Chat was the very first three-dimensional avatar world to become widely available on the Internet. It worked so well that it inspired a whole generation of worlds, many of which appear in this book. I was using Worlds Chat from its early days, and I did some investigation on how it was put together.

Worlds Chat team

A super team put together Worlds Chat, including Dave Leahy, Andrea Gallagher, Wolf Schmidt, Judy Challinger, Syed Asif Hassan, Farshid Meshgali, Kurt Kokko, John Navitsky, Naggi Asmar, David Tolley and many others. Jeff Robinson (a.k.a. Scamper, the Combat Wombat) working with Helen Cho was Worlds Chat's first artist, and is responsible for much of the "better-lit alien" look of the space station. Jeff's strange fascination with penguins and love of clever lighting illusions have left their permanent mark on Worlds Chat. Visit Jeff's home page at **http://www.scamper.com/** and see his great Worlds Chat Tour at **http://www.scamper.com/art/wc/wctour01.html**.

Worlds Chat history as told by Wolf Schmidt

Wolf Schmidt, a member of the team, kindly offered us the following history and stories from the world's first 3D avatar virtual world.

> "Worlds Chat was meant as a demonstration of our multi-user technology, and as an active laboratory of what our servers could do. We had done corporate demos before April 1995, but they had never been widely distributed enough to get hundreds of people logged into the server at once. Dave Gobel (Worlds founder) was interested in the social computing aspects of the technology, and it was jointly decided that a good application of the technology would be to provide a 3D graphical parallel to the IRC and other chat popular on the Internet as of January 1995. The first WC came out in April 1995, and went through several versions on the client side, and meanwhile we occasionally changed the server and protocol in the background. The user base went from hundreds to thousands-plus, though our record for simultaneous users is still just under 1,000 real users at once. As a sort of plug here, no other multi-user servers to our knowledge can scale that well or carry that much load. Tests with bots (automated avatars) have run even more users at once."

Wolf tells the saga of Tokie-D-Bear

> "About eight months ago, there was this guy who called himself Tokie-D-Bear. He modified the cutesy 'Blue Bear' avatar such that it was, from alternate angles, holding a large bong and a "phat" reefer, with a perpetual cloud of purple haze

obscuring the head region. He put together a page called the Worlds Chat Tabloids, wherein he doctored Worlds Chat-related screen shots under headlines such as, 'Vampire Moths seen attacking HubCenter,' (with a screen shot of a boy avatar being decapitated by a menacing butterfly avatar), 'Penguin Gangs on the Prowl,' (with a screen shot of a penguin avatar holding an incriminating spray can near fresh graffiti in hub corridor), and 'Tokie's Secret Crop Busted,' (with a screen shot of plentiful marijuana fields pasted near the Infinite Plain Castle in Chat version 08). Each article ran about eight paragraphs and featured amusing bogus quotes from 'Worlds security personnel.' It ran for maybe three Web issues, and every time one came out, Dave L. and I would check it out and be rolling all over the floor. Scott Benson (our webmaster) remembers this page, too, and remembers that Tokie had an access log on his pages. Tokie's log could be accessed by clicking the link to see who the last 20 people to get high with Tokie were. So, of course Benson clicks the log and there's my name, Leahy's name, all 'getting high with Tokie' with our e-mail addresses, and the worlds.net domain. And now Benson's name is there too! Oops! Well, we promise we didn't inhale."

Digi's Diary:
The Rise of the Homo Cyborgiens

Digi's Diary

Wolf Schmidt's story of Worlds Chat hacker, Tokie-D-Bear, tell us something that the cyberpunks have known for years: there is a new species of human being on the loose: *Homo Cyborgiens*. What are cyborgiens? A cyborgien is a hybrid of the highest form of hacker, an ambidextrous communicator, and an impersonator and artistic impresario par excellence. And cyborgiens' mutation occurs in the mind as the cortex purrs with bit pulses, and its folds reach through limits of space and time to stroke the great dark sinewy body of the Net. In the coming century and millennium beyond, cyborgiens will step further beyond what the rest of us understand as normal consciousness. Cyborgiens will affect our lives, the future of humanity, and the Earth's biosphere more than we can now know. You cannot go into space and see the Earth from orbit, or the moon, and remain unchanged. Astronauts have taken us to that place through their photographs and words, and changed the daily reality of millions of people who will never see the sun rise or set in the same light again. Cybernauts entering digital space in the spacecraft of their own minds may bring us to frontiers of abstract and complex worlds which will so change us, that we just might be able to survive in a truly abstract and complex universe.

The Palace
CHAT COSMOS

Our drama in digital space is opening now, as we pull the good ship *Avatar* away from the Worlds Chat Space Station and head out into the cosmos...the Chat Cosmos, to be precise. We are entering what looks like a meteor cloud. Flying mountains whiz by us, and we notice that strange flat beings are moving around on their surfaces. There ahead of us is the Palace, the great centerpiece of this constellation of chat worlds. The Palace is a great stone edifice with glowing windows and a huge crowd of wafer-thin avatars dancing around its front gates.

Send out your space probes and explore the cosmos of worlds around the Palace. In the Palace, you can put on a whole virtual theater production with your own props, design and build your own avatars, construct your own Palace world, and above all, chat, chat, and chat.

Your Guide to the Palace Cosmos

WORLD GUIDE

WORLD SKILL LEVEL	Beginner
BUILDING CAPABILITY	Yes
SYSTEM REQUIREMENTS	Mac OS 7.0 or greater; Windows 3.1, Windows 95/NT
AVATAR CREATION CAPABILITY	Yes
DEPTH	2D
SOUND SUPPORT	Music, sound effects, voice, read text on Mac

MINIMUM MACHINE

OPERATING SYSTEM	Windows 3.1 or Mac OS System 7.0
COMPUTER	PC: 386 or better with 256-color VGA display Mac: any machine running System 7.0 with 13-inch color monitor
RESOURCES	PC: 4MB RAM, 5MB free disk space; 16-bit sound card optional for music and sound effects Mac: 2MB RAM
CONNECTION	SLIP/PPP Dial-up to the Internet at 14.4 kbps or a LAN

The Palace: So You Want to be a Star in the Chat Cosmos?

The Palace is a vast constellation of tiny virtual worldlets spreading across the chat cosmos. In the Palace, you can design your own avatar (if you are a registered user), collect props, play group games, program fun behaviors with scripts, and even create your own Palace worldlet. Above all in the Palace, there is chat, and lots of it. The Palace is jam-packed with people wanting to talk. Let us start your epic journey in search of the ultimate chat in the Mansion (as seen in the following figure), and then set off visiting some of the hundreds of Palace worlds.

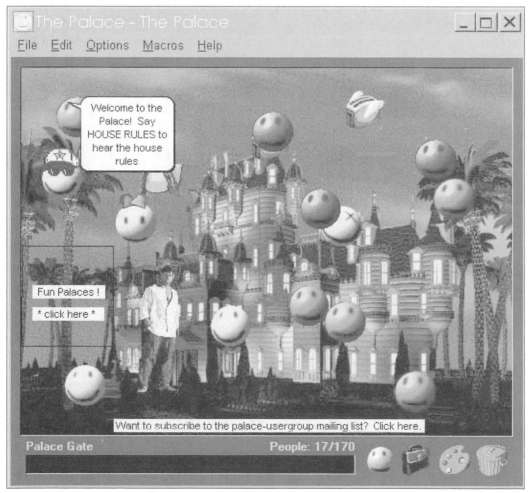

Outside the Mansion is the gateway to the Palace.

How the Palace (Net) Works

The Palace is really a large network of Palace sites running on individual computers, local area networks (LANs), and on the Internet. The Palace is known as a *client/server* system. This means that your experience in the world is maintained by two cooperating pieces of software known as the client and the server. The client runs on your machine, and the server runs on a remote machine. The client is the interface window into Palace worlds. Servers run behind each world and help coordinate the people in the world, and what they see on their clients. The Palace client software you run can communicate with any Palace server. This allows you to wander through hundreds of different worlds by pointing your client at new servers.

The Palace is completely cross-platform, which means that it can be used by both Windows and Macintosh users. On Macintosh computers, the Palace software can run on a local AppleTalk network, or it can access the Internet using MacTCP or Open Transport. Windows users can run the Palace software on either a TCP-based LAN or on the Internet via a SLIP or PPP connection. Palace servers running on local area networks, which are hooked to the Internet, allow interaction between people on the LAN and folks coming in via the Net.

Installing

Installing the Palace Client

What do I need to use the Palace?

You can run the Palace on either a Macintosh or a Windows PC. You will need about 5MB of free hard disk space for storing the executable files, data files, sounds, and pictures for the original Palace Mansion site. If you plan on traveling to other Palace sites, you'll need additional hard disk space to store the art that these servers use. This new art will be downloaded from the Internet and stored on your hard disk.

Mac users

To run the Palace, you will need a color Macintosh with at least 2MB of free memory. The Palace requires Macintosh System 7.0 or later. The Palace will (someday) work on a 12-inch monitor, but currently works best on a 13-inch monitor or larger.

Windows users

To run the Palace, you will need a 386 PC or better with at least 4MB of RAM, running Windows 3.1 or above. You also need a 256-color display. The higher the resolution on your monitor, the better; a minimum of 800 by 600 pixels is recommended, but not required.

Software and connection requirements

The Palace client software is all you need. It is called Palace on the Macintosh and palace.exe on PCs. This client program is specially designed to communicate with the Palace server program (typically running on someone else's machine, but possibly on your own). There are a number of different ways to get connected to the Palace:

- Use the Palace client on a LAN; you don't need any additional software.

- Use the Palace client on the Internet; you need a *Winsock* stack. (Short for Windows Sockets, Winsock is a standard interface for Microsoft Windows applications and the Internet.)

- Use the Palace client with a modem over the Internet; you'll need a SLIP or PPP connection of 14.4 kbps.

In general, if you can use Netscape, you should be able to use the Palace. You can't use the Palace through Windows-based, on-line services like America Online, CompuServe, Microsoft Network, or Prodigy, unless they support direct Internet access through the 32-bit Winsock. Winsocks allow communication between Windows Web browsers, e-mail clients, IRC clients, or any other Windows Winsock applications and the TCP/IP. See, "Setting Up Your On-Line Service to Connect Directly with the Internet," in Appendix B. If you have further problems, contact your on-line service for help.

Getting started and a few disclaimers

The Palace is easy to install, and as a *guest user*, it is free to use for a limited time. You are not charged for the time you spend talking in the Palace, but you could be charged for the hours you are online from your *Internet service provider (ISP)*. Check with your ISP on monthly free hours and rates. If you become a *registered user*, for a fixed yearly fee, you will have access to many more features. To learn how to become a registered user, see the section, "How do I become a registered user of the Palace?" in the FAQ on the companion Web site to this book.

The Palace is constantly evolving, and may have changed since this chapter was written. I placed the very latest version of the Palace on the book CD, so it may be somewhat different from what is described here. These differences will be minor, and this chapter will still be a great guide to the Palace and its worlds. If you see new features or changes, check for information under the Help menu in the Palace. When you first log on to the Palace, you may be asked to upgrade to a new version. You can download an upgrade, or a completely new version of the Palace from the Internet by following the instructions in, "Installing or upgrading the Palace from the Internet," later in this chapter.

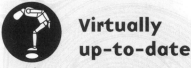

Virtually up-to-date

Help   As a special service for readers of *Avatars!*, I have a home page on the World Wide Web devoted to keeping you up-to-date on your favorite worlds. Find news about software updates, social events held within these virtual worlds, and brand new worlds you might want to try at **http://www.digitalspace.com/avatars**. Bookmark it!

If you have questions or problems

If you have questions or problems installing or running the Palace, consult the companion Web site to this book. If this does not help you, check the excellent Palace home page at **http://www.thepalace.com**, especially the Tech Talk pages at **http://newbie.thepalace.com**, which have host discussion groups, and contain on-line manuals, related sites, and tech support pages.

I appreciate your feedback on *Avatars!*, but I don't have the resources to provide technical support. I would be happy to hear about your experiences in the Palace. Contact me through the *Avatars!* book Web site at **http://www.digital space.com/avatars**.

UNIX and OS/2 versions

At this writing, there are no versions of the Palace client program for UNIX or OS/2. Check the Palace and the *Avatars!* book Web pages for updates on new versions which might support these platforms. You also may be able to run the Palace client using a Windows emulation system on non-Windows machines. Note that if you are considering hosting a Palace world, the server software runs on a wide range of UNIX systems (as well as PCs and Macintoshes).

Installing the Palace from your Avatars! CD

If you have a CD-ROM drive on your Macintosh or PC, you can install the Palace directly from the book CD-ROM. If you don't have a CD-ROM drive, skip right to the section, "Installing or upgrading the Palace from the Internet." In "The Book CD-ROM" chapter, I provide a step-by-step example of installing from the CD-ROM. I suggest you refer to it and follow the same steps for the Palace. Once the installation program on your CD-ROM has started, return to this chapter and find the section, "Running the installation."

Installing or upgrading the Palace from the Internet

If you want the very latest version of the Palace, or were informed that you had to upgrade the version found on your *Avatars!* CD, then you must download files from the Internet. If you haven't done this before, don't panic; it is easier than you might think!

❶ Connect to the Internet (dial up with your modem or make sure your Internet connection is active).

❷ Start your Web browser, such as Netscape Navigator or Microsoft Internet Explorer.

❸ In the top of the browser, you will see a long text box called Location, where you can enter text.

❹ Click in this box, delete the text inside, type http://www.thepalace.com, and press Enter.

❺ After a few moments, the home page for the Palace should appear. If nothing comes up for a long time, check to see that you are online.

❻ If the Palace page is not available for some reason, try entering the location for the *Avatars!* home page, which is http://www.digitalspace.com/avatars. This page may contain more up-to-date links for the Palace.

❼ Once you are at the Palace home page, follow the instructions for downloading or upgrading the Palace virtual world chat software for the PC or Macintosh. At one point, you will click on a link and be prompted for a place to save a file. In response to the dialogue box, click Save to Disk (Netscape) or Save As (Internet Explorer), and save the file to a folder or a place on your desktop. You must choose a folder where you will remember to find the new file, and note the name of the file. You can use the folder that your Web browser gives you, or move back up and select another. I put all downloaded files in a folder I call \download on the PC, and Download on the Mac.

❽ Wait patiently while the download progresses (about 3.5MB). You can do work in other applications, but be careful not to interfere with the connection. Try not to do more on-line work (such as Web surfing) on the Internet while the download is progressing. If you are using your regular telephone line for the modem, don't make a telephone call.

❾ After the download is finished (about 40 minutes for a 28.8 kbps connection, and about 80 minutes for a 14.4 kbps connection), open the folder into which the file was downloaded and double-click on it to start the installation. Go to the section, "Running the installation."

Running the installation

Whether you are running the installation from the CD-ROM, or from the file you downloaded from the Internet, use this section to guide you through the installation. Note that if you downloaded the Palace from the Internet, the installation process may have changed. If this has happened, refer to instructions on the Palace Web site.

❶ The installer setup program will run and prompt you at each step. First, read and accept the license agreement terms.

❷ You will be prompted for the folder into which the Palace will be installed. The default folder on a PC is \palace, and on a Mac, Palace. You can change this or accept the default (recommended).

❸ You will be prompted to install the Palace client and server (both are check-marked On by default in the PC version). If you do not plan to host your own Palace area, I recommend installing only the Palace client, and checking Off the server. On the Mac, choose the Easy Install option to just install the client. Note that you can install the server later, if you like.

❹ The installation should complete successfully if you have enough disk space (you need about 5MB free). The installation program should have created a Palace entry on your Start menu (in Windows 95), or a program group (on Windows 3.1), or its own folder (on the Mac). The Palace should be easy to find.You may also be prompted to view the readme file, which is a good idea. This file contains notes about the latest Palace software.

Files created by the installation

It will be useful later to know the names of files created for the Palace client software. On the Mac, a folder called Palace will be created, which contains the following files:

- Palace–an executable file: the Palace client software

- Palace.prp–a binary file containing prop data used by the Palace client

- Cyborg.ipt–a text file containing a cyborg script

- Mansion script–a text file containing the script for the Palace Mansion

- Pictures–a folder containing the artwork for the Palace Mansion

- Sounds–a folder containing the sounds for the Palace Mansion

- Plug-ins–a folder for storing Palace-aware, add-on applications

On the PC, a subdirectory called \palace will be created, which contains the following files:

- palace.exe–an executable file: the Palace client software

- palace.prp–a binary file containing prop data used by the Palace client

- cyborg.ipt–a text file containing a cyborg script

- Pictures–a subdirectory containing the artwork for the Palace Mansion

- Sounds–a subdirectory containing the sounds for the Palace Mansion

Cleaning up after installation

If you downloaded the Palace installation file from the Internet, you can delete it after the installation is complete. Do not delete the palace.exe by mistake, as this is your running version of the Palace client software. (On the other hand, I often keep the original installer around just in case I have to reinstall it.) Of course, you also have the CD with the original installers, so you do not need to take up valuable hard disk space with them.

Getting Started and Learning the Interface

First Steps

After double-clicking on the Palace client alias, shortcut, or file, you will see the Palace startup screen. The next step is to make sure your connection to the Internet is active; choose File ➪ Connect.

The Connection dialogue specifies your name (Guest, as you are not a paid, registered user), the Hostname (which you can change later if you want to go directly to Palace servers other than the Mansion, where everyone starts), and other settings such as port (leave unchanged). Press Connect, and at the very bottom of the Palace client application window, you will see several messages appear. You should eventually see the message, "Connected via TCP" (if you are connecting through the Internet). If an error message such as, "Connection Refused" appears, chances are the server is down, and you'll just have to try again later.

Connect by using the Palace connection dialogue.

If the Palace repeatedly fails to connect, check that your Internet connection is actually working. If you can visit Web sites with your Web browser (running independently of your on-line service), then you should be connected to the Internet. If you still cannot connect, see the FAQ on the companion Web site to the book, or the technical support section on the Palace home page at **http://www.thepalace.com**.

A Palace primer

The Palace is a large network of individual Palace sites running on individual computers, local area networks, and the Internet. Each Palace site has its own theme, design, artwork, and music. The theme may determine the clientele and kinds of conversations you will have there. Each site can have dozens of *rooms* for you to explore. As the Palace is a two-dimensional world seen from above, all rooms consist of a background image with two-dimensional avatars sliding about. You could make the same thing by cutting out a magazine photograph and then placing small clippings of people and other things on top of that picture. Moving around in this digital version of *Flatland* (the name of a 2D imaginary world described over 100 years ago in a book by Edwin Abbott), is as easy as pointing and clicking. As you can move your avatar, so you can click through doors and visit new rooms, or whole new Palace sites.

Getting to know your sweet interface

When you first connect to the Palace, the first scene you will see is the Palace front gate. The great building in the background is called the *Mansion,* and it is your first stop in the Palace chat cosmos. There are a lot of avatars outside the front gate. They are not locked out or protesting—this is simply a popular gathering place and a drop zone for *newbies* like us. Often the world will greet you as you arrive at the gate, saying something like, "DigiGardener has arrived," to make you feel welcome. But before we rush into the Mansion or converse with these avatars, let's have a quick interface lesson. We are green newbies, but the rest of the Palace society does not have to know it right away!

The figure on the following page shows the Palace client software interface in all its grandeur. Let's go through the interface, step-by-step.

View screen

The interface is dominated by a large, rectangular area known as the *view screen.* This is where all graphic action takes place. As you move from room to room within a Palace site, the view screen is filled with a picture representing the background of that room. All avatars and props in the room appear on top of this background.

The Palace client displaying elements of its interface.

Input box

The long, thin box beneath the view screen is known as the input box. This is where you type in what you want to say, press Enter, and then watch as the text magically appears above your avatar's head in a cartoon bubble. Registered members can enter IptScrae commands from this box as well (more on this later). To activate the input box, simply click anywhere in it; the box lights up and a cursor bar appears, awaiting your input. You can toggle the program's focus back and forth between the input box and the view screen by pressing Tab.

Find yourself in the crowd

When I first entered the Palace, I could not see which avatar was me, so I just typed in some text saying, "hey guys . . . ," and I could see the text appear in the cartoon bubble above my avatar. When I first started, I was given a yellow smiley face (known in the Palace as a *roundhead*) and a name badge reading, Guest 453. I became a registered user after deciding I liked the Palace, and so I got to choose my own name, and came in with a red roundhead. After that, I could change my avatar. (More later about how to become a registered user and change your avatar.) For now, you will start life in the Palace as a yellow roundhead.

Status bar

The area just between the input box and the viewing area is known as the *status bar*. On the status bar you can see the following items displayed:

- The name of the current room

- Two numbers: one representing the number of people in the current room, and the other representing the number of people on the current server

- The name of the person you are talking to if you are whispering (see "Whispering sweet nothings," later in this chapter)

- The Special Feature icons

Special Feature icons

To the right of the input box are four icons which allow you to access many of the Palace's special features. These icons include the following:

Face icon

This icon is obscured in the preceding figure because I have clicked on it to open the *face picker,* which allows you to change your facial expression and color.

Satchel icon

Clicking on this icon opens the *prop picker,* which gives you access to the current collection of props. Props are special pieces of art that allow you to decorate your environment, your avatar, or to give as gifts. This window allows you to add props to your avatar and remove props from your collection. Registered members can also use this window to edit existing props, or create entirely new ones.

Paint Palette icon

Clicking on this icon opens the *Painting window,* which gives you access to a number of special tools used for painting on the Palace screen. With the painting tools, you can draw right on top of the artwork in a Palace room, and everyone else there can see what you are doing. It is like a shared digital canvas. This drawing does not have a permanent effect on the room art itself. When you come back in later, it will be gone. Note that this function is turned off in some Palace rooms. Note also that unregistered guests are able to look at the tools in the Painting window, but are unable to use them. Such are the benefits of membership!

Trash Can icon

This icon functions much like the traditional Macintosh or Windows 95 trash can; dragging a prop here gets rid of it. Clicking on the Trash Can icon does nothing.

The File menu

Use the File menu to enter and leave the Palace, or to issue file-oriented commands, such as logging your conversations and commands. The File menu commands include the following:

Connect: This command is used to sign on to a Palace server via TCP/IP. Clicking here will cause a dialogue box to appear, which asks for the address to which you wish to connect. The previous four Palace addresses that you visited will appear as choices in the pull-down entry box. In Windows, if you are running the server locally (on the same machine), you can hold down Shift when selecting this menu item to log in via DDE (Direct Data Exchange). The client will determine the IP address of your server automatically.

Connect via AppleTalk (Mac version only): This command is used to log onto a Palace server running on an *AppleTalk* local area network.

Disconnect: This command disconnects you from the current Palace server without closing the client program.

Open log file|Close log file: This command toggles the Log file open and closed. A Log file records all chat text and commands received by the client to a file on your hard disk. Clicking here brings up a standard dialogue box, which allows you to name the file (a default appears which uses the current date and time as a name for the file).

Child lock: This command brings up a dialogue box which allows you to set a password on the Palace client to child-protect your software. Do not forget this password—you will be asked to supply it every time you log on to the client. To remove the password, simply delete the contents of the password text box and click OK. This resets the password (to none).

Reload script: This command reloads your cyborg.ipt file, the only Palace data file you can edit while online. You can edit the cyborg.ipt file at any time with any ASCII word processor (running in another window), save it, and return to the Palace client. Your changes will not take effect until you select Reload Script.

Register: This command allows you to lock in your unique serial number, which is supplied when you register the software with The Palace Inc. Locking in this number gives you access to the advanced members-only features of the Palace client. Once the registration process is complete, your serial number appears in the client program's splash screen (instead of the words, Unregistered Version).

Quit (Mac version) or Exit (Windows version): This command disconnects you from the current Palace session and closes the client.

The Edit menu

The Edit menu contains the standard editing commands used to manipulate text, as well as the Preferences command. The Edit menu commands include the following:

Undo (Mac version only): This command allows you to undo the previous editing operation (i.e., to revert back to the way things were just before your last editing operation). This works only in the Prop Editor.

Cut: This command allows you to cut text from the input box or the log window. Mac users can also use this command for graphic functions, such as when working in the Prop Editor. The hot key combination for this command is Ctrl+X (on the Mac, Command-X).

Copy: This command allows you to copy text from the input box or the log window. Mac users can also use this command for graphic functions, such as when working in the Prop Editor. The hot key combination for this command is Ctrl+C (on the Mac, Command-C).

Paste: This command allows you to paste text into the input box from anywhere. Mac users can also use this command to paste an image when working in the Prop Editor. The hot key combination for this command is Ctrl+V (on the Mac, Command-V).

Clear: This command clears the current contents of the input box. You can do the same thing by pressing Esc.

Preferences dialogue box

Choosing the Preferences command from the Edit menu displays a dialogue box that allows you to set many options. Some of the most useful include:

Name: This is the name that others see attached to your avatar. You can see the names of others in the room by simultaneously holding down Command-Option (for Mac users) or Ctrl+Alt (for Windows users).

Balloon Delay: These checkboxes allow you to modify the length of time that cartoon chat balloons are displayed on the screen. Three durations are available: slow, medium, and fast. The duration of any message is based upon the length of the message, modified (locally) by this setting.

Show User Names: This command allows you to toggle the display of user names in the viewing area. You can make these names appear only temporarily, by holding down F3.

Tinted Balloons: When checked, this command causes all cartoon balloons to appear filled with color. They are white by default.

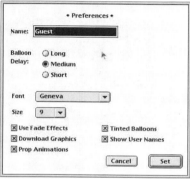

Text Display Font (Mac version only): This pull-down menu allows you to set the font used to display the text in cartoon balloons, user names, and hotspot names.

Text Display Font Size (Mac version only): This allows you to set the size of the font used to display the text in cartoon balloons, user names, and hotspot names.

The Preferences dialogue box (Mac version).

The Options menu

The Options menu contains various commands for controlling the behavior of the software, as well as several means of transportation throughout Palace sites. The Options menu offered to Macintosh and Windows users are significantly different, so I discuss them separately in the following section:

Macintosh version

Draw: This command toggles the Painting window open and closed (you can do the same thing by clicking on the Palette icon). The Painting window is a floating window which contains special tools for painting directly on the screen. Only registered members can use these tools.

Show Names: This command toggles the display of nameplates beneath all users in the room with you. You can make these names appear only momentarily by holding down Command-Option.

Sound Volume: This command opens the Sound Volume control.

Speak As: This command displays a submenu of available voices from the Apple Speech Manager (PlainTalk 1.4.2).

Full Screen: This command toggles between a full-screen display and a windowed display.

Iconize: This command minimizes the Palace client without disconnecting, and reduces the display to an icon on your desktop.

Go Back: This command moves you back to the previous room you visited.

Log Window: This command toggles the log window open and closed. This is a floating window which stores all the text messages that the client receives (both speech and commands). This text can be saved to disk by selecting Log to File from the File menu.

Find User: This command toggles the *user list* open and closed. This window is shown in the adjacent figure, and displays a list of all users logged into the current Palace site, and the names of the rooms they are in. Clicking on a user's name in this window causes you to enter *telepathy mode* with that person; you may now speak to that person just as if you were whispering—no matter how far apart you are! To instantly teleport yourself to another person's location, double-click on their name. Exception: Rooms marked Private cannot be entered (except by wizards and gods).

The user list.

Goto Room: This command toggles the *rooms window* open and closed. This window displays a list of all rooms in the current Palace site, and the number of users in each room. To instantly teleport yourself to another room, double-click on the room's name. Exception: Rooms marked Private cannot be entered (except by wizards and gods).

Wizard: This command opens a dialogue box asking for the *wizard* (or *god*) password. Wizards and gods have special powers and capabilities beyond those of registered members. There are different wizards and gods (and passwords!) at each Palace site.

Windows Version

Show Names: This command allows you to toggle the display of user names in the viewing area. You can make these names appear temporarily by holding down F3.

Sound: This command toggles sound on and off. The hot key combination for this command is Ctrl+S.

Full Screen: This command toggles between a full-screen display and a windowed display. You can do the same thing by clicking on the Max button in the upper right-hand corner of the Palace client window.

Go Back: This command moves you back to the previous room visited. The hot key combination for this command is Ctrl+B.

Find User: This command toggles the *users window* open and closed. This window displays a list of all users logged into the current Palace site, and the names of the rooms they are in. Clicking on a user's name in this window causes you to enter *telepathy mode* with that person; you may now speak to them just as though you were whispering—no matter how far apart you are! To instantly teleport yourself to another person's location, double-click on their name. Exception: rooms marked Private cannot be entered (except by wizards and gods). The hot key combination for this command is Ctrl+F.

Goto Room: This command toggles the *room list* (shown in the adjacent figure) open and closed. This window displays a list of all rooms in the current Palace site, and the number of users in each room. To instantly teleport yourself to another room, double-click on the room's name. Exception: rooms marked Private cannot be entered (except by wizards and gods). The hot key combination is Ctrl+G.

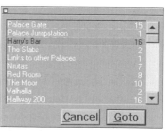

The room list.

Log Window: This command toggles the *log window* open and closed. This is a floating window which stores all text messages the client receives (both speech and commands). This text can be saved to disk by choosing File ⇨ Log to File. The hot key combination for this command is Ctrl+L.

Draw: This command toggles the Painting window open and closed (you can do the same thing by clicking on the Palette icon). The Painting window is a floating window containing a number of special tools for painting directly on the screen. Only registered members can use these tools. The hot key combination for this command is Ctrl+D.

Prop Window: This brings up a floating Prop Picker window which allows you to accessorize your avatar with props. The hot key combination for this command is Ctrl+P.

Wizard: This invokes a dialogue asking for the wizard password. If the password is entered correctly, a Wizard menu is added to the menu bar. The hot key combination for this command is Ctrl+W.

Record Macro: This command opens a submenu which allows you to select a number for the macro you wish to record, which will correspond to the assortment of props currently on your avatar. You can record up to 10 different macros.

Play Macro (0-9): These commands allow you to recall quickly a particular macro; your face color, expression, and props will instantly change to those recorded in the corresponding macro.

The Wizard menu

The Wizard menu provides access to a set of advanced functions, beyond the needs and rights of mere registered members. Wizards and gods are the managers and proprietors of the various sites in the Palace network. Anyone with the server software and an IP address can open a Palace site and become its god, and can give the site's wizard password out to trusted individuals. Each Palace site has its own god, and many sites have wizards as well.

The commands in this menu provide wizards (or gods) with various superpowers in the form of special commands and authorial control over their Palace sites. Since proper utilization of these commands requires an in-depth understanding of the server software, this topic is not treated here. For information on wizard commands and the Wizard menu, see "The Palace Server Software Manual," at **http://newbie .thepalace.com/documentation/server-doc.htm**.

The Help menu

The Palace client's Help menu consists of a number of links which, when clicked, will take you to the appropriate page at The Palace Inc.'s Web site at **http://www.thepalace .com**. The topics covered include:

- User guide
- FAQ (Frequently Asked Questions)
- Palace directory
- Software updates
- Discussion groups
- Palace home page

If these links fail to work correctly, try again while your web browser is running in the background.

Journeys in the Palace: Getting Lost in the Labyrinth

The Palace is a big place! Palace members have put up over 1,000 Palace sites full of interesting rooms. For a small fee, you can also host a Palace site for a limited number of users. Visit The Palace Inc.'s home page for details at **http://www.thepalace.com**.

Move that avatar's body!

Moving an avatar around is very simple: just click on the area in which you want your avatar to be moved. Be careful of hotspots (described later in this section), or you may also fall into another room. You can also use the arrow keys to make small vertical and horizontal avatar movements (note that if the input box is currently active, the arrow keys won't work this way; press Tab to toggle back to the view screen).

Jumping to a specific room

Another convenient way to move is to use the Goto Room command (Command-G for Mac users, or Ctrl+G for Windows users). This opens the rooms window, which lists all the rooms (by name) under the Palace site that you are currently visiting. Note that you will only be able to go to rooms that are public and unlocked.

Joining a specific user

If you are looking for a particular user, you can use the Find Somebody or Find User command (Command-F for Mac users, Ctrl+F for Windows users). This opens the window and lists all the users currently visiting a particular Palace site. Double-clicking on the user's name will take you to the room where he or she is located, or was located at the moment the command was issued. As you'll see, people can move pretty quickly around the Palace! Pressing Command-F (Ctrl+F for Windows) refreshes the display.

Hotspots and doors

By far, the easiest way to travel between Palace rooms and whole Palace sites is to click on the *hotspots*, which are like magic doorways built into Palace rooms. Hotspots are also sometimes called *doors*. Some hotspots are obvious, as the image of a slightly open door suggests that you could click there and go through. Whole directories of links, like the one shown in the following figure, let you visit many Palace sites by simply clicking. An easy way to find hotspots is to move your mouse over the Palace room. The mouse cursor will change to a pointing hand wherever there is a hotspot.

A Palace site links room with
hotspots.

Clicking on the hotspot will send you to a new room or Palace site. Note that using the arrow keys to move onto a hotspot does not activate the hotspot.

So many sites, so little time

Of the more than 300 servers in the chat cosmos of the Palace, the vast majority are personal sites. A few companies have put up beautifully adorned sites with elaborate themes. Cybertown (**http://www.cybertown.com**) has created a spectacular, spacey Palace site and one of its rooms appear in the following figure.

Cybertown Palace's Space Bar.

Let's Chat: The Good Life as a Guest

There are several levels of citizenship in the Palace; that of guest, registered user, and the highest level, wizard. In this section, I will cover features that are available to guests (and everyone else). See the section, "How do I become a registered user of the Palace?" in the FAQ on the companion Web site to this book.

Even if you are only a guest, you can still do what most people come to the Palace to do: chat, chat, chat. The Palace software provides you with a number of ways to express yourself. To chat, you just click on the input box, an area at the bottom of the Palace client window, and then start typing. Your words will appear in the input box. You can also press Tab instead of clicking on the input box to start typing again. When you push Enter (sometimes called Return), your text in the input box will appear in a cartoon balloon near your avatar's head.

You can control the length of time text stays up on your screen by setting the balloon delay (Edit ➪ Preferences). Mac users can also control the font and font size used in the cartoon balloons.

Using special balloons

You can change the way your words appear on the screen by typing special characters in front of your text. The table on the following page describes each of these prefix characters.

Whispering sweet nothings

By clicking directly on another person's avatar, you enter Whisper mode. In this mode, all other avatars on the screen become slightly darker, and the phrase, "Talking to:" appears in the status bar above your input box. At this point, the person you have clicked on has no idea that they have been selected. To whisper to this person, simply type your message into the input box, as usual. Both you and the other party will see your message appear on the screen in italics, but no one else will see the message. Subsequent messages continue to be private until you deselect the person by clicking on the status bar (the area just above the input box) or select another person.

Balloon prefixes

PREFIX CHARACTER	WHAT IT DOES
:	This gives you a thought balloon, instead of the normal talking balloon
!	This gives you an excited-looking spikey balloon
^	This gives you a rectangular sign balloon, which stays up until you move or say something else. Sign balloons are useful for saying things like BRB (Be Right Back) or On the phone.
@x,y	This allows you to place your cartoon balloon wherever you want on the screen. X and Y are the numeric coordinates of the location from which you wish the balloon to appear. The view screen is 512 pixels wide (X) by 384 pixels high (Y). This feature can be used for *spoofing* (putting words in people's mouths); however, anyone who looks at the log window would be able to see who the real speaker was. This feature doesn't work for guests.
; my message	This results in your message appearing only in the log window

If you are a registered user, you can also whisper to people in distant rooms. This is called *telepathy*. To send a telepathic message, simply open the user window by choosing Options ⇨ Find User. Next, click once on the name of the person you wish to speak to. Regardless of their location, they will see your message in italics (and no one else will). Note that your message cannot enter a locked room. Sounds and special balloons do not work in Telepathy mode.

Sending messages telepathically via the user window.

Shortcut keys for chat

There are shortcut keys that enable you to streamline your chat sessions. The following table describes each one.

Shortcut keys

KEY	WHAT IT DOES
Tab	Toggles between the input box and the viewing area
Up Arrow	Pages back through your previously typed statements
Down Arrow	Pages forward through your previously typed statements
Esc	Clears the input box

Sounds like chat

Want to express yourself a little more brashly? The Palace has a built-in set of audio files which everyone can use. These files are located in the Sounds folder (which is within the Palace folder), and they are recorded in 22 KHz, 8-bit mono WAV format. All you really need to know is:

To make a sound, type a right parenthesis followed by the name of the sound, like so:

>   )applause

You can even follow a sound with spoken text, like so:

>   )applause He shoots! He scores!

The current list of available sounds includes: amen, applause, belch, boom, crunch, debut, guffaw, kiss, no, ow, pop, teehee, wet1 (I don't know what this means—try it and see!), wind, and yes. Try 'em all!

The Face window

As a guest, you come into the Palace wearing the default roundhead, or yellow head avatar. Although you cannot make your own avatar (or change the color of your head) until you become a registered member, there are still a number of things you can do to personalize yourself for better communications.

The Face icon at the bottom of your screen brings up a pop-up window which can be used to change your facial expression and color (if you are registered). This window may be kept open while you are maneuvering around in the Palace, so you can change your appearance almost instantly. A rapid sequence of facial expression changes can be a hilarious way of communicating with your avatar buddies. If you have an extended keyboard (with a separate numeric keypad on one side), you can use your number keys to rapidly change your expression, as well.

These expressions serve much the same function as emoticons in e-mail messages. They are a convenient means of displaying emotion in a medium which cannot convey all the subtleties of human communication. In fact, some of the expressions can be triggered by typing various emoticons straight into the input box, as shown in the adjacent table.

Emoticons	
WHEN YOU TYPE...	**YOU GET THIS EXPRESSION...**
:)	Smile
:(	Frown
:|	Normal
;)	Wink
:[	Angry

Making Your Own Avatar and Creating Props in the Palace

I loved my roundhead, but now that I am a registered user and have my own name DigiGardener, I want my own avatar. One of my favorite avatars is Leola the tiger from OnLive! Traveler, but how do I bring her into the Palace? I would really like to just walk through a door from Traveler and enter the Palace, taking my avatar, personal information, and collected objects with me. It would be wonderful to port from world to world seamlessly, but I have a feeling this may not be possible for a while. Everyone has their own way of doing things, and making it all fit together is just too difficult at the moment. I know of two projects, one called Universal Avatars and another called Living Worlds that are working together to make this possible. If you are interested in these avatar standards projects, see Appendix A: "Projects, Groups, Events, Philosophers, News and Predecessors in Avatar Cyberspace."

Step 1: Get the image you want to make your avatar

So, back to Leola! The Palace has made it very easy for you to create your own avatar using the images you love. To capture Leola, I ran Traveler and used the PC Print Screen (PrtScr) to capture the Traveler screen which shows Leola. On a Macintosh, you can also capture the screen by pressing Command-Shift-3. Then start your trusty paint program, (any paint program will work, including good-old free MSPaint or MacPaint), and paste the screen into a blank canvas.

Step 2: Use a paint program to make the image the right size

In the paint program, crop out just the Leola tiger (seen in the following figure) and then resize her to a single tile of 44-by-44 pixels. You can also make avatars by fitting multiple tiles together, but that is an advanced avatar building topic. The 44-by-44 tile will fit just perfectly into the space normally taken up by a roundhead happy face avatar. After making it the right size and doing some cleanup, copy it to the Windows (or Mac) clipboard again.

Step 3: Create a new prop

Run the Palace client software and click on the Satchel icon to bring up the Prop Picker window. On the Prop Picker window, press New to make a new prop, and the Prop Editor window pops up. Next paste the 44-by-44 pixel Leola tile into the Prop Editor window (by pressing Ctrl+V on the PC or Command-V on the Mac). As you can see from the adjacent figure, Leola is now squarely

I paste my new avatar into the Prop Editor.

on top of the old roundhead avatar. You can use the arrow keys on your keyboard to move the image up, down, left, or right, which is what I did here to show you the roundhead underneath Leola.

Step 4: Try out your avatar for size

My avatar is just a little too high on the old roundhead avatar.

In the Prop Editor window, select the item Head so that it is checked. This means that the prop you are making will become your new head. You can also type in a name for your prop instead of NewProp, such as MyNewHead. Now select OK, and you will return to the Prop Picker window. The last step is to double-click on the new prop, which should appear at the top of the Prop Picker window. By double-clicking, you assign that prop to your avatar. You can assign any other prop to your avatar in the same way. As you can see from the following figure, the new Leola tiger is riding a little too high on the old roundhead avatar. I returned to the Prop Editor to move Leola down. Note that I temporarily turned the Head option for this prop off so that the original roundhead was still showing underneath for comparison purposes.

Step 5: Preen your avatar

When you're happy with how Leola was placed as your avatar, return to the Prop Editor to do some cleanup. I used the eraser tool to clear away the original backdrop. You could use this to remove Aunt Thelma from that great avatar picture of you. After making certain the Head option was checked on, you're ready to try on your final avatar, and voilà! Leola, small cute tiger!

Voilà! Just the avatar you wanted

A quick avatar facelift: Changing your face color

If all of this prop and custom avatar stuff is getting you confused, and you simply want a little more expression on your avatar, you might consider more easily changing your facial expression or color. Beneath the array of 16 expressions in the Face window (shown in the following figure), you will see a palette of 16 colors. Clicking on one of these colors causes your roundhead avatar face to change to that color. Face colors can be used to great effect in signifying emotional states, especially when used in conjunction with appropriate expressions (i.e., red plus the angry face, blue plus the sad face).

If you have an extended keyboard (with a separate numeric keypad on one side), you can use the plus and minus keys on the keypad to change your face color as well.

You can change your facial expression and color.

More about props

Props are little 44-by-44 pixel graphic objects that you can move around with the mouse, or attach to your avatar. You can combine up to nine objects at a time. Props are selected from the Prop Picker window by double-clicking on them. Although registered members can pick up any loose props that they find lying around in a room, guests are restricted to handling only those props which appear by default in the Prop window (they were put there by the Palace site designers, not other users). You can take a prop off your avatar by double-clicking on it again in the Prop Picker window, or by dragging and dropping it into the Trash icon.

Recording and playing macros

A macro corresponds to a specific costume (including face color, expression, and props). By playing back a pre-recorded macro, you can rapidly change your costume. When you've created a look that's right for you, you probably will want to save it as a macro, so you can recall it with a simple keystroke. The Macros menu allows you to record up to 10 costume changes, and instantly recall them by using a corresponding hot key combination (Command-0 through Command-9 for Mac users; Ctrl+0 through Ctrl+9 for Windows users).

For example, when you select Record Macro/5, your current costume is saved as Macro #5. From then on (until you record another macro over #5), you can instantly recall that particular look by pressing the hot key combination (Command-5 for Mac users; Ctrl+5 for Windows users).

Using the painting tools

Clicking on the Palette icon opens the Painting window, which displays a collection of painting tools. Any registered member can paint in the Palace, and everybody in the room sees what you are painting. Wizards and gods can turn painting off in particular rooms, however. Some Palace operators consider painting to be a nuisance activity, and turn it off.

The following painting tools are available:

Pencil/Filled Region

This Tool button toggles between two states: pencil and filled region. The Pencil tool (which is selected when no colored area appears around the pencil on the button), allows you to draw in various colors and thickness. The Filled Region tool (which is selected when a colored area does appear around the pencil on the button) operates similarly, but turns the drawn region into a closed shape. In the Mac version, it also fills this region with the selected color.

Line Sizer

This tool is used to change the width of the Pencil and Filled Region tools. The current size is the one in the center of the icon. To increase the pencil size, click in the upper right-hand corner of this button. To decrease the pencil size, click in the lower left-hand corner.

Detonator

When clicked once, this button deletes the most recent drawing command. When double-clicked, it deletes all drawing on the screen.

Layerer

The Palace allows you to draw on two layers: Behind Avatars and In Front Of Avatars. This button allows you to toggle between these two layers.

Palette

The Palette tool allows you to select from the 236 drawing colors of the *M-and-M Palette*. The colors are organized into six slices of an RGB cube, next to a ramp of grays.

Eyedropper

Although not visible as a tool in the Painting window, there is an Eyedropper tool available for selecting colors directly off of the screen image. The cursor changes to an eyedropper when you hold down Option (for Mac users), or Ctrl (for Windows users), and press the mouse button down anywhere in the view screen (no matter what tool is selected when the hot key is pressed); the color under the mouse pointer becomes the current drawing color in the Paint window. This function can be useful for extending a particular color you see on the screen.

The Painting window.

Interacting with loose props

Props, when not waiting patiently in your satchel, are found either attached to people's faces, or scattered around loose in various rooms; that means they can be picked up by any registered member. The easiest way to create a loose prop is to first put it on (by double-clicking on it in the Prop Picker window), and then pull it off your face and drag it into the room. There are a lot of things you can do with loose props, such as:

- Move them by grabbing them with the mouse and dragging them around. You will notice that you can't put a prop on somebody else; they have to pick it up and decide to wear it. Similarly, you can't grab a prop that somebody else is wearing; they must give it to you by dropping it (of course, it is possible to grab props by doing a screen capture).

- Make a copy of a loose prop (leaving the original behind) by holding down Option (for Mac users) or Ctrl (for Windows users) when you drag it.

- Add a loose prop to your collection, by dragging it to your Satchel icon.

- To add a loose prop to your collection, and simultaneously put it on by dragging it onto yourself.

- Dispose of a loose prop by dragging it to the Trash.

Making your own props

Registered Palace members can create their own custom props. You saw earlier how to make a custom avatar. An avatar is just another single prop or set of props. To work with your collection of props, you first have to open the Prop Picker window; simply click on the Satchel icon at the bottom of your screen.

To create a new prop, choose Props ⇨ New Prop, or press the New button in the Prop window. The *Prop Editor* will appear.

To edit an existing prop, choose Props ⇨ Edit Prop, or press the Edit button in the Prop window. To modify an existing prop while retaining the original (unedited) version, first duplicate the prop by using the Duplicate command on the Props menu (or press the Copy button in the Prop window), then select one of the pair, and choose Edit. This action also causes the Prop Editor to appear.

Prop Editor

You first saw the Prop Editor when we were making the custom Leola tiger avatar. This section will give you a little more information about the Prop Editor, describing its tools in detail.

Pencil tool

This tool, as you might expect, is used for drawing new props, or adding color and detail to existing props. There are a number of special hot key options you can use (see the following table); simply hold the appropriate key down while using the Pencil tool:

Pencil tool hot keys

Mac	Windows	Function
Shift	Shift	Constrains the pencil to the nearest straight line
Command	Alt	Turns the pencil tool into the paint bucket
Option	Ctrl	Turns the pencil tool into an Eyedropper tool

Selector Box tool

This tool can be used to select and move rectangular sections of your prop. In the Mac version, it is automatically selected when you paste a picture into the Prop Editor. In the PC version, it is automatically selected upon entering the Prop Editor, and it must be the selected tool before you can paste in a picture.

To select a rectangular section of your prop, simply press down at one corner of the desired area, drag the cursor to the diagonally-opposite corner, then release the mouse button. The indicated area may now be dragged around within the editing surface, and will be locked into place upon selecting any tool. The drag-copy hot key option is also available to Mac users: Pressing Option drags a copy of the selected area (leaving the original in place).

Eraser tool

This tool is used to erase parts of your prop. Erased portions are transparent; they allow the underlying face and/or background to show through. The optional hot key allows you to pour transparency (the gray pattern that will show as transparent when your prop is used) into solid-colored areas of your prop. Pressing Command (for the Mac) or Alt (for Windows) turns the cursor into an eraser paint can which pours the transparency.

Eyedropper tool

Although not visible as a tool in the Prop Editor, there is an Eyedropper tool available for selecting colors directly off the prop. Hold down Option (for Mac users) or Ctrl (for Windows users) and press the mouse button down anywhere in the image (no matter what tool is selected when the hot key is pressed); the color under the mouse cursor becomes the current drawing color for the Pencil tool.

Paint Can tool

Also not visible as a tool in the Prop Editor, there is a Paint Can tool available for pouring colors (and transparencies) directly into the prop image. The cursor changes to a paint can when you hold down Command (for Mac users), or Alt (for Windows users), while the mouse is anywhere in the image (this occurs no matter what tool is selected when the hot key is pressed, with the single exception of the *selector box*).

Line Sizer tool

This tool is used to change the size of the Pencil and Eraser tools. The current pencil size is the one in the center of the icon. To increase the pencil size, click in the upper right-hand corner of this button. To decrease the pencil size, click in the lower left-hand corner.

Palette

The palette is used to select a drawing color. This color will be used by all pencil operations until another color is selected via the Palette or the Eyedropper tool.

Prop Name

This text box allows you to give your prop a name. For registered members, this feature is especially important, as there are IptScrae commands (see "IptScrae: Better Living Through Scripting" in this chapter) which can be used to automate props, as long as their names are known.

Cancel

Clicking Cancel closes the Prop Editor without saving any changes you have made to your prop.

Save

Clicking Save saves your work and closes the Prop Editor. Edited props are saved in their original positions in the Prop window; new props appear at the top of this window.

Check off the type of prop you are making

Head props

In addition to normal props, such as those available to all Palace guests, members may use various head props to completely change their avatar's appearance. A head is a prop which completely replaces the roundhead. Any prop can be made into a head prop. Mac users can do this by selecting the *Face flag* on the Props menu. Windows users can do the same thing by clicking on the Head option box at the bottom of the Prop Editor window. For both platforms, this causes the background smiley head in the Prop Editor to disappear.

Ghost Props

A *ghost* is a semi-transparent prop, meaning that the underlying head prop and background art will be seen faintly through the image of this prop. Any prop may be made into a ghost prop. Mac users can do this by selecting the *Ghost flag* on the Props menu. Windows users can do the same thing by clicking on the Ghost option box at the bottom of the Prop Editor window.

Rare Props

Although this feature had not been implemented at the time I wrote this chapter, it will eventually be used to provide for a class of props which cannot simply be copied and dragged away. This will allow for one-of-a-kind personal possessions, and will exponentially increase the value of certain items. For now, however, making a prop rare has no effect at all.

Prop editor background color (Mac version only)

The Prop menu contains commands which will change the background color displayed in the Prop Editor. That can be useful at times to make the prop stand out.

Pasting into the Prop Editor

As you saw in the previous section, in which we made the Leola tiger avatar, you can cut and paste pictures from other sources into the Prop Editor. Simply select the image you want (using Photoshop, Paint Shop Pro, or any other quality graphics software), and copy it. In the Palace client, open the satchel and click on New to open the Prop Editor. Simply paste the image in and save it; that's all there is to it! Mac users can use the Edit menu for this operation; for Windows users, the hot key combination for pasting is Ctrl+V.

If the picture is up to 44-by-44 pixels in size (i.e., the height and width of a single prop), it will retain its original size when pasted in. If the image is larger than 44-by-44 pixels in size, it will be altered. Macs and PCs handle this differently: the Mac client will scale the image down to fit into a 44-by-44 area, while the Windows version will merely paste the upper left-hand 44-by-44 pixels into the area.

Note to Mac users: If you don't want the image to be scaled down as previously described, hold down Shift as you paste the picture in.

Creating oversized props and avatars

Throughout the Palace, you will often see people wearing images that are quite obviously larger than the default 44-by-44 pixel size of a single prop. These oversized props are actually comprised of several (up to nine) normal-sized props, and are created by offsetting the props' relative positions in the Prop Editor.

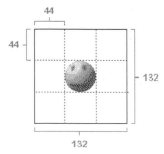

The total prop area shows how to tile props together.

As shown in the illustration to the left, the area in which you may place a prop is actually comprised of nine 44-by-44 cells. Any prop may be saved anywhere in this 132-by-132 square.

While the Prop Editor is open, and the selector box is the active tool, the arrow keys can be used to move the image vertically and horizontally, relative to the central prop space (i.e., the location of the default roundhead). It is this feature which allows the creation of oversized props. Here's how to do it:

1. Create several 44-by-44 pixel partial images to serve as the individual parts of the oversized prop. Since you can get up to nine (3-by-3) props on your avatar at one time, this means that the oversized prop must not exceed 132-by-132 pixels in size. You might want to keep your graphic editing program open while performing these operations, so you can grab new pieces of the oversized image as needed.

2. Use the arrow keys to move these individual props as required. If they are all 44-by-44 pixels in size, this is particularly easy; simply slide them as far as they will go in the direction you need to move them. Cartoon balloons always display close to the center of the central cell. Try to consider where you will want your cartoon balloons to appear when you speak while wearing the oversized prop, and place the individual pieces accordingly.

For example, let's say you're creating an oversized prop which is a picture of a clock face, measuring 88-by-88 pixels (equivalent to four normal prop tiles). You might decide to use the four upper-left cells, which would make your cartoon balloons display from the lower right-hand corner of your oversized face. You would paste in the upper left-hand corner of your clock image and use the arrow keys to move it 44 pixels to the left, and 44 pixels upward (as far it can go in those directions), saving the prop in this position. Then grab the next 44-by-44 pixel piece from my graphic editing program and paste it into the Prop Editor, moving it 44 pixels upward and saving it. The lower left-hand piece is moved 44 pixels to the left and saved, while the lower right-hand corner (the fourth and final piece) is saved in its default position (the central cell). Later, when you double-click on these props to put them on, they will appear in their offset positions, together forming the completed image of your oversized clock face. That's it!

Don't forget to define all of the props you just assigned to the macro. This will allow you to quickly re-clothe your avatar in its new props.

Creating Your Own World with the Palace Server

The Palace server is a user-friendly, do-it-yourself home 2D virtual world kit. With the Palace server software, you can open your own place and become a Palace operator.

While most of the powers and options available to you as a Palace operator are easy to learn and easy to use, an endless number of advanced interactive tricks and short-cuts can best (or only) be achieved by mastering IptScrae, the programming language that comes with the software.

With the Palace, you can go as deep as you want: advanced interactive worlds may require months of detailed and incremental development, while basic Palace environments may be set up in an hour or two. In fact, you can open your own carbon-copy of the original Palace Mansion in minutes—without even changing an option or writing a single line of code!

Creating whole Palace sites is beyond the scope of this chapter, so I encourage you to look at the documentation on the server, and the IptScrae programming language at **http://newbie.thepalace.com** under Tech Talk.

Godhood

The penultimate power in a Palace site rests in the hands of its god(s), who are generally also the owners and operators. Godhood brings with it some responsibility as well, since it is the god of the site who ultimately must take responsibility for the look, feel, mood, pace, and ongoing activities associated with the site in the minds of others.

To help them shoulder some of this cosmic responsibility, Palace gods have been given a special set of commands above and beyond the ordinary wizard powers.

Doings in the Palace

What is going on in the Palace? It turns out . . . quite a lot! This next section will give you a sampling.

Meet the Natives

Interviews

I have been interviewed twice in the Palace. One reason the Palace is so good for interviews is that you can save the log of all conversations. Another reason is that many people can get into the interview area and participate. The first interview I did was for *Artificial Intelligence Watch,* a British computer science newsletter. I was able to do this while on vacation in July 1996, up in the woods outside Seattle, on a friend's Internet connection. This also saved huge telephone charges (to call London).

Minds Palace, as a first-rate social spot in the Palace cosmos, holds regular interviews and publishes them later on their Web site at **http://www.minds.com**. I was recruited for such an interview, so I showed up early in the dressing area of Minds Palace. You can connect to Minds Palace by choosing File ⇨ Connect and entering minds.palace.com.

Digi gets a dressing down

I had arrived early at Minds Palace for my interview, nervous as a mare in the springtime. It wasn't exactly like appearing on the *Tonight Show,* but I still wanted to look my best. Minds Palace has a great prop wall, where you can collect and use props to dress up your avatar. The prop wall must have seen me coming, because it had just the accessories for an out-of-breath, red-faced roundhead like me. I dragged and dropped a wonderful set of rubbery arms and legs into my Prop satchel, opened it up, and found them all nicely stashed there. From that point, I could just drag the props onto my avatar's body, and use the Edit window to adjust them and voilà: Digi's got legs!

I plopped my new prop legs onto old roundhead!

Snatching a crown and a funny thing that looked like a crumhorn (my voice is pretty soft, so I need to get attention somehow), I was off to my date with destiny . . . famous author interviewed (well, famous in his own computer room, anyway).

Expand your mental capacity in Minds Palace

In Minds Palace, you can make your own character from a large collection of outrageous body parts and, if you're lucky, get your 15 minutes of fame in their monument to cool avatars. Drop in, enjoy the view, and pursue good conversation with other like minds. Find the Minds Palace home page at **http://www.minds.com/palace/**. Connect directly with Minds Palace by entering palace.minds.com into your Connect dialogue box.

Games! Charebus

Zenda studio, working with Minds Palace and The Palace Inc. has produced *Charebus*, a combination of charades and rebus in which you solve picture puzzles while chatting with other players from around the world. A new twist on charades, pictionary, and rebus puzzles, Charebus is currently played in the Minds Palace at 5 p.m. each Saturday. Groups of five or more can play at the same time. Each Charebus puzzle features a different mystery phrase (movie, song, TV show, etc.). To solve the puzzle, you must guess picture clues related to that mystery phrase.

Find information about Charebus and other games in the Palace at Zenda Studio's home page at **http://www.zenda.com/**. You can even submit your own puzzle ideas for future episodes of Charebus.

Avatar fashion shows

So many Palace citizens (registered users) have created their own avatars that it seems like a real pageant. Some citizens have created multiple avatars, which they change in and out of in the course of the avatar parade. Take Turbodog, for example.

Roundheads are the ubiquitous smiley faces everyone starts with as a guest in the Palace. When you become a registered user, you get a red roundhead and the power to create your own avatar. Turbodog, whom I met one day, is a student from the Bayou country of Louisiana, and a total pro in the avatar creation game. Take a look at his turbo-charged round-head here!

Turbodog, the turbo-charged roundhead.

Avatars often take the form of TV or movie characters. These are called avamarks, otherwise known as avatar trademark violations, and they abound in virtual worlds. As avatars are still small potatoes in the world of entertainment, we have yet to see hundreds of blue-suited avalawyers chasing down avamarks and serving them with avasuits.

In the adjacent figure, Turbodog is showing off one of his more practical avatars, the famed BRB (be right back). One has to eat sometime, lest the Palace eat up your whole life!

A BRB avatar is very useful for personal survival.

Using macros to switch between various sets of grouped props is the way to create an avatar fashion show.

IptScrae: Better Living Through Scripting

Scripting with the Palace's very own programming language, affectionately known as IptScrae (pig Latin for Script), is a powerful way to automate yourself, create bots, and have a whole lot of fun. I used the *snowball* script built by Turbodog to chuck this hunk of white at my fellow avatars. Snowballs work both ways, so I did get it back in my cheery face.

Snowball script in action . . . gotcha!

Oops! I got it back!

Describing all the details of IptScrae is beyond the scope of this chapter. If you are an ordinary user, you might be satisfied with running scripts that other programming nerd types give to you. If you are afflicted by deep nerd thought, you may want to learn IptScrae by checking the references in the Palace FAQ on the companion Web site to this book.

Bots: It's the Borg!

Appearing more often in virtual worlds are things called bots (a virtual world shorthand for robot). In other types of computer software, bots are called agents or angels. Bots, agents, and angels are all pieces of software that run on their own, and sometimes look just like other users who communicate with us. However, there is no person behind a bot (apart from the programmer of the bot, who may not be around). Bots can be very helpful, as greeters or guides, or sometimes they can tell you who has been in a particular area in the last 24 hours. However, some bot builders are pretty devious, and design their bots to trick people into thinking that the bot is a real person.

Talking bots can be designed to mimic Eliza, which could make for embarrassing situations when real users discover that they have been talking about their deepest, innermost feelings with a bot for an hour (especially if it was a good-looking one!). We in the virtual worlds business have been racking our brains for years to come up with a standard symbol for bot so that no user is tricked (if people will use the symbol). After finding nothing suitable, users came up with one for us: the eye piece on the *Borg* characters, as depicted on the *Star Trek: The Next Generation* TV series. As you can see in the adjacent figure, a user is proudly displaying a Borg avatar (in this case, representing a real user). This kind of bot facial marking (black ring around the right eye as you are looking at it) is now being used increasingly to signify a bot.

Is it a bot? Or has the Borg arrived to assimilate us?!

Community Behavior in the Palace

Like any community, the social life at Palace sites can be spoiled by a few rotten roundheads (rudies or avapunks). Most Palace sites, including the main Palace server, have community standards posted that pop up when you enter. The Cybertown standards are shown in the adjacent figure.

Recently, hostility by registered users toward guest users has grown, with guests being denigrated, and as shown below, sprayed with a treatment of anti-guest repellent. This repulsive behavior can only discourage more guests from becoming active members and contributors. How do you fight back if you are a mere roundhead? Newbie revolt! Use the pen over the sword, and keyboard your displeasure. Ask for help from fellow citizens, newbie or registered alike! Who knows, you might even try calling for a wizard (see the following section on wizards). Also, see the section, "Palace Community Standards," in the FAQ on the companion Web site to this book, for the Palace's official guide to community behavior.

Getting a community standards notice at the entryway to Cybertown.

An example of anti-guest roundhead hostility.

Wizards: so you want to rule the world?

Dr. John Suler, a psychologist studying the Palace community, has paid special attention to the role of wizards. The following is a short excerpt from his full paper, which you can read on the Web at **http://www1.rider.edu/~suler/psycyber/palacestudy.html**.

> "The ultimate badge of prestige at the Palace is to be chosen as wizard. Wizards possess special abilities that ordinary members don't (like being able to kill, gag, and pin misbehaving users). They also participate in decision-making about new policies for the community. Many members, secretly or not, wish they could attain the social recognition, power, and self-esteem achieved through this promotion. To get it, one must demonstrate commitment to the community, which includes spending a considerable amount of time there. Wizardship can become a very enticing carrot that stimulates addictive attendance. For those few who do attain that position, it can powerfully reinforce one's efforts, and further bolster one's loyalty and devotion to Palace life. Even though the position does not include a salary, many wizards see it as a job (for) which they are responsible. The wizard now has a viable reason for being so "addicted." As one user stated the day after receiving his surprise promotion, "I WORK here."

Fine-Tuning Your World

Seeing other people's names

Even if you have the Show Names option turned off (see Preferences under the Edit menu), it is still possible to see the names of all the people in the room with you: if you're a Mac user, just hold down Command and Option simultaneously. If you're a Windows user, simply hold down F3.

Seeing doors

Want to see all doors in the current room? By holding down Ctrl (for Mac users), or Ctrl+Shift (for Windows users), you cause the outlines of all doors in the current room to become visible.

Hot Spots

Hot Spots

The following table lists many of the most popular sites related to The Palace.

The Palace official pages and ftp sites
http://www.thepalace.com **The Palace home page.**
http://www.thepalace.com/palace-faq.html **The Palace FAQ.**
http://www.thepalace.com/discussion-groups.html **The Palace Community Standards Discussion Group. (Please post your experiences, insights, and suggestions for the benefit of all Palace users).**
http://mansion.thepalace.com/cgi-bin/directory.pl **The Palace Directory.**
http://www.thepalace.com/downloads.html **Available Palace downloads (software and multimedia assets).**
http://www.thepalace.com/documentation.html **Palace documents (manuals).**
http://www.thepalace.com/web-pages.html **Palace-related Web pages official link page.**

http://www.thepalace.com/register.html

Description of how to register for the Palace.

Unofficial citizen pages

http://callisto.syr.edu/~alrubin/palace/palace.html

Adam's Palace Pro Shop (Is It Eating Your Life Too?).

http://www.itsnet.com/home/lminer/palace/

Chris Miner's Palace Tutorial for Windows Users.

http://www.ultranet.com/~rover/

Rover's Doghouse.

http://www.chatlink.com/~peanut/iptscrae.html

Eric D's IptScrae Resource Center.

Nathan Wagoner's Palace hot list

http://www.ducksoup.net

Nathan Wagoner is an avid Palace pro and designs art for Palace sites. His company is DuckSoup Information Services.

http://rogue.northwest.com/~gb1018/welcome.html

The Palace Everything Page.

http://desires.com/2.0b3/Toys/Palace/palace.html

An article in *Urban Desires*.

http://desires.com/2.0b3/Toys/Palace/palace.html

Dr. Xenu's Guide to Props and Bots—lot's of help for building Palaces.

http://rogue.northwest.com/~gb1018/related.html

A list of helpful links.

http://www.itsnet.com/home/lminer/palace/

Very helpful beginners' tutorials.

http://www1.rider.edu/~suler/psycyber/palacestudy.html

A large study by Dr. John Suler, a psychologist whose focus is on the Palace.

http://www1.rider.edu/~suler/psycyber/psycyber.html

The main page, with many other related resources by Dr. Suler.

http://www.geocities.com/SiliconValley/Park/5049/palacering.html

The Palace Ring of WWW sites.

Digi's Diary

Digi's Diary: What to do About all Those Naked Pix

Well, you can't hide it. Sooner or later in the Palace you will see either avatarts (scantily clad female avatars) or avahunks (male avatars of the same persuasion). I met one ten-year-old in WorldsAway who said his parents would not let him use the Palace any more because of "all those naked pix" (WorldsAway's avatars are built from carefully chosen parts). In the Palace, you can make your own avatars; put anything on a scanner and you have an avatar. What is there to do about it? Where is all this going? Do we need community policing? Do we need parental controls? Do we need a "naked pix patrol?"

Lady G is a fine avatart (with clothes).

Since it is a global medium, we have to consider that in some cultures all of these pix would not be seen as particularly offensive. Many advertisers in print and on TV produce images far more suggestive than anything I have seen in avatar land. While naked pix might be offensive to some in the English-speaking world, they would be egregiously so to a devout Muslim, for example.

So what can we do? Maybe Freud was right—that sex is the basic drive in human (and virtual) societies. If naked pix do disturb you, you can always choose another virtual world. But perhaps another approach might be to change the way you look at it. Psychologist John Suler wrote a marvelous paper on the psychology of the Palace (**http://www1.rider.edu/~suler/psycyber/palacestudy.html**), which addresses these issues. He writes, "The Palace often feels and looks like an ongoing cocktail party—and like any good party, there is a hefty dose of natural, playful flirting." So perhaps you could look at it as flirting, and not take it *too* seriously.

Dr. Suler goes on to report that, "When I ask people why they keep coming back to the Palace, the most common response is, "I like the people here."

When it comes down to it, if you liked more people than you disliked in your visits to the Palace, it is probably worth returning. Sometimes people put on a facade and act out a role which is not really who they are. Giving people the benefit of the doubt is also a good rule of thumb. Don't be afraid to talk to the avatarts and avahunks, and ask them why they are dressed that way!

AlphaWorld and Active Worlds

GREEN PLANET

(T)he good ship *Avatar* is going into a parking orbit around AlphaWorld, a large green planet in a planetary system of virtual worlds called Active Worlds. From our vantage point in orbit, you can see its numerous cities, built by some of its more than 200,000 citizens. It is apparent from this height that AlphaWorld is a very advanced civilization.

Get ready to *teleport* your landing party down into AlphaWorld. In this chapter, you will experience the sights and social scene of a huge digital city. Together, we will crash an avatar block party, attend a virtual wedding, sightsee at major tourist traps on the planet, and build a base of our own on this alien digital landscape.

Your Guide to
AlphaWorld and Active Worlds

WORLD GUIDE

WORLD SKILL LEVEL	Advanced
BUILDING CAPABILITY	Yes
SYSTEM REQUIREMENTS	Windows 95, Windows NT
AVATAR CREATION CAPABILITY	No, unless you host your own world
DEPTH	3D
SOUND SUPPORT	Music, sound effects

MINIMUM MACHINE

OPERATING SYSTEM	Windows 95
COMPUTER	486DX 66 MHz PC; 256-color VGA monitor or higher
RESOURCES	16MB RAM; 24MB free disk space; 16-bit sound card is optional for music and sound effects
CONNECTION	SLIP/PPP Dial up to the Internet at 14.4 kbps

AlphaWorld and other Active Worlds: Living and Building in the Digital City

The Active Worlds are some of the most advanced virtual worlds in digital space. Users of avatar worlds are called *citizens,* a sign that they should be respected as members of a community. In AlphaWorld, you can chat with other citizens and attend social happenings. Above all, you can *build* in AlphaWorld! Building can be done by any citizen on any free land or by special arrangement in a number of parallel planets called Active Worlds. In fact, AlphaWorld is just one of over 200 Active Worlds.

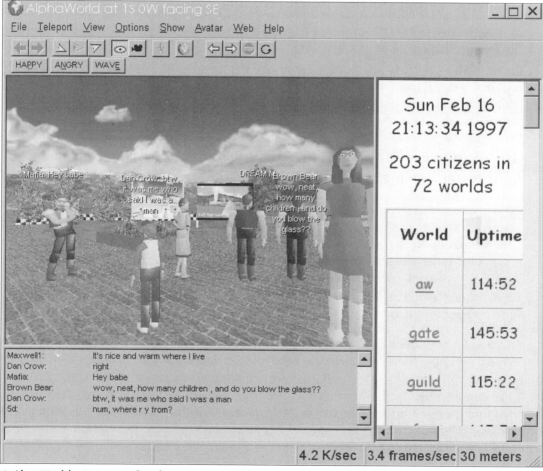

Active Worlds Browser showing an avatar block party at AlphaWorld Ground Zero.

Visiting AlphaWorld, you will learn how to travel and meet people in a very large three-dimensional virtual world and homestead your own place in cyberspace. AlphaWorld is as unpredictable as the real world—as unpredictable and unique as the individuals who create it. Each time you enter AlphaWorld, there will be new buildings, towns, and cities, and there always will be new community members to meet. Get ready for a real adventure in avatar cyberspace!

Installing

Installing and Immigrating into Active Worlds

What do I need to visit Active Worlds?

To visit AlphaWorld and other Active Worlds, you must have a PC running Microsoft Windows 95 or NT. As shown in the *minimum machine* table at the beginning of this chapter, you need a 486/66 MHz PC running Windows 95 and a direct connection to the Internet. Your PC should have at least 16MB of memory. A Pentium machine with plenty of memory (24MB of RAM or more) will run this world much faster, but is not required.

Using Active Worlds through AOL, CompuServe, and other on-line services

You can't use Active Worlds through on-line services unless they support direct Internet access. For example, you can use Active Worlds through America Online, the Microsoft Network, and CompuServe 3.0 as they do provide this service. To do this, you must be able to configure your on-line service to access the Internet through Winsock (the tool Windows uses to communicate with the Internet) and then run Active Worlds. See Appendix B: "General Questions and Answers," for on-line connection advice.

If you can connect directly to the Internet by a dial-up SLIP or PPP connection of at least 14.4 kbps, then you should be ready to run Active Worlds. If you are at work or a place where you have a PC on the Internet full time (such as a university or college), you can also use Active Worlds. Connecting from work might require you to check on your firewall and proxy server restrictions. See the section on "Questions and Answers About Connecting" in the FAQ found on the book companion Web site at **http://www.digitalspace.com/avatars**.

Getting started and a few disclaimers

The Active Worlds Browser is the software you need to enter AlphaWorld and other Active Worlds. The Active Worlds Browser is easy to install and easy to use. You will install Active Worlds Browser either from the CD in this book or by downloading it from the Internet. Getting Active Worlds Browser installed is easier than you might think and soon you will be building your own *Metaverse*. Metaverse is the name for the virtual world described in Neal Stephenson's 1992 classic novel *Snow Crash*. I highly recommend that you beg, borrow, or steal this novel and compare Stephenson's Metaverse with your experience in AlphaWorld. *Snow Crash* is listed in the bibliography.

Active Worlds Browser is experimental shareware software. As long as its creator, Circle of Fire Studios, supports it, it will be free to use (you have to accept the terms of your free license during installation). You are not charged for the time you spend exploring, chatting, and building in AlphaWorld and other Active Worlds, but you could be charged for the hours you use from your Internet service provider (ISP). Check with your ISP for its monthly free hours and rates.

Active Worlds is constantly changing

Active Worlds Browser is constantly evolving, and will likely have changed since this chapter was written. I placed the very latest version of Active Worlds Browser on your book CD, and it may be somewhat different from what is described here. In fact, when you log on, you will likely be asked to upgrade to a new version. Upgrading is easy and is described in the section, "Active Worlds is asking me if I want to upgrade." The differences from your running version of Active Worlds Browser and what is described here will not be major and this chapter will still be a great guide to Active Worlds. If you see new features or changes, you should check for information under the Help menu in the Active Worlds Browser.

Active Worlds is now owned by its users!

At the time of this writing, Worlds Incorporated (the original company that developed Active Worlds) had just sold Active Worlds (including AlphaWorld) to a group of users working with Circle of Fire Studios. This is exciting to me as it means that Active Worlds will continue to evolve and grow, driven by the people who love it most, its users! The new home for Active Worlds is at **http://www.active worlds.com**. Please see your Avatars book home page at **http://www.digitalspace.com/ avatars** for the latest news on Active Worlds.

If you have questions or problems

If you have questions or problems installing Active Worlds Browser or running any Active World, you should consult the "AlphaWorld and Active Worlds FAQ," on the book companion Web site. If this does not help you, check the Active Worlds home page at **http://www.activeworlds.com**, and the Active Worlds Support page at **http://www.activeworlds.com/support.html**.

Help

Virtually up-to-date

Keep up-to-date with your favorite worlds; visit your *Avatars!* Web site.

As a special service for readers of *Avatars!*, I have a home page on the World Wide Web devoted to keeping you up-to-date on your favorite worlds. Find news about software updates, social events held within these virtual worlds, and brand new worlds you might want to visit at http://www.digitalspace.com/avatars. Bookmark it!

To contact the Active Worlds team at Circle of Fire Studios directly with your suggestions, bug reports, or comments, email them through their homepage at **http://www.activeworlds.com**.

Another good source of information on how to use Active Worlds is the on-line Windows Help file. Just press F1 while using Active Worlds and use the table of contents or index to find your topic of interest.

I appreciate your feedback on *Avatars!* but I don't have the resources to provide technical support. The Active Worlds Team and I are happy to hear about your experiences with AlphaWorld and other Active Worlds. Contact us through the *Avatars!* book Web site at **http://www.digitalspace.com/avatars**.

Macintosh, UNIX, and OS/2 versions and running under Windows NT

At this writing, there are no native versions of the Active Worlds Browser for the Macintosh, UNIX, or OS/2. Check the Active Worlds and *Avatars!* book Web pages for updates on new versions which might support these platforms. You may also be able to run the Active Worlds Browser using a Windows emulation system on non-Windows platforms. Active Worlds may run under Windows NT, but the Active Worlds team reports that you may also experience problems. Check the Active Worlds Web site for assistance with operation under Windows NT.

Bear with me through the following step-by-step instructions and soon you will be experiencing life as an avatar in digital space!

Do you have a previous version of the Active Worlds Browser installed?

If you have previously installed the Active Worlds Browser, it may be wise to delete it before installing your version from the CD. If your version of the Active Worlds Browser is more recent than the one on the CD, you may want to stick with it.

In Windows 95, you can remove a program this way: Open the Control Panel, double-click on the Add/Remove Programs icon, scroll down to Active Worlds, highlight it, and click on the Add/Remove button to delete it from the system. You can also do this by deleting the folder in which the Active Worlds Browser resides.

Installing the Active Worlds Browser from the Avatars! CD-ROM

If you have a CD-ROM drive on your PC, you can install the Active Worlds Browser directly from there. If you don't have a CD-ROM drive, skip to the section, "Installing or upgrading the Active Worlds Browser from the Internet." In "The Book CD-ROM" chapter, I provide a step-by-step example of installing from the CD-ROM. I suggest you refer to this chapter and follow the same steps for the Active Worlds Browser. Once the installation program on your CD-ROM has started, you can return to this chapter to the section: "Running the installation."

Installing or upgrading the Active Worlds Browser from the Internet

If you want the very latest version of Active Worlds, or were informed that you had to upgrade the version found on your *Avatars!* CD, then you must download it from the Internet. If you haven't done this before, don't panic, it is easier than you might think!

❶ Connect to the Internet (dial up with your modem or make sure your Internet connection is active).

❷ Start your Web browser, such as Netscape or Internet Explorer.

❸ In the top of the browser, you will see a text box called Location, where you can enter text.

❹ Click in this box, delete the text inside, and type in **http://www.activeworlds.com**. Press the Enter key.

❺ After a few moments, the home page for Active Worlds should appear. If nothing comes up for a long time, check to see that you are online.

Avatars!

❻ If the Active Worlds page is not available for some reason or is not carrying the Active Worlds software, try entering the location for the *Avatars!* home page, which is **http://www.digitalspace.com/avatars**. This page may contain more up-to-date links for Active Worlds. Once you are at the Active Worlds home page, follow the instructions for downloading or upgrading the Active Worlds Browser. At one point, you will click on a link and be prompted for a place to save a file.

❼ A few seconds after clicking on the link, you will be presented with a dialogue box. Click Save File (Netscape) or Save As (Internet Explorer) to download the file to disk (or you can save it on your desktop).

❽ You will be prompted to choose a folder in which to save the downloaded file. Note where you chose to save the file and the name of the file itself (it could be called something like awb152.exe). You can use the folder designated by your Web browser or select another. I put all downloaded files in a folder which I call \download.

Wait patiently; this download is not large (about 1.2MB). It should only take about 15 minutes, depending on the speed of your connection. While waiting, you can run other programs, but be careful about interfering with the connection. (Try not to do more work on the Internet while the download is progressing, and if you are using your regular telephone line for your modem, don't make a telephone call.) If you have a call-waiting feature, you may want to turn it off before beginning the download. If someone calls in, this could interrupt your download.

❾ After the download is finished, you must open the folder where the file was downloaded and find that file. To do this:

- Open the My Computer icon on your desktop.

- Open the MS-DOS C: icon representing your hard disk.

- Open the folder into which you saved the file (in \download).

- Close all other programs except your Internet connection and keep this folder open.

- Double click on the file named something like "awb152.exe" that looks like a little diskette and hard drive.

Find the file you downloaded.

❿ Go to, "Running the installation," in the following section.

Running the installation

Whether you are running the installation from the CD using your Web browser, from the CD file you directly copied, or from the file you downloaded from the Internet, use this section to guide you through the installation. Note that if you downloaded Active Worlds from the Internet, the installation process *may have changed*. If this has happened, refer to instructions on the Active Worlds Web site.

❶ It is a good idea to close other programs before you continue with the installation. You can do this by clicking on the running application icons on the task bar and then closing them. You can also use Alt+Tab to go to other running applications even when the installer is waiting for your input and you cannot see the task bar. Simply hold down Alt while pressing Tab and select the icon representing your running application. You can leave your Internet connection running.

❷ Start the installation program. You will be prompted to accept the terms of a license agreement; read them and, if you agree, accept the terms.

❸ You will be prompted to select the folder, or destination directory into which the Active Worlds Browser will be installed. I recommend that you just accept the given destination directory (Active Worlds).

❹ After the installation is complete, there might be a shortcut to the Active Worlds Browser on your desktop. You can also find the Active Worlds Browser in your Start ➪ Programs ➪ Active Worlds folder under your Start menu.

❺ For all the settings to take effect you might be asked to reboot your computer. If you are installing the Active Worlds Browser for a second time, you may not have to reboot. To reboot, click on the Start button, select Shut Down, and then Restart the Computer.

❻ After the computer restarts, I recommend that you do the following cleanup of files before you start getting absorbed in AlphaWorld. After this, you will be ready to get started.

Cleaning up after installation

If you copied the Active Worlds Browser installation file onto your desktop, into a folder, or you downloaded it from the Internet, you can delete it after the installation is complete. It should have a name like awb152.exe. You can keep the original installer around just in case you have to reinstall it. Of course, you will have your CD with the original installers, so you do not need to take up valuable hard disk space (1.2MB just for the Active Worlds installer).

The help files

There will be files called Help placed in your Start menu folder. If you open these files, you will find general information about this release of the Active Worlds Browser.

Some words before you go . . .

AlphaWorld is just one of many virtual worlds available under the Active Worlds Browser. The Active Worlds Browser is the software provided on your *Avatars!* book CD. With it you can explore many different virtual worlds. AlphaWorld was the original, and still is the largest, of these worlds. Once in AlphaWorld, you can visit other worlds in the Active Worlds Browser universe. This chapter will focus on AlphaWorld and give you a look at other Active Worlds Browser worlds.

Starting the Active Worlds Browser

Before starting up the Active Worlds Browser, you must re-establish your connection to the Internet. Once you are connected (test your connection by seeing if your Web browser works), double-click on the Active Worlds Browser icon to start the browser. In Windows 95, you can find the Active Worlds Browser on your desktop, under the Start menu ⇨ Programs ⇨ Active Worlds. You can also look in the folder called Active Worlds where you can find the Active Worlds Browser program directly.

Active Worlds is asking me if I want to upgrade

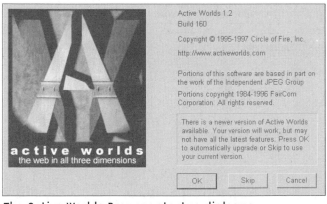

The Active Worlds Browser startup dialogue.

As soon as you start Active Worlds Browser you may see a message like that shown in the figure to the left. This message may read "there is a newer version of Active Worlds available. Your version may work but may not have all the latest features. Press OK to automatically upgrade or Skip to use your current version." I recommend you press OK and receive the upgrade. This will not take long and will ensure you are using the latest version. After Active Worlds downloads its upgrade (usually 100 or 200KB) it will upgrade itself and then restart.

The version of Active Worlds Browser installed from the CD will require upgrading in this way. You may be asked to upgrade in several steps, depending on how old your version of Active Worlds is. In the event that you are told that you must download a whole new version of the Active Worlds Browser, return to the previous section, "Installing or upgrading Active Worlds Browser from the Internet."

What! You don't have your immigration papers?

When you enter the Active Worlds universe you can enter either as a tourist or become a citizen through a process called *immigration*. When you enter for the first time, these choices are presented to you in a dialogue box like the one shown in the following figure. Entering as a tourist allows you to communicate and explore but not to build. I recommend immigrating right away. If you don't choose to immigrate right away you can change your status from tourist to citizen by selecting Change to from the Citizen menu in Active Worlds Browser, and then immigrate. If you do enter as a tourist, you must select a nickname by which you will be known. If you want to immigrate, follow these three simple steps.

Immigration Step 1: Supply your nickname, e-mail address, and password

If you choose to immigrate right away or opt to immigrate after you have visited Active Worlds as a tourist, the procedure is the same: you have to fill out a *form* (nothing changes, even in the virtual worlds!).

Enter a name for your tourist visa or immigrate and become a citizen.

Don't panic, immigration into this virtual world is much easier than crossing national boundaries! As the following dialogue shows, all you have to do is enter your nickname (some fanciful name you would like to be known by in the world), your e-mail address, and password (enter it twice for verification). In the example above, I entered my customary nickname, DigiGardener, an email address **digispace@aol.com**, and a password I won't forget. When you type in the password, you will not be able to see it, just "*" symbols. This is done to hide the password. Be careful when you type it in. I use the old hunt-and-peck method, pressing each key with one finger and watching the keyboard thus giving me fewer chances to make a mistake. When you enter Active Worlds in the future, you will not have to enter this password again, but it is good to record it somewhere in case you need it.

The citizenship application to immigrate to Active Worlds.

Note that all of this information (except your password) is stored in a file called *aworld.ini* which can be found in your Active Worlds folder. You can save this file as a safe backup for your identity. For more about the aworld.in file, see the section, "Questions and Answers related to Your Identity" in the FAQ for Active Worlds on our companion book Web site. Lastly, if you forget your password, there is an option in the Change To option under the Citizen menu which will request the Active Worlds server to send you your password by e-mail.

You are not anonymous in this world

Note that by supplying your e-mail address, you are not *anonymous* in any Active World you visit. The Active Worlds team made the decision to require this immigration process so that they could count how many people join AlphaWorld, keep in touch with citizens about upgrades and changes, and encourage people to be responsible. If your identity is known, you are less likely to do or say anything offensive in the greater community.

Immigration Step 2: Verifying that your nickname is available

After you press OK in the preceding dialogue, the Active Worlds citizen server goes into action, checking to see if the nickname you entered is available. It is important to have your name be unique in every active world, as this is the only way to reach you. You might receive the message: "Sorry, the name 'DigiGardener' is already in use by another citizen. Please try another name" (tip: try something really creative!) which means that your nickname is already taken. With almost 200,000 registered users, you can bet that every name of a fantasy character from books like Tolkien's *The Hobbit,* or science fiction or names of rock stars are already taken. You can keep trying to enter new nicknames (like sting99 or sting999) until one is accepted.

If the Active Worlds server is down (which is rare), you may be given the message "Active Worlds Immigration Office Closed Until . . . ." In this case your best option is to come back later and try again.

You can actually run Active Worlds without being connected to the Internet. You will be given the option to enter in "stand-alone mode." In this mode you will be able to travel around in a world alone and visit places you have previously visited (as they have already been downloaded onto your hard disk). I often use stand-alone mode to show people Active Worlds and Sherwood Forest on my laptop computer. I don't have to go scurrying around for a phone jack.

Immigration Step 3: Arriving in the world!

If all has gone well, you will now enter Active Worlds. After a few seconds, the Active Worlds entry dialogue should say "Starting . . . " and then disappear to be replaced by a new window, the Active Worlds client window. You will then land at the Ground Zero point of one of the Active Worlds known as The Gate. A Ground Zero point is the universal place of entry for everyone in a virtual world. There are ways to come into different points in Active Worlds, called *teleports*, which we shall explore later in this chapter.

It may be hard to tell when you are at Ground Zero because not much of the world may be visible for a few seconds. The Active Worlds server, to which you are connected, is busily sending you a whole set of little pictures. These pictures will be put together by the Active Worlds Browser to show you the world and the people in it. After a few seconds, you should start seeing the area around Ground Zero. When you enter new Active Worlds areas you have not visited before, all you will see for a few seconds is a sea of little black triangles. These black triangles are *anchor points* where the picture objects will be placed. If a triangle moves, it might indicate that an avatar is associated with that point.

These little pictures are called Renderware or RWX objects. These are the basic building blocks of AlphaWorld and all the other Active Worlds. If you want to get into the details of Renderware objects, you should view the help documents in the Active Worlds Browser or on the Active Worlds Web site. As these objects arrive over the Internet, they are stored on your hard disk. This is called *caching*. Once you have many objects cached, you will not have to wait so long for scenes in the world to download.

Active Worlds just grow and grow

The more you travel in AlphaWorld and the other Active Worlds, and the more objects you get in your cache, the faster travel becomes. As you travel, you will also pick up more city data; all those anchor triangles to which the objects are attached. All this means is that the more journeys you take, the more disk space is taken up for AlphaWorld and other Active Worlds. You can easily consume 40MB or more. In the Settings dialogue found under the Options menu, you can set the Disk Usage to limit how many and how long objects are stored on your hard disk.

Now that you are finally "in the world," let's move on to start exploring the Active Worlds universe!

First Steps

Stranger in a Strange Land: First Steps into a New World

Once you land in Active Worlds, you will be in a place called The Gate (see the following figure). Here you are truly a stranger in a strange land! Moving around in front of you are *avatars*, the digital personalities representing other people in Active Worlds. In The Gate everyone looks like a grey alien. The Gate is like a Grand Central Station to worlds within the Active Worlds universe. I suggest you head straight for the original world, AlphaWorld. To do that, you can move yourself forward (by pressing on your up arrow cursor key) to the gate labeled AlphaWorld and then pass right through it. Don't worry about bumping into other avatars, you will pass right through them and this is not considered rude! You can also use your mouse to click on the gate marked AlphaWorld to go directly to that world. If you have a sound card and your speakers are turned on you might well hear the sound of the teleport as you pass through.

Landing in AlphaWorld you will have to wait while objects stream in. Everything will look like floating black triangles for a few seconds. Eventually you will see a scene much like the one portrayed in the figure at the very beginning of the chapter. This scene shows a little boy avatar, a woman in a green dress, and some chunky looking dudes in the distance. All these avatars represent someone online using the Active Worlds Browser, but the size or gender of the avatar may have nothing to do with the real person behind it.

The dude standing by the green lady has some text over his head that reads: "Brown Bear: wow, neat, how many children, and do you blow the glass??". This text is also shown in a window at the bottom of the window, and is obviously part of an ongoing conversation. The person who chose the chunky guy avatar took the name Brown Bear and is talking to one or all of the other avatars. Threads of conversation are always going on and can get confusing.

In the area around the Ground Zero point, you can see several billboards and smaller signs. Signs are a useful part of AlphaWorld and you can often pass through them to visit areas they advertise. Around Ground Zero there are several dark structures that look like a cross between an obelisk and a telephone booth. These are *teleporters*. As you might guess, if you walk into a teleporter, you are transported instantaneously to distant lands. Ground Zeros in most worlds are surrounded by teleporters.

Beyond the square around Ground Zero, you will see an expansive green plain and a mountainous horizon. Those mountains are an awfully long way off (I have never reached them, personally). Spread out on the green plain is a vast cityscape, or rather, a whole series of cities.

The initial Active Worlds Browser window is quite small to start with, but you can resize it to get a better view. You can even make it fill your whole screen. This is quite dramatic, but it might make your movement a bit slow. The larger the window, the more work your computer has to do to paint the scene as you move through the virtual cities in AlphaWorld (so the slower you will be able to move). If you have a fast computer you can use a bigger view. You can fine-tune the performance of your world under the Options menu, but this is a detail you don't have to worry about now.

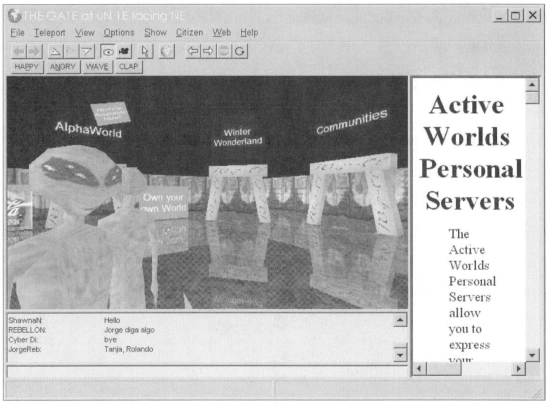

At Ground Zero in The Gate.

Avatars in AlphaWorld.

Choosing Your avatar

There are a range of avatars in AlphaWorld, including surfer dudes, karate kids, tourist women, strongmen, svelte model women, geeks, birds, and other assorted characters, as shown in the preceding figure.

If you have immigrated as a citizen, you can choose your avatar from the avatar gallery, available by clicking on the Avatar menu (see adjacent figure) at the top of the Active Worlds Browser window. If you do not choose an avatar, you are assigned the default avatar (named Cy), which looks a little like a storefront mannequin. Once you choose a new avatar, everyone in the world (after 10 or 20 seconds) will see the change take effect. You may see some avatars which are not listed in the Avatar menu. These are custom-built avatars. Custom built avatars are a new experimental addition to Active Worlds. Expect to see more of this in the future, including a way for you to build your own avatar.

Avatar
Cy
Cybot
Barbra
Birde
Butch
Caldius
✓ Dredd
Harold
Helmut
Hotep
Kelly
Ken
Marsha
Shanubia
Shred
Tanya
Willy

Choose your avatar from the Avatar menu.

Badge of honor, badge of shame

Like two society women who discover they are wearing the same dress at the ball, it can be embarrassing and confusing to see so many avatars that look like you (see following figure). To help, most worlds provide a name tag called a name badge.

In Active Worlds, this badge is shown above the heads of avatars. It appears just after you have entered some text. In the following figure, you can see the name badges of avatars called **North, DigiGardener** (that's me!), and **ChillyDog**. You will also notice that other text appears under the name badges. This is the text which the real people behind North, DigiGardener, and ChillyDog, typed in. (I'll talk more about communi-

cations later.) Like Internet addresses, name badges (sometimes called user IDs or nicknames), are unique in each world. As in the real world, in the virtual you can also bring honor or shame to your name. In Active Worlds, you also must supply your e-mail address during citizen application. This can make Active Worlds citizens quite responsible, except for some dramatic cases, as you will see in our later section on crime.

Look-alike avatars can be confusing!

OK, now what?

The very first thing you must do in Active Worlds is get away from Ground Zero! If you are standing there, you cannot carry on a decent conversation because people are constantly landing on top of you! But hold your horses, you ask, how do I move? In the next section, I introduce you to smooth moves in the virtual block party.

Navigating in AlphaWorld

Moving around in the world

If you have used a computer for any length of time, you will find that moving around in AlphaWorld is easy. If you have used computer games in arcades or at home, especially three-dimensional ones like Doom, you will find moving around in AlphaWorld a snap!

Clipping along by keyboard

Even in this era of the mouse, nothing beats the versatility of a good keyboard command set. Active Worlds Browser's designers chose a very logical and simple set of keyboard keys for motion, as shown in the following table.

Keyboard keys used for motion

KEY	EFFECT
Forward Arrow	Moves you forward into the scene
Backward Arrow	Moves you backward out of the scene
Left Arrow	Turns you to your left
Right Arrow	Turns you to your right
Keypad Plus Key	Flies you up
Keypad Minus Key	Parachutes you down
Page Up Key	Turns your "head" to look up
Page Down Key	Turns your "head" to look down

As with many computer games, you can use these keys in combination. For example, if you want to turn in a circle, you can hold down the forward arrow and left arrow keys at the same time. The keypad plus and minus keys (different from the plus and minus keys above the numbers on your alphabetic keys) are the most fun. As kids (or maybe you are a kid now?), we dreamed of flying; well, now you can! As you keep your finger down on that plus key, you will see yourself rising up. This can give you a feeling of exhilaration. These virtual environments, even without goggles or fancy gloves, give you the feeling of being inside them. People have even reported a sense of vertigo and fear of heights while using virtual worlds. You might laugh at these people, sitting comfortably in front of their computers, but recall your own feelings in movie theaters, or at some of those huge screen IMAX productions where you felt like you were going to tip right out of your seat.

Mousing it at ground level

If you want to use your mouse to control movement, you can go into "mouse mode" by clicking on the small pointing cursor icon on the toolbar. Your mouse movements will carry you around the world until you click again to release the mouse. AlphaWorld and many other worlds did not support devices, such as joysticks, at the time of this writing.

The toolbar

The Active Worlds Browser has a toolbar which makes some common operations simple to reach. The left and right arrows on the left-hand side of the toolbar allow you to move back or forward. Whenever you travel with a teleporter (more on this

later), your previous position is recorded. You can go back to this position by pressing on the left arrow on the toolbar or by selecting Back under the Teleport menu. You can reverse your steps using the right arrow or Forward under the Teleport menu. You will find these features very useful as you explore the Active Worlds.

The Active Worlds toolbar.

The next three buttons on the toolbar show eyes looking up, straight ahead, and down. Clicking on these buttons allows you to tilt your avatar's head viewpoint up and down, or come back to a level position. You can also change your viewpoint by using the Page Up and Page Down keys or the View menu (see adjacent figure).

Use the View menu to change your point of view.

Had an out-of-body experience? You'll like this one!

Next on the toolbar are the eye and camera buttons. Clicking on the eye button will let you see the world through your avatar's first-person point of view. Picking the camera will let you move out of body into a third-person *bird's eye* or *god* view. These options can also be activated by pressing the Home and End keys or selecting choices from the View menu. Many AlphaWorld citizens find that floating at some distance above the ground (by pressing + or -) is the best way to get around. You can combine flying and third-person view for a truly dramatic effect.

Seeing yourself from overhead can be very useful. In god view you can see what you look like and what is in your surroundings as you move along. God view is also a very good way to "see" conversations being directed at you by more than one avatar. Hitting the End key more than once pulls you out of your body even farther. Even though you are out of body you can still use all the same keys to move and communicate or even build.

When you are tired of being so all-seeing and want a more intimate viewpoint, hitting the Home key or pressing the eye button on the toolbar will bring you back into your avatar's body.

In the adjacent figure I (as DigiGardener) am leading a tour and talking at the same time. The right-side set of buttons on the toolbar will appear only if you have the built-in Web browser option installed. More later in the section, "Built-in Web options."

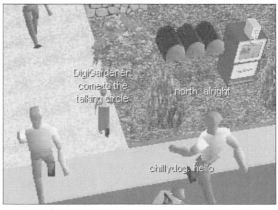

I'm leading a group on a tour in god view.

Gesture gesticulation

| HAPPY | ANGRY | WAVE |

Pressing gesture buttons makes your avatar gesture.

You may notice that avatars around you are making this strange series of gestures. Some of these gestures are automatic and others you can control by clicking on buttons like the ones shown in the adjacent figure. The gestures you can make depend on the avatar you have selected. Some worlds have avatars with no gestures at all. See the section, "Did you see that . . . avatar move?!" later in this chapter, for a funny karate sequence of avatar gestures.

Speed Freak? We've got just the key combinations for you!

You may find the pace in AlphaWorld a bit sedate. To pump up the RPMs and rocket around, try pressing Ctrl with the motion keys to speed up, or pressing Shift and the motion keys to pass through objects.

Ctrl: the ten-speed key

This key moves you along at a good clip, 10 miles per hour in traffic. With this combination, the Active Worlds Browser still bothers to paint the scene as you go along.

The Teleporter: a 50,000 KPH rocket scooter

To travel really fast, I recommend you select the To option in the Teleport menu. Here you can enter coordinates for some far distant place or even teleport to a whole new world.

See the section on "dive bombing" under "What in the World is There to Do?" for using ultrafast modes that would make Evel Knievel proud!

Am I at the edge of the world?

As you motor further away from Ground Zero, you will notice that the built-up areas seem to end abruptly about half a city block ahead of you (see figure on next page). This does not mean there is nothing beyond this point. This point is a sort of *artificial horizon*, beyond which the Active Worlds Browser does not paint the scene. You would need a pretty powerful computer to be able to show the city out to the distant mountains. The Active Worlds Browser compromises by giving you a closer and more limited horizon. This is necessary, but it is one of the most disconcerting features of this world. Your commonsense brain is constantly saying: "there is nothing more there," while your higher virtual worlds brain has to disagree and reason: "no, there will (or will not) be something more shown there when we get closer." As you build up a mental model of familiar spots in AlphaWorld, you will begin to imagine the shape of the area beyond the horizon and saunter forth without fear that you will suddenly run smack into a wall!

You may also notice that you are stopping and starting as you move. This is happening because the Active World Server has to send you new city information. As you visit areas, this data is saved on your hard disk, and your journeys through this area again will go much faster. Sometimes the server will have to deliver a new object that is not in your library. If you press F3 or select Downloads from the Show menu, you can see what objects the Active Worlds server is sending you.

Experience the horizon effect.

Are you being served?

Other information can be shown, such as frame rate, bandwidth, and visibility (distance to the artificial horizon).

You will notice that objects being downloaded are displayed as tiny black pyramids called *anchors*. At the top of the Active Worlds Browser window you might see a message "Waiting for Server" or "Sent 1552 bytes of 8096." After city data or objects are downloaded, the Active Worlds Browser software will take a few seconds to paint this new object into the scene. After you have received a large number of objects, your travels will become faster and easier. Bear in mind that as the Active Worlds Browser runs, it will take up more disk space. It will not take a large amount, but it is good to keep at least 20MB of free space available at all times.

Show	Avatar	Help
✔ Position		F11
Visibility		F2
Frame Rate		F12
Bandwidth		F4
Downloads...		F3
✔ Toolbar...		

Use the Show menu to see more Active Worlds Information.

Whoops, I stubbed my toe!

It might come as no surprise that in Active Worlds, you can run into a wall. If your avatar suddenly stops moving, you could be trapped against an obstruction. If you look down (with Page Down), you might notice an object at your "feet." These worlds are made up of millions of "objects." These are images of real-life things such as shrubs, sidewalks, doors, and beer mugs. As in real life, you would expect some objects to be more solid than others. As you might expect, you can pass through objects like shrubs but will be stopped cold by a stone wall. To pass through objects, press Shift together with the motion keys.

They say that any sufficiently advanced technology is indistinguishable from magic. Why bother with doors when you can just Shift through the walls. It is so common for avatars to blast through the masonry that many builders in AlphaWorld don't bother with doors or roofs on their buildings. Beware of Shift, though, you can find yourself underground, looking up at the bottom of AlphaWorld (a curious but harmless situation).

Let's Travel!

Some people never venture beyond the bounds of Ground Zero, and are content to mill about and chat within this tiny area. But there is a vast hinterland in AlphaWorld, with major cities, and other Active Worlds you can reach. So take up your old kit bag and catch the wanderlust of this vast virtual planet.

Ground Zero is laid out as a large town square with routes leading out to many destinations. Some of these routes are by land; you just move in that direction. Roads tend to travel only a short distance. Hey, this is cyberspace; where we are going, there are no roads! Expect to be hedge hopping before long. The best way to explore by land is to fly to a certain altitude and zoom along. You can take any direction you like out of Ground Zero, and you can fly for a very long way before you will run out of city. Is there any order to it? Because AlphaWorld citizens just built where they found land, there is not much rhyme or reason to the cityscape. It is a kind of unplanned virtual Los Angeles. You do find some semblance of neighborhood in concentrated areas. Someone lays down a pattern, like a river, a pathway, or a bit of street, and others tend to build around it.

Cartesian universe

After a while you will ask the inevitable question: where am I? In a dynamically changing and enormous environment like AlphaWorld, there is no map. In this universe of the world, Columbus was wrong, the world *is* flat and it has an edge off of which you can fall! AlphaWorld is not a sphere but is actually a huge green plain. Get out your old high school math and geography books and blow off the dust; welcome back to the Cartesian coordinate system! If you are not in high school yet, you will be able to blow your teachers away!

At the top of the Active Worlds Browser window you will see text displayed which might say something like, "AlphaWorld at 23N 37E facing SW." This means that you are 23 units north and 37 units east of Ground Zero and you are facing southwest. Knowing this type of latitude/longitude location system is essential for getting around in AlphaWorld. As you move, notice how the numbers change. In our current position, if we continue in the southwesterly direction, we will see both the north and east numbers decreasing. In fact, we will be headed back toward Ground Zero (at 0N, 0E). When you are moving very fast, these numbers really roll by.

It is big out there!

AlphaWorld is huge! Once you learn to speak Cartesian, you can say to someone, "Come and see my place at 8326S, 9665W." One AlphaWorld unit corresponds to about 2 feet (0.6 meters) in "real" terms. After traveling around AlphaWorld for almost a year (does the author have any real social life, you might ask?), I have yet to reach the edge (those sunny distant hills will never be explored). This is tiring, you might exclaim, as your finger holding down Ctrl goes numb; is there a better way to get around? Yes, there is a better way; see the following section on teleports!

Teleports: Scotty, beam me around!

A whole generation growing up with *Star Trek* and hard core science fiction is about to live its collective fantasies; the teleport is here! And you don't have to wait until the twenty-fifth century to use one! Teleports are a public art form, just take a look at these beauties . . .

In-world teleporting

Teleports are handy ways to jump from one point in AlphaWorld to another. You can also jump

A modern suburban teleport.

A citizen entering a futuristic teleport in Alpha Colony.

between totally different Active Worlds. There are many ways you can teleport. The first is by entering one of the in-world teleport booths, as shown in the previous figures. These booths look different, but they all do the same thing: move you quickly to another location. Large collections of teleports, in *telestation halls* or in *teleparks*, are handy points from which to explore the universe of Active Worlds.

Telestation halls have teleports that take you to points in a common area, like the eastern part of AlphaWorld. In halls, teleports are arranged in pairs, the outbound port on one side and the inbound on the other. You can enter the outbound port and will see people coming back from the locations through the inbound ports. Move the mouse cursor over a teleporter and you will see a description of where it will take you. If you have a sound card installed you will hear a distinctive teleporting sound as you emerge from a port into a new area. You may have to wait a moment while the server gets you set up to see the new scene. If a world has many new objects, you might have to wait a minute or so before you see much.

Built-in dial-a-teleport

The Teleport menu.

Another way to teleport is by using the built-in teleporter. This was pioneered by the AlphaWorld Police Department as a teleport cruiser used to get to crime scenes quickly, to track down vandals, or assist citizens being subjected to *avabuse* (verbal abuse). Choose Teleport ⇨ To, and enter your coordinates, as in the following figure.

Enter your coordinates in the Teleport dialogue.

Don't forget to enter the NEWS (North, East, West, or South) letters after your numbers. You can enter decimal precision (like 105.8N). If you enter a third number which has no letter with it, it sets your *skew*, or the direction you will be facing when you land (for example, 180 means you will be facing 180 degrees off the normal east-west line). If you enter a number followed by the letter A, it will set your altitude in units above the ground. You can also directly enter the name of an Active World.

Other ways to enter the world: The Web teleport

A third way to use teleports is through Web pages. Many AlphaWorld citizens have built Web sites about their AlphaWorld creations. They have included special types of links which, when clicked on, launch an Active World and land you right where they want you. I have used this extensively in an AlphaWorld town building experiment called Sherwood Forest, sponsored by the Contact Consortium, of which I am one of the founders. The following figure shows Web teleports to the front gate and many private properties on the site. Citizens use Web teleports to get to their homesteads, to give tours, or draw in people for shared events. The consortium used Web teleports and special signs that you could walk through at Ground Zero to draw in hundreds of guests to a big experimental social mixer we held in July 1996. If you are interested in taking a look at how we did this, see the special Web page at **http://www .ccon.org/events/mixup1.html**.

The Web teleport is a portent of things to come. Most virtual worlds, including OnLive! Traveler, Comic Chat, and others allow you to Web teleport. The Web is becoming like a road map and publishing medium for virtual worlds. It is acting like a two-dimensional travel guide from which you can drop into three-dimensional virtual worlds and meet people.

See the section "Questions and Answers about Linking Active Worlds to web pages," on the book companion

A Web page teleport goes to Sherwood Towne and AlphaWorld Ground Zero.

Web site, which describes how to set up Active Worlds Explorer as a helper application within your Web browser so that you can do Web teleporting.

Built-in Web options

If you have installed Microsoft Internet Explorer version 3.0 or later, the Active Worlds Browser will include a Web browsing window automatically. If you have the built-in Web option, you will have a new set of buttons on the toolbar allowing you to control your Web browser. You will have options to enter a Web URL, go forward, back, or stop loading. You can even perform a search of the Web from within the Active Worlds Browser. I happened to come upon this avatar of *Star Trek's* Captain Jean-Luc Picard (see following figure). We can search the Web and navigate through links to our hearts' content using the toolbar buttons or the choices on the Web menu.

These menu options permit full navigation of the World Wide Web.

If you come upon a link to a Web page (sometimes attached to little newsstands) and click on it, the Web page will come up right inside the Active Worlds Browser. If you have a Web browser other than Microsoft Internet Explorer, it will be started in a second window.

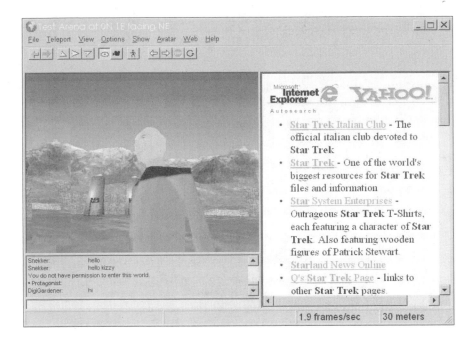

An Active Worlds Browser showing the built-in Web browser.

The Gate to new worlds

If you click on the World icon on the toolbar, the Web browser window on the right will update statistics about all the worlds and the people in them. Clicking on the name of the world will have the same effect as taking a teleport in the Gate; it will land you in the world (if you have permission to enter). Not all worlds are open to the public, and some are not opened up until they are fully developed.

You can enter these into the Coordinates dialogue under the Teleport menu. For example, I am caretaker of an Active World called TheU Virtual University and I can go there by entering **alphaworld.worlds.net:7023 0N 0W**, where **alphaworld.worlds.net** is the Web address, **7023** is the port, and **0N 0W** is the coordinate of Ground Zero in TheU. Note that these addresses are always changing, so the most reliable way to find new worlds is to visit The Gate.

A Web of Worlds

There is a whole web of Active Worlds worth visiting. At the time of this writing, there were over 200 separate Active Worlds. Later in this chapter, in the section "What in the World is There to Do?," we will take a peek inside some of these worlds, such as Circle of Fire's Yellowstone Park and Titan Guild's Winter Wonderland.

You too can have your own world

You can build your own Active World. This would require you to purchase the Active Worlds Server software and developer's kit. You would also have to support your own server on a Windows NT or UNIX computer and develop your own objects and content. Many people are taking the plunge and hosting their own worlds. You can find more information and documentation on creating your own Active World on the Active Worlds Web site at **http://www.activeworlds.com**.

Citizen to the rescue: AlphaWorld Atlas

Elliott Lee, an enterprising AlphaWorld citizen, went to the trouble of creating an atlas for AlphaWorld. You can find it on his Web site at **http://www.cs.cuc.edu/~sopwith/aw/awatlas/mapif.cgi**. We hope it is still active as you read this book. If you cannot find it, your *Avatars!* book Web site at **http://www.digitalspace.com/avatars** should contain more up-to-date links for AlphaWorld.

The AlphaWorld Atlas is simple: citizens with a site to advertise make entries into the atlas, giving its world coordinates, and indicating its structural type (town, business, etc.). Atlas users then enter coordinates and can see small colored dots (like radar spots) representing sites of interest in the area.

Clicking on the dots, users are shown the Atlas listing for that structure. Also there is the AlphaWorld Teleport Station which allows you to click on a huge overhead image of AlphaWorld and then land in AlphaWorld on that spot. Find the Teleport Station at **http://kozmo.yakima.net/alphaworld/teleport.html**. See this image reproduced in the color pictures in the center of this book. We also talk about this in the section "What Hath They Wrought, Builders and Their Creations?" later in this chapter.

Communicating

Can you repeat that? I couldn't see what you were saying!

Communicating with another person in AlphaWorld is as easy as typing text into the long message area across the bottom of the Active Worlds Explorer window and then hitting Enter. After a few seconds, you should see your message appear in the chat box just above the entry area. As soon as the text appears there, it will also appear nicely perched above your avatar's head where everyone can see it. Having both the text chat box (which you can use to scroll back and track the threads of conversations) and text above avatars' heads allow you to easily follow conversations.

The talking circle shares thoughts at Sherwood Towne

Note also that if you are not looking at other avatars, you might miss what they are saying. Carrying on conversations in god view, as shown in the following figure, allows you to follow many threads of conversation at once. This figure shows a *talking circle* which I built out of floor tiles and pots at the entrance to Sherwood Towne. A talk leader can place his or her avatar at the center; other talkers situate themselves around the leader next to the pots. If all of the users go into god view, they can see the text of the talk leader and each other without worrying about the text overlapping and becoming unreadable.

Text lag

There can be a delay of several seconds while your text is shipped across the world to all the other users who are in your vicinity. The AlphaWorld server has to do quite a lot of work just to determine where you are, and who and what you should be looking at, so please be patient!

Many AlphaWorld veterans find that this simple method of communication is too limiting, so they install a conferencing system such as Powwow (available free of charge at **http://www.tribal.com/**), Microsoft NetMeeting, or CuSeeMe, which allows better text chat, voice, or even video to supplement the Active Worlds Browser. See your *Avatars!* book Web site at **http://www.digitalspace.com/avatars** for other links to valuable free communications tools.

What in the World is There to Do?

Bored just chatting and exploring? Well, AlphaWorld citizens are continually inventing new ways to have fun. Let's go along with several citizens on activities from photo shoots to the equivalent of the virtual bungee jump!

Meet the Natives

Virtual road trips to that virtual summer vacation!

There are no maps or roadside assistance in AlphaWorld yet, but this should not stop you and your family from getting in the virtual minivan and heading out for excellent adventures. Best of all, there is no gas to buy, and the bathroom is always handy! Many families have hooked up two or more computers to separate accounts through multiple telephone lines (that teen phone is useful for something) and toured as a group.

You can call on the homes of friends (rarely is anyone there, but sometimes you may be surprised), or prowl undetected through a virtual Beverly Hills. There are no security services and guard dog bots in AlphaWorld yet, but you can't take anything, anyway!

Circle of Fire Studios (find it at **http://www.channel1.com/users/fire/**) made a wonderful virtual version of Yellowstone National Park, which is in Wyoming in the U.S. It comes complete with a faithful geyser, a lodge with a fireplace, and grizzlies fishing in streams. As the following figure shows, you can do things in the virtual world that you would not dare attempt in real life. Some have fallen into the geyser, and are now traveling inside magma chambers in the bowels of the Earth.

A virtual tourist snaps photos of Yellowstone's Old Faithful geyser.

Whoops! You can fall into the lava pools under the Yellowstone geyser.

We stop by the chair lift for a picture of that gorgeous scenery!

You stand warned. As you get close to Old Faithful, a park ranger's voice calls out, "don't go near the geyser, it's dangerous!"

Hit the slopes!

Avatars slalom down the slopes in Titan's Guild Winter Wonderland, an Active World dedicated to fun in the white fluffy stuff. This world comes complete with chair lifts, runs from bunny to diamond level, and some pretty good jumps and moguls. When will we see the AlphaWorld skiing world cup?

Winter Wonderland also has a lodge with a crackling fireplace, a skating rink with plenty of Santa Claus avatars, and cheesy skating rink radio shows piped in through RealAudio (if you have RealAudio installed).

Group photos and photojournalism

Writing this book transformed me into an avatar photojournalist. You too can document your adventures in virtual worlds. Hundreds of citizens have created Web sites showing their travelogs (or *avalogs*). Will the avalog replace those very interesting home movies or fascinating slide shows we all love?

Like the scene in Stanley Kubrick's *2001, a Space Odyssey*, in which the astronauts line up in front of that monolith on the moon, you can engage in the cheesy but engaging exercise of avatar group photographs. The figure on the next page shows just how confusing it is to get everyone facing in the same direction at one time. And when it is all ready, say cheese! To take a picture, just press the Print Screen or PrtScr key on your PC keyboard, and then paste the resulting image into a paint program or word processing document.

Some AlphaWorld citizens have become fanatical photojournalists, shooting hundreds of pictures of just about every spot, and every social gathering in the world. See, "A Day in the Life of AlphaWorld," later in this chapter for shots of an actual wedding held within AlphaWorld.

Shared building

Shared building is a very common and rewarding activity in Alpha-World. Whole communities have been constructed this way (see the

Lining everyone up for a shot can be tricky!

section, "What Hath They Wrought? Builders and Their Creations"). Due to permission restrictions, citizens engage in shared building, with many people using the same avatar. To do this, you must share the aworld.ini file found in your Active Worlds directory folder. This process is described in the section, "Using aworld.ini for collaborative building," on the book companion Web site.

Did you see that . . . avatar move?!

If you haven't already noticed, avatars in AlphaWorld and other Active Worlds move. Avatar articulation sequences are a form of entertainment in themselves. My photojournalistic shutter was quick enough to catch the following frames of sensei KaiOhShin in the digital dojo.

KaiOhShin, martial artist of AlphaWorld, shows off his moves.

KaiOhShin in a stance.

KaiOhShin stands tall.

KaiOhShin takes a bow.

Boogie down at the avatar dance

A very popular activity in AlphaWorld is DJ-ing (disk jockey-ing). A host will attach music (MIDI or WAV files) to objects so that everyone in the area can hear it. People "sing" along and dance, moving their avatars back and forth in variations of the Avatar Slam, Bit Boogie, Virtualese Waltz, and Raster Rasta. The adjacent figure shows a scene from one late Friday night party at Ground Zero. Protagonist, Active Worlds co-creator Ron Britvich in real life, sings and dances along to a favorite: *Pixels in the Wind*. Another old saw is, *We are the AlphaWorld*, a virtual variant of *We are the World*.

Active Worlds co-creator, Protagonist, puts on a Top 10 hit: *Pixels in the Wind.*

Let's party!

If you have music, avatars, dancing, and scintillating conversation, then you have a party! I was involved with a group of AlphaWorld citizens in throwing a big summer bash on July 13, 1996, at Laurel's Herb Farm in Sherwood Forest Towne, a collective building area. As Laurel had created such a beautiful garden, we decided to throw a party there. On top of that, we built a virtual redwood tree grove next door, and held a poetry reading there with poets in-avatar from my hometown of Boulder Creek, California. And on top of all that, we held a big physical get together at the beautiful hilltop home of my friends and neighbors here in town.

In AlphaWorld, hundreds of avatars showed up by jumping through the sign (shown in the following figure on the right), which was actually a direct teleport to Sherwood Forest Towne. We had a DJ for music, professional party hosts, poets, and even the

A summer garden party at Laurel's herb farm.

The sign and teleport to the garden party from Ground Zero.

AlphaWorld Police Department in case of trouble (which we had). We held simultaneous parties in both the Palace and Black Sun Interactive's Passport. Lots of people, wine, song, poetry mixed with computers, and partygoer avatars joined us virtually, and made themselves heard. This mixing of physical and virtual parties was a lot of fun, and I expect to see more of this in the years ahead. Why don't you try it? You can find out how we did it at **http://www.ccon.org/events/mixup1.html**.

Dive bombing

Dive bombing is one of the strangest and most thrilling activities in AlphaWorld. AlphaWorld citizens pick a favorite spot and then, usually with a partner cybernaut, rocket to high altitude using a combination of Ctrl and Keypad Plus. It is more fun to do this out of body in the god view. To do this, press End before you start your ascent.

You will see your avatar shoot upward, and you will track right along behind it. When you finally let your fingers off the thruster controls (Ctrl+Keypad Plus), you will be at a dizzying height. Go back into your avatar's body by pressing Home, and then look around. You may or may not see your partner, but you will see the horizon and realize how high you are. Use Page Down to tilt your viewpoint straight down, and you will see a tiny area below. That is the section of the city you just left, an isolated island within its display horizon. There is actually much more city below, but the Active Worlds software is just not showing it.

Next you can begin your powered descent. Looking straight down, press Ctrl+Keypad Minus and watch how the city comes up underneath you. Finish your descent by just holding down Keypad Minus. Be careful not to approach ground too fast or you will blow beneath the world. If you do this, you can look up and see the underside of the city. You will have to come back up by pushing Shift+Keypad Plus. Finally, use Page Up to tilt your head up. Congratulations on a fine landing!

Hide-and-seek

It may seem silly, but good old hide-and-seek can be a fun form of virtual chase. As avatars can be seen through buildings and at long distances, the finding is easy, but the catching is not. The chase is on, and may the fastest CPU win!

Romance!

In any medium where people interact, romance can bloom. I have met many new and fascinating people through interactions inside AlphaWorld. When I have taken the trouble to telephone or visit these people, they have almost always surprised me . . . they were not what I expected from their virtual personae! People have met in AlphaWorld and fallen in love in real life. In "A Day in the Life of AlphaWorld," I cover a full-scale (and real-life) wedding, complete with bridesmaid, best man, and minister.

The Dark Side of AlphaWorld

Vandalism and other crimes in the virtual city

As AlphaWorld is a builder's mecca, the capital crime there is vandalism. If you are building on an area (a pure green homestead plot), and happen to leave some of it uncovered by floor tiles, road, or walkways, then vandals can strike! In the adjacent figure you can see graffiti plastered all over an empty lot by the notorious Kyoti. King Punisher and his gang are another set of hooligans in Alpha-World who have been known to set sites on fire by attaching animated flames. As there is no fire department in AlphaWorld (as of this writing), this is a big problem. There is, however, a police department.

The AWPD

The AlphaWorld Police Department (AWPD) patrols AlphaWorld in search of vandalism and avabuse. Founded by citizen **NetGuy**, the AWPD has built an impressive headquarters, as seen here. It also has a

Birds fall in love.

The Kyoti graffiti vandal strikes.

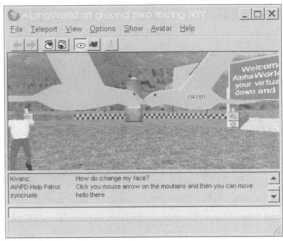

AlphaWorld Police Department has an impressive precinct building.

good set of Web pages in which police reports are filed regularly (see your *Avatars!* book Web site for links to the AWPD). The police are an all-volunteer group of AlphaWorld citizens. They also offer a very friendly help patrol at Ground Zero.

Natural disasters

"Natural" disasters occasionally strike AlphaWorld. The most traumatic of all is the *meteor strike*. This is a rare occurrence, but can happen when the main AlphaWorld server crashes, or has to be rebuilt because the format of the world is changing. In this event, all buildings are demolished. The last time this happened was mid-1995, as reported in the first issue of the *New World Times* (as seen in the preceding figure), and is not

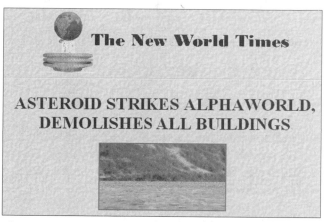

The *New World Times* reports on an asteroid impact.

likely to happen again soon. I hope that AlphaWorld will go on forever, but there may come a day when it is time for an end-of-the-world party.

Another temporary natural disaster is known as the *upgrade fire*. This occurs when you move to a whole new level of Active Worlds Browser software, which requires the server to send you (gradually) all of the objects to repaint the world. The server sends you the anchor points first (seen as black pyramids). These are the points to which objects attach. It takes some time before the objects themselves appear, so in the interim, you seem to be moving around in a barren, charred landscape like that of a burned forest. Don't worry when you see this, for all of the trees and city will come back!

Avabuse

Avabuse, the abuse of a person in-avatar, can take several forms. One is just plain bad language and outright deception! This is a social world of free speech, and our neighbors may not always treat us as we would treat them in return. Another form of avabuse is related to body language. The figure on the next page shows a case in which an aggressive (or bored) AlphaWorld citizen was constantly shadowing me and blocking my views of all conversations. Repeatedly passing back and forth through someone's avatar is called an *avattack,* and is the virtual form of assault and battery.

Avabuse is in your face!

Please do not discount the feelings you have when something like this happens. The power of inhabited virtual world environments is that they *make you feel like you are there with other people*. Your feelings are valid, just as the intent to offend you was real. Just stay calm and teleport or run out of areas where you feel you are in trouble or not wanted. There is no shame in this, just as there is no shame in similar real-life situations.

Gender-bending, race-shifting, and generally not being yourself

As you may have seen in on-line chat rooms, participants assuming a character of the other sex and leading people on is a common occurrence. In AlphaWorld, you can combine this with the selection of racially different avatars, or choose to be a little kid, or a hulking giant. In Neal Stephenson's *Snow Crash*, people were not permitted to select an avatar taller than they were in real life. No such social mores hold in AlphaWorld.

Part of the most thrilling and enticing aspect of the virtual experience is to live the fantasy of being another person. Perhaps there is an actor or actress in all of us. There is a dark side of gender-bending or race-shifting, however. The old adage still applies: "Oh what tangled webs we weave when we practice to deceive."

Starbright World and the liberation of the virtual

There is a positive side to a free choice of digital personae. There are AlphaWorld citizens who are bedridden, hearing impaired, or confined to a wheelchair. Being able to communicate with others and fly through landscapes is reported to give them a tremendous sense of liberation. The Starbright World, designed for sick children in the hospital, is used as a liberator and play environment. Starbright is not detailed in this book because it is not available to the general public, but it is perhaps the most poignant example of how virtual worlds technology can help enrich the quality of human life. For more details on the Starbright World, see Appendix A.

The power of accountability

AlphaWorld is an environment which does not permit anonymity. When you became a citizen, you provided your e-mail address. Bear in mind that you could be identified and contacted if you are causing someone grief. For a guide to good citizenry, see Dataman's AlphaWorld netiquette guide in *Netiquette, The World Manners Guide*, on the book companion Web site.

A Day in the Life of AlphaWorld

Witness a (real) virtual wedding

On May 8, 1996, at 9 p.m. Central Standard Time, history was made with the world's first Internet-hosted wedding held inside a multi-user graphical virtual world. The happy couple, Tomas Landhaus, 27, and Janka Stanhope, 31, were married in real life inside AlphaWorld in a pavilion specially constructed for the occasion. They had first met at AlphaWorld Ground Zero, then met later in person, and fell in love. They felt it was only appropriate to host their wedding back in AlphaWorld, and invite all their AlphaWorld friends.

Organizing this event took the efforts of many people—to build the pavilion, to rehearse, to arrange music (piped in through MIDI files), to design special custom avatars for the bride, groom, and best man, and to script the ceremony.

Avatar wedding album

An ecstatic groom and best man.

The bride says, "I do."

The happy couple sneak a kiss.

Estimates are that 50 or more friends and onlookers showed up for this event, which was advertised by word of mouth in AlphaWorld. The minister, *New World Times* editor **Dataman,** presided and kept the aisles clear. NetGuy, AlphaWorld's police chief, served as best man, and friend **Yellow Rose** served as a bridesmaid.

Citizens floated their avatars down the aisle, crowded the altar to witness the words "I do" from both the bride and groom, and then flooded in around the couple to wish them well. The event was assisted by a live Powwow (a conferencing system from Tribal Voice) conference running on the side. The festivities went on for about an hour after the ceremony. When the bride tried to toss her bouquet, she discovered that it was permanently glued to her avatar. Immediately after the wedding, the groom drove 3,100 miles from San Antonio, Texas to Tacoma Washington to kiss his bride.

The wedding of Janka and Tomas felt real. I fell asleep that night exhausted and fully believing that I attended this wedding. You may think me mad, but any kind of community and culture, real or virtual, is about presence and communication. Both were there that day in AlphaWorld.

The story of two dudes

Another story involves two surfer dudes I met one day in the hinterlands. The two of them came sailing over the horizon to join a Sherwood community build. They were both named **Drumgod,** obviously an *avatwin* (a shared avatar). "Where's the beach," they asked. "There is the famous Seth's Surf Shack," I said. "Been there, done that," they replied. So I offered to give them land at Sherwood Towne. They agreed to settle in town, and the Sherwood Clan agreed to throw a building lesson into the bargain.

As an Avatwin, two surfer dudes (from Alabama, it turns out) share an avatar for common building on one site.

They were in luck, for one of AlphaWorld's luminaries and pro builders also showed up. **BlackThorne** is a real surfer from Brisbane, Australia, who spends his nights in AlphaWorld. BlackThorne agreed to give them a pro building lesson. What do they want to build? "A beach," the avatwins replied in unison.

The surfers built for 10 hours, created a surfer's beach bazaar, and then took off late in the evening (Central Standard Time in the U.S.). Talk about surfing the Internet!

What Hath They Wrought?
Builders and Their Creations

Getting tired of just jabbering with the socialite set? Then you may be ready to become a creative force in AlphaWorld. When Worlds Inc. opened AlphaWorld for business in the summer of 1995, there was just a Ground Zero, a few buildings, and a seemingly infinite green plain. Over the next year or so, some of AlphaWorld's 200,000-plus citizens took it upon themselves to fill it. And fill it they did. The original AlphaWorld got so big that teleports were invented to carry people to new outlying cities. Now there are whole parallel worlds. AlphaWorld is now made up of about 12 million objects, all placed there one at a time by people. AlphaWorld builders have arranged these objects into structures such as a Roman Coliseum, an underground city, and a popular bar in the shape of a glass pyramid—the largest Lego construction project in history.

An amazing satellite image (see color section in center of book) was taken from a very high altitude above the center of AlphaWorld. It shows a 10 kilometer by 10 kilometer area around Ground Zero. Traveling up this image is the same as AlphaWorld north, down is south, left is west, and right is east. It took only a few minutes to find Sherwood Forest Towne (which I will show you later). This image was made by the creators of AlphaWorld, who processed the city database and painted colors for each type of object they found. See if you can find the airport (hint, look in the northeast) and the Roman Coliseum.

You can find this remarkable map at the AlphaWorld Teleport Station at **http://kozmo.yakima.net/alphaworld/teleport.html**. At the teleport station, you can click on this map, and land in different spots in AlphaWorld. Like the quote from Neal Stephenson's *Snow Crash*, which we reproduced here, AlphaWorld has realized the dream of a digital street in a shared virtual city. Stephenson's fictional *Metaverse* may not be far from reality, and you can do your part to build it!

Just do it

The builders of AlphaWorld are no different from you or me; they are just ordinary people, often working from home. Laurel (her world nickname) has beautified many areas of AlphaWorld with spectacular flower gardens, waterfalls, and rockeries. She has done all this on her laptop computer sitting at her kitchen table at home in Louisiana in the U.S. AlphaWorld builders range in age from under 10 to over 80, and come from all walks of life. One of the best features about life in digital space is that your skin color, race, sex, size, religion, or age does not matter; nei

"Like any place in Reality, the Street is subject to development. Developers can build their own small streets feeding off of the main one. They can build buildings, parks, signs, as well as things that do not exist in Reality, such as vast hovering overhead light shows and special neighborhoods where the rules of three-dimensional spacetime are ignored."

—Neal Stephenson, *Snow Crash*

academic degrees you have. If you want to be an architect and learn how to build beautifully for the virtual realm, you can just do it.

So much is built every day that it is impossible to show you all of it. By the time you read this book, there might be a dozen new cities completed. I suggest you go into AlphaWorld and tour around. Use your *Avatars!* companion Web site at **http://www.digitalspace.com/avatars** as an up-to-the-minute guide to the hottest spots in AlphaWorld.

Let's take a look at some great buildings, and some great builders, in AlphaWorld.

This is your office in cyberspace.

BlackThorne (his AlphaWorld name) has built his home office in cyberspace. The computer on his desk doesn't work (but it just might one day). You might recognize that the screen shows a view of AlphaWorld Ground Zero. Perhaps one day we will use simulated workspaces like this to do our real work (all we need are those little sticky notes in there).

It was so wonderful when there were no cars in AlphaWorld, and then someone had to go and build one. The AlphaWorld Police Department may figure out one day how to issue parking fines! This car owner is lucky, because his hot rod is parked in Colony Alpha, a separate Active World hosted by citizen Moria, where the AWPD has no jurisdiction. Why have streets and cars in a world where you can just sail through the air? Because nothing works as well as the familiar. In the beginning, metaphors within this new form of real cyberspace will probably stick close to the familiar . . . but wait!

This sleek batmobile is parked at the Black Sun Café and Bar in Colony Alpha.

Cyborg Nation

Cyborg Nation is an Active World built by **Dataman,** longtime AlphaWorld citizen, and editor of AlphaWorld's first community newspaper, the *New World Times* (see **http://www.synergycorp.com/alphaworld/nwt/**). Cyborg Nation is an experimental world which is *not* made of streets and towns and mailboxes. Cyborg Nation features weird geometric scenes, stunning visuals and, we expect, cyborgs. Bots, or automated avatars, are not common in virtual worlds yet, so maybe Cyborg Nation is the place where some will evolve. Cyborg Nation is constantly changing.

Another Active World is TheU Virtual University, hosted by the Contact Consortium (of which I am a part). A real architect and AlphaWorld citizen, **San Marco,** who

TheU Virtual University development center.

lives in North London in Great Britain, is serving as the coordinator of a global architecture competition to build a functional virtual university in three dimensions. This project grew out of consortium members' prior experience with MUDs (Multi User Domains), the text-based interactive worlds used in education, which are very widespread on the Internet. San Marco has built a university development center in TheU, which is shown in the preceding figure. On the walls are images representing links to Web sites. Clicking on these images will bring up your Web browser and point it to a particular Web site. We use this space for discussions, in-world meetings, and as a shared information library about TheU project and other virtual education projects. For more information on TheU, see **http://www.ccon.org/theU/index.html**.

Sky Cities

Necropolis City, in AlphaWorld, is a marvelous creation of transparent glass panels and terra cotta brick. Do avatars go there to die? I don't know, but Necropolis is certainly inspired, and inspires citizens to practice *dive bombing* over the area, which I described earlier in this chapter. One unique feature of cities like Necropolis is that they are built partly underground. You can descend into subterranean vaults. You can also travel through the ground (it is transparent) and see the vaults connecting together like rabbit warrens.

Nothing says you just have to build on the ground, and so there are plenty of floating palaces. Anti-gravity not invented yet? No problem, you can lift a whole virtual city to great heights. Be careful in approaching the edges of these towns, the vertigo effect is very convincing!

The Story of Two Builders

Tazunu Inoue and his Japanese palace and gardens

Tazunu Inoue is a dedicated Alpha-World builder and citizen from Japan. This is Tazunu's story, in his own words, and a look at his magnificent creations. These include palaces and castles in a very Japanese style, and a water garden with rocks set in the shape of a map of the Japanese home islands. You can find Tazunu's property at 7786S, 7964E facing north in AlphaWorld, and on his home page at **http://www.sun-inet.or.jp/ ~inoue/aworld/index.html**.

Tazunu Inoue's elaborate palace.

Tazunu's own words

It was in February 1996 that I came to AW for the first time. A virtual world that is quite like the real world came into my eyes. Everything seemed to be exciting. But I could not manipulate my body freely. I was not good at reading or writing English (and the situation has not changed much). So I was like a child.

The interior of one of Tazunu's creations.

One day, a kind person led me to this place (North of Lock Heaven, over 100 kilometers far away from Ground Zero). He showed me his house and taught me that I would be able to build my own home, too. He was very patient. (He is one of my neighbors now.)

I have been building my house since then. It is a Japanese castle. I did not mean to build a big home from the beginning. But a castle is an originally big thing, which is why my castle is still under construction.

Tazunu Inoue

By the way, there are two reasons I made this home page. One reason is that there are too many objects to see all of my castle at a glance. You might say our computer is suffering from nearsightedness. Another reason is my poor English . . . It's not so easy to explain everything about my castle in English while we are in AW.

Like Tazunu, citizens tiring of brick and mortar return to a natural state of gardens, waterscapes, park land, and bird-song sounds (see Laurel's story below). Plenty of water shapes let the builder go off the straight and narrow. Avatars building a river together have been known to instruct each other to "hand me the flowing stream, two-by-two, stat!"

Laurel and the greening of cyberspace

Laurel (her nickname), a resident of Louisiana in the American Deep South, and a master builder in AlphaWorld, created this beautiful herbalist's farm and shop in the Sherwood Forest community. Inside is a wonderful rustic setting that would please any merry man and his lady. Laurel specializes in beautiful, natural outdoor architecture and landscapes throughout the Active Worlds universe. Visit her Web site at **http://www.intersurf.com/~bocan/garden.htm**, where you will find Web teleports to her many creations.

Laurel's own words

Once upon a time, there was a woman who loved gardens and natural places. One day while wandering through this new realm called cyberspace, she happened upon the most wondrous place she had ever seen. This new place was called AlphaWorld. She was enthralled by the opportunity to create as many gardens and parks as she could stay awake to build. The following is an account of her creative endeavors.

Laurel

Laurel's Herb Farm in Sherwood Forest Towne.

The Mountain

When Laurel first arrived in AlphaWorld, she gazed in wonder at all the lovely buildings. But as she spent more and more time in this enchanting realm, she realized that there was something it lacked. Although the buildings and little flowers were lovely, the land was absolutely flat! Where were the hills and streams that she longed to walk beside? So Laurel set out to build the world's first mountain.

The Interim

After the mountain was finished, Laurel was very pleased at all the lovely visitors that came. But she was also very tired and so she rested for a long, long while. Besides, after creating a mountain, whatever could she do that would compare? She planted a little garden here and a little garden there, while she thought of what else she might do.

Moving to Town

Laurel met many wonderful people as she wandered around in AlphaWorld. Solus and Dataman helped her with all her many questions and kept her company. One day, she met some people who were building a special community called Sherwood. They were part of a group called the Contact Consortium and all seemed very nice. They invited her to come and live in their community of Sherwood, so one day she started building a little cottage, and then a little garden there. Laurel loved herbs and decided that her garden would contain them.

An Invitation

Not long after she had settled into her new little cottage, Dataman told her that there was to be a very special event in AlphaWorld. Tomas and Janka were getting married, but they needed someone to build them a pretty place to hold the ceremony. Laurel smiled happily and said that she would be thrilled to help. After many long hours, the pavilion was created. Tomas and Janka got married there and made history as the first couple to be wed in a virtual world.

The Future

What will Laurel's future hold? Planting more gardens in AlphaWorld, I'm sure; but Laurel is intrigued by the emergence of this new phenomena of worldlets, and would love to help build in them. If you've looked through her galleries and like what she's done, why don't you tell her? If you'd like to share your AlphaWorld sites with her, why don't you write to her? If you or your company has need of a person like Laurel, why don't you let her know? She is anxious to get on with her mission of the greening of cyberspace.

Cities Within Cities: the Community Building Phenomenon in Suburban AlphaWorld

The Sherwood Forest community is an experiment of the Contact Consortium. Sherwood brings together a large number of people to craft a community space for the purposes of beauty, function, and personal expression. Members of the Sherwood clan include anthropologists, architects, urban planners, teenagers, homemakers, university students, writers, artists, a rabbi, a government economist, and many others. Cartographer Steven Hanly created a series of maps of Sherwood Forest Towne as it was being built. The following figures show the pace of growth between March and May 1996. Our goal with Sherwood was to create a space in which builders would have to cooperate closely (the building lots were kept very small), and to create an area of AlphaWorld that people would want to revisit. Find Sherwood at coordinates 105.4N, 187.8E, 180 skew and see the Sherwood Web page at **http://www.ccon.org/events/sherwood.html**.

The community has its own newspaper, the *Towne Crier,* which documents life in a real inhabited virtual town. Lessons learned in Sherwood are helping consortium members to enrich the experience of culture and community in digital space. Sherwood is an attempt to overcome the "build and abandon" phenomenon that leaves so many ghost towns in AlphaWorld. Sherwood is ongoing, and you are welcome to join the merry townesfolk. Find information at the Consortium Web site at **http://www.ccon.org**.

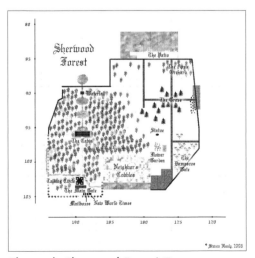

The early Sherwood Forest Towne.

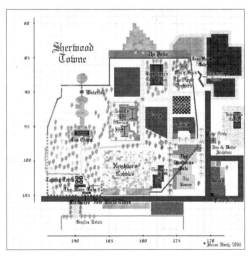

Sherwood Forest Towne after just two months of building.

The mad rush into digital space and away from our communities of place?

Human beings have always dreamed of creating the perfect society and the most beautifully designed utopian city. Like the sooners of Oklahoma, we rush madly into the digital promised land to stake our homestead. There are those who question this. They claim that the growth of virtual communities is a symptom of a loss of the community around us. They say that we all yearn for the neighborly contact we had in "the good old days," yet today we sometimes distrust or avoid our neighbors. Many of you now reading this book will end up as avatar devotees and spend hours online having a great time, rather than spending time with your neighbors.

There is a balance to everything. Writing this book has required me to spend hundreds of hours in virtual worlds, and I have met hundreds of wonderful people there whom I never would have met otherwise. I have had the good fortune to meet some of these people in person, and they have often surprised and delighted me. Perhaps the virtual world, like the telephone, is just another way to make contact with fellow human beings. The telephone has extended our community of friends and family, overcoming the isolation of distance, while bringing humanity closer together. I believe that the virtual worlds of avatar cyberspace will be as important to the twenty-first century as the telephone is today. I also believe it is important to get out of that seat every once in a while and hug your spouse, kid, parent, cat, dog, or neighbor.

Digital Homesteading: Have I got a Real Estate Deal for You!

After seeing some of what AlphaWorld citizens have built, you might be asking: how can I create my own digital homestead? Land in AlphaWorld is cheap; you just go out and find it. Like any other art form, the hours and effort you put into it creates the real value. Any plot of land that has an astroturf green color with no objects on, above, or below the surface, is available for you. To put your stake in the ground, merely copy some adjacent object onto this land (be careful not to let the object overlap with another object already existing there). I describe homesteading and building in detail in the section, "Virtual Building 101," later in the chapter.

I recommend that you visit the many Web sites built by Active Worlds citizens to see examples of what they have built, and for tips on building. Your *Avatars!* book Web site has up-to-date links to these sites.

Building supplies yard

The following figure shows a building supplies yard where you can learn what objects are available for building in AlphaWorld. There are several construction companies in AlphaWorld that feature building parts yards. Note that visiting any one of them will require Active Worlds Browser to download and cache all the objects, which can use up disk space. The benefit of this is that you will not have to wait for these objects again. Now we are ready to start you as a freshman in the University of the Virtual. Let's enroll in Virtual Building 101.

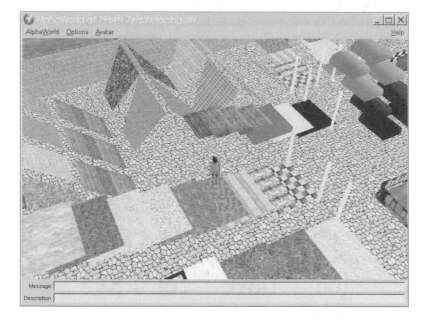

The building supplies yard is located at 7984N, 7998W.

Virtual Building 101: A Step-by-Step Guide

It's time to go back to school and learn how to build in AlphaWorld. You will be surprised at how fun and easy this is. I give building lessons in AlphaWorld all the time. One day, I asked the students if they would mind posing for a few pictures along the way. Miss **Toon Smith** was pleased as peach about being in this book, and happy to share her lesson with us.

Background information

AlphaWorld is made up of three parts: the *world* (the green plain and all the space above and below it), the *people* (all the avatars), and *objects*. You will hear the word object all the time. Objects are just parts. Examples of objects include a piece of grass, a section of road, a roof, a length of fence, or a big palm tree. In AlphaWorld, you have several hundred objects to choose from. What can you do with an object? Here are just some of the things:

- You can put an object on the ground or float it in the air.
- You can rotate an object and fit it together with other objects.
- You can overlap objects or sink them below the ground.
- You can change an object into any other object.
- You can link an object to a person's e-mail address or World Wide Web page.
- You can attach music or sounds to an object for people to hear as they approach.
- You can give an object actions, such as making it rotate or flash.
- You can remove an object (if you are the one who put it there in the first place).

Objects are made of two basic components: a *model* (the way the object looks, how big it is, and how many sides it has); and *properties* (how the object is placed, its name, and what actions are connected to it).

To build, you simply move through the world, find a place where there are no objects, and then put some of your own objects there. It is as easy as that. In the year and a half after the birth of AlphaWorld (from the summer of 1995 until the end of 1996), over 10 million objects were placed inside AlphaWorld by people just like you and me.

Building on a place gives you ownership of the land occupied by your objects, and all the space above and below it. Look for objects underground. Other people's objects under your site can interfere with building, so you may want to look there first before making grand plans. Remember, if someone else's object is there, you cannot move it, delete it, build above it, or below it. I recommend that if you are just playing around with building, that you delete all your objects when you are done to leave space for someone else. AlphaWorld is big (there are over 4 trillion square meters), but as in the real world, digital land is not a resource that should be wasted.

Getting started

If you can arrange to meet an experienced (and patient) AlphaWorld citizen to help teach you to build, you will be lucky. I was taught by an 18-year-old student from Finland to whom I owe an eternal debt. But if you cannot find an in-world helper, this section will get you building in no time! Please note that there is an excellent help system built right into Active Worlds Browser, which can act as a supplement for this guide.

Toon Smith, our eager student with a camera ready.

Circle of Fire Studios sells its Active Worlds server software and services to help you build your own worlds. For more information, visit the Active Worlds Web site at **http://www.worlds.net**.

Step 1: Find a place to build

Find a place where you can build. To do this, travel some distance from Ground Zero using high-speed travel over land, or by taking a teleport ride. You can build on the open green plain in areas where there are no other objects on, above, or below the ground. It is best to allow yourself more space than you think you will need (imagination has a tendency to grow). I sometimes pick building areas that are next to roadways or walls because it is likely that my neighbors will not want to build there.

Step 2: Pick the starter object

The area Toon Smith and I have chosen is by the side of a road put down by someone else, and between the properties of two other builders. This can be a good spot, as it will allow us to go over to either property and see the objects they used to build it. We know we can build here because the area is covered by the same green color you see all over the open spaces of AlphaWorld. Having a road nearby is good too, as it suggests access to our property and good frontage. Roads often serve to draw in visitors.

Choose your starter object, in this case, a piece of road (see the following figure). Click once with the right mouse button on the piece of road. The starter object should be highlighted with a yellow frame, just like the piece of roadway. In addition, a special dialogue box, called the Object Properties dialogue, should pop up on your screen.

Right-click on your starter object.

The Object Properties dialogue box

The Object Properties dialogue gives you all the information you need to change or move an object in AlphaWorld. This dialogue will stay displayed as you pick and act on several objects. As the following table shows, the buttons on the dialogue allow you to delete, duplicate, shift, raise, lower, or rotate the selected object. These same actions are available through the pull-down Object menu, and can also be done by using simple keyboard shortcuts.

The Object Properties toolbar enables you to change or move an object.

Object Property dialogue buttons, functions, and shortcut keys

BUTTON	EFFECT OF CLICKING ON THE BUTTON	KEYBOARD SHORTCUT
Delete button	Permanently deletes the selected object	Del or Delete
Duplicate button	Makes a copy of the selected object, and makes that copy the currently selected object	Ins or Insert
Move Away button	Moves the selected object away from you	Up arrow
Move Toward button	Moves the selected object toward you	Down arrow
Move Left button	Moves the selected object to the left	Left arrow
Move Right button	Moves the selected object to the right	Right arrow
Move Up button	Raises the selected object upward	Keypad+ (plus)
Move Down button	Lowers the selected object downward	Keypad– (minus)
Turn Left button	Rotates the selected object 15 degrees counterclockwise	Page Up
Turn Right button	Rotates the selected object 15 degrees clockwise	Page Down

The object name, owner, and build date

The object name is the all-important name of the Renderware file which contains the description of the object. To change this object into another object, you have to type the new object name (complete with the .rwx file extension). There are hundreds of objects with which to build in AlphaWorld. There are tools you can download from Worlds Inc.'s home page to see a visual list of these objects. A complete list of object names can be obtained through the Help menu options, by listing the contents of the directory, \active worlds\aw\models, or by visiting the Web site which has building instructions and a complete list of objects for AlphaWorld at **http://www.activeworlds .com/alphaworld/aw-build.html**. If you have trouble finding this list, see updated links on your *Avatars!* book Web site at **http://www.digitalspace.com/avatars**.

The *owner* of an object is the citizen number of the person who placed the object there. In the future, this will be used to allow you to contact that person. This should be of great assistance in resolving property disputes and vandalism. The *build date* is when the object was placed in the world . . . useful for the coming science of digital archaeology!

Step 3: Make a copy of the starter object

Now press the Duplicate button on the Object Properties dialogue or the Insert or Ins key on your keyboard. This will make a *copy* of the piece of road, offset slightly from the starter object. Next, use the movement buttons on the Object Properties dialogue, or the cursor keys on your keyboard, to move the piece of road to the right. You must get the piece completely clear of the original road, although it can end up right up against the road. Remember to only move a copy of your starter object. The original belongs to someone else, and if you move it, you will receive a message from the building inspector that it is someone else's property.

Move the duplicate object clear of the starter object.

Voilà! The starter object is safely placed on your land.

Once you have placed your starter object safely on a green patch a short distance away from the original object, you should be able to click on the next object (or close the Object Properties dialogue) and *serve* this new object into AlphaWorld. If, after 20 seconds, you do not get a warning from the building inspector (a daemon that talks to you through text chat), you have successfully homesteaded in cyberspace, and the land you just covered is "yours!" If you do get an *encroachment* warning, the starter object will disappear, and you will have to try again. I recommend moving your starter object completely clear of the original object you copied, so that you can see some green between the two objects. If you keep getting encroachment warnings, look around for trees or other overhanging or overhead objects. If you keep experiencing trouble, you might want to find another place to build.

Step 4: Pick an object to change your starter

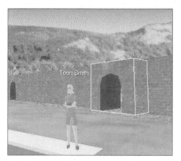

Look around for another object into which you would like to change your starter.

With your own starter object in place, you can continue to make copies of it and cover more land, or you can start to change these objects into different forms. The adjacent figure shows how I found a lovely brick arch on the Moroccan Palace behind my building area. Right-clicking on it will bring up the Object Properties dialogue again.

To change the starter object into this arch, simply make note of the name of the arch file (in this case, arch22.rwx), and then just right-click back on your own object and enter the same name into the Object area. In this example, I will delete the name street1.rwx, and replace it with arch22.rwx. Once this is done, you can close the dialogue box and the section of street will magically change into the arch. Holy cow!

Object Properties come from the neighbor's arch.

Like magic, the road becomes an arch!

Step 5: Set up the object description and actions

You may have noticed two more entry areas on the Object Properties dialogue: Description and Action. You should enter something in the Description field (such as your initials) to easily identify your objects. The next copy you make of these objects will automatically save your description. I recommend using a very short description, just two to five characters, as descriptions take up valuable space, and can reduce the number of objects you can place on your land. The Action field allows you to give this object actions, such as rotating it, or linking it to a Web page. I will discuss object actions in more detail later in this chapter, and in the section, "Questions and Answers about Action Commands," on the book companion book Web site.

Step 6: Manipulating your objects

If you select the arch, you can move it from side to side, up or down, or rotate it using the buttons in the Object Properties dialogue or the keyboard keys. In the following figure, I am rotating the arch. Make another copy of the arch and try raising it up to stack it on top of the first arch. You might find it easier to build while in god view or from far overhead looking down.

Rotating the arch.

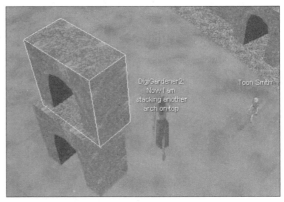

Put another arch on top of the first one while in god view.

Note that if you are lowering an object, you might actually lower it right through the ground level of AlphaWorld. There is nothing wrong with this, and people have built underground cities this way. It can be confusing, however. You can sink underground by holding down Shift and pressing minus (-) on your keypad. Take a look under the floor of AlphaWorld to make sure that no one else's objects occupy that space. If there are objects there, you will not be able to build above them.

Step 7: Reserving your land

Using a flooring or walkway you like, cover your land to preserve it for future building. As the adjacent figure shows, you have to be careful not to encroach on another person's property. The AlphaWorld building inspector will just bump your offending objects back.

Reserve that land!

Step 8: Identify your property

Put a mailbox on your property.

Finally, as seen in the adjacent figure, you should add a mailbox object (with the name mailbox1.rwx) to your site. In the Action field of the Object Properties dialogue, if you enter the command, mailto:myaddress@myserver.etc, in which myaddress@myserver.etc is your e-mail address, then people visiting your site can identify who it belongs to and, by clicking once with the left mouse button on the mailbox, can send you a message. Adding the object, news1.rwx will give you a handy newspaper stand which is traditionally linked to a World Wide Web home page by including the address of the home page in the Action field (for example, **http://myhomepage.etc**). Note that in order for the mailbox to work, you may have to set up the mail program in the Web browser. See the browser help files for instructions on how to do this. For links to the World Wide Web to work, you may have to run the Web browser while you are running Active Worlds Browser.

The last and most important thing about identifying your property is to note the coordinates where it is located. It can be embarrassing and frustrating to forget where you built your virtual log cabin (like losing your car in a parking lot).

Step 9: Take a look at what others have built

A tour through AlphaWorld and other Active Worlds is the best way to learn what can be built—from the large scale (as in the pyramid and floating crystal building) to

A huge glass pyramid and a floating crystal building.

The Hansen family's home under construction.

the humble (the Hansen family's humble home under construction). Clicking on their sign, we visited the Hansens' home page and sent them an e-mail. We received a surprised and pleased answer the next day.

Step 10: You have graduated!

If you have reached this far, congratulations. You have graduated from Virtual Building 101. Now go out and show the world what is in your dearest Tinker Toy dreams or Lego fantasies. It's time to be a kid again (or just be a really rad kid in digital space)!

A happy graduate (Toon Smith) of Virtual Building 101.

Building 202: Advanced Building Tips

Build over large areas quickly

Use the same starter object over and over. Before you start cloning your starter object, make sure it's at ground level and oriented straight north and south, east and west . . . it's easy to get confused by a starter object that was skewed and/or raised off the ground. Then use the same starter object to clone more objects whenever it makes sense. That way, if you go off a little at some point, the error won't proliferate throughout your whole project, and will be much easier to fix.

When you press the Ins key, the new object you create is placed $1/2$ meter away from the original . . . so when you are making a long wall or a lake, or anything that requires mass duplication, make it work for you. Line up your sight so that you can build and shift objects away from you in just a few repeated steps. Avoid problems with object density by using short descriptions and actions. Here's how it works: you are limited to about 25 objects per 10-by-10-meter cell. But the limit of total storage is about 1,000 bytes per 10-meter cell. Descriptions and actions take 1 byte per character, so if you have 20 objects with a 20-character description in each, you are using up 40 percent of the storage for the cell just with descriptions!

Avoid the Area Full error

It is possible to overload an area with too many objects. The limit is pretty high, but if you're building something that's several stories high, or has a lot of overlaps, you might occasionally get the message: "This area is full." Try building somewhere else.

There are things you can do to avoid the Area Full error if you're building a really elaborate structure. The area sampled measures 10-by-10 meters, so if you use lots of small objects, the Area Full error can be a problem. One suggestion that AlphaWorld regulars have made is to use the largest objects possible. Another thing is to empty the Description and Action fields of these objects or make them smaller; it's actually the data that's counting against you. You can just fill in descriptions and actions for prominent objects like the mailbox, or the tower, or the door of your central structure. Another trick: try deleting the current object, and then rebuilding it again from scratch. That sometimes works.

Whenever possible, use big objects like the double panels so they won't count against your object limit. Sometimes you'll get error messages when building, or your request might take a while to go through. Keep trying, and when all else fails, delete the particular object that's giving you trouble and recopy a new one.

Use Shift to move objects in smaller increments

Use Shift when moving or rotating objects to cut the distance or rotation to 10 percent of normal. This is not recommended for beginners because it can be difficult lining things up once they are off by just a little. It's harder to make rotated objects line up nicely with each other. Use Shift to make smaller adjustments in the rotation. You can also use Shift when you're joining seams between two different types of objects.

Use pop-up labeling and sound effects

When you use the *pop-up labeling* feature, every description assigned to an object will appear in a pop-up label as your mouse cursor moves over the object. As for music and sound effects, there is an extensive collection of original MIDI and WAV audio files that you can attach to anything. Sound is 3D and stereophonic; the audio gets louder as you approach an object, and softer as you move past. There is ambient audio such as birds and water, and other intriguing sound effects.

Be a good neighbor

Because AlphaWorld is an evolving community, there are no perfect safeguards to keep land disputes from occurring. Most encroachment issues have been worked out, including building above and below the land. But it's still up to AlphaWorld citizens as individuals to be polite to each other. For instance: *Call before you dig.*

If you are considering building next to someone else's property, try to figure out if the other property owner is done, or if they're still working. If in doubt, look for a mailbox and drop them a line. Ask if they'd mind a new neighbor. That little amount of courtesy can save you both a whole lot of grief. Remember to put a mailbox on your own property, too!

Better yet, build somewhere farther out, where everyone can build to their heart's content.

Build smart

Try to keep the object count as low as possible. Obviously, if you're building something large or elaborate, this might be hard to do. But if you create something with hundreds of needless extra objects that take forever to render, nobody's happy. Avoid overlaps, use big objects, use the best object for the job, and clean up your mistakes and loose ends before you quit for the day.

Be careful with those sounds and animations!

Sounds and animations will cause the biggest slowdowns in the rendering and running speeds of your (and everyone else's) computer. These will be annoying, especially to people who are viewing AlphaWorld with a minimum platform (low RAM or a slow '486). Avoid placing animations in heavily traveled areas like Ground Zero, or close to the street. And don't clutter up your whole property with sounds—the seams between the sound regions will make strange sound jumps and slow down other people's machines.

Dataman, tireless host of AlphaWorld, and editor of the *New World Times,* has compiled an on-line building models reference and some advanced building tips. Dataman's catalogue of objects includes animation panels, arches, awnings, building panels, stairs, roofs, trees, flowers, walls, walks, floors, and miscellaneous objects such as statues. It can be found at **http://www.activeworlds.com/alphaworld/awbuild.html**.

Fine-Tuning Your World and Other Tips

Object actions

The Action field of an object allows you to attach behaviors to your objects. For example, you can play a sound, link an object to a hypertext page, or make objects appear or disappear in certain ways. An object can even have more than one action. To create an action, right-click on an object until you see the Object Properties dialogue. Next, enter text into the Action field. Commands have the following three parts:

- The *trigger* that starts the action

- The *command* that describes what action will occur

- The *arguments* for the command, which further specify what action will take place

If you break apart an example action message, it would look something like this:

Example action: BUMP   VISIBLE   OFF

What it does: The command takes place when you collide with the object. It makes the object invisible, where BUMP is the trigger, VISIBLE is the action, and OFF is the argument.

You can enter commands in either upper- or lowercase, and you can include more than one action in a single Action field. Actions are described more fully in the section, "Questions and Answers about Action Commands," on the book companion Web site. Also, see The Active Worlds Web site for more on actions.

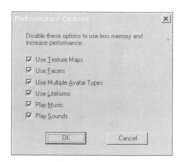

Use Performance options to optimize your experience in an Active World.

Performance options

If you find that AlphaWorld or any other Active World just runs too slowly on your computer, select Settings from the Options menu and then select the Performance tab. Just click on the checkboxes next to options such as Use Texture Maps or Play Sounds, and you will reduce the amount of work Active Worlds Browser has to do. I suggest that you experiment then select with Performance tab options until you are comfortable.

Multimedia streams in Active Worlds

At this writing, Circle of Fire Studios has just added support for multimedia streams inside Active Worlds. Students at the Massachusetts Institute of Technology integrated a live Web camera into a sign in an Active World. This allowed us to watch the students in their dormitory on a Saturday night. Their Web camera updates a JPEG image on the Web, which we see in the virtual world changing every minute or so.

The following figure shows an innovative use of image streaming in Active Worlds to create a model of NASA Mission Control. Live images of STS-80, a mission of the Space Shuttle Columbia, are updated into an Active Worlds area. Needless to say, this is only a hint of how virtual worlds could be used for work applications.

If you are interested in using advanced multimedia commands, see the object actions and other commands referenced under the Help menu found in Active Worlds Browser.

A live telecast of NASA's STS-80 Shuttle Mission uses image streaming.

Hot Spots

Hot Sites: What in the World is Going On?

In AlphaWorld, the newsstand objects often point to a site on the World Wide Web. Just have your Web browser running, left-click on a newsstand, and you will launch that Web site! One very important Web site to visit is the *New World Times* at **http://www.synergycorp.com/alphaworld/nwt/**, which is AlphaWorld's first and still most popular newspaper. The adjacent figure shows an advertisement from the *New World Times*, which gives you a good idea of what some citizens are up to.

An advertisement in the *New World Times*.

Paul Klee built and hosts an art gallery in Colony Alpha, another Active World which you can reach from The Gate. Paul features new artists and holds regular openings. He captures the work of a featured artist by scanning in photographs of paintings, and placing the resulting images on the walls of his gallery.

Paul Klee's art gallery is in Colony Alpha.

The following magnificent sculpture garden was constructed by students as a project for Dr. Derrick Woodham, in a class at the University of Cincinnati. The garden features modernistic, geometric, and urban sculpture.

Active Worlds is evolving many new services all the time. I suggest you check out the *New World Times* or your *Avatars!* book Web site for up-to-date links.

A sculpture garden constructed by University of Cincinnati students.

Hot AlphaWorld Web Site Services

Note that some of these Web page links may have changed, or the Web pages may have been discontinued. Consult your *Avatars!* book home page at **http://www .digitalspace.com/avatars** for a more up-to-date list of links.

Official pages

http://www.activeworlds.com
Active Worlds home page.

http://www.synergycorp.com/alphaworld/nwt/
The *New World Times.*

http://www.ccon.org
Contact Consortium Sherwood and the U Pages.

Unofficial citizen pages

http://www.spam69.demon.co.uk/aworld.htm
Good Web links and teleport links for AlphaWorld.

http://www.sun-inet.or.jp/~inoue/aworld/index.html
Shows a little of his phenomenal Japanese castle . . . definitely worth a visit.

http://www.luna.co.uk/~gevans/pages/ca.htm
Colony Alpha open for business!

http://www.daap.uc.edu/soa/dwoodham/piazza.htm
A preview of what's coming in a new world!

http://www.intersurf.com/~bocan/garden.htm
Shows some really cool stuff.

http://www.interlog.com/~donaldb/alpha/tribe.html
A must for Powwow users!

http://together.net/~raylou/motor.htm
Shows some innovation with basic models doing interesting stuff . . . CARS!

http://www.noord.bart.nl/~pldejong/alphaen.html
Shows some evidence of building skill. (Also linked to a Dutch version.)

http://users.aol.com/nkingtodd/alphaworld.htm
Is just starting; stay tuned for more!

http://www.geocities.com/CapitolHill/2333/
Includes the AlphaWorld Police Department; page and information about vandalism.

http://wasabi.cs.vt.edu/~josec/alphaburg/
An interesting project.

http://www.luna.co.uk/~gevans/pages/necro1.htm
The coolest Web page about AlphaWorld yer gonna see, folks. With Netscape version 2.0 or above, you can link to Necropolis.

http://www.cs.cuc.edu/~sopwith/aw/
Sopwith's AlphaWorld page is making my job easier! It includes Web page teleport directions, a tour of AlphaWorld, the new AlphaWorld atlas, and more!

http://www.voicenet.com/~drager/dave.htm
The Neo-AlphaWorld Page is just starting up, and has some cool pictures of Neophyte's house.

http://pages.prodigy.com/visual_echo/club319.htm
Interesting links and humor.

http://www.networkpros.com/awcontentsf.htm
A very useful tool during construction!

http://www.sentex.net/~hogarth/lencelotville
A brand new community newspaper for Lencelotville.

http://www.tiac.net/users/bdwilson/a/alpha01.html
Shows some of Dharma Bum's outstanding work in AlphaWorld.

http://www.ldl.net/~ryoma/awpage.html
Ryoma Sakomoto's AlphaWorld page is new, improved, and cool! Ryoma is the builder of Legacy Palace. If you haven't seen it, check it out! (72S, 30W way high up)

http://www.avault.com/
One of the most innovative on the Web. Use Netscape 2.0, or better yet, use Microsoft Internet Explorer to see it at its best. Also see the New Improved Adrenaline Vault in AlphaWorld; it's subterranean with an entrance above ground at 8S, 24E.

http://www.connecti.com/~queue/
Queue's Adventure Page is a VR-happening spot.

http://www.connecti.com/~queue/awcool/
Cool Spots in AlphaWorld page is a good place to list your site.

http://www.geocities.com/TimesSquare/3349/aworld.html
Grover is one of AlphaWorld's oldest citizens and is also the mayor of a new town, and can be found at Lock Haven at http://www.geocities.com/TimesSquare/3349/lh.html.

http://together.net/~raylou/ray3.htm
Get Loose with Louie at Louie's Bar and Grill, featuring cool MIDI files.

http://www.worldonline.nl/~karel/aworld.html
The Duke Of Zircon's AlphaWorld page has enough royalty for several worlds.

Digi's Diary: Our Future in Digital Space

Digi's Diary

Where will the lure of the virtual lead us? Your guess is as good as anyone's!

During the creation of this book, I spent months going in and out of AlphaWorld, and every other virtual world I could find. Because I could build and leave my own mark in AlphaWorld, I experienced first-hand my own psychological and emotional attachment to the spaces I created. Building my own sites changed the way I looked at the world. I would catch myself saying, "my those trees and shrubs are arranged beautifully—wait a minute, that's a real forest!" I found that working and living in digital space puts a heavy workload on the mind, a kind of virtual brain fatigue. In the coming years, new equipment such as affordable stereovision goggles will make the experience in virtual worlds almost totally immersive. Everywhere you look, you will see the digital landscape. The only thing that seems guaranteed is that these worlds will become richer, and that many more people will be drawn into them.

Where will the siren song of the virtual eventually lead us? Off this world and into the digital space? Out of our bodies and into a higher mind? Your own journey into digital realms will be a very personal experience, unlike anyone else's. Perhaps the answers to these questions will emerge within a *collective mind* we create through this medium.

DigiGardener marches on. See you in the next world!

WorldsAway

IN THIS DREAM YOU CAN FLY

WorldsAway : one

"You wouldn't give your flesh and bone head to anyone, would you?"

"If you don't like your looks, log out now and start over."

[Entering Locale: Cypress Street]

NuYu

Visitor's Center

Our cybercraft flies across the waves of spacetime en route to a place shrouded in mystery. Drifting for what seems like an eon, something comes into our forward viewing screens. Before us lies a shimmering, silvery veil. Engines come to a full stop. All that is known about this place is that those passing through enter into a dream state, and many never return. Captain Digi, goes to impulse drives and takes the ship through the veil.

As the ship presses against the folds of the veil, we start to feel heavy with fatigue, our eyelids press down, and the entire crew falls into the deepest sleep. Some great time later (or is it just an instant?), the captain and crew slowly wake up to the sound of a ship's bell, gently clanging in the breeze. We find ourselves on the deck of an ancient wooden sailing ship. The ship is drifting slowly on an aquamarine sea toward a distant shore. Are we dreaming, or have we arrived at some fantastic new place in virtual space? You are digital dreaming, and are about to enter the WorldsAway Dreamscape!

Your Guide to
WorldsAway
and the Dreamscape

WORLD GUIDE

WORLD SKILL LEVEL Intermediate

BUILDING CAPABILITY Yes, you can decorate your own apartment

SYSTEM REQUIREMENTS Macintosh, with System 7.0 or greater; PC with Windows 3.1, Windows 95/NT

AVATAR CREATION CAPABILITY Yes, from components available

DEPTH 2.5D

SOUND SUPPORT Music, sound effects

MINIMUM MACHINE

OPERATING SYSTEM Macintosh with System 7.0 or greater; Windows 3.1 or greater

COMPUTER Macintosh or PC 486DX; 256-color monitor

RESOURCES 8MB RAM; 25MB free disk space; 16-bit sound card optional for music and sound effects

CONNECTION 2,400 bps modem connection via CompuServe; 14.4 kbps dial-up to the Internet for Internet version

WorldsAway Dream Worlds

WorldsAway's Dreamscape from Fujitsu Software Corp. bids you to enter a flourishing virtual community with a dreamlike setting. In WorldsAway, there is a lot to do. You can try your hand at costuming your own avatar. Getting tired of that out-of-body shape? Want a face-lift? In a WorldsAway world, you can pick out a new body, head, clothing, and accessories (I only wish this were so easy in real life!).

If you are a natural-born tycoon, you can try your hand at wheeling and dealing in the WorldsAway virtual economy—earning tokens, buying, selling, and trading, and even renting and decorating your own apartment.

There are plenty of social gatherings, citizen organizations, and even games you can play with other WorldsAway community members. Above all, citizens in WorldsAway communities are *helpful,* and you will meet many new friends who will take you on tours of your new world.

Meet the Flying Pub Sisters in WorldsAway's Dreamscape.

The Dreamscape is WorldsAway's first and most popular virtual community. By the time you read this, many new worlds will be open on WorldsAway. I will devote most of this chapter to exploring the Dreamscape, but most of what you learn here will serve you well in other WorldsAway communities.

WorldsAway is available for both the Macintosh and Windows PCs in two versions: to members of the CompuServe on-line service and to users connected directly to the Internet. This means there are many ways to visit the Dreamscape and other WorldsAway Worlds.

Installing

Installing WorldsAway

What do I need to play in WorldsAway?

To join the WorldsAway community, you must have a Macintosh computer running System 7 or later, or a PC (minimum 486) running Microsoft Windows 3.1, Windows 95, or Windows NT. As shown in the minimum machine table at the beginning of this chapter, your computer must have at least 8MB of memory, 25MB of free disk space, and a 256-color monitor. A more powerful computer (Power Macintosh or Pentium PC) is a definite plus, but is not required.

Getting started and a few disclaimers

WorldsAway is easy to install and easy to use. You can get the WorldsAway software either from the CD in this book, by downloading it through a CompuServe account, or directly from the Internet. There are two versions of the WorldsAway software on the CD, one for use through CompuServe, and one for use directly on the Internet.

WorldsAway for CompuServe

If you wish to use WorldsAway through CompuServe, and you are not a member of CompuServe, you will have to subscribe to it first. The easiest way to do this is to call CompuServe directly and order the latest version of the software. You will have to arrange for payment, probably by giving them your credit card number. CompuServe has operations in many countries. In the United States, you can call CompuServe toll free at 800/524-3388. If you have access to the Internet already, you can visit the CompuServe home page at **http://www.compuserve.com**. You may be able to download the CompuServe Information Manager (CIM) directly from the home page.

If you are using WorldsAway with CompuServe, you will be charged for the hours you spend beyond your free hours per month. Check for CompuServe's monthly free hours and rates. WorldsAway can be addicting, so you may want to consider investing in a flat-rate, unlimited use plan.

WorldsAway for the Internet

If you decide to install the version of WorldsAway that works directly with the Internet, you may be able to use it free of charge for some period of time. More information on the amount of free time available will be contained in the software.

More about the companion CD software

WorldsAway is constantly evolving, and may have changed since this chapter was written. I placed the very latest version of WorldsAway on your book CD, and it may be somewhat different from what is described here. These differences will not be major, and this chapter will still be a great guide to WorldsAway. If you see new features or changes, you should check for information under the Help menu in WorldsAway.

If you have questions or problems

Virtually up-to-date

Help

As a special service for readers of *Avatars!*, I have a home page on the World Wide Web devoted to keeping you up-to-date on your favorite worlds. Find news about software updates, social events held within these virtual worlds, and brand new worlds you might want to try at **http://www.digitalspace .com/avatars**. Bookmark it!

If you have questions or problems installing or running WorldsAway, see "WorldsAway and the Dreamscape Frequently Asked Questions (FAQ)," on the companion Web site to this book. If this does not help, check the WorldsAway home page at **http://www.worldsaway.com**, the WorldsAway known problems page at **http://www.worldsaway.com/Worldsaway/mac/known.html** for Mac users, and **http://www.worldsaway.com/Worldsaway/win/known.html** for PC users. Note that if CompuServe is connected, you can access the Web through its built-in Web browser.

If you are experiencing problems with CompuServe, and can still access the Internet, I suggest you visit the CompuServe home page at **http://www.compuserve.com**. If you cannot access the Internet or CompuServe, try calling CompuServe for technical support in your country.

Another good source of information on how to use WorldsAway is the on-line help files. Just select the Help menu in WorldsAway, and use the table of contents or index to find the topic you are looking for. In addition, the WorldsAway Quickstart Guide, found on the Web at **http://www.worldsaway.com/quick/**, and the WorldsAway

Dreamscape User Guide, found at **http://www.worldsaway.com/Worldsaway/userguide/ dreamscape/guide.html**, are excellent WorldsAway references.

I would appreciate your feedback on *Avatars!*, but I personally don't have the resources to provide technical support. We would be happy to hear about your experiences in the WorldsAway Dreamscape. Contact us through the *Avatars!* book Web site at **http://www.digitalspace.com/avatars**.

UNIX and OS/2 versions

At this writing, there are no native versions of WorldsAway for UNIX or OS/2. Check the WorldsAway and *Avatars!* book Web pages for updates on new versions which might support these platforms. You may also be able to run WorldsAway using a Windows emulation system on non-Windows platforms.

Installing WorldsAway on your computer

If you are a member of CompuServe, and have your CompuServe Information Manager installed (MacCIM 2.4.2 or greater for Macintosh users, or WinCIM 1.4 or greater for PC users), you are ready to install and enter WorldsAway. If you have a direct connection to the Internet, or a dial-up PPP connection, you can install and enter the Dreamscape without first having to subscribe to CompuServe.

You can obtain your WorldsAway software in one of three ways:

1. From the book CD

2. By downloading it through CompuServe, or by installing it from your CompuServe 3.0 CD, where it can be found in the Extras folder

3. By downloading it from the Internet

Bear with me through the following step-by-step instructions, and soon you will be experiencing life as an avatar in the WorldsAway Dreamscape!

Installing WorldsAway from Your Avatars! CD

If you have a CD-ROM drive on your Macintosh or PC, you can install WorldsAway directly from the book CD-ROM. If you don't have a CD-ROM drive, see "Downloading, installing or upgrading WorldsAway through CompuServe," or "Installing or upgrading WorldsAway from the Internet." In "The Book CD-ROM" chapter I provide a step-by-step example of installing from the CD-ROM. I suggest that you refer to this chapter and follow the same steps for WorldsAway. Once the installation program on your CD-ROM has started, you can return to this chapter to the section, "Running the installation."

Downloading, installing, or upgrading WorldsAway through CompuServe

If you are a CompuServe customer, you can download the WorldsAway software through your account. To do this, follow these simple steps:

1 Start CompuServe and connect.

2 Select the Services menu and choose Go.

3 A dialogue is displayed; enter the word AWAY and click OK.

4 You will see the WorldsAway dialogue box. This is your main gateway into WorldsAway from CompuServe. Select Download WorldsAway Software. This starts the download process. As the file is 14MB or larger, you will have to wait an hour or longer (depending on the speed of your connection to CompuServe). Go and grab a book to read while you are waiting. I recommend a good fantasy like J.R.R. Tolkien's *The Hobbit*, which will put you into a good frame of mind for the Dreamscape. Neal Stephenson's *Snow Crash*, is also an excellent primer for avatar adventuring. Note that the time spent on Compu-Serve downloading WorldsAway is free. You will not be charged for this time. Go next to the section, "Running the installation."

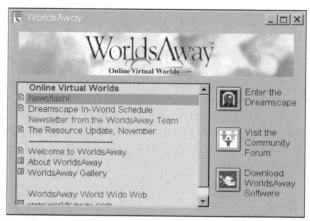

The WorldsAway dialogue; select Download WorldsAway Software.

Installing or upgrading WorldsAway from the Internet

If you have an Internet connection and want the very latest version of WorldsAway, or were informed that you had to upgrade the version found on your *Avatars!* CD, then you can just download it. If you haven't done this before, don't panic; it is easier than you might think!

1 Connect to the Internet (dial up with your modem or make sure your Internet connection is active).

2 Start your Web browser, such as Netscape Navigator or Microsoft Internet Explorer.

❸ At the top of the browser window you will see a long text box called Location, where you can enter text (the addresses of Web pages).

❹ Click in this box, delete the text inside, type in **http://www.worldsaway.com**, and press Enter.

After a few moments, the home page for WorldsAway should appear. If nothing comes up for a long time, check to see that you are online.

If the WorldsAway page is not available for some reason, try entering the location for the *Avatars!* home page, which is **http://www.digitalspace.com/avatars**. This page may contain more up-to-date links for WorldsAway.

❺ Once you are at the WorldsAway home page, follow the instructions for downloading or upgrading the WorldsAway software. You can download versions of WorldsAway for the Macintosh, Windows 95/NT, or Windows 3.1. In addition, you should select either the version for CompuServe (if you are a CompuServe subscriber), or for use directly on the Internet.

❻ You will be presented with a dialogue box which will allow you to download the WorldsAway installer program to your hard disk; click Save File (Netscape) or Save As (Internet Explorer) to download the file to disk (or you can save it on your desktop if you are running a Macintosh or Windows 95).

❼ You will be prompted to choose a folder in which to save the downloaded file. Note where you choose to save the file, and the name of the file itself (it could be something like wawin.exe, the Windows version of WorldsAway). I put all downloaded files in a folder which I call \download on the PC, and Download on the Mac.

❽ Wait patiently; this download is large (about 14MB). It could take well over an hour, depending on the speed of your connection. You can do other work on the computer, but be careful not to interfere with the connection. Try not to do more work on the Internet while the download is progressing, and if you are using your regular telephone line for an Internet connection, don't make a telephone call. You may want to turn off any call-waiting feature you might have on your telephone line before starting the download. If someone calls, this could interrupt your download.

❾ After the download is finished, open the folder into which the file was downloaded and find the file. You are now ready to install WorldsAway. Go to the section, "Running the installation."

Running the installation

Whether you have obtained your WorldsAway software from the book CD, through CompuServe, or from the file you downloaded from the Internet, use this section to guide you through the installation. Note that if you downloaded WorldsAway from CompuServe or the Internet, the installation process may have changed. If this has happened, refer to the instructions on the WorldsAway Web site at **http://www.worlds away.com**. The following steps take you through the installation process.

❶ Close other programs before you start the installation. For the Macintosh, pick each running application from the application menu and close it. In Windows 95, you can do this by clicking on the running application icons on the task bar and then closing them. In Windows 95 and Windows 3.1, you can also use Alt+Tab to go to other running applications even when you cannot see the task bar. Simply hold down Alt while pressing Tab and select the icon representing the running application. If you are logged into CompuServe or the Internet, you should be able to leave the connection running while you install WorldsAway.

❷ If you downloaded WorldsAway, there should be a large file (14MB or more) in your download folder or subdirectory. The file should be named something like wawin.exe on a PC or WA (version #) Mac Install, on the Macintosh. Find this file from inside CompuServe by using the Find File extension on the Mac, or through the file manager on your desktop for the PC, and open or double-click it. A setup program will run and take you through the WorldsAway installation.

❸ During installation, you will be presented with a license agreement and terms of service. I recommend reading and accepting them (the installation will not proceed if you don't). Note that the installation may vary for the CompuServe version and the Internet version, but both should be simple and not take long.

❹ If you need assistance with installation of your CompuServe version, or have any other questions, visit the WorldsAway Community Forum on CompuServe (click on the Community Forum icon in the WorldsAway dialogue where you picked Download WorldsAway Software, and leave a message for the forum staff in the Help Desk message section). For the Internet version, you can find assistance and a list of frequently asked questions on the WorldsAway home page at **http://www.worldsaway.com**.

5 After completing the installation, locate the folder in which you downloaded the WorldsAway program (in \fjwa on a PC, WorldsAway on a Mac). You can create an alias for WorldsAway on your Macintosh desktop or create a shortcut on your Windows 95 desktop. WorldsAway will create an entry in Programs under the Start menu. If you are running Windows 3.1, you can find WorldsAway in its own program group.

6 I recommend that you do the following file cleanup before you start getting absorbed in WorldsAway. After this, you will be ready to get started.

Cleaning up after installation

If you downloaded or copied the original WorldsAway installation file onto your desktop or into a folder, you can delete it after the installation is complete. You might also keep the original installer around just in case you have to reinstall it, but it is a large file (14MB or more), and it will take up valuable hard disk space.

The readme files and other WorldsAway documentation

There will be files called, "WorldsAway Readme," and "WorldsAway User Documentation," inside the folder where WorldsAway is installed. If you open these files, you will find general information about the current release of WorldsAway.

Voyage on the Argo: Joining the Dreamscape Community

First Steps

The Dreamscape is just one of many virtual worlds available through WorldsAway. With WorldsAway, you can explore many different virtual worlds. Dreamscape is the original, and largest of these worlds. Once you have WorldsAway running, you can visit other worlds in the WorldsAway universe. Find out about the latest worlds on the WorldsAway Web site at **http://www.worldsaway.com**.

This chapter will focus on the Dreamscape, but you will find that after graduating from the Dreamscape, other worlds will be a snap. The folks from Fujitsu have done a wonderful job designing the Dreamscape, and thousands of Dreamscape citizens have made it a place worth visiting. You will start your adventure by taking a voyage on the good ship *Argo*.

Starting WorldsAway and entering the Dreamscape: All aboard!

Before starting up WorldsAway for CompuServe, you must make sure that you are connected with CompuServe Information Manager. If you happen to be using the Internet version of WorldsAway, you must establish your connection to the Internet. Once you are connected, double-click on the WorldsAway program icon to start up the WorldsAway application. The Internet version may require you to start your Web browser before connecting. Instructions on starting the Internet version will be given at the end of the installation process.

The CompuServe dialer, Information Manager, and WorldsAway icons on a Windows 95 desktop.

On the Macintosh, you should be able to find the WorldsAway program icon in its own folder. If you are using Windows 95 or Windows NT 4, you can find WorldsAway on your desktop, or by choosing Start ➪ Programs ➪ WorldsAway. In Windows 3.1, find WorldsAway in its own program group or look for the fjwa.exe file in the \fjwa directory. WorldsAway for the Internet may be found in the \wa20 folder.

When you start up WorldsAway, it may start updating itself. If for some reason this update stops in the middle (your connection may have been lost), just reconnect to CompuServe or the Internet and restart WorldsAway, and the rest of the update will come in.

Immigrating to Kymer: Your voyage on the good ship Argo

To get to the Dreamscape, you first must travel on a virtual sailing ship, the *Argo*. The *Argo* is your gentle passage to the Dreamscape. Instead of just a parachute landing into this world, you are given time to learn about how to move around, communicate, and do things. Your patient guide on the *Argo* is Hermes, a teacher parrot from the land of Morpheus. The *Argo* is taking you to the mysterious island of Kymer, described as, "the ancient island of reverie." On that island is a city called Phantasus, where you will find many other dreamers like you.

Arriving on the deck of the *Argo*.

As you can see in the following figure, that is me, or rather my *avatar,* standing there and looking rather plain. In WorldsAway, you start out with a simple avatar like this one, and while on board the *Argo* (and later in Kymer), you can choose a different body and head. Wait, that bird—that's the famous Hermes! What is he saying to me? I can see his words in cartoon bubbles floating up above us both. He is saying a whole lot of things between wing flaps. But is Hermes a person—well, I mean, does Hermes represent a real person? Nope, Hermes is one of those strange critters you often find in virtual space called a *bot,* short for robot. Hermes is built just to respond to your questions, rattle off advice, and ask for a cracker or two!

Hermes is a bot. *Awwwk!*

Wait, Hermes just told me about a special gift behind the door to the left. Are we on a game show here? Well, if it is a free gift, then the price is right, so how do I go through that door? Hermes is right there telling me to just click on the door. As you can see in the figure on the right, clicking on anything in WorldsAway brings up a little pop-up menu. You will get used to this trick.

The menu choices look pretty straightforward. I pick Pass Through, and my avatar walks right on through the door (after it opens, of course; I would hate to get a black eye for everyone to see in Kymer!). And inside?

Well, I went through, and I found my gift! But I don't want to spoil it for you by telling what it is. You've got to do it for yourself. All I can tell you is, don't pass up that gift. Boy, did I find it to be valuable later on!

Oh, the secret door; but how do I go in? Just click and find out.

By the way, if you have a sound card and speakers on your computer, you will hear all kinds of great sound effects, like the sounds of the ship as it plies toward Kymer, and squawks from Mr. Hermes. And before you go inside anywhere, you can ask about it, and get a bit of information read to you by the world itself. This is kind of like talking to yourself, except that the universe talks back. Don't worry about exploring various places in the Dreamscape, you can't be killed, and you won't be trapped against your will.

Click anywhere outside an object, get a pop-up menu, and go!

Well, I was getting anxious to start wandering around the *Argo,* so I clicked my mouse on the deck, and got a pop-up menu like the one in the preceding figure. Choosing Cypress Street caused my avatar to walk off to the right. The scene dimmed for a moment, and then voilà: I was in a new part of the ship.

The world is talking to me, and telling me that I have to choose my body, head, and name here on the promenade deck. What looks like a twenty-first century Thai telephone booth turns out to be the body-changing chamber! I click on it and get the choices of male/female, athletic/stocky, and some other body type (well, overweight then).

Well, even though I am actually a man, I kind of like the idea of trying virtual life as the other gender. The avatar WorldsAway gives you in the Dreamscape is the medium-build female. I also like the athletic body shape I was given by the world (I am lanky and definitely not athletic in the real world), so I'll just stick with what I was given. Signs near the body booth tell me that bodies on the island of Kymer cost 1,000 tokens, so I am glad I could choose mine now. Gee, tokens—it seems that there is an economy in the Dreamscape.

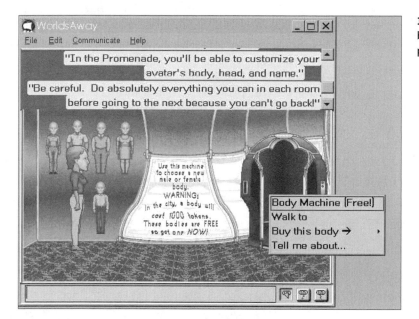

I can choose a new body on the *Argo* promenade deck.

Well, darling, let's get you a new wardrobe!

Rolling right along the promenade deck, you can see two other interesting machines. One turns out to be an ATM (short for Automated Token Machine). Clicking on this allows you to withdraw money from the private bank account you were given when you first arrived in WorldsAway. As you will see later, you can earn more tokens for the time you stay in the Dreamscape through good old-fashioned wheeling and dealing. I rush past the ATM to the head vending machine. Vending machines, sometimes called *vendos,* offer you things to buy, and are scattered all over Kymer. I really want a new head. No more plain-Jane for me!

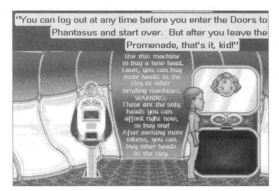

"You can log out at any time before you enter the Doors to Phantasus and start over. But after you leave the Promenade, that's it, kid!"

Use this machine to buy a new head. Later, you can buy more heads in the city or other vending machines. WARNING: These are the only heads you can afford right now, so buy one! After earning more tokens, you can buy other heads in the city.

An ATM and head changer vendo are located on the promenade deck.

Head Machine [9 of 9 / 50 T]
View next item
View previous item
Buy this item
Tell me about...

Click on the vendo, and roll through the items inside.

Clicking on the vendo lets me view each item inside, as shown in the figure on the left. In two clicks, I found the head for me. Buy that, I said, and was left standing, head in hand! This seemed like a ridiculous situation, so I clicked on me to see if there were options . . . and found a lot, including one option to wear what I was holding. Bingo! I am getting ahead in this world! There are a lot of options you can access by clicking on yourself. You can turn your avatar's body, gesture (I love jumping), put things you have into your pocket, check on your status (including the tokens you have), and become a ghost (lurk in the background—a useful skill I developed for parties in real life).

Rolling along to the right, I come across the name registry where I can pick my avatar's name. As always, I am DigiGardener, a kind of Janet Appleseed, putting down roots in virtual space.

Hermes again! We are pulling into the Port of Phantasus on the isle of Kymer, and this is the last chance to change your identity before entering the city.

Buy that head... a head in the hand is worth two in the bush!

avatar151
Gesture ▶
Turn ▶
Put into ▶
Wear
Status ▶
Become a Ghost
Tell me about...

Put that head on!

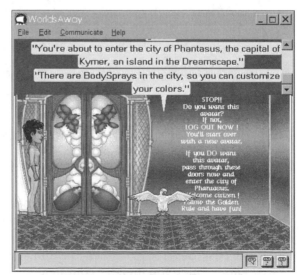

WorldsAway
File   Edit   Communicate   Help

"You're about to enter the city of Phantasus, the capital of Kymer, an island in the Dreamscape."
"There are BodySprays in the city, so you can customize your colors."

STOP!! Do you want this avatar? If not, LOG OUT NOW! You'll start over with a new avatar.

If you DO want this avatar, pass through these doors now and enter the city of Phantasus. Welcome citizen! Follow the Golden Rule and have fun!

Docking at the Port of Phantasus on Kymer; permission to go ashore, Captain!

If you really don't like what you see, or think you missed a step, you can close WorldsAway and restart it. You will then land back on the deck of the *Argo,* and can go through the previous steps again.

Take a deep breath . . .

Take a deep breath just before you go in. You will be entering a living, breathing community of people. Just because it is called a virtual community, that makes no difference; you will be talking and sharing experiences with real people from many cultures all over the world. I suggest that you take a glance at "WorldsAway Guidelines for Community Oriented Behavior," found in the FAQ on the companion Web site to this book. The main thing to remember in any virtual world is the good-old golden rule: *treat others as you would like them to treat you in return.* Follow that one, and you can't go wrong.

Whoops, what if I can't get in?

If you find at any point that you cannot get into WorldsAway or the Dreamscape, there may be a technical problem, such as a lost network connection, or the world may be too full. I suggest that you try again a little later.

Entering Kymer: All Ashore Who's Going Ashore!

Meet the Natives

Alighting on the magic soil of Kymer, my shipmates and I walk out into the hustle and bustle of Cypress Street. But wait, where are the people? Where are we? Phantasus is a sizable port town, so we have to walk around a bit to find the hot spots. This book serves as a great map. Oh, you are a well-prepared tourist! Take a look at the map in the color section of the book. The map can also be found under the Help menu in WorldsAway, and on the WorldsAway Web site at **http://www.worldsaway.com**.

Walking around the hustle and bustle of Cypress Street in Kymer's Phantasus City.

Wandering through the dolmens of Cypress Street, I arrive at the central

I found some folks at the fountain!

To talk normally, just type and press Enter.

Put out a few thought balloons.

You can insert emoticons into your speech.

The Edit menu options.

fountain where, lo and behold, there are some people (or at least their avatars). These are real people, not bots, and they all greet me as I come in. You can see me on the right, and the world is telling me I am entering the West Fountain. They see me come in (the world tells them something like, DigiGardener is here), and they start saying, "Hi Digi," (my nickname).

Jabberwocky all day

I have so many questions for these folks . . . but how do I talk? It is a very simple procedure. At the bottom of the WorldsAway screen is an area for typing in text. If you put something in there and hit Enter, it will be displayed in a cartoon bubble over your head for all to see. On the right-hand side of the text entry area, there are three little icons (as you can see from the adjacent figures). The first means speak normally (which we just did). The second allows you to cast your words out there as a cartoon-style thought balloon. The third button allows you to ESP (short for extra sensory perception), which is a kind of walkie-talkie radio system within the Dreamscape. Using ESP, you can send a private message to only one person or to a group of your friends. You will see an example of ESP soon.

The Edit menu allows you to switch between these different modes of communication. It also allows you to insert gestures, called *emoticons* (emotional icons look like the old 1970s smiley face), as in the Happy Days text line in the figure at the top of this page.

Avatars just kept striding in, and one curious fellow, a duck in a cowboy hat, started tossing around wonderful streams of confetti. Everyone wanted to know where it came from, and he said it was from the recent Dreamscape New Year's party, which celebrated the Dreamscape's first year online. It turns out that he was from the Duckolytes, an informal Dreamscape welcoming association, modeled on the official Dreamscape helpers, called *acolytes*. He said that you could not buy confetti—you just had to be at

the New Year's celebrations to get some. Boy, I have been here only five minutes, and already I have learned so much. The people here are really helpful, and this place is hopping!

There are lots of in-world groups dedicated to helping new members. One group, the SunRays, even has charity events to raise *tokens* for victims of crimes and crashes. All these helper groups really demonstrate both the generous character of the Dreamscape and the complexity of the society.

Avatars join in the confetti toss at the WorldsAway Dreamscape first-year anniversary party.

Digi discovers the virtual economy

I am starting to get excited; I can really talk to people here and do things! For better or for worse, as in the real world, it seems you need money here (called tokens). As mentioned before, you can earn tokens just by staying in the Dreamscape (note that you may be paying real CompuServe or Internet service provider on-line charges while you do this). You can also earn tokens by selling things. But what have I to sell? I just got off the boat!

Well, Kymerians to the rescue. A beautiful avatar named Daira tells me that I am probably carrying around my newbie head (the one I substituted with my beautiful head), and that I can sell it to a pawnbroker next to the V-Mart. I click on me, get the menu, and remove this old head from my pocket.

Daira kindly agrees to take me over to the V-Mart. "But how do I follow you," I ask? She says, "Just click on me and select Follow." I do this, and then she walks off stage left. Magically, I follow along, like I am tied to her as

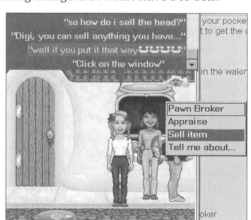

Sell, sell, sell. The pawnbrokers are outside of the V-Mart.

if by one of those toddler cords! We arrive a couple of screens later at the V-Mart (on the corner of Orchid and Cypress Streets), and there is the pawnbroker's window. A lot of people (well, their avatars at least) are going up to the window and leaving with smiles on their faces. I click on the window, choose Approach, then click on Appraise to find out that this head is worth 80T (tokens). What a deal for a useless head; I quickly choose Sell Item and pocket this small fortune. I find out later in the V-Mart that 80T doesn't buy much!

Daira teaches me how to ESP.

Daira says she has to go, but teaches me how to reach her in the future by using ESP, the radio system within the Dreamscape that lets people communicate privately with each other. "Just click on the third button on the bottom left," she says, "and then put in my name, Daira, where it says To. Then you can put in any message you want and send it to me anywhere in Kymer when you press Enter." I try this and it is sooo easy!

Attention all V-Mart shoppers!

OK, got tokens, will travel to the V-Mart. Through the doors I find a vendo with what looks like a set of cool baskets and bags. Rolling through the selections, my eyes roll at the price—250T! I suppose I could sell my new head . . . but no, I saw people walking around the Dreamscape headless, and it is not conducive to good conversation. Actually, someone told me later that those unfortunate newbies were talked out of their

heads. Warning: *do not give your head to anyone, for any reason!* Many newbies are really shocked when they are targeted by thieves, and don't know that there are lots of support organizations set up to help them get a head.

Love that basket . . . but not the boutique price!

I love the basket shown in the previous figure, but I just cannot afford it, and there are no credit cards here. Virtual worlds encourage good money management and balanced budgets (I wonder how long that will last?).

Another vendo is more in my price range: a key to your heart, only 15T! I didn't know I was such a cheap date! I clicked on myself to get my own status menu, and found that I had 55 tokens to my name. Well, that would be enough to be able to brag to friends that I had shopped at the V-Mart.

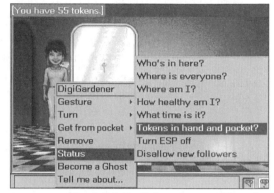

Can you afford this? Click on yourself and find out.

Ghosting my way into the virtual Vegas

Down to one thin 40T, I was kicking at old confetti litter when I moseyed right into the middle of a sort of virtual Vegas (see the gambling avatars in the color section of the book). Gambling, the chance at fast fortune, yes, I'm going to own this town one day! But wait, where did I go? "This game is full," said the dealer, "and besides, you have been ghosted!" True, my avatar was not in the room at all, but hiding in the small eye-cloud in the right corner. It turns out that everyone goes into Ghost mode when a room is too full. As a ghost, you can hear everything, communicate only by ESP, and actually travel much faster through the world (your avatar is spared all that walking). Being a ghost is like being a lurker in a chat room or on a mailing list . . . just reading everything, but never speaking up to the whole group. If you click on the cloud, you can try to un-ghost (if someone has just left the room). You can also see how many people are ghosted along with you in that little cloud.

Tycoon not! Back to having fun!

Hopes for fortune dashed, I then asked myself, "What is life really about, anyway?" How about flying! These virtual worlds are good because you can do things here that you can't in real life. It's like being in your own theater. I spooked around Kymer for a while as a ghost, and decided to materialize in an empty spot. Right then and there, another avatar walked in who was me, or at least looked like me. I said to her, "wait a minute, you are me, I mean, I am you!" She laughed and then flew like a bird. "How did you do that," I asked. She said that I just had to double-click on myself, and I, too, could fly.

Express yourself!

Select your expressions by choosing Gesture ➪ Communicate.

Another pair of citizens was watching us, too. The Flighty Twins told me about other gestures I could make by pressing special keys on the keyboard or by choosing Gesture ➪ Communicate, as shown in the figure to the left. They also told me about turning your avatar's back to the screen if you are doing something somewhere else, or not paying attention to the computer. They said this is polite to the other citizens who otherwise might try to talk to you.

Get creative with your choice of clothing and heads at the Nu Yu, including body sprays to change your body and skin color. The couple in the following figure got very spooky for Halloween by painting their faces gray.

You can make your avatar fly.

A wild and crazy couple!

Gullible's Travels: Through the Dreamscape

New friends in the StarWay Café

To collect new friends, choose File ➪ Friends List.

If you take the time to really explore the city, you will meet so many great people along the way. As you collect new friends, add them to your Friends list. I met someone I really enjoyed talking to in the StarWay Café. I added this person by choosing File ➪ Friends List. The Friends list will give you a list of avatar names of people who are currently using the Dreamscape. You can pick out the name of a new friend and add it to your Friends list. The Friends list is great; you can ESP everyone on the list when you come into the Dreamscape to find out who among your friends is around.

Bingo, games, and other add-ons

Well, I finally did it; I got into one of those games in the Dreamscape. This time it was bingo in the CompuServe version of WorldsAway. This is more my speed. I could see everyone else playing (by the calling of letters and numbers, and the occasional "bingo!"), but then I discovered that the bingo game itself was a separate program you had to download. The others told me I could go off to the WorldsAway area (GO AWAY in CompuServe), enter the community forum, and there I would find libraries of software for WorldsAway. So, I found the bingo game, downloaded it onto my hard disk (CompuServe places it in its own folder called Download), then I double-clicked on the file bingo1.exe, which starts the game right alongside WorldsAway. Whenever the bingo caller (who in this case was Cinnamon Cupc@ke, the girl avatar between Mr. Duck and Mr. Macho Cowboy in the following figure) typed the letter-number sequences, I could press the Auto button and my bingo squares would be colored red. It took me a little while to learn the ropes, but I eventually won at bingo!

There are many other games and add-ons to WorldsAway which have been created by ambitious citizen-programmers. I encourage you to ask others about them, and give them a try. Virtual worlds like WorldsAway are mainly used by people to socialize or create things together. Gaming worlds like The Realm and Meridian 59 were designed as games, but they have a lot of social interaction between the fist and knife fights ("excuse me, but I must interrupt this story of our lives to go and fight that dragon over there").

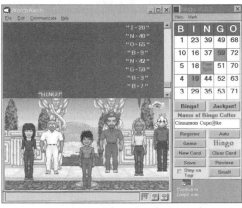

A bingo game; now that's more my speed!

Web touring

One of the best features of the Internet version of WorldsAway is the Web tour that you can host. To do this, just click on your avatar, pick Web Tour, and then select Start Web Tour. Everyone in the room will see a message that a Web tour is starting, and click on your avatar to join (by selecting from the Web Tour pop-up menu). You will get your Web browser window and then be able to visit Web pages. Other WorldsAway users will see these same pages displayed in their Web browsers. You can end a tour at any time by clicking on your avatar and selecting Stop Web Tour.

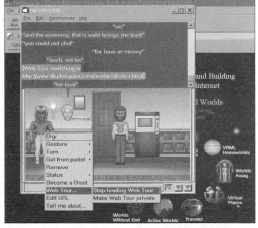

Web tours abound in the Internet version of WorldsAway.

Web touring is a great social activity. It gives you a chance to show off your favorite sites, or your own creative work. Another virtual world that has this Web touring capability is Virtual Places, described in a later chapter.

Nu Yu has a whole new wardrobe

Spray it on . . . and get a whole new look!

A Texas fashion consultant with a teddy bear really helped do me up, forever leaving plain-Jane on memory lane. Today, it was a trip to the Nu Yu—where I could pick up body sprays—the quickest and cheapest makeover in Kymer.

Choosing a violet body spray for only 15T, I clicked on myself and applied it to my top. Next, I got rid of those khaki pants forever by buying a blue spray and turning them into blue jeans. My host approved, and took me outside to dry. I sold the partly used spray canisters to the pawnbroker.

© 1995 Fujitsu Cultural Technologies

Get a head! Here are just some of the avatar head choices in the Dreamscape.

Elsewhere in the Nu Yu, you will find vendos (vending machines) selling new heads. The adjacent figure shows just some of the hundreds of choices of heads available here. Heads can be expensive, so save your tokens before you get your hands on that vendo lever! Remember that you should never give your head to anyone, no matter what they say they will do for you. This was one of the earliest scams in the Dreamscape. It was a crying shame, seeing all those headless avatars wandering around. No one would talk to them; they might as well have been wearing dunce caps.

Turfs: A place of one's own!

This is the story of a man named Jim Duckolyte and a woman named Stayce Jaye, and their family of six little duckolyte avatars! Well, so it isn't the *Brady Bunch*. But if you grew up in the 1970s, and are none too happy that you can't afford a house and a baby-sitter for your six kids, then a piece of the virtual turf may be the best you can hope for. So, this is the story of Jim and Stayce from Utah, who have a cute two-room

Jim Duckolyte and Stayce Jaye have a little two-room turf (apartment).

turf (apartment) at the Temple Street Terrace Apartments in Phantasus (maybe along with six beautiful little ducklings). Meet our couple, Jim Duckolyte and Stayce Jaye, a real-life, virtual-life couple (see the following figures).

Stayce and Jim stand at the elevator to their own turf.

I click on the elevator to go up to Jim and Stayce's.

We are in the lobby of the apartment building, about to take the elevator up. Stayce and Jim must go up first, go into their turf, and then invite me to come up. This is like one of those fancy apartment buildings in New York City. You cannot even go up in the elevator without an appointment. I click on the elevator, put in the name of their apartment, and go on up.

Give and ye shall receive

Jim and Stayce's two-room apartment is just filled with stuff! It looks like a living room on Christmas afternoon. Their combined stuff, including nifty floating balloons, sure took this newbie by surprise. Stayce said most of the stuff was hers and Jim's, bought with tokens, or given as gifts. I turned red with embarrassment when I realized I had not brought a gift (a must-do in duckolyte and WorldsAway society).

You can easily give something to someone. Just click on yourself and take something from your pocket. When you have something in hand, you can just click on someone else's avatar and give it to them. They will be given a notice that you have given them an object. Once, I was standing next to someone, and they put down a heavy chest they were carrying. I bent down and opened the chest to see what was inside. I picked up a soccer ball (football for the world outside of the U.S. and Canada). The owner of the trunk said, "Oh, can you please give this back to me when you are done."

In the turf with Stayce, I see so much stuff, and it isn't even Christmas yet!

I then realized I could have just walked off with it. I wanted to be honest and well-thought-of in my new world, so I dutifully gave it back to him, whereupon he said, "you are honest; for that you can have the ball." I was very thankful, and told him that it was the first thing I had been given in Kymer. Off to the right start in the virtual world.

My own turf . . . but can I afford the rent?

Well, I was so excited about turfs that I hoofed it over to the manager's office to inquire about rentals. As you can see in the following figure, rentals can be pretty stiff for a newbie like me. I will just have to keep visiting that ATM machine, or maybe set up a bingo parlor of my own.

At the manager's office inquiring about turfs.

Avatar affection

You will really meet some nice people. This is not a shoot-'em-up world, and when you come back, people will remember what you did the last time you visited. You will be surprised at how many people you will run into time and time again. And if you feel like it, you can give them a big hug. This is usually done by standing face-to-face (click on yourself and select Turn until your avatar's back faces you), and then typing in something like (((hugs))) or ((((((((HUGS)))))))) if you feel really affectionate toward someone. Of course, you should ask them if you can do this beforehand, or they might think they are being avabused, or worse, avattacked!

Is there true love in the Dreamscape? It's no rumor; there have been hundreds of virtual weddings here. I know of one wedding that was carried out in the real world at the same time! According to reports, on Valentine's Day 1996, groom Joseph Perling, with his laptop computer in lap sitting on Venice Beach, California, was wed to Victoria Vaughn, who was logged in from Hollywood. The groom's father, the Reverend R. John Perling, presided over the ceremony from his church in Beverly Hills. Their friends and other uninvited guests jacked in from all over the country and the world to witness the ceremony, and join in the festivities. Of course, the couple knew each other in person, and now live together, but like the wedding in AlphaWorld (see the "AlphaWorld and Active Worlds" chapter), virtual worlds are providing a glorious means of bringing people together.

Love at first sight?

Rumor also has it that people get married in WorldsAway even though they are married to entirely different people in RL (real life)! There are even professional wedding decorators in the Dreamscape who will set up everything you need, such as the altar, wedding dresses, and confetti.

Fine-Tuning Your World

Under the Help menu, there is an option called Page Acolyte. Acolytes, and other community members called *hosts,* are your helpers inside WorldsAway. Most of the time, there is someone around, but if you don't get an answer to your page, you can also search for a duckolyte, a member of the unofficial helper citizen group.

You will find the WorldsAway preferences under the File menu. You can set the idle timeout (the time when WorldsAway will automatically sign you off if you have been inactive). You can also turn off WorldsAway's music or sound effects to allow spouses or siblings to sleep.

The WorldsAway for Internet preferences are also under the File menu. You can set your idle timeout, and sound on/off. You can also set up the Web Tour preferences. These preferences allow you to either bring your Web browser forward or leave it behind the WorldsAway program window as you are Web touring.

Set up WorldsAway for the Internet with the Preferences dialogue.

Hot WorldsAway Sites

Hot Spots

Fun areas in the Dreamscape

The Nu Yu is a big vending machine area where you can buy a whole new look. Select from a wide choice of bodies, heads, accessories, and sprays. You'd better have a good pocket full of change before going to Nu Yu, because makeovers can be expensive, and they don't accept charge cards! Meditation Park is an area I have heard about, but have never visited. I will leave that one for you to discover.

More WorldsAway worlds will be operational by the time you read this book. Check the *Avatars!* book Web site at **http://www.digitalspace.com/book**, or the WorldsAway Web site at **http://www.worldsaway.com**, for updates.

Visit the Nu Yu for a complete makeover.

WorldsAway Community Forum on CompuServe

Click on Services ⇨ Go and enter AWAY, and then click on Community Forum. This contains live chat, newsgroups, downloads of pictures, writings, and game plug-ins for WorldsAway. When you enter the community forum, look for the following topic areas:

Library: software and information archives for WorldsAway

Conference: for live off-world chat on various WorldsAway subjects

Messages: lists posted messages from such WorldsAway user groups as WorldsAway Internationale, for non-English-speaking users of WorldsAway

I recommend that new users check into the forum regularly, to get a feel for the community. Also, almost every new and exciting event in the Dreamscape is posted in InWorld Events, so it's a great tool for people who are trying to find their niche in the Dreamscape.

WorldsAway Web Home Pages

Official pages

Note that some of these Web page links may have changed, or the Web pages may have been discontinued. Consult your *Avatars!* book home page at **http://www.digitalspace.com/avatars** for a more up-to-date list of links.

http://www.worldsaway.com
The WorldsAway home page.

http://www.compuserve.com
The CompuServe home page.

http://www.compuserve.com/down/cim.html
Download the CompuServe Information Manager software and sign up for CompuServe.

http://www.worldsaway.com/founding1.html#software
Download the WorldsAway Dreamscape software.

http://www.worldsaway.com/members/
The WorldsAway member list. This is a very useful compendium of e-mail addresses and Web pages of WorldsAway community members. You can also register yourself in this telephone directory for WorldsAway.

http://www.worldsaway.com/quick/
Find the WorldsAway Quickstart Guide.

http://www.worldsaway.com/Worldsaway/userguide/dreamscape/guide.html
The WorldsAway Dreamscape User Guide.

http://www.worldsaway.com/Worldsaway/clarion/
The *Kymer Clarion* newspaper for the Dreamscape.

http://www.worldsaway.com/Worldsaway/download1.html
The Dreamscape photo gallery.

http://www.worldsaway.com/Worldsaway/newsletter/
The Dreamscape Team Newsletter.

http://www.communities.com
Electric Communities home page is the Web site belonging to Chip Morningstar and Randy Farmer, the creators of Habitat, and great-grandfathers of WorldsAway. Read all about where WorldsAway came from at this site.

http://www.communities.com/habitat.html
The Habitat history page.

Press blab about WorldsAway

http://www.hotwired.com/wired_online/4.06/metaworlds/index.html
Wired magazine's article about Metaworlds.

http://zeppo.cnet.com/Content/Features/Dlife/Chat/side3.html
Where Worlds Collide, a C|Net review of WorldsAway and other virtual worlds.

Unofficial citizen pages

http://web contact.com/wa/ducks/
The official home page of the Duckolytes.

http://web contact.com/wa/
The Duckolyte links page, Kymer Web.

href=http://ourworld.compuserve.com/homepages/GermanGiant/
See the WorldsAway Yellow Pages at GermanGiant's WorldsAway page.

http://users.aol.com/MajorEvent/Bloodline/bldintro.htm
The Bloodline, the surviving members of the original Club Caribe, Quantum Link tribe.

http://ourworld.compuserve.com/homepages/sabertooth/
Saber's Cyber Site.

http://ourworld.compuserve.com/homepages/Doggie_Wings/wapage.htm
SS Chang's WorldsAway page.

http://ourworld.compuserve.com/homepages/cosmocat/
CosmoCat's final resting place, the story of a beloved acolyte.

http://home.sprynet.com/sprynet/steve04/
Steve Hall's WorldsAway pages.

http://ourworld.compuserve.com/homepages/oraclesRcool/
The Oracle Oddities home page.

http://www.lemonde.fr/multimedia/sem2496/textes/enq24962.html
C'est Sage, a page about WorldsAway en Français (in French).

Digi's Diary

Digi's Diary: Avaddiction

Another sermon from lay preacher DigiGardener. You may have heard about *avaddiction*, or addiction to leading life as an avatar. So let's face it, maybe our social lives were not that great before we discovered avatar living, but what about now? Well personally, I find that if I replace TV time (little human interaction there, unless you enjoy fighting over the remote control) with avatar time, it is probably a step up. Some people can watch TV and avatar at the same time, but hey, other avatars like me can detect your glazed expressions when you do that . . . atten-hut!

Life as an avaddict.

So what about avaddiction? As the old Greeks tell us, "all things in moderation!" Well, those old Greeks didn't have this wonderfully addicting technology. I treat my avatar time as a teaser for some real, sit-down, human, face-to-face interaction. On-line chat stimulates my desire for yet more communication. After I figure out that my cat really doesn't understand or care about my rantings, I pick up my jacket and head into town for coffee with friends. Yes, life on the avatar cyberspace beat can be strange, but I have met so many interesting people from around the world (some of whom I later met in person), that I feel the avatar experience has grown and enriched my social web.

OnLive!
Traveler
MYSTIC VOYAGES THROUGH SOUND

Ⓐs we maneuver our cybercraft toward a strange, bright orange planet, we hear distant voices hailing us. Approaching the surface in our shuttle, we are awestruck by the brilliant skies, distant mountains, and great cityscape below. Windsong and ethereal music drift up to us as we come in for a landing. Got the gift of gab? You are going to need it, as the natives are all very talkative. Welcome to Utopia, gateway to the worlds of Traveler.

Your Guide to Traveler, Utopia, and other Worlds

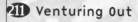

WORLD GUIDE

WORLD SKILL LEVEL	Intermediate
BUILDING CAPABILITY	No
SYSTEM REQUIREMENTS	Windows 95
AVATAR CREATION CAPABILITY	No, but it supports customization of existing ones
DEPTH	3D
SOUND SUPPORT	Voice, Music

MINIMUM MACHINE

OPERATING SYSTEM	Windows 95
COMPUTER	Pentium-based PC; 256-color monitor supporting VGA or SVGA
RESOURCES	16MB RAM; 13MB free disk space; SoundBlaster 16 or compatible 16-bit sound card, with Windows 95 driver and speakers/headphones
CONNECTION	PPP dial-up to the Internet at 14.4 kbps; 28.8 kbps recommended

Traveler: A Journey Through Sound

Traveler is your gateway to many intriguing worlds of sound and voice. Remember Citizens Band (CB) radio, or perhaps you are a HAM radio operator? OnLive! Traveler brings that experience to the new avatar cyberspace. In a Traveler world like Utopia or MTV Tikkiland, you choose an avatar (which looks like a giant head, or a costume party mask), fly around in three dimensions, and when you see other talking heads or hear their voices, you can join in the conversation. Because the sound is also *three dimensional,* you can tell when someone is talking from your left or right side, or when a conversation is right in front of you or at a distance. You will feel as though you have really visited with your friends in Traveler. Any way you look at it, Traveler is a fantastic journey through sound.

View of OnLive! Traveler in action at the Stonehenge talking circle.

Installing OnLive! Traveler

Installing

What do I need to use Traveler?

To run Traveler and visit all of its worlds, you need a Pentium PC running Windows 95 and a direct connection to the Internet. You can't use Traveler through on-line services like America Online, CompuServe, or Prodigy, unless they support direct Internet access through the 32-bit *Winsock.* (Short for Windows Sockets, Winsock is a standard interface for Microsoft Windows applications and the Internet.)

For example, you can use Traveler through the Microsoft Network, CompuServe 3.0, and AOL for Windows 95, as they do provide this service. There is more information on using Traveler through on-line services in the FAQ on the book companion Web site.

The best way to use Traveler is to be directly connected to the Internet by dial-up PPP connection with at least a 14.4 kbps connection (28.8 kbps is recommended). If you are at work or a place where you have a PC on the Internet full-time (such as a university or college), you can also use Traveler. Connecting from work might require you to check on your *firewall* restrictions. (See "Firewalls and Proxies," in Appendix B for more information.)

To use Traveler, you must also have a sound card installed (SoundBlaster 16 or compatible is recommended), speakers, and a PC-style microphone (with a $1/18$-inch plug) plugged into your sound card. The sound card must have Windows 95 compatible drivers installed. Future versions of Traveler will support text chat, but we highly recommend you use the sound options (you can purchase complete kits for $150 or less) to get the full experience of Traveler. The recommended minimum machine specifications shown at the beginning of this chapter give you an idea of the system you should have to run Traveler.

Getting started and a few disclaimers

Traveler is easy to install, and if your sound system is set up properly, you will be talking in no time. Another plus is that Traveler is free to use (you have to accept the terms of a free license during installation). You are not charged for the time you spend talking in Traveler, but you could be charged for the hours you are online from your *Internet service provider (ISP)*. Check with your ISP on monthly free hours and rates. If you are paying toll charges on your telephone line to call your Internet service provider, you could be billed for the hours your line is used to chat on the Internet. Check with your phone company and try to get a flat rate for this line.

Is it time to switch to digital telephony?

It is important to note that you can use Traveler to talk to people all over the world, as long as they are also running Traveler, and are on the Internet. The quality of voice transmission can resemble a forest fire fighter's radiophone, especially when talking to someone who is many server steps away. Voices traveling between Europe and North America or Australia may be difficult to understand at times. See the sidebar, "How Traveler works," later in the chapter for a better understanding of how your voice gets from you to another person. You might ask: Can I switch from my long-distance telephone company and just communicate by voice via a virtual world? The answer is not clear yet. If a close friend or family member is on the Internet frequently, and uses OnLive! Traveler, this might be an option. Until most people have access to digital telephony, you will have to keep that phone right next to your computer.

The version of Traveler you will find on the *Avatars!* CD is the one described in this chapter. However, Traveler may have evolved since this chapter was written, so when you log on, you may be asked to upgrade to a new version. If you download an upgrade from the Internet, or a whole new version of Traveler, it may look somewhat different from what I describe here. To download an upgrade, or a completely new version of Traveler from the Internet, follow the instructions under, "Installing or upgrading Traveler from the Internet," later in this chapter.

Virtually up-to-date

Help

As a special service for readers of *Avatars!*, I have a home page on the World Wide Web devoted to keeping you up-to-date on your favorite worlds. Find news about software updates, social events held within these virtual worlds, and brand new worlds you might want to try at http://www. digitalspace.com/avatars. Bookmark it!

If you have questions or problems

If you have questions or problems installing or running Traveler, consult the "OnLive! Traveler FAQ," on the book companion Web site. If this does not help you, check the OnLive! home page at **http://www.onlive.com**, and its special support page at **http://www.onlive.com/beta/support.htm**, for help with common problems. To contact the OnLive! Traveler team directly with your suggestions, bug reports, or comments, fill out the feedback form at **http://www.onlive.com/beta/feedback.htm**. Sending e-mail to **support@onlive.com** is also a good way to get help.

I appreciate your feedback on *Avatars!*, but I don't have the resources to provide technical support. We would be happy to hear about your experiences with Traveler. Contact us through the *Avatars!* book Web site at **http://www.digitalspace.com/avatars**.

Macintosh, UNIX, and OS/2 versions

At this writing, Traveler is not available for the Macintosh, UNIX, or OS/2. Check the OnLive! and *Avatars!* book Web pages for updates on new versions which might support these platforms. You also may be able to run Traveler using a Windows 95 emulation system on non-Windows machines. Note that if you are considering hosting an OnLive! server, this software runs on various UNIX systems and Windows NT.

Sound card detection and setting up your sound system

Traveler will try to detect the presence of a sound card during the installation and when it starts to run. If Traveler cannot detect a sound card, it will let you know, and may not continue any further. If this happens, you may have to reinstall the software drivers for your sound card. Make sure you have a sound card recommended by OnLive! (check the list on the Web site at **http://www.onlive.com**). SoundBlaster 16 or compatibles should be no problem. Make sure you have Windows 95 drivers for your card. You may want to install these drivers using the Add New Hardware icon in your Windows control panel. You will be prompted to insert the proper driver installation disks. You can also get up-to-date drivers from the manufacturer of your sound card.

Once your sound card is set up correctly, make sure your PC speakers and microphone are plugged into the correct jacks on the card, on the back of your PC. You can tell whether your speakers are working with the sound card, as you will begin to hear common Windows sounds through them (startup, error sounds, etc.). You can test your microphone by running the standard Microsoft Sound Recorder applet found in Accessories/Multimedia programs in your Start menu.

If you have a Windows PC like the one described above, complete with sound system, you are ready to go!

Registration

OnLive! is collecting information about its users so it can design better products and contact you with important update information. I encourage you to visit their Web site at **http://www.onlive.com/cgi-bin/travreg.cgi**, and fill out the on-line registration form. Filling out this form is valuable for another reason: it is a checklist to make sure that your configuration meets the minimum specifications.

Do you have a previous version of Traveler installed?

If you have previously installed Traveler, go to the Windows 95 control panel and double-click on Add/Remove Programs. Scroll down to Traveler, highlight it, and click on the Add/Remove button to delete it from the system. Before beginning the new installation, also make sure to delete the old Traveler folder. The previous release is normally installed in \program files\onlive, unless you had selected a different option. You must delete the entire folder called onlive. This will help make the new installation as trouble-free as possible.

Installing Traveler from your Avatars! CD

If you have a CD-ROM drive on your PC, you can install Traveler directly from the book CD-ROM. If you don't have a CD-ROM drive, skip right to the following section, "Installing or upgrading Traveler from the Internet." In "The Book CD-ROM" chapter, I provide a step-by-step example of how to install from the CD-ROM. I suggest you refer to this chapter, and follow the same steps for Traveler. Once the installation program on your CD-ROM has started, you can refer to "Running the installation," later in this chapter.

Note that on other parts of the CD, Web pages are links to sites for OnLive! Traveler and other virtual worlds, including the home page for *Avatars!* at **http://www.digital space.com/avatars**. If you are online while you have the CD open, you can click on these links and explore the universe of virtual worlds on the Internet.

Installing or upgrading Traveler from the Internet

If you want the very latest version of Traveler, or were informed that you had to upgrade the version found on your *Avatars!* CD, then you must download files from the Internet. If you haven't done this before, don't panic; it is easier than you might think!

❶ Connect to the Internet (dial up with your modem and make sure your Internet connection is active).

❷ Start your Web browser, such as Netscape Navigator or Microsoft Internet Explorer.

❸ In the top of the browser window, you will see a long text box where you can enter text.

❹ Click in this box, delete the text inside, type: **http://www.onlive.com**, and press the Enter key. After a few moments, the home page for OnLive! should appear. If nothing comes up for a long time, check to see that you are online.

If the OnLive! page is not available for some reason, try entering the location for the *Avatars!* home page, which is **http://www.digitalspace.com/avatars**. This page may contain more up-to-date links for both OnLive! and Traveler.

❺ Once you are at the OnLive! home page, follow the instructions for download-ing or upgrading Traveler. At one point, you will click on a link and be prompted for a place to save a file. In response to the dialogue box, click Save to Disk (Netscape) or Save As (Internet Explorer), and save the file to a folder on your hard disk (or save it on your desktop).

❻ You must choose a folder that will be easy to remember, so that you can find the new file, and also note the file name. You can use the folder that your Web browser gives you, or move back up and select another. I put all down-loaded files in a folder I call \download. Now wait patiently. You can do other work, but be careful not to interfere with the connection. Try not to do more on-line work (such as Web surfing) on the Internet while the download is pro-gressing, and if you are using your regular telephone line for the modem, don't make a call.

❼ After the download is finished (it takes about 45 minutes with a 28.8 kbps connection, and about 90 minutes with a 14.4 kbps connection), open the folder into which the file was downloaded and double-click on it to start the installation. Go to the section, "Running the installation."

Running the installation

Whether you are running the installation from the CD-ROM, or from the file you downloaded from the Internet, use this section to guide you through the installation. Note that if you downloaded Traveler from the Internet, the installation process may have changed. If this has happened, refer to instructions on the OnLive! Web site.

❶ After the software has been downloaded, close your browser, and go to the directory (or desktop) location where you saved the file. OnLive! Traveler is packaged as an executable WinZip compressed file. Double-click on the file, which will launch the WinZip or another Zip format extractor application. If you get a message that the file type is unknown, you may have to download and install WinZip (see "Downloading and Installing a Zip Program," in Appendix B).

❷ WinZip will prompt you to extract all of the Traveler files. You should choose to place these files in a temporary directory. I have made a directory called \temp, which I use for this kind of thing. Sometimes the files will be placed in your default temporary directory (usually this will be the \windows\temp directory). After selecting the destination directory, verify that "When Done Unzipping Run: Setup" is selected and click Unzip to extract the files. After the files have been unzipped, click OK.

❸ The installer setup program will run and prompt you at each step. Accept the license agreement terms, if you agree, and accept the folder into which Traveler will be installed (or enter your own path). The default folder is \program files\onlive. You should make a note of the path to the folder where Traveler is installed.

❹ You will be prompted to install the full-duplex driver if you have a 100 percent compatible SoundBlaster 16 card. When prompted to install a sound driver, click Yes to install the full-duplex driver. (If you know that you have the latest full-duplex driver, click No.) If you install the driver, click OK to close the window that confirms this installation.

❺ The installation should be successful if you have enough disk space (you need about 13MB free).

❻ When the installation is complete, you must reboot your system to run the Traveler application. You can either reboot now or later. Make your selection, and click OK.

Finding the installed software

The installation program should have created a shortcut to OnLive! Traveler on your desktop, and possibly also a program group in your Start menu. If you cannot find the new software, you can open My Computer and the C: drive. The folder for this new program might be listed in the C: disk or found under the Program Files folder. Open that folder, and you will find the program.

Use the following instructions to create a shortcut to Traveler on your desktop, or in a folder of your favorite applications. Open \program files\onlive, or the folder you selected during the installation of Traveler, as shown in the following figures.

Step 1: Find the folder in which Traveler was installed.

Step 2: Open the Apps subfolder to find the Traveler program.

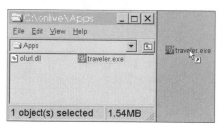

Step 3: Drag and drop the Traveler icon to create a shortcut on your desktop.

Find the file called traveler.exe in the Apps subfolder.

With the right mouse button down, drag and drop the icon onto the desktop, and select Create shortcut(s) here, when prompted.

Cleaning up after installation

If you copied the Traveler installation file onto your desktop, into a folder, or you downloaded it from the Internet, you can delete it after the installation is complete. It should have a name like onlive.exe. Do not delete traveler.exe by mistake, as this is your running version of the Traveler program. (On the other hand, I keep the original installer around just in case I have to reinstall it.) Of course, you also have the CD with the original installers, so you do not need to take up valuable hard disk space. You may also have to delete files you unzipped into your temporary directory. I always check for this just in case files are left behind. After the installation is complete, you do not need to keep these files around.

Portal Through the Wormhole

First Steps

Starting up Traveler

Before you start Traveler, you should connect to the Internet (dial up with your modem, or make sure that your Internet connection is active). Once you are online, you can start Traveler by double-clicking on the shortcut on your desktop, or by selecting Start ➪ Programs ➪ OnLive! Traveler.

Through the stargate

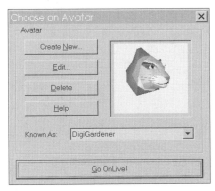

The gate to Traveler.

When Traveler first starts up, it presents you with the Choose an Avatar dialogue box (see the adjacent figure). The first time in, you might want to consider leaving everything as OnLive! has set it. If you do want to change things, here are the options and what they will allow you to do:

Create New: This option allows you to change the name (nickname) you use with your avatar. You initially start out as a guest. You should start customizing your avatar by giving it a name, and then choosing Edit to select its look and behavior. You can create many different names associated with different avatars. In this way, different members of your family can choose their favorite or customary avatars when they run Traveler.

Edit: This option allows you to edit the features of the avatar, including the avatar model itself, voice, profile, and options (see "Customizing or changing your avatar," later in this chapter).

Delete: This option will delete the name you have given to your avatar, and revert you back into a guest, or assign a new name using Create New.

Help: This option will send you right into the Traveler help system (which will launch its Web site inside your Web browser).

Known as: This option shows you the nickname that you selected. You can change to a different nickname, which has a different avatar and personal information.

Go OnLive!: Pressing this button will start the process of connecting you with OnLive! First, your Web browser should start (if it does not, start it before running OnLive! Traveler). As the following figure shows, you will be presented with several Traveler worlds. Select Utopia.

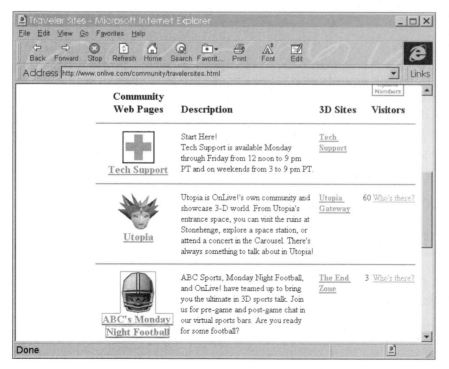

The Web site gate to Traveler.

Clicking on the link called Utopia (which ends in .sds), should launch the Traveler software and start you teleporting into the Utopia gateway world. After clicking on a Web link to a Traveler world, you may be prompted to Open or Save a file. Choose Open; this is the file used to start Traveler. You should see something like the figure to the right. These expanding wire frames represent your teleportation journey into the world. If you don't see something like this, click on

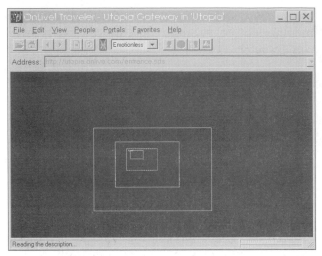

Going through the space portal.

your Traveler software (or start it if it is not already running) and then select File ⇨ Travel to Start Place. (Start Place is the entry area where you initially land in Traveler, normally the plaza at Utopia.) This should give you another try. If this does not seem to help, see the "OnLive! Traveler FAQ," on the book companion Web site.

On your way!

Traveler may take a few minutes to download information about Utopia and the people in it, and then it will drop you right into the fray! You have no choice but to wait and slowly become mesmerized by the graphic tunnel through which you are traveling. You can watch the tiny messages and progress bar at the bottom right-hand side of the window to get an idea of what is happening. If the OnLive! or other server is busy or otherwise unavailable, you will be given a message and asked to try again later.

Connecting to other Traveler worlds

If you want to go directly into other OnLive! Traveler worlds (and there are many), you have several travel options:

- Enter Utopia, and then fly through the portals there (this is described later in the section, "Going places . . . far!").

- Start Traveler, and then pick a destination from the Portals menu.

- Enter a world portal address directly into your Web browser's Go To Location field, which has the same effect as clicking on a link.

Traveler worlds Web addresses

WORLD DESCRIPTION	SPONSOR	WORLD PORTAL ADDRESS
Utopia	OnLive!	http://utopia.onlive.com/entrance.sds
Virtual Vegas Inc.	Virtual Vegas	http://onlive.virtualvegas.com/vvegas/vvcasino.sds
MTV Tikkiland	MTV	http://mtvtikkiland.onlive.com/tikki/entrance.sds
Frighteners World	MCA/Universal	http://www.mca.com/universal_pictures/onlive/ frighteners/entrance.sds
Best's Internet Resort	Best	http://www.best.com/best_resort/entrance.sds
Concentric Corp.	Concentric Cafe	http://home.concentric.net/cafe/cafe.sds

Later in this chapter, in the section, "Hot Worlds," I will tell you more about these other Traveler worlds.

Watch out, I'm coming in for a landing!

Entry into Utopia, OnLive!'s gateway world, is dramatic. As the following figure shows, you are suddenly through with the portal journey, and now are falling into the cityscape of Utopia.

Coming in for a landing at Utopia Gateway.

Altar of the great god portal of Utopia.

Landing with a resounding bump, you find yourself facing in the general direction of the great god avatar of Utopia. Don't worry, this great leader won't do anything ungracious to you. Instead it serves as an oracle and gateway to other worlds. If you are lucky, you will land in a crowd of fellow Utopians. As you fall, you might even see the heads of other Utopia members online, and already in conversation.

No room at the inn?

At this writing, Traveler has a limit of just under 20 people per area. If that area is full when you try to connect, you will be sent back to the room you left on your last visit. If the Utopia gateway is full when you are first logging on, you will be sent into a duplicate gateway. Therefore, you can be present in a second (or even third) Utopia. These will be named something like, Utopia Gateway #2, and indicated at the top of your Traveler window. If you are trying to meet someone in Utopia, you should be aware of this.

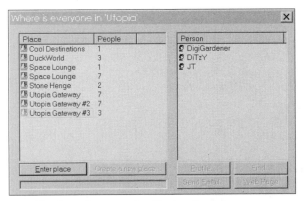

Use the People menu to find out where everyone is in Utopia.

As the adjacent figure shows, you can tell who is in which duplicate of a room by selecting the Where Is option on the People menu. If you see friends in another room, you can try to enter that room when you see the number of people there drop below the allowable limit. Alternately, if you could get a message to them, they could join you in your less crowded area. This whole duplication of rooms is a little confusing, but just remember, if rooms get full, identical rooms are created.

Let's Talk!

Meet the Natives

As you can see, the other members look pretty strange (don't forget that you probably look just as strange to them). "Hey fish! What is going on here?" you might want to say, and guess what, you *can* say it. Just bend over to your microphone (make sure it is on), press the space bar on your keyboard, and speak.

Mr. Fish may be considerate enough to answer you (if he got your drift). It is best to be quite close to another Traveler member, and to be facing them, before you talk. You should take a moment to determine if that avatar is in conversation with someone else. Butting into these conversations would be considered no less rude than doing it in a face-to-face situation.

Chatting it up with the fox and friends.

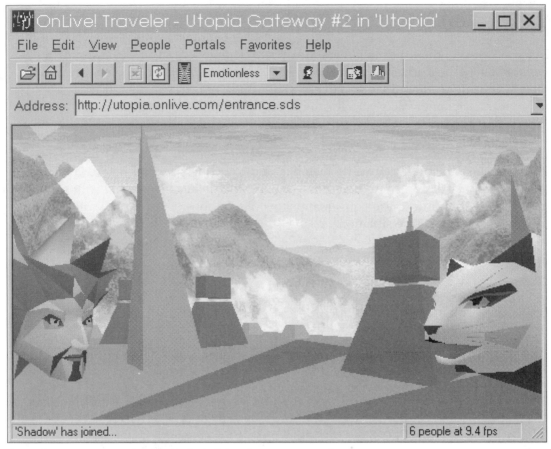

Sunset Dawn, a Traveler Host, is talking to a new guest.

In the preceding figure, two members are talking intensely. The printed page does not convey how exciting this looks and sounds on the screen. The mouths and facial expressions of both avatars actually move in tune to their voices. This is accomplished by a small miracle of sound processing inside the Traveler software. Note that another miracle provides you with three-dimensional sound, which means that the volume changes depending on your distance from other talking members. In addition, the stereo effects provide different sound out of your left and right PC speakers. This helps you figure out the direction from which someone is addressing you, and even if someone is talking from *behind* you!

Help, I need a host!

The members talking in the preceding figure are actually formal *hosts* in Traveler worlds. Hosts are often dedicated users who just spend a lot of time helping people in Traveler worlds. They may not be working directly with OnLive!, the company that supplies Traveler, but they are often encouraged and supported by OnLive!. Hosts are often your best source of help and tips on Traveler etiquette. Often, OnLive! engineers will show up inside a world to give direct technical support. This is quite an improvement over going to the old, dusty manual or struggling with the help system; your tech support lives inside your software!

OnLive! says technical support engineers are available Monday through Friday from 12 to 9 p.m., and on weekends from 3 to 9 p.m. Hours are Pacific Standard Time and are subject to change.

Just who am I talking to?

Traveler seems to suit a particularly American skill or sensibility of just being able to walk up to a stranger and start talking. In nearly every other culture, people want more of an introduction. Unless you are meeting someone you know in a Traveler world, and that person can introduce you, this is not an option. That is why the designers of Traveler built in a Visit card feature (as it is known in Europe). This is like a personal business card. Before you even approach another avatar, you can read their visit card, called a *profile*. As shown in the adjacent figure, to read someone's profile, just right-click with the mouse on top of their avatar and select Show Profile.

Who *are* you? Right-click on a member to find out.

The profile you see might look like the one in the figure to the left.

When you think about it, this is pretty exciting stuff! You can talk with people of so many different cultures, and it is all on a level playing field. Race, handicaps, and physical appearance do not enter into the picture. Gender can, however, unless you choose *voice disguising* (see the section, "Fine-Tuning Your World," later in the chapter). Try to be conscious that the person with whom you are speaking may not understand your culture, and may have a very different world view than you.

A typical member profile . . . this person is Japanese! This might be an interesting cross-cultural conversation.

The pop-up menu you get by right-clicking on another avatar also allows you to:

Go in Front Of: It moves you so that you face this person's avatar (you can also do this by double-clicking on that avatar).

Go Near: This gets you closer to the avatar, without invading his or her personal space.

Ignore: This is a powerful feature to be used with discretion. It means that a person (who obviously has offended you in some way) will no longer be able to speak to you, nor you to him or her. See the section, "Trouble in Traveler City," for more information on ignoring.

Send Mail To, Show Web Page: This will send an e-mail to someone, or show their Web site. Note that this will only work if that person has entered their e-mail and Web site address in their profile.

Postcards from the cyberedge

Perhaps an environment like Traveler is not so different from real business meetings. For example, by dragging and dropping a shortcut from your desktop (a bookmark for a Web site, a document, etc.) onto someone's avatar, you can e-mail that shortcut reference, or even the document to that person. This will require setting up your default mail client (Eudora or Netscape, for example) for OnLive!. To do this, see "OnLive! Traveler FAQ," on the book companion Web site.

This kind of sharing of practical information could mark the beginning of serious collaborative uses of virtual worlds in business and education. Why take that red-eye flight to Milwaukee when you could carry out your project review in a digital work space? (Stand by, folks!)

Why some voices sound better than others

Any message traveling through the Internet between two Traveler users passes along a daisy chain of lines, which go from one server to the next. The more steps, the more the chance that pieces of voice will be delayed, come in out of order, or even be lost. Talking with people who are many steps away, or who are in an area with slow Internet connections, can be difficult. I have found that talking with people in Europe from here in California can be difficult at times. In addition, during working hours, or early evening in time zones where Internet use is heaviest (United States time zones), congested packet traffic on the Internet can interfere with clear, consistent Traveler voice delivery.

How Traveler works

The story of how Traveler works is fascinating. When you lean over, press the space bar, and begin to speak into your microphone, the following complex set of steps happens:

1. Other conversations and the background sound are cut out temporarily so you don't get feedback (old radiophone standard practice). If you have a full-duplex sound card (e.g., SoundBlaster 16), you don't have to press the space bar to start speaking. It is just like speaking on the phone.

2. Your voice input is processed by the sound card and put into a buffer.

3. The Traveler software picks up the buffer of bytes representing your voice and compresses it.

4. This voice data is then processed for vowels and converted into mouth movements. These are then included piggyback-style on top of the voice packets.

5. These bytes are then converted into smaller packets and shipped out through your Internet connection.

6. The packets stream through the Internet, pausing occasionally at servers before being pushed onward.

7. The packets begin to arrive through your own local server, and are put back together in sequence, and passed on to a buffer in your conversation partner's Traveler software, running on their PC.

8. The Traveler software on the other end then decompresses your voice data and looks for phonemes, vowels, and word breaks.

9. Traveler then streams your voice out through your partner's sound card and speakers while at the same time drawing and redrawing your avatar, showing face and mouth movements corresponding to the distinct vowel sounds in your voice stream. If you say the letter E, your avatar's mouth makes the shape of what would look like an E. If you say the letter O, your avatar's mouth would open up to make the shape of an O.

And all this is done so that *you* can jabber away with strangers!

Improve your reception and voice quality with better microphones or a headset

Selecting a reasonably good microphone will affect how others hear you. I use the microphone that came with my SoundBlaster 16 card, and it works just fine. Other avid Traveler users have purchased headset microphones, known as *boom mikes*. These are telephone headsets with a mike that swings out in front of your mouth. Note that some headsets only have one ear piece. As Traveler delivers stereo sound (different sound to your right and left speakers), it is important that if you want to use a headset instead of speakers, that you get one with two ear pieces. The main advantage of a boom mike and headset is that the mike will be very directional, that is, only pick up your voice instead of sound in the room.

You can improve how you are heard in Traveler by keeping your room noise or ambient sound low. You may not want to listen to the stereo while using Traveler, as this will be piped directly to the other members. Another tip is to turn down the ambient background sound in Traveler itself to keep the room noise and voice echo to a minimum.

Pump up the volume (or turn it down a little)

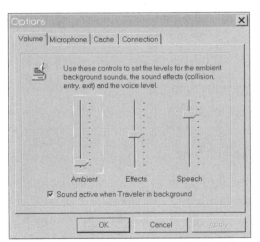

Use the Options dialogue to set Traveler volume controls.

The adjacent figure shows the options for setting Traveler's volume controls. These important settings include the following:

Ambient: This controls the background music and sounds you hear in Traveler worlds. Set this one low to reduce the pickup of these sounds by your own mike as you speak. Traveler members often turn this back up when they enter a brand new area so they can listen to the new background sounds. Usually, each world has its own background ambient sound.

Effects: This controls the volume level for special sound effects, such as when you enter (your entry chimes), collisions with other members or objects, and when you exit (exit gong or transporter/teleport hum). I recommend that you keep these sound effects toned down as a courtesy to the other people in the room or house.

Speech: You can raise and lower the volume at which other members' voices are played back. This is a useful feature, especially when using Traveler at a party to jam with virtual guests.

Sound active when Traveler in background: It is a good idea to set this on, as it will keep Traveler transmitting members' voices even when you switch to another application or minimize Traveler (so that it is placed onto the task bar). This will allow you to follow conversations, a kind of digital talk radio, while doing other work. Steal those packets from the Internet!

Venturing Out

You may be all raring to join the hottest conversation circles, but you just can't . . . move! Navigation in Traveler is easy; it's all in the finger action. The following table lists the keyboard keys you can press to move, and where they take you. There is no joystick support yet (a good feature to add), but keyboard keys are actually a pretty good way to get around (as millions of *Doom* players can tell you). Note that the key combinations such as Ctrl+Left Arrow indicate that you have to hold down the first key (in this case, Ctrl) and then press the second key.

Key combinations and how they move you

KEY	EFFECT
Up Arrow	Move forward
Down Arrow	Pull back
Right Arrow	Turn to the right
Left Arrow	Turn to the left
Alt+Up Arrow	Rise up
Alt+Down Arrow	Sink down
Alt+Left Arrow	Slide to the left
Alt+Right Arrow	Slide to the right
End on your number keypad	Puts you upright again (use this if you really don't know which way is up)

Want to be *really* dramatic? You can use the following keys to tilt your head up or down.

Note that you cannot roll all the way around like a stunt airplane doing the loops.

Common communication protocols	
KEY	**EFFECT**
Page Up	Tilts your head up
Page Down	Tilts your head down

Going places . . . fast!

If you are tired of the leisurely pace in which you are moving, just hold down the Shift key together with any of the above key combinations, and you will move *much* faster.

Whoops! I bumped into something (or someone)

In Traveler worlds, you can travel right through most things. You cannot go below the floor of a world. You also cannot pass through another avatar. This is an interesting feature, as many other virtual worlds allow you to whisk through other people like ghosts in the night. When you bump into someone in Traveler, you will hear a distinct bump sound. Not only will you hear your bump, but you will *budge* their avatar, moving it a short distance. This helps you to know when *you* are being bumped. Bodily contact is an important part of our culture as higher primates (speaking for myself, of course). By letting avatars have body contact, Traveler's creators have given us another thread to weave into a richer social experience inside virtual space. As with any social situation, however, there are those who abuse others (see the section, "Traveler Tips: Headbangers and Boomboxers," later in this chapter).

Going places . . . far!

Traveler can take you to many different places. Utopia is just a waystation, the first stop on a tour of a constellation of worlds. The main way to get to these places is through *portals*. In the beginning of this chapter, the section, "Connecting to other Traveler Worlds," described how to enter Traveler worlds through your Web browser. There are other ways to do this directly inside Traveler.

The wondrous portals

This red pyramid, vaguely reminiscent of the *Tardis* in the science fiction TV series *Dr. Who,* is actually a portal, Traveler's way of getting you somewhere far . . . fast. When you come upon a portal in a world, just right-click on it to see the following options:

Activate: This takes you through the portal.

Go Near: This takes you up to the portal so you can check it out.

Properties: This will tell you where the portal goes, before you take the jump.

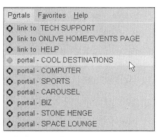

Right-click to find the options for a portal.

You can activate a portal just by passing into it. Be careful that you don't collide with one by accident; there is no easy way to stop a portal from taking you away!

A pull-down of portals

An even more convenient (if less dramatic) way of going through a portal is to select from the list of portals on the Portals pull-down menu. As the adjacent figure shows, there is a selection of links and portals. Links will take you to a Web site (i.e., start your Web browser and make it view a Web page), whereas portals will land you into a new virtual world. Some portals take you to an entirely different world, and others take you into a space within the current world. When traveling through a portal, you will see the same *space tunnel* graphic that you saw when you first entered Utopia through Traveler. Let's take a tour of some new worlds.

Click on the Portals pull-down menu to move to other destinations.

Worlds within worlds

We will go on a tour of interesting worlds within the OnLive! universe. The address of each world is given in the section, "Hot Worlds and Building Your Own," later in this chapter.

For our first stop, we will visit the technical support space within the Utopia world. Here, you will almost always find technicians from OnLive!, as well as expert users to help with your technical questions.

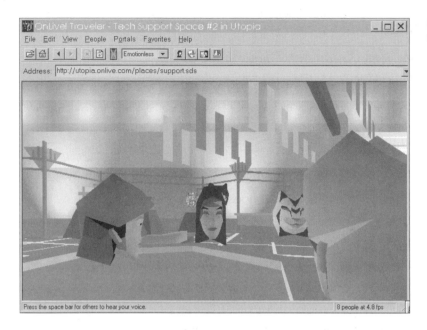

A technical support
area within Utopia.

Next, let's go to the Grand Central Station of Traveler, known as the *Cool Destinations* area. In Cool Destinations, you can fly through portals into whole new worlds in the Traveler cosmos, such as MTV's Tikkiland. There are also people congregated in Cool Destinations. Often, you can get advice about great destinations or events happening in other worlds just by asking people in this area.

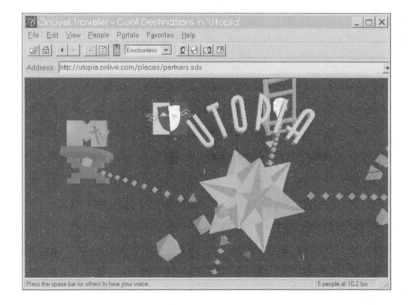

The Cool Destinations
portal cluster.

It's all made out of tikki takki . . .

MTV's Tikkiland: mass media meets cyberspace!

Is it kitsch, or will it be seen as high original art when unearthed by digital archeologists in the next millennium? Either way, MTV's Tikkiland will go down in history as one of the first places where the new cyberculture meets traditional pop broadcast media.

Once in Tikkiland, practice using your fast navigation (hold the Shift key down) and moving up and down (with Ctrl+Up Arrow and Ctrl+Down Arrow) and sail around Tikki Island. Staying at just one level is boring; learn to fly. Be forewarned that you could also end up underneath a world (as you can see in the adjacent figure), which is an adventure in itself!

Flying underneath Tikkiland.

What goes on here? There is music (this is MTV); there are music celebrities (schedule posted on MTV's Web site); and there is much to talk about. I haven't seen Ren or Stimpy or Beavis or Butthead yet, although there seem to be an awful lot of avatars named Beavis here. Of course, there is the beach, the swaying palms, the sun, the Tikki (what is Tikki, anyway?) and of course, the pool. The pool is a great place to congregate and (what else?) talk. I would love to practice my backstroke but, hey, I am just a head!

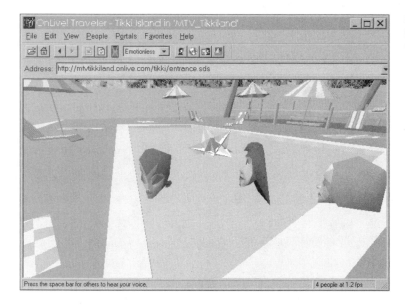

Avatar bathing beauties hang out at the pool in Tikkiland.

There are many more worlds to explore and people to meet. Be sure to check out the section, "Hot Worlds and Building Your Own," at the end of this chapter, and visit the OnLive! Web site at **http://www.onlive.com**, for news of new worlds and special happenings inside the Traveler universe.

Where is everybody?

The simplest way to see where people are in Utopia is to fly high up over the area and look for all the talking heads. Be careful when you land in a group of people, they can get pretty upset if you clobber them on their heads.

Flying over Utopia.

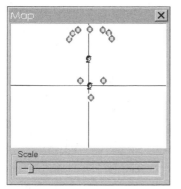

A map displaying people and portals.

Under the View menu, there is a Map option which brings up a map of the whole area, showing people (as tiny heads) and portals (as diamonds). You can click on people or portals with your right mouse button, and take many actions, such as going near them. The map is a very handy tool in Traveler.

Under the People menu, there is a choice called, Where is everyone in. Selecting this will list everyone in your present world. The following figure shows a listing of everyone in Tikkiland. When you have this list, you can do a number of things, such as click on the different areas of Tikkiland to see who is in which area. You can also find out information about people, and send them e-mail without having to enter their area. The figure below shows a listing of people in a particular place in Tikkiland.

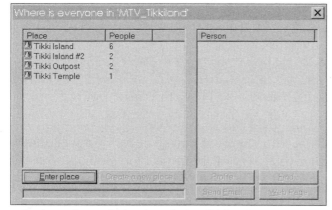

A listing of people in the whole Tikkiland world.

A group of people in a particular place in Tikkiland.

Hello . . . Earth to avatar!

When someone has minimized Traveler (put it onto the task bar), or is busy in another application, you will notice that their avatar's eyes close. This is a very sensible and useful feature. Remember, if someone is not responding to you, do not become irritated or shout—they may be having a problem with their connection, or *you* may be having a problem with your connection!

Fine-Tuning Your World

Customizing or changing your avatar

The most common thing people want to do is to customize or change their avatars. You can find the avatar customization options under the Edit menu. Note that if you entered Traveler for the first time, you probably did not set up your avatar's name. You may have to quit Traveler and restart it, selecting Create New on the very first dialogue. You can then enter a name for your avatar. Once you have a name, you will be allowed to modify your avatar.

Avatar customizing options under the Edit menu.

The dialogue box in the following figure displays the array of avatar models to choose from. Note that I have chosen Leola and given her a smile. We also could have given her a fierce tiger scowl. You can also color different parts of your avatar by selecting Appearance. This selection will open a palette of colors. Dragging a color over the top of an area in your avatar will color that area. A famous avatar in OnLive! is an all-white tiger (except for the eyes and mouth) used by Sunset Dawn.

Once you have chosen your look, you should choose your voice. Traveler offers you the limited ability to disguise your voice. The figure at the top of the next page shows how you can change the pitch of your voice. This is like those interviews on TV crime shows where they electronically disguise a person's voice. You can make yourself sound male or female (although the disguising might be obvious).

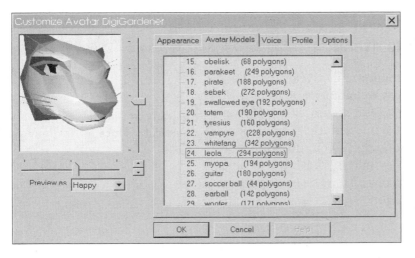

Choosing the Leola tiger avatar from the Customize Avatar dialogue.

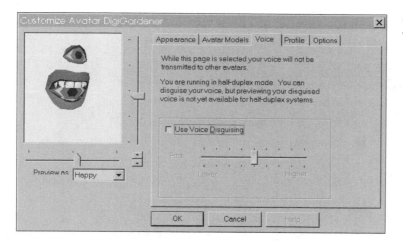

Customize your avatar's voice.

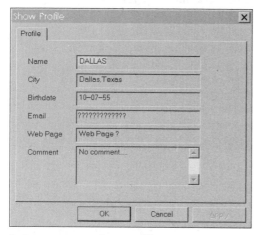

Set up your avatar profile.

Another useful avatar customization option enables you to set up a profile. As the adjacent figure shows, you can give your real name (if you choose to), your nickname (which you also would have been asked for when you started Traveler for the first time), your e-mail address, Web page address (if any), and a brief description of yourself. In the above figure, there is a profile of a Utopia citizen from Dallas, Texas, who chose not to enter an e-mail address, Web page, or comments.

Select Options from the View menu.

Many Traveler citizens forget to fill out their personal information, but it can be very useful in starting conversations. I always fill out this information, my theory being that if I had anything to hide, I would not be talking inside virtual worlds for anyone in the real world to hear!

Other options

Traveler has several other useful options found under the View ⇨ Options menu, including volume, microphone, cache, and connection (see the figures on the next page).

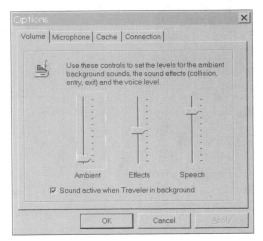

The Volume Options dialogue.

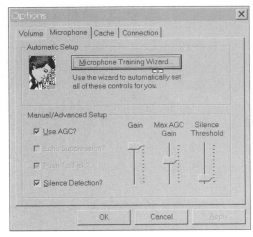

The Microphone Options dialogue.

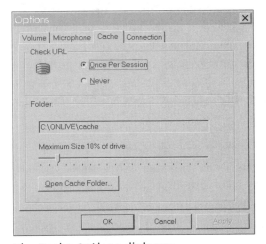

The Cache Options dialogue.

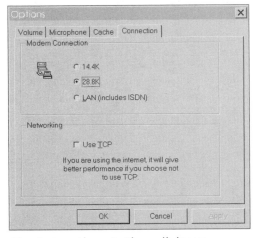

The Connections Options dialogue.

Saving favorite places

Use Favorites to save your favorite places.

If you had a particularly good time in a Traveler room, you can save it as a *favorite* by selecting Favorites ⇨ Add to Favorites. You can then open the favorite area later with Favorites ⇨ Open Favorites, or stow your favorite room right on your desktop by selecting File ⇨ Create Shortcut. When connecting to Traveler in the future, your favorites will be shown. Favorite is one of my favorite features.

Traveler Tips: Headbangers and Boomboxers

Ham, CB, and radiophone: Protocols and etiquette from other technologies come in handy

Are you Hamming it up in your off hours? Did you keep on truckin' with your CB radio long after the 70s were over? Or were you a sad sack in the Army for too many years? If so, you probably have learned some pretty good protocol and etiquette from other communication technologies that you can now recycle in the Traveler environment. Of course, two law enforcement officers talking in Utopia may be unintelligible to the rest of us! And as any radio operator would tell you, if you have to cough or sneeze (or yawn) don't do it into the open microphone! Here is a sampling of protocols that may come in handy:

Common communication protocols

You say	It means	Comes from
Ten Four	I got that	CB, police radio
Say or Come Again	Please repeat that	Everyday life
Over and out	Good-bye	Radiophone, CB

Excess noise, echo, and open microphones

On occasion, you will be having a nice, orderly conversation, and then someone will come into your area with a lot of static or background noise. They might not be doing this on purpose; their microphone might just be open all the time. How does this happen? Seasoned Traveler users can be heard asking open-mike offenders to push the P key on their keyboards to shut down the microphone. That person can then talk normally by pressing the space bar down when they want to speak. If you have the ambient sound set too high, or your speakers set too loud, you can cause feedback to the other listeners through your own open mike. If you or they hear a voice echo, then someone has a problem with speaker feedback. A solution is to turn the speaker volume down, or to try to better isolate the microphone from the other speakers. Many users get microphones that have excellent local pickup, such as the boom mikes on headsets. These microphones will sense the speaker's voice and little else.

Little Billy is mute!

If someone cannot get their sound to work, and they cannot hear you, you can ask them to just nod or shake their heads in a kind of simple sign language. If you find you can hear people but cannot send them your own voice (you don't have a microphone), just use the Left Arrow and Right Arrow to shake your head, and the Tab+Up Arrow and Tab+Down Arrow to nod.

Don't fall down a manhole

Be careful not to back into a portal. Portals often resemble pyramids or telephone booths. If you do back into one, you will be swept away rather unexpectedly with no way to stop yourself. This can lead to rather abrupt endings to conversations!

The server is getting loaded

If you are in an area where it becomes very hard to talk or hear anyone, check the People ⇨ Where is dialogue. The server supporting this area may be getting overloaded. Sometimes you . . . have . . . to . . . talk . . . very . . . slowly so that your voice will go through. This is often the warning of an overloaded server. It is a good idea to get out while the getting is good, and travel to a different area supported by a different server.

Are we still on the air?

If suddenly you notice that nobody seems to be talking or moving, you may have experienced a *soft disconnect*. This means that you have lost your connection between the Traveler client and its server. You may still be connected on the Internet. A telltale sign of a soft disconnect is when some avatar heads just spin around, indicating *idling*. If you think this has happened, select View ⇨ Reenter, or press Ctrl+R. If this does not work, you may have to shut down and restart Traveler.

Trouble in Traveler City

Dirty mouths. Rotten language can spoil a party, and there are people out there who will try to do just that. You can click on their avatars and *ignore* them (this cuts off their sound), and encourage others to do the same. It is better if you and the others can reason with this person. Try not to stoop to their level and resort to their language, or worse, to *headbanging* (described later in this chapter). Communities are forming in the new digital streets, and they are self-policing for the most part.

Gaming worlds (see the "Gaming Worlds" chapter) and traditional all-text MUD and MOO environments frequently give individuals (often called wizards or gods) special powers.

The social virtual worlds like Utopia, on the other hand, often treat everyone as equals, and let community norms evolve. I believe that it is a good indication for our future in digital space; if you just give people equal access to a world, and equal powers there, and let them communicate face-to-face, they create a functioning, decent, and sustainable environment for themselves. For more tips on how to better get along in virtual worlds or manage your own community, see "Netiquette and Community Hosting" on the book companion Web site.

Boomboxers

Boomboxers are users who turn their music up next to their computer and come into a Traveler world with their microphone open. Boomboxers are often not listening to anyone's conversations, so the best thing to do is to ignore them by right-clicking on their avatar and selecting Ignore. It often takes a minute or two to identify the boomboxer. Usually, they are targeted by users working together ("I think he just went past me..."). You can also go away from the sound and engage in a private conversation with someone far away from the troublemaker.

Headbangers

Another set of hooligans found in Traveler worlds are the *headbangers*. These pranksters roam around, and when you are not looking, start to bump you around. They usually come from behind or above, and just hammer away. It can be very funny if it isn't you trying to have an intelligent (or even not-so-intelligent) conversation. Solution: bump back, complain, or just ignore that person. You can also call for help from others in the world; you would be surprised by the effectiveness of a community voice, even in this "artificial" reality (but how artificial is it, really?).

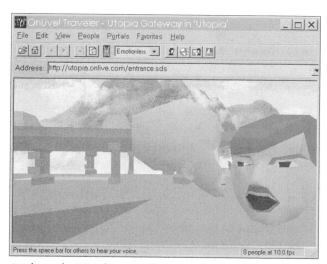

Avabuse in Utopia. Headbangers hurt, OW!

Where are the cops when you need them?

You can report offending users (if they have a profile) to OnLive! or look for hosts or OnLive! technical support within a Traveler world, who may be able to come to your rescue on the spot. Most OnLive! technical support people have the ability to kick people out of the world, but they must witness the offending person in the act.

Meet the Natives

Meet the Utopians

In this section, you will meet some citizens of the Traveler universe, sometimes called Utopians, after the gateway to all the Traveler worlds. First I will chronicle the amazing family of Sunset Dawn and Razz, and tell you the story of the youngest human to use the Internet! After that, we will present an interview with P.J.S. The Cat, a well-known Utopian country music star.

The Kindrick story: the family that travels together

Sunset Dawn's avatar.

The Kindricks are a family in Virginia in the U.S. Sunset Dawn and Razz (their avatar names) have two lovely children, Matthew, 5, and Mark (or Markee, as everyone calls him), just born at the time they were using Traveler. Markee got out of his crib one day and climbed up to the microphone. With nobody watching, he put his thumb on the space bar and opened the microphone, which he then put into his mouth and started sucking. Markee wanted to be part of the fun he had watched since the day he was born. Other avatars heard this sucking sound and came over to find out what was happening. They must have thought that this avatar was trying to imitate the little baby from *The Simpsons,* and doing a pretty good job of it! Markee had got what he wanted, his own private communication with the faces on the screen. As far as I know, Markee is the youngest person to ever use the Internet.

In their own words: Sunset tells her part

"We were sitting one night watching TV, and we were watching a program called C|Net. We just started getting into the computer and HTML. We wrote down the URL for OnLive! (http://www.onlive.com). We downloaded the program, and it gave us a password. It was like that for a little while (with the passwords). We made up our avatars. I was Sunset Dawn and my husband was Razz (our Net names). I was the cat avatar and Razz was the dog. When we started going to Utopia, it was a site to see. At the time, there were just a few of us. I remember the first day I went there. JM (a person from OnLive!) said, "hmmm, Sunset Dawn, I haven't seen that name before." And things went from there.

A few months later my two sons were a part of Utopia, too. Mark was 6 months old, and he loved trying to make sounds through the microphone, and he loved watching the avatars and the colors. Mark liked this program from the first time we let him see it. He started making sounds at OnLive! at around five months old, through the microphone.

Matthew's avatar.

We have another son, Matthew. He started picking his own avatar at five years old. He really liked the guy with brown hair, then through the months, he liked the pony. And he loved getting on OnLive! and helping people with their moves . . . and telling other people how to use the program. From this program, my son Matthew had learned how to read, write, and spell peoples' names. Matthew has learned to talk with people on their level. He is like a little man.

A few months after we had become a part of Utopia, OnLive! asked us to be a part of a new program called the Host Program. We were so happy and honored that we said yes. All we had to do was talk with people, host events—like playing music, and things like that. At the time, Hazel Holby was the leader in the Host Program for OnLive!. We talked on the telephone and through e-mail as to what we were going to host. I decided to host a tour for OnLive!. Show people around and give them history about how OnLive! started. People loved it. I have made a lot of friends. Wally was a part of helping with the tour. We would take people to all the places in OnLive!, and they loved it. We started at the Utopia Gateway, then from there we would go through all the places in Utopia. Razz decided to start Name That Tune With J.R. . . . . They would play a little byte of music, and people would have to guess the name of the song.

A few months later, OnLive! decided to do a new program called the Test Drive Program. The Test Drive Program was created to test the OnLive! server, see how many people the server could hold, help the new users, talk with people, make OnLive! a better place to make friends, teach people how to use the program, and help people out with problems. OnLive! asked me and Razz to work in the Test Drive Program for two months and get paid for it. I was happy and honored again because OnLive! made us feel as part of their own team. It's a great feeling to have, knowing the people at OnLive! let us work with the OnLive! team.

The whole Kindrick family, including baby Mark, the world's youngest avatar user.

While I, Sunset Dawn, was doing the Test Drive Program, I made a lot of new friends, and had a lot of fun. I was there every day and did my job as if I was out in the field working. I really enjoyed those two months. After the two months ended, I still went to OnLive! to help out. I love the program. It has helped us become a better family, and we can't get too much of OnLive!."

Razz adds his two bits

"Hi, Razz here. When I think back to when we got our PC, about a year and a half ago, to when we got connected, which is about a year and three months, to now, I feel that OnLive! Traveler has to be the best thing that has happened to us since we have been on the Net. With OnLive!, I feel that the whole family has come a long way. OnLive! has made it so easy to communicate with our friends, and to make new ones almost each time we log on. One of the best experiences that stands out for me was when I just got a new hard drive. I put in the drive, and had it all together to turn on the PC. The PC

Razz's avatar.

saw it as it booted up, but when it got to Windows 95, it did not know that it had another drive. I, being new to all this, wasn't sure what to do. I knew I had a friend at OnLive! named HD Rick, so I logged on and saw him there. But to make a long story short, he helped me finish installing my hard drive while I was logged on to the Net at OnLive!. With OnLive!, we are able to learn many neat things on the Net, in a short amount of time."

An interview with a star Utopian

I reproduce this interview with P.J.S. the Cat, a well-known Utopia citizen, with the kind permission of OnLive! Technologies. She tells us about her nightly experiences in Traveler worlds, and weekly country music jamming sessions.

Interviewer: Tell us what P.J.S. the Cat stands for.

P.J.S. the Cat: Contrary to popular belief, it does not stand for "peanut butter and jelly sandwich." Actually, it is the initials of my name.

Interviewer: Why do you think so many other Utopians chose you as a featured personality?

P.J.S. the Cat: Well, I think probably because I'm always happy and keep a positive attitude. Also, I've had many comments that everyone likes my laugh—and I laugh a lot.

(Author's note: P.J.S.'s laugh is definitely contagious.)

Interviewer: What's your favorite time to visit Utopia?

P.J.S. the Cat: I like all hours—both day and night, but nighttime is busier, so I usually end up spending three or four hours in Utopia. There's so many interesting people to meet.

Interviewer: Is there any experience or event in Utopia that stands out from the rest?

P.J.S. the Cat: Actually, one of my favorite events is on Friday nights in Mitzi's Lounge, where there is a weekly country music concert in Utopia—two guitar players and a harmonica player get online and play . . . and they're quite good!

Interviewer: I'm sure you've met many Utopians—is there someone in particular who you see often, or who you enjoy talking to?

P.J.S. the Cat: There is one man—JimBob, I think, who is very entertaining. He comes into Utopia and usually talks about BBQ ribs and BBQ chicken. He also is a CB operator, so he talks with some CB slang, and says things like, "Did you copy that?" Everyone really enjoys his company.

Hot Activities

Space flight

One fine evening in Utopia (after a certain time of day, your own local time or California time, I am not sure), the sun sets in Utopia. After the sun suddenly sets (no sunset or dawn here), you can see the stars beyond Utopia. Tonight, I noticed a tiny moving speck in the heavens.

Leave Utopia behind.

The Utopia colony against the night sky.

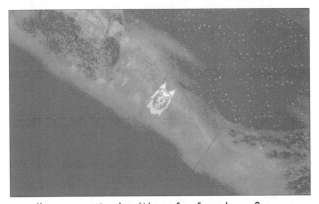

An alien, or a Utopia citizen far from home?

Finding our way back to the Utopia waystation.

Was this a moon of Utopia? I flew out farther from the warmth and light of Utopia's main plaza than I had ever gone before.

I turned around and saw the amazing sight of Utopia, like some space ship adrift in the cosmos, far behind and below me.

I finally arrived at the "moon," and it turned out to be another Utopian. "Wow, what brings you way out here on such a fine night," I asked. The other avvy (avatar) was very friendly, and told me he was a postman in England. "Wow," I said, "I just met someone who works in a chocolate factory in Germany. I guess it is not just engineer geek types like me who are into avatars!"

He agreed, and said he wondered if the world would still need postmen in the future, or if they could just talk through avatars. We raced each other back to Utopia and called it a night.

Avatar masquerade

With several pretty wild avatar models available, and the ability to stretch or shrink them and change their colors, you can really customize yourself and strut through the avatar masquerade.

By the time you read this, Traveler may let you import your own avatar models in VRML (Virtual Reality Modeling Language), and then you may see a truly strange range of characters flowing through the space.

Wild fashion show in
Utopia.

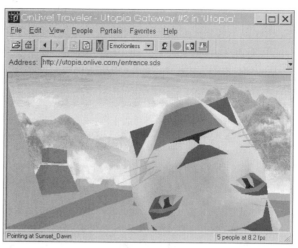

A love affair with the Cat Lady.

You may meet someone really chic, like the white tiger created by Sunset Dawn, shown here rolling herself around by pressing the Tab+Arrow keys.

Sport zone . . . ten hut!

Sunset Dawn, as a Traveler Host, took me on a tour of one of her proudest creations: the sports bar where avatars play interactive games, usually once a week. Here are some examples:

Team sports in Utopia.

- **Soccer and football:**
  Players use a "dead avatar head" for a puck, put there by the good folks at OnLive!. A coach flies above two teams of three or four each while they are on the field (see the preceding figure). If a team can bump the head through the goal posts, it scores a point. Games run up to 15 or 20 points, winner take all. If you know how modern-day soccer actually originated, you should get a kick out of this newest version!

- **Sumo wrestling:** There is a wrestling ring where avatars have three turns to push each other out of the ring, with a coach looking on. This is truly hilarious to watch!

- **Basketball:** To make a basket, you have to raise yourself (your avatar) up and bring it down through the hoop. Your avatar is the ball. Hope you don't mind being bumped around!

More games are being invented all the time; check the Utopia calendar of events.

Sunset's sports bar has inspired a larger event: the End Zone Monday Night Football (as seen in the preceding figure). In this area, you can listen to football games broadcast live into Traveler. Who knows, you may soon be butting heads with Joe Montana. Check it out! Find the End Zone at **http://www.onlive .com/**.

Other activities

The great avatar statue in Utopia points to the events calendar home page at **http://www.onlive. com/utopia/**. Here is a sampling from a recent calendar:

Monday: Host Wally runs a photography session in which screen captures are taken, developed, and put on a Web page, all instantaneously!

Friday: Razz hosts Name That Tune in which users play a section of music from a CD while their microphones are on, and others have to name the group and song. Everyone gets a turn to play their own music.

Sports lounge: Interactive games once a week (scheduled soccer, wrestling, basketball, and other games).

Traveler as the perfect voice supplement

I have found people using Traveler to give them a live voice conference while they do another activity, like play bridge in the Internet Gaming Zone (you can download it at **http://igz2.microsoft.com**). These players can play board games using the Gaming Zone, and communicate by voice by running OnLive! Traveler at the same time. The other Gaming Zone players who are just communicating with text chat will not know that the other team has a voice connection. Those with the voice feature could have a chance to cheat, as the text-only players will not pick up on what they are saying, but hey, where is the fun in that?

Other communication tools to use with Traveler

Some use ICQ (shareware that enables instant messaging over the Internet) to supplement Traveler (you can download it at **http://www.mirabilis.com/**) to find and chat with friends online while running Traveler. You can also use MUDs, MOOs, Microsoft's Net Meeting, Powwow, or Internet Relay Chat as a supplement to Traveler to make communications easier. Having text chat directly in Traveler would be useful, and this feature may be included by the time you read this book.

Hot Spots

Hot Worlds and Building Your Own

Utopia

http://www.onlive.com/utopia/
Utopia is OnLive! Technologies' community site. From Utopia, you can travel out and explore different areas and worlds, including the mystic ruins at Stonehenge, or the wacky Duckworld. Download Utopia at this site.

http://utopia.onlive.com/entrance.sds
Go directly to Utopia (if you have Traveler already installed).

http://www.onlive.com/utopia/
The Utopia special events calendar.

http://www.onlive.com/community/travelersites.html
A listing of Traveler sites.

http://www.olgate.com
Great new Traveler worlds at OL Gate.

Tikkiland from MTV

http://mtv.com/tikkiland/
This is a special, supercyber, 3D virtual chat space. You can be anything from a parakeet to a skeleton floating around talking-not typing-to a bunch of other freaky users in a place that looks like a possessed jungle, called Tikkiland. Find MTV's Tikkiland at this site.

http://mtvtikkiland.onlive.com/tikki/entrance.sds
Go directly to Tikkiland (if you have Traveler).

Best Internet's Resort

http://www.onlive.com/3Dcommunities/index.htm
This resort features a cybercabin complete with working fireplaces, domed skylights, and views of the surrounding redwood forest and mountain skyline. Find the resort at this site.

http://www.best.com/best_resort/entrance.sds
Go directly to the resort (if you have Traveler).

Concentric Cafe

http://www.onlive.com/3Dcommunities/index.htm
Be sure to visit Concentric Cafe for a virtual cup of espresso and casual conversation with friends. Enjoy the cafe's warm ambiance and explore its rooftop lounge! Find the cafe at this site.

http://home.concentric.net/cafe/cafe.sds
Go directly to Concentric Cafe (if you have Traveler).

Virtual Vegas

http://www.onlive.com/3Dcommunities/index.htm
Try your luck at Virtual Vegas, a full 3D rendered cybercasino. Wander through comfortable Vegas-style chat lounges that are enhanced with the background buzz of a busy casino. Find Virtual Vegas on the Web at this site.

http://onlive.virtualvegas.com/vvegas/vvcasino.sds
Go directly to Virtual Vegas (if you have Traveler).

So you want to build your own world?

At the time I was writing this chapter, OnLive! Technologies was offering its world developer kit and five user licenses for free. To create your own OnLive! world, you must have a Windows NT or Sparcstation UNIX server. It is quite a lot of work to build your own world and all the avatars in it (far harder than building a Web page). See the OnLive! Technologies Web site at **http://www.onlive.com** for details on the Traveler world development kit.

OnLive! Technologies tells me that Traveler will soon be using Virtual Reality Modeling Language (VRML) to create its worlds and avatars. This means that the number of worlds you can visit through Traveler will be always growing, as more and more VRML sites spread across the Internet.

Traveler Web Pages

Note that some of these Web page links may have changed or the Web pages may have been discontinued. Consult your *Avatars!* book home page at **http://www .digitalspace.com/avatars** for a more up-to-date list of links.

Official pages

http://www.onlive.com
OnLive!'s home page.

---

http://www.onlive.com/help/guide/guide.htm
Traveler's online user guide.

---

http://www.onlive.com/beta/support.htm
The OnLive! support page.

---

http://www.onlive.com/tech/
The OnLive! tech support and feedback page.

---

http://www .onlive.com/utopia/
See who is in Utopia at any given time.

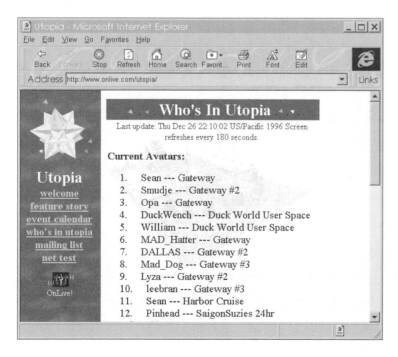

See who is in Utopia.

Press Blurbs

http://register.cnet.com/Content/Reviews/Hands/082096/onlive.html
CINet reviews OnLive! Traveler and Tikkiland.

Unofficial citizen pages

http://www.efn.org/~j_r/utopia.html
J.R.'s OnLive! Traveler ring of Web pages.

http://www.pionet.net/~dave/index.html
Dave's index of Traveler citizens and OnLive! main page.

http://www.ncn.net/~dave/pics/ index.html
Photo gallery (real pictures) of Traveler citizens.

A ring of OnLive! Web pages.

http://www.qtm .net/~rckclimbr/
RcK's home page.

http:/ /www.geocities.com/Area51/8993/index.html
Don and Michael's page.

http:// www.geocities.com/BourbonStreet/3918/
P.J.S. the Cat's home page.

http:// www.geocities.com/HotSprings/2837/
Josh's Traveler Page.

http://www.hdsne .com/seth/
Seth's home page allows you to download new test avatars.

http://www.davecentral.com/conf3d.html
DaveCentral's great listing of 3D worlds.

Digi's Diary: A Revolution from Your Own Living Room

Digi's Diary

One thing is very different about the avatar revolution now sweeping the Internet. Past revolutions, such as the World Wide Web or Java, have come from the bowels of university laboratories or sprawling company campuses. This time, the revolution is starting right in your own living room! The avatar worlds have been built by small companies, or small groups within large companies. However, all of the companies that host a world have told me the same thing: They are amazed, and were completely unprepared for what the users did in their world. It is the participants that have made the medium and who now drive it forward.

The story of Sunset Dawn and Razz and their family (in the section, "Meet the Utopians," earlier in this chapter) tells it all. Sunset Dawn used her powers of communication and organization to create various activities, and even a sports bar area where avatars could play football or bang each other about in Sumo wrestling. The OnLive! company listened to its Utopia citizens and helped them make it a better place to visit. One other unique thing about this revolution is that women will have a large role. Sunset Dawn, and many women like her, will be instrumental in creating activities, and fostering the high level of community and communication that will make avatar worlds a success. Well, let's face it; if you get a bunch of guys together in-avatar (communicating via avatars), sometimes all they have to say is, "so, what speed of computer are you running?"

Will you become a legend in your own living room? Certainly to the small group in your avvy (avatar) community! And if a five-month-old baby can communicate with his own avatar, I personally think that millions more people will be using avatar worlds soon. That small group will not stay small for long.

Virtual Places

GRAND CENTRAL STATION OF THE WEB UNIVERSE

On our voyage of discovery in digital space, we have traveled through parallel universes. Up ahead lies the intersection of two great universes. The cyberspace time continuum folds around as avatar worlds cross over the Web to create a million virtual places. Avatars slide around on top of Web pages; Web pages ripple and change under avatars.

So what are we going
to see

Your Guide to
Virtual Places

WORLD GUIDE

WORLD SKILL LEVEL	Beginner
BUILDING CAPABILITY	No, use your Web site as a chat room
SYSTEM REQUIREMENTS	Windows 95, 3.1, NT, Mac OS
AVATAR CREATION CAPABILITY	Yes, use your own picture
DEPTH	2D
SOUND SUPPORT	Sound effects only

MINIMUM MACHINE

OPERATING SYSTEM	Windows 3.1, 95 Mac OS 7.5.3 or higher
COMPUTER	PC 486; 256-color video supporting VGA or SVGA; Mac 68030 supporting System 7.5.3 or higher
RESOURCES	PC: 8MB RAM; 12MB virtual memory, 3MB free disk space; sound card optional for sound effects Macintosh: 12MB RAM, 4MB virtual memory. Microsoft Internet Explorer 3.0 or Netscape Navigator 3.0 is required
CONNECTION	PPP dial-up to the Internet at 14.4 kbps, or subscription to America Online

Virtual Places: Cruisin' the Web Cosmos

Imagine being able to take your friends in a tour bus that drives on top of the World Wide Web. Imagine turning any Web page into a chat room, and inviting hundreds of avatars to your own personal cyberbash. Welcome to the world wild web of Virtual Places. Someone had to do it; combining the virtually infinite spaces of the World Wide Web with the unlimited ability of Internet citizens to chat. Virtual Places lets you cruise the Web cosmos in style. So what are we waiting for? Let's go surfin'.

Virtual Places on the Macintosh.

The Virtual Places Communities

Virtual Places (VP) has an interesting history. Created by an Israeli company named Ubique (which continues to develop VP to this day), it was first hosted by GNN, an *Internet service provider* in Berkeley, California in late 1995. At about the same time, America Online (AOL) entered the picture. AOL already had a very successful business with chat rooms (30 to 40 percent of their customers' on-line time was spent chatting), and it needed a visual avatar chat space. AOL bought Virtual Places (and ultimately bought GNN), so Ubique built a completely integrated version of VP which runs inside AOL. Lastly (or at least when this chapter was written), Ubique brought out another new version of VP (version 2.1) that runs as a separate application with Microsoft Internet Explorer. This version is hosted at **http://talk.excite.com**, and is a follow-up to the original 1.0 version that runs with Netscape Navigator. More versions of VP are emerging, which will give you plenty of choices!

Which community should you select?

If you subscribe to America Online, and you do not have any other connection to the Internet, you should choose the AOL version (this works best with version 3.0 of AOL for Windows 95). If you have a direct connection to the Internet, and you are using a Macintosh, and have Netscape 2.0.2 or later, you should go with version 1.0. If you have a Macintosh with Internet Explorer 3.0, try the Excite VP. If you have a PC with Windows 3.1 or 3.11, and any version of Netscape Navigator, try version 1.0. If you have a PC with Windows 95 and Internet Explorer 3.0 or higher, and a connection to the Internet, try version 2.0 or Excite's VP version 2.1. Excite is an on-line service that supports Web searching and has recently branched out into chat and online communities.

The AOL versions of VP tend to have more moderation and parental controls in place. The open communities tend to be more of a free-for-all.

Community characteristics

VP VERSION	COMMUNITY	HOST SITE	USER POPULATION	COMMENTS
AOL Version 2.0	Virtual Places for America Online	Log on to AOL and go to keyword: VP	Averages 700 to 1,500 members during peak hours	Best viewed with AOL 3.0 for Windows 95
Excite Version 2.1	Excite's VP	Download from http://talk.excite.com	Averages 300 to 500-plus members during peak hours	Beta, works with Internet Explorer 3.0
Internet Version 2.0	Small but growing community hosted by VPchat	Download from www.vpchat.com	Averages 100 to 250-plus members during peak hours	Requires Internet Explorer 3.0 or later
Internet Version 1.0	The earlier VP chat client and community on the Internet	Find it also at www.vpchat.com	Averages 250 to 500 members during peak hours	Best viewed with Netscape 3.0

Just want pure chat?

The good folks at Virtual Places have created their own version of Virtual Places in Java. This version does not support avatars, just pure chat and group tours of Web sites. It is much easier to get started in this kind of chat and then move on to avatar worlds if you really dig the experience. If you want to experience VP's Java Chat, just point your Java-enabled Web browser (Netscape Navigator 3.0 or Microsoft Internet Explorer 3.0) at **http://talk.excite.com**, and select "Go right to live chat." In about 30 seconds you will be chatting.

Installing and Downloading Virtual Places

What do I need to use Virtual Places?

Installing

To use Virtual Places, you need either a PC with a 486 processor and Windows 3.1, or a Macintosh with a 68030 processor and Mac OS version 7.5.3 or higher. There are many flavors of Virtual Places (as you saw in the preceding section) which may require more powerful computers. If you are an America Online subscriber, you can get into Virtual Places directly through AOL. If you have a direct connection to the Internet (dial-up or local network) you can use the other versions of VP listed in the "Community characteristics" table.

Software and connection requirements

Along with the Virtual Places client software, you must run a Web browser, such as the browser in AOL, Netscape, or Internet Explorer. Various versions of VP work with various browsers, so check the preceding table to match the appropriate browser to the VP version you use. You can get your Virtual Places client software from the CD-ROM in this book, download it directly from the Internet, or get it through AOL.

If you use another on-line service such as CompuServe, Microsoft Network, or Prodigy, you may be able to use an open (non-AOL) version of VP if your on-line service supports direct Internet access through the 32-bit *Winsock*. (Short for Windows Sockets, Winsock is a standard interface for Microsoft Windows applications and the Internet. Winsocks allow communication between Windows Web browsers, e-mail clients, IRC clients, or any other Windows Winsock applications and the TCP/IP). See, "Setting up your on-line service to connect directly with the Internet," in Appendix B. If you have further problems, contact your on-line service for help.

Getting started and a few disclaimers

Virtual Places is free to use (you have to accept the terms of your free license during installation). You are not charged for the time you spend exploring or interacting in VP, but you could be charged for the hours you are online from your *Internet service provider (ISP)* or from America Online (if you are using AOL VP). Check with your ISP or AOL on monthly free hours and rates. Of course, you should remember that you are also charged by your telephone company for using the phone line while you are using a modem.

Help

Virtually up-to-date

As a special service for readers of *Avatars!*, I have a home page on the World Wide Web devoted to keeping you up-to-date on your favorite worlds. Find news about software updates, social events held within these virtual worlds, and brand new worlds you might want to try at http://www.digitalspace.com/avatars. Bookmark it!

More about the companion CD software

Virtual Places is constantly evolving, and may have changed since this chapter was written. I included the very latest versions of Virtual Places on your book CD, and they may be somewhat different from what is described here. These differences will not be major, and this chapter will still be a great guide to Virtual Places and its worlds. If you see new features or changes, check for information under the Help menu in Virtual Places.

If you have questions or problems

If you have questions or problems installing or running Virtual Places, consult the "Frequently Asked Questions (FAQ)," on the companion Web site to this book. If this does not help, check the Virtual Places home page at **http://www.vplaces.com/vpnet**, especially the excellent tutorial at **http://www.vplaces.com/vpnet/support**. You can find a reference guide, technical support, and release notes at **http://www.vplaces.com/vpnet/help/**. Another important page for VP users is **http://www.vpchat.com/**, which contains avatars, gestures, help sections, and pointers to all available versions of VP.

To report a bug to the VP folks, simply fill out the bug report form for the version you are using on the Web site at **http://www.vplaces.com/vpnet**.

I appreciate your feedback on *Avatars!*, but I don't have the resources to provide technical support. I would be happy to hear about your experiences in Virtual Places. Contact me through the *Avatars!* book Web site at **http://www.digitalspace.com/avatars**.

UNIX and OS/2 versions

At this writing, there are no versions of Virtual Places client program for UNIX or OS/2. Check the Virtual Places and *Avatars!* book Web pages for updates on new versions which might support these platforms. You also may be able to run the Virtual Places client using a Windows emulation system on non-Windows machines. Note that if you are considering hosting your own Virtual Places community, the Virtual Places community server runs on standard UNIX platforms, and connects with any version of VP on Windows or the Macintosh.

Installing Virtual Places from your Avatars! CD

If you have a CD-ROM drive on your PC or Macintosh, you can install Virtual Places directly from the book CD-ROM. If you don't have a CD-ROM drive, skip to the section, "Installing or upgrading Virtual Places from the Internet," later in this chapter. In the chapter, "The Book CD-ROM," I provide step-by-step instructions for installing software from the CD-ROM. Refer to this chapter, and then follow the same steps for Virtual Places. Once the installation program on your CD-ROM has started, you can return to this chapter to the section, "Running the installation."

Installing Virtual Places through America Online

If you use AOL and wish to use Virtual Places directly inside AOL, follow these steps to get chatting in the Web cosmos under AOL:

1 Start and log on to AOL.

2 Go to keyword (select the Go To menu and keyword, or press Ctrl+K on a PC, or Command-K on a Mac).

3 Enter the letters VP and press Go. You will be presented with an AOL Virtual Places dialogue. You can take a sneak preview of VP or avatars, or just go to Explore Virtual Places Now.

4 AOL will present you with more dialogue boxes, explaining terms of service, and then you can begin downloading the Virtual Places software. This will take between 20 minutes and an hour, depending on the speed of your connection.

5 Once the download is finished, AOL will prompt you to install VP. VP will run and download further components (mostly artwork), and then start. You will be asked to enter your personal information and set your avatar. This procedure is pretty much the same in all versions of VP, and it is covered in a section called, "Your First Steps into the Web Cosmos," later in this chapter.

Installing or upgrading Virtual Places from the Internet

If you want the very latest Internet version of Virtual Places, or were informed that you had to upgrade the version found on your *Avatars!* CD, then you must download files from the Internet. If you haven't done this before, don't panic; it is easier than you might think!

❶ Connect to the Internet (dial up with your modem or make sure your Internet connection is active).

❷ Start your Web browser, such as Netscape or Internet Explorer.

❸ In the top of the browser, you will see a text box called Location, where you can enter text.

❹ Click in this box, delete the text inside, type **http://www.vplaces.com/vpnet**, and press Enter. After a few moments, the home page for Virtual Places should appear. If nothing comes up for a long time, check to see that you are online. You can also try VPchat.com's home page at **http://www.vpchat.com**. If you are downloading the version of VP for Excite, get it from **http://talk.excite.com**.

❺ If the Virtual Places or other home pages are not available for some reason, try entering the location for the *Avatars!* book home page, which is at **http://www.digitalspace.com/avatars**. This page may contain more up-to-date links for Virtual Places.

❻ Once you are at the Virtual Places home page, follow the instructions for downloading or upgrading the Virtual Places software for your particular platform (Windows 3.11, Windows 95, or Macintosh) and your particular Web browser (Netscape 2.0, 3.0, or 4.0, or Internet Explorer 3.0 or 4.0). At one point, you will click on a link and be prompted for a place to save a file. In response to the dialogue box, click Save to Disk (Netscape) or Save As (Internet Explorer), and save the file to a subdirectory folder or a place on your desktop. You must choose a folder where you will remember to find the new file, and note the name of the file. You can use the folder that your Web browser gives you or move back up and select another. I put all downloaded files in a folder I call \download. Wait patiently while the download progresses (about 2MB to 3MB). You can do work in other applications, but be careful not to interfere with the connection. Try not to do more on-line work (such as Web surfing) while the download is progressing, and if you are using your regular telephone line, don't make a call.

❼ Macintosh-specific instruction: After you download the file (which should have the suffix .hqx), Netscape should unpack it to a file called VP Installer.

If Netscape has a problem expanding the .hqx file, you can get a free copy of StuffIt Expander from various Web sites, including Aladdin Systems at **http://www.aladdinsys.com/consumer/expander2.html**. This expander can be used to produce the file called VP Installer, self-extracting—just double-click on it to produce the VP Installer.

❽ After the download is finished (30 to 50 minutes for a 28.8 kbps connection, and about twice that long for a 14.4 kbps connection), open the folder into which the file was downloaded, and double-click on the file to start the installation. Go to the following section, "Running the installation."

Running the installation

Whether you are running the installation from the CD-ROM or from the file you downloaded from the Internet, use this section to guide you through the installation. Note that if you downloaded Virtual Places from the Internet, the installation process may have changed. If this has happened, refer to the instructions on the Virtual Places Web site. The following are installation instructions for both the PC and Macintosh platforms.

For the PC

❶ Double-click on the file to start the installation.

❷ InstallShield should start and bring up an interface to install VP.

❸ Read and accept the terms of the license agreement (if you do not, the installation will stop).

❹ Accept the folder into which VP and its settings will be installed and the other settings. InstallShield will then install the files onto your hard disk.

❺ You will be prompted to start VP at the end of the installation. If you have the Web browser for this version of VP, and you are connected to the Internet, you can choose to start VP now.

For the Macintosh

❶ Double-click on the VP Installer file which was downloaded and expanded.

❷ Read and accept the terms of the license agreement (if you do not, the installation will stop). The Virtual Places folder, called VPlaces x.x (where x.x is the version number), will be installed by the MindVision VISE installer, which handles installation on your hard disk. You can change the folder's location if you wish.

Memory requirements for the PC

PCs generally require 8MB of RAM for VP and your Web browser, although 16MB is recommended (especially if you are running Windows 95).

Memory requirements for the Macintosh

Virtual Places requires 3MB of RAM (4MB is recommended), and works with a Web browser which requires an additional 8MB of RAM. In the current beta version of the Macintosh software, there is no support for the Microsoft Internet Explorer browser. A future release of the software will support Internet Explorer.

You may need to use virtual memory for VP to work on your Macintosh. Check your Macintosh documentation for instructions on using virtual memory on your computer.

Files created by the installation

If you are running Windows 95, a shortcut to Virtual Places will be placed on your desktop as well as a folder called \program files\vplaces. In Windows 3.1, you will find VP in a program group called Virtual Places and a directory called \vplaces. On the Macintosh you can find VP in a folder called Vplaces.

Cleaning up after installation

If you downloaded the Virtual Places installation file from the Internet, you can delete it after the installation is complete. Do not delete the Virtual Places program you just installed by mistake.

First Steps

Your First Steps into the Web Cosmos

Step 1: Starting up Virtual Places

As there are many versions of VP for different platforms, there are many ways to start the program.

Starting VP in Windows 3.11

1. Locate the Virtual Places program group.

2. Double-click on the VPlaces icon.

Starting VP in Windows 95

Double-click on the shortcut to Virtual Places (or Talk! by Excite) or choose Start ⇨ Programs ⇨ Virtual Places.

Starting VP on the Macintosh

Double-click on the VP icon on your desktop or in the folder in which you installed VP.

As I describe the VP interface, I will be using the open community under VP 2.0 and 2.1. I will occasionally show screens from the AOL version. Most VP versions are so similar that you should have no trouble with the descriptions here matching your version.

Step 2: Creating your identity

In all versions of VP, you will be asked to create your identity. This involves filling out a few dialogue boxes and choosing your starting avatar.

Fill out the Identity dialogue to immigrate to Virtual Places.

As the adjacent figure shows, the Identity dialogue is pretty simple. You have to fill in your nickname and your e-mail address. The other information is optional. The second tab in this dialogue allows you to give more information about yourself, such as gender, hobbies, etc. In the AOL version, your identity is already tied to your AOL screen name.

Next, you should select your own avatar. You could, of course, stay with the default avatar (the masked man), but who wants to be walking around looking like some kind of strange face on Mars? You can select your avatar from the stock library or personal library. Stock avatars are provided by Virtual Places, but these are pretty generic looking. Personal avatars have more character, and you can import custom-made avatars from several personal avatar libraries on the Web, or by scanning them in from pictures or artwork. I detail how to do this later in the chapter.

Note that you can always change your avatar and identity at a later time. Simply right-click (click and hold on the Macintosh) on your avatar and select Identity.

Select an avatar from the Personal Avatars dialogue.

Step 3: Attaching to the browser

After you have started Virtual Places and created your identity, it should have started your Web browser and then automatically connected to the default community server. This "attach to the browser" phase is important, as VP cannot run without a Web browser. Versions 2.0 and 2.1 run entirely within Internet Explorer 3.0. The AOL version starts up a Web browser inside AOL itself. The other versions start Netscape on its own and build windows around it to provide the interface. If VP cannot attach to a Web browser, you may have to reinstall that browser. Make sure you have the right browser and right version installed for your version of VP (see the "Community characteristics" table earlier in this chapter).

Step 4: Connecting to a community server and entering a room

Next, the VP software will attempt to connect to a community server and bring up the Web page associated with the entry chat room for that server. After that, VP will try to place your avatar into the entry room for that community.

If you cannot connect to a community server, or if a room is full, I recommend that you try again later, as the server may be down. If you cannot join the entry room for that community server, you will be presented with a dialogue box called the Places Directory (also called the Places Selector). This will allow you to select and go to a room that is not full. There is a room occupancy limit of 25, which keeps the pace of chat down to a readable level. If you want to wait for a chance to enter the full room, you can cancel the Places Directory dialogue and opt to become an observer.

The Preferences option under your Tools menu will also let you change the default Web page, and the Community Servers options allow you to set the community you want to enter when you first connect to Virtual Places.

Step 5: Joining the community

If all has gone well to this point, you should be looking at a scene much like the one in the following figure. This is the mixed community server Virtual Places 2.0 lobby. It is an open VP community running in Microsoft Internet Explorer 3.0. The first thing you will notice is several windows. In the upper left is a Web browser window, showing normal Web pages. Below that is the Chat window, for the threads of chats in the current room, or on the selected Web tour. To the right is the People window, listing the nicknames of all the avatars in the current room, the avatars not able to get into the room and observing, and the active Web tours.

The Virtual Places
open community 2.0
for Windows 95.

Entering or exiting a room

If you are an observer, and want to enter the room (if the number of participants falls below 25), you can right-click (or click and hold, on the Macintosh) on your name under Observers and choose Enter Room. Alternately, you can click on the Enter Room icon on the toolbar across the top of the Virtual Places program. If you are in a chat room and wish to become an observer, just right-click on your avatar and select Exit Room.

Observers cannot chat in the room, but they can watch all the activity and wait for a chance to enter the room. Remember, even if you are an observer, you are not hidden; anyone can click on the Other Observers icon in the People window and see your nickname listed there.

Room occupancy limits

To keep screen crowding to a minimum, Virtual Places limits the number of avatars and chat participants on a Web page to 25, and automatically opens the Places Directory window when you arrive at a full room. You can still watch the action, but you can't chat or put your avatar on the page. All is not lost, however. You can exchange IMs with any person on the screen. You can check the All Places window to find out where others are hanging out and seek action elsewhere. Or you can wait for a vacancy in the room and fill it.

It's All About Communicating

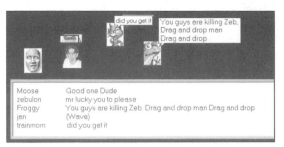

There's an avatar crush one fine day in VP chat space.

Now that you are in a room, it's time to start doing what everyone is here to do: communicate! To chat, simply click in the text entry area, type some text, and press Send (or press Enter on your keyboard). In a second or two (depending on how much chat is going on), your words should appear above your avatar in a cartoon bubble. Note that as you start typing, a small bubble appears over your avatar.

This tiny bubble is very handy and indicates to others that your are composing a new message or reply. As the following figure shows, VP chat can get dramatic, (the avatars are trying to rescue some poor fellow being crushed by another avvie).

Moving your avatar around

As the preceding figure suggests, you can move your avatar by simply clicking the left mouse button down (clicking and holding the mouse button, on the Macintosh), dragging your avatar around, and dropping it somewhere inside the Web page window. Other people will see your avatar move suddenly some seconds after you drop it. Be careful about dropping your avatar right down on top of someone else's, as this is considered rude.

Gestures

If you want to send an emotion along with your message, click on the Gestures button on the right-hand side of the text entry area. There is a palette of gestures and emotions (see the adjacent figure). Picking one of these gestures will ensure that it flows out with your next message (like the hand-waving good-bye shown).

The VP gestures selector—say it with panache!

You can double-click right on the gesture palette to preview what a gesture will do. Try to avoid testing gestures where people are conversing. It can make things very confusing. These are not the only gestures available to you. Some VeePsters (the name for pro users of Virtual Places, discussed later in this chapter) have begun to build others.

Hand-waving good-byes.

Sending an instant message to someone

You can initiate a chat with someone using instant messaging in several ways:

- Click on their avatar with the right mouse button and select Send Instant Message.

- Select Send an Instant Message from the Tools menu.

- Drag and drop your avatar onto the other person's avatar.

- Click on the person's nickname entry in the People window and press the IM icon at the bottom of the People window.

If the user agrees to the chat in this way, they will type something in response and send it back to you. Instant messaging is a kind of private conversation. Note also that if you are an observer you can still send instant messages to other observers.

The Instant Message dialogue.

Ignoring someone

If you are really being bothered by someone, you can ignore them by following these simple steps:

1. Right-click on that person's avatar.

2. Select Ignore from the menu.

From this point on you will not see their chat (and they will not know you have ignored them, either).

Saving chat transcripts

If you want to save the last chat you had since you entered a room, you can save it to a text file using the following steps:

1. Click on the Room or Group tab (at the bottom of the chat area).

2. Right-click (or click and hold, on the Macintosh) in the Chat window and choose Save As from the menu (you can also choose Save Dialogue As from the File menu).

3. Fill in file name and click on the OK button to save the chat transcript.

Finding someone

To find someone in the chat room or any other room in this VP community, simply follow these steps:

1. Choose Find from the Tools menu, or click on the Locate icon at the bottom of the People window.

2. Type in the nickname, or first name, or last name, or e-mail address of the person you are trying to find. You can even enter the first few letters of the name, and VP will find all people with similar names.

3. You will be presented with a dialogue box (see adjacent figure) which lists all people found and their corresponding locations (if they are in VP at the moment). You can then send them an instant message or go to their location. This Locate feature is a very important social interface in VP.

Locate someone in the community.

Finding out about someone

If you want to find out about someone you are chatting with, just right-click (or click and hold, on the Macintosh) on their avatar and select Identity, and you will see a dialogue box like the one in the figure on the right. Whether you choose to *believe* what people write in as their identities is another story!

Selecting someone's avatar helps reveal their identity.

The cowboy seems like he is a true bronco buster!

Finishing off the interface: The VP menus

The menus at the top of your Virtual Places program window allow you to perform many functions quickly, and access advanced services. Note that I am describing the menus for VP version 2.0, running the open communities. The menus may be slightly different for your version of VP.

- The *File* menu allows you to Enter Room, Attach to Browser (which is usually done automatically), Close Instant Message, Save the current chat log, and Exit.

- The *Edit* menu has the basic Copy, Past, and Clear commands.

- The *Go* menu controls normal Web navigation functions such as returning to previously visited Web pages.

- The *Avatars* menu allows you to set controls for your avatar. Here you can edit your identity, flip your avatar horizontally or vertically, or set the mood of your avatar (some avatars come in sets of views, which assign an avatar picture to a particular mood). If your avatar has a set of moods, you will be able to choose between them here. You can also toggle Show Avatars (to show or hide all the avatars). Lastly, the Avatars menu lets you switch between large and small avatars. If there is a big crowd in a chat room, small avatars may be better.

- The *Guided Tours* menu has a Set Up a Tour command, letting you choose a tour size, icon, and name for the tour. You can then select Guide a Tour, which puts your Tour icon in the current VP room with you as the driver. If you are a passenger on a tour, and you somehow get left behind (if you get off the tour and it moves on), the Sychronize with Tour option will usually get you back on the tour that dumped you.

- The *Games* menu will be used to plug games into VP (this was not yet implemented in VP at the time this chapter was written).

- The *Tools* menu lets you choose and connect to your community server, open the Places Directory (also done via an icon on the toolbar), send an IM (instant message) to someone whose nickname you know but is not visible, find someone on VP whose nickname you know (you can then IM them, see their Identity, or Go to the URL where they are located), set a parental control password to keep your kids from using VP without your approval, and set several preferences for VP. Note that the Start Audio/Video option is not yet working in the current versions.

- The *View* menu hides or shows the Gestures palette, and allows you to enlarge the chat window in case you want to see more chat and less Web and avatars. You can use the Reset the View settings and save them if you like.

- The *Help* menu will bring up Web pages, including a complete manual for using Virtual Places.

Taking the Grand Tour

Navigating around in the VP Web cosmos

In Virtual Places, every Web page becomes a kind of simple virtual world, a backdrop on top of which the drama of avatars can be played out. You can bring avatars to your own Web pages by running a guided tour, which I describe in this section. If your page becomes a popular spot to hang out, it will start appearing toward the top of the Places Directory. The more people visit your Web page, the more they will want to get in. This sets up a kind of snowball effect. Some people have set up Web pages just having interesting backdrops, such as romantic scenes for virtual weddings. These Web pages (VP Spaces) are listed in the "Hot Sites in VP Land" section, later in this chapter.

The VP toolbar

The Virtual Places toolbar, sitting at the top of the window just under the menus, is your key to navigating Virtual Places spaces. As with the menus, I am describing the toolbar icons for VP version 2.0 running in the open communities. These icons may be slightly different (in different positions) on your version of VP.

The toolbar in Virtual Places.

- The first four buttons from the left will move you forward and back, and let you stop or reload Web pages you have visited during this VP session.

- The Home button will take you back to the home page associated with this community.

- Favorite Places will bring up a menu that allows you to set pointers (called *bookmarks* or *favorites*) to some of the Web page rooms that you like most. You can then click on Favorite Places and quickly re-enter those rooms.

- The Enter Room icon will move your avatar out of the Observers list into the current room (if the room is not full).

- Places to Chat will bring up the Places Directory, shown earlier in this chapter. From the Places Directory, you can go to new chat spaces within the current VP community server, join active tours, or see how many people are in every chat space. To see all active chat spaces (with at least one avatar in them), you must click on the All Places tab. Cool Places, Special Events, and your previously selected Favorite Places can also be listed in the Places Directory. Once you have selected a place, you will be connected. The small file folder tabs at the lower left-hand corner of the screen will then list the chat room you are in, and other tabs for What's Hot (announced activities), and active tours.

- The Layout icon allows you to select alternate layouts, like showing just the Web page or just the chat, or returning to the classic Virtual Places layout. The View menu described previously has similar options.

- The question mark (?) icon will take you to VP help documents.

Web touring—an important social activity in VP

In this section, I describe how to tour the Web in style through Virtual Places. Setting up or joining a Web tour is easy, and it is one of the most unique and powerful features of VP.

Start a guided tour by selecting the Guided Tours menu and the Set Up a Tour option. You will be presented with a dialogue box like the one in the adjacent figure. You can set the name of your tour, and the size of the tour. I always choose the 11-person "Peace Bus" (this is my name for it because I live in an old hippie zone in Northern California).

Preparing to host a tour in the Set Up a Tour dialogue.

After you set up your tour, select Guide a Tour from the Guided Tours menu, and your bus will appear in the chat room for all to see. As you can see from the following figure, my bus is pretty obvious, but it remains a challenge to convince people to join my

The tour bus preparing for departure.

tour. I sometimes spend several minutes calling out, like a hawker in a market, "join a great tour to avatar worlds . . . bus is departing in two minutes." After awhile, depending on how adventurous the current crop of avatars feels, people will start appearing on your bus. To join a tour, all you have to do is simply drag and drop your avatar onto the tour vehicle. You can also right-click (or click and hold, on the Macintosh) on the tour vehicle, and select Join from the menu that appears.

It's a miracle—no it's server push!

When you decide to pull your bus out of the Web station, a miraculous thing happens. As soon as you enter a new Web address, and your Web browser window in Virtual Places moves to that site, the other people on the tour will start seeing the same Web page. This is the miracle of *server push,* which means that your travels are pushing Web pages to your tour group through their Web browsers.

I always take groups of avatars to the Avatar Teleport (your book home page at **http://www.digitalspace.com/avatars**), because this is a gateway to all avatar worlds, and these people are probably interested in avatar worlds! On this particular tour, I took the group to the overhead "satellite" image of the AlphaWorld cityscape. This is located at **http://kozmo .yakima.net/alphaworld/teleport.html**. Nobody could believe that this was an image of a huge 3D avatar city. Some of my tour mates jumped ship and started exploring, and I was left with only tim28 and tinkerbell.

Flying high in a VP bus over the AlphaWorld cityscape—hello, Sherwood Towne!

You can end a tour by choosing Stop Tour from the Guided Tours menu. Anyone can leave your tour by simply dragging their

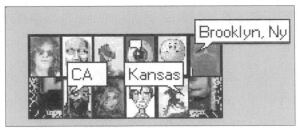

Where is everybody from? A common question on board a tour.

avatar's icon off your vehicle. They will then be free to explore the Web page upon which they landed.

Tours are very popular activities in VP, and some are regularly scheduled by VP citizens (VeePsters, as they are known). Many tours have a theme, such as science and nature, where Web sites featuring great science pages are visited. If you are a kid, parent, or just an unsuspecting VeePster, ask the tour guides where they are going before you join. Unscrupulous VeePsters have been known to run porno tours.

Getting dumped

If you are a passenger on a tour and you somehow get dumped (i.e., you got off the bus and then it pulled out of town), you can select Synchronize with Tour (on the Guided Tour menu), and this will usually bring you back to the group.

The tour garage

On the Set Up a Tour dialogue, you can select the Change button and change the picture of the tour vehicle. This will take you to a tour garage, which is a directory of GIF files. You can copy any GIF file into this directory (which is set in the Tools menu Preferences dialogue box), and it can be used as the tour vehicle. The GIF files must measure 48 by 40 pixels for small tours; and 144 by 64 pixels for large tours. Graphics of up to 150 by 75 pixels in GIF format will be adjusted to these sizes.

Parental Controls and Community Behavior in Virtual Places

Parental controls

Virtual Places, like any chat environment, can fall prey to the lowest common denominator. If people become bored, they often drift into more banal forms of conversation. In addition, some parts of VP come with their fair share of "naked pix" avatars. If you are a parent, you may want to set a password to restrict your children's access to VP. Do this by choosing Parental Control from the Tools menu. You can block access to VP unless you are there to supervise. Think of it as one of those TV channel blockers that screen out certain TV shows from kids, or restrict their viewing hours.

Community behavior

Some VP communities have moderators or published community rules which tell people the behavior expected of them. As with parental controls, nobody can stop certain behaviors if someone really wants to be obnoxious. The best defense is a strong community. If you don't like what is happening, speak up! Recruit others to speak up, too; you might be surprised to find out that they share your feelings. Remember the old saying: It only takes one bad apple to spoil the cider.

In the America Online versions of VP, you are expected to follow their terms of service (in AOL, go to keyword TOS). If you violate these, you could be kicked off your AOL account, so be careful. You can report offensive Web pages (to which someone may be leading tours) to AOL by sending an e-mail to **tosweb@aol.com** with the Web page URL.

As is recommended by AOL, but true for every VP community, the best way to deal with offensive members (short of talking them out of it or recruiting help from the community) is to ignore them. To quote America Online's advice below:

> "If you are offended by a member's avatar, chat dialogue, or IMs (Instant Messages), you can choose to ignore a member. To do this in a Windows version, simply right-click on the offending member's avatar and choose Ignore from the pop-up menu (that avatar will now appear to you as a generic face, their dialogue will be hidden from you, and their IMs blocked). The same can be achieved on the Macintosh version by command-clicking on the offending avatar to bring up the menu. If you receive unwanted IMs and prefer to block all IMs, you can choose to ignore all of them. Simply select the Tools menu and Preferences and turn off IMs on the General Preference dialogue box."

Meet the VeePsters

In this section, you will meet some of the *VeePsters,* or dedicated veteran users of Virtual Places. Their stories illustrate the kind of masterpieces you can paint on the canvas of the World Wide Web when you are part of a strong community.

Meet the
Natives

The story of Webtown

Webtown is a community set up so that VeePsters (citizens in the Virtual Places universe) can share a common Web space, newsgroups, and an event calendar. One of the great features of Webtown is its VP apartments. This is a great Web site, hosted by CyberSurfer, which allows you to select components and fit them together into an "apartment" (or flats, for you members of the former British Empire). After filling out some forms and pushing buttons to select your furniture, the view out of the window (and even what is in the refrigerator), you are presented with your very own Web page which shows the image of your custom-built apartment.

The following figure shows my apartment in VP Towers West, complete with a view of the Golden Gate Bridge in San Francisco (I wish I could afford such an apartment in real life!). I superimposed the view of my refrigerator (which is shown on another part of my Web site) in the lower right, and included my life's motto and favorite Web sites. Thousands of people have created their own apartments in VP Towers and other parts of the CyberSurfer Webtown site. After creating your apartment, you can invite friends there by simply running Virtual Places and taking them (through their avatars) to this Web site. Events held in Webtown residences are often posted on the Webtown site.

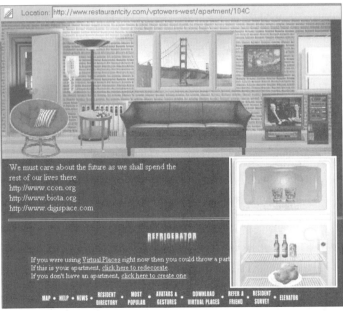

This is my apartment in VP Towers, Webtown.

Find Webtown@VP at **http://www.cyberclay.com/webtown/**, the *Webtown News* at **http://freeweb.nethead.co.uk/Devalin/Webtown/news.htm**, and CyberSurfer Studios' Restaurant City & Web Towers (VP apartments) at **http://www.restaurantcity.com/**.

Gekko and Webtown

Nabih Saiba, or Gekko, as he is known in Virtual Places, is the original creator of Webtown. He has agreed to tell his story for readers of *Avatars!*

Nabih Saliba, the creator of Webtown.

"Hello,

I'm the guy who created Webtown. CyberClay (which housed the site) is a Web design firm that was just getting started a little over a year ago. I was a consultant for them as well as a designer. I stumbled across Virtual Places one day when there were only about zero to 15 people using the beta software. It was great! After using the client for about two hours, I thought, "Hey! What a great tool for building a community," and set to work on Webtown version 1.0. At first, it was nothing more than five stark pages with names denoting some form of location. Then I ran Web tours like mad trying to get people to explore the possibility of forming a true on-line community; one we could build, promote, and manage ourselves. It worked, as I found I was not alone in this dream. Like true pioneers, people using handles like The Q, Editrix, Stu, and Wyvern, banded together in a cyberfrontier to build a community of Web sites. Our virtual town grew rapidly from 10 or 15 to a total population of almost 500 within the space of three months.

Gekko's Virtual Places avatar.

The beauty of combining chat with Web browsing is that the power to create interactive environments is extremely simple. Webtown was founded on the principle that anyone could build anything and link it into the spirit of a unified community. Since its inception, there have been many Virtual Places Web sites created by those that know and love the software. As my personal career occupied more of my time, I had to limit my involvement with Webtown. It's still out there doing its thing, and I hope people still find enjoyment in its pages, and interactive wonder with Virtual Places. The Web is plenty big for all of us and the spirit and culture of online communities will continue to bring the human touch to a sterile technology. As Gekko used to say in his profile, 'Take from life what is pure, and for living what is sufficient.'"

Nabih Saliba
a.k.a. Gekko

For Pro VeePsters

Pro or veteran VeePsters frequently sport their own avatars. Making your own avatar is simple. Use a paint program or scanner to create an image. You must make a GIF file out of this image (just a plain old GIF, not the transparent kind). This GIF file cannot be any larger than 48 by 64 pixels.

Design tips when making an avatar

Virtual Places and America Online have provided the following tips for building your own avatar in VP:

- Try not to make the image too complex, and avoid a lot of detail (it will be lost at this size).

- Try to avoid multicolored schemes.

- Head shots work best.

- Create big images, then size them down to 48 by 64 pixels.

- Keep TOS (Terms of Service . . . common decency) standards in mind.

Tools often used to make images for avatars include:

- AOL's built-in image editing feature.

- PaintShop Pro (enter keyword in AOL: PaintShop Pro). You can also download PaintShop Pro from the Internet (there is a shareware version available) at **http://www.jasc.com/psp.html**.

- JASC Image commander (keyword: JASC).

- Adobe Photoshop from Adobe Systems Inc.

- An image scanner to transform an image from paper into pixels and then edit it using the above tools.

All you have to do is make a GIF file with the above specifications and place it into your personal avatar folder. The location of this folder is set in the directories section of the Preferences dialogue, found under the Tools menu. For example, in Windows 95, this personal avatars folder is located at: \program files\vplaces\exts\gallery.

Note also that if you are using the 32-bit VP client, the stock avatars that came with your VP client have moods. Point your mouse at your stock avatar and click the right mouse button (or click and hold on the Macintosh). Choose the mood you want from the pull-down menu, and your avatar's expression changes instantly. Moods are currently not supported for personal avatars.

Avatar galleries

You can get plenty of pre-made avatars from dozens of avatar galleries created by VeePster users on the Net. VP maintains a listing of galleries at **http://www.vplaces.com/vpnet/support/support2.html**. See the section "Hot Sites in VP Land," at the end of this chapter for a comprehensive list of avatar galleries and VeePsters who build avatars. Visiting these galleries and selecting an avatar is easy. Simply go to the Web page, select the image you like with the right mouse button (or click and hold, on the Macintosh) and save the image into the directory or folder indicated in the Preferences dialogue under the Tools menu.

Private rooms and auditoriums

A recently added feature now allows private rooms and auditoriums. To view an auditorium, see "Digi's Diary," at the end of this chapter. Private rooms are a new feature which is not yet finished in versions of VP documented for this book. It should be complete by the time you have this book.

Other webworlds

Virtual Places is often referred to as a *webworld*. Webworlds are virtual worlds in that they have people represented as avatars or chat handles in a shared space. Webworlds are also unique in that the backdrop for the community is built out of Web pages. Webworlds are easily built as citizens just link in their own home pages. Common styles, icons, and means of navigation characterize webworlds. VP and Webtown are not the only webworlds. In Appendix A, you can read about De Digitale Stad, one of the original webworlds.

Fine-Tuning Your World

There many options to fine-tune VP, allowing you to configure your community server, general settings, and the places where VP gets all its resources. It is possible to host your own Virtual Places community, but this is beyond the scope of this book. I suggest you visit the virtual places home page at **http://www.vplaces.com/vpnet/index.html** to find out more.

Configuring Virtual Places community servers

A community server provides its community with co-presence capabilities for the entire World Wide Web. For example, using such a server on AOL, AOL members can meet on any Web page in the world, chat, and go on guided tours of the Web together. People may belong to multiple communities, depending on their interests. You can configure a community server for each community of which you are a member.

How the community server works

If Virtual Places can attach to an appropriate Web browser, the following occurs:

1. The Communications Manager is automatically tied with the Web browser and the People Manager.

2. You are automatically connected to the default community server. (You can change communities and set a different default community at any time during the session.)

3. Your Web browser navigates to the default place, as defined in the Preferences dialogue box found in the Tools menu.

4. The Virtual Places indicator is then displayed in the top right-hand corner of the browser window, which means you are live on the Web with Virtual Places.

As the preceding figure shows, you can use the Community Server dialogue to select from a set of servers or modify their settings. Community server management is beyond the scope of this book. Please see the VP home page about this topic and about hosting your own VP community.

Setting Virtual Places preferences

The Preferences dialogue box (found under the Tools menu) contains startup and general settings for Virtual Places. There are two parts to this dialogue box: General and Directories. Following is a description of these settings.

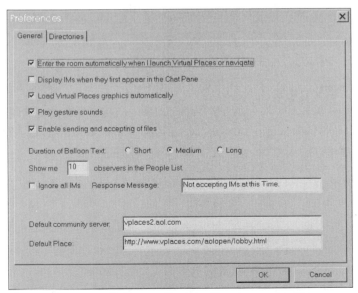

The Preferences dialogue displays the General settings.

General preferences

The General preferences settings inlcude the following:

- Enter room automatically when I launch Virtual Places or navigate: When selected (default), this enters your presence into the room automatically as you navigate from room to room. If deselected, your presence will be as an observer; when you navigate to a new room, you must explicitly enter each room to participate. Note that if you are a passenger on a tour, you will enter the room even if this option is not selected. This prevents you from getting left behind on a tour.

- Display IMs when they first appear in the Chat pane: When selected, Instant Messages, once answered by the recipient, are displayed in the Chat pane, rather than in a stand-alone window.

- Load Virtual Places graphics automatically: When selected (default), the avatars of people in the room are automatically loaded. If deselected, the avatars are not loaded from the Virtual Places server, and you must select Retrieve Picture from the shortcut menu on someone else's presence.

- Play gesture sounds: This determines whether you want to hear accompanying sounds for gestures. Sound is not available for default gestures.

- Enable sending and accepting of files: This allows you to send and accept avatars, gestures, and other files.

- Duration of balloon text: This determines how long the display of chat text is displayed in the Web browser window. The options are: short, medium, and long, where short is four seconds, medium is six seconds, and long is eight seconds.

- Show me nnn observers in the People List: This determines the number of observers displayed in the People pane, where nnn is the number of observers. The maximum number of observers allowed is 200.

- Ignore all IMs: Select this to ignore all Instant Messages and send the response message defined in the Response Message field.

- Response Message: A message sent in response to an IM received when Virtual Places is set to ignore all IMs. The default message is: Not accepting IM at this time.

- Default Community Server: The name of your default community server (for example, vps1.arena1.aol.com). When you open Virtual Places, it automatically connects to this community server.

- Default Place: The initial URL displayed by the Web browser when Virtual Places is launched, and when selecting Home from the Go menu.

Directories preferences

Directories preferences determine where Virtual Places gets it resources. They include the following:

- Stock Avatar Gallery: The directory containing the graphics for your avatar. The graphics in this directory are displayed in the avatar gallery when you select Stock when changing your avatar picture. The default is \vplaces\exts\gallery.

- Personal Avatar Gallery: The directory containing graphics for your avatar which you have added. The graphics in this directory are displayed in the Avatar Gallery when you select Personal when changing your avatar picture. The default is \vplaces\exts\gallery.

- Tour Vehicle Gallery: The directory containing the graphics for your tour. The graphics in this directory are displayed in the Tour Garage when you change a tour graphic. The default is \vplaces\exts\tours. Feel free to add GIFs of your own to this directory.

- Gesture Gallery: The directory containing your animated gesture files.

- Community File Pathname: This is your Virtual Places community list file name. This file contains the information you enter when you configure your community servers in the Community Servers dialog box.

- License File Pathname: This is your Virtual Places license file name. There should be no need for you to change the location of your license file.

- Favorite Places List File: This is your Virtual Places list file name. This file contains a list of your favorite Virtual Places as defined in the Places Directory dialogue box.

A note from Santress V (Joanne Ascunsion), creator of Vplace

"The Virtual Hangout was first started in 1995 as an idea inspired by some very kewl VeePsters. It started out as a need for a place to hang out—well, an alternative place to the dreaded start page for VP, anyway. The AV gallery idea was inspired by Shari, who wore the wonderful Gen13 Sarah Rainmaker avatar. (Thank you Shari; it was you who started it all!)

Predawnia Gallery is a super VP resource at http://www.predawnia.com/gallery/index.html. Spellsinger's Place is at http://best-com.com/target.htm, and is a great help facility for VP and links to just about everything concerning VP and avatar galleries. Stormsinger's Virtual Place also has avatars, gestures, tours, and awards, and can be found at http://members.gnn.com/stormsingr/index.htm.

Scenes from the Active Worlds Universe

The East Gate telestation in AlphaWord. This is a grand central teleport hall that takes avatars to distant parts of AlphaWorld. The teleports on the left are outgoing and those on the right are incoming. You can stand here and watch the hustle and bustle of avatar humanity flowing through.

Yellowstone National Park inside Active Worlds, built for the National Park Service by Circle of Fire Studios. This is a beautiful and popular spot to hang out. Watch out for those grizzlies!

Avabar Scene

Roger Zuidema's Avabar Scene shows avatars from a variety of virtual worlds in a digital mixer. As you can see, the bar in the good ship Avatar is a popular place to take a break from the duties of exploring the new worlds of digital space.

Satellite of AlphaWorld Cityscape

An overhead view of the AlphaWorld cityscape. Building started in the summer of 1995 from the central Ground Zero point. The square white border around ground zero is the December 1995 boundary. When the new land was added, growth exploded as new towns, roadways, and forests were created by some of the 200,000 user citizens. Teleport stations fueled growth around popular drop points.

See if you can find the airport, the circular "land art" formations, the freeway, Sherwood Forest Towne, and "Lee's least wandered path," which emerges from Ground Zero and wanders around the entire 1995 AlphaWorld.

First Steps into Digital Space Aboard the Worlds Chat Space Station

A force field in the Worlds Chat observation deck designed to keep "newbies" at bay!

Helen Cho's gingerbread baby avatar arriving at the hub in the Worlds Chat space station. Veteran users strut their stuff in custom designed avatars.

The Social Scene

OZ Virtual street scene with avatars in a virtual Reykjavik, capital of Iceland.

OZ Virtual street scene.

The Wedding of Tomas and Janka in AlphaWorld, May 8, 1996. See their story in the chapter on AlphaWorld and Active Worlds.

Touring Through the Worlds

A stylistic Virtual Paris with teleportation drop sites in Deuxième Monde.

Floating outside Farmer John's house in OZ Virtual.

Flying beneath MTV Tikkiland in Onlive Traveler. This island is home to MTV hosts, and plenty of teen-leaning avatar chat and "boom boxing" music.

Avatar Antics

Avatars doing battle with Ogres and each other in Sierra's The Realm. The avatar which has lost his clothes is waiting for the outcome of the battle, after which he will try to scoop up the loser's belongings!

French avatar in La Deuxième Monde virtual Paris.

Skiing avatars in Titan's Guild Winter Wonderland in Active Worlds. This world features plenty of ski slopes, skating rinks, and a lodge with beer, pizza, and a fireplace to toast chilly avatar feet.

More Avatar Antics

A drama
playing
inside
Neutron.

The Flying Pub
Sisters in
WorldsAway
Dreamscape. A
group of skilled
flying avatars can
do "the wave."

Onlive Traveler Party Scenes

Playing chicken and staring down a Hoofer avatar from Alabama.

Tulips flirting in a float-o-rama high above Condor Summit in Onlive Traveler.

More Onlive Traveler Party Scenes

Big crowd of mostly animal avatars in the Utopia Gateway Plaza.

Mirthful moment while talking with Professor Sandy Stone of the University of Texas at Austin (tigress). We are having a conference with Captain, her trusty tech-op, about setting up a community for the U.T. fall courses.

Biota: Bots and Virtual Pets

Two Norns fighting over food in Cyberlife's Creatures world.

Floops in his very first episode.

More Biota: Bots and Virtual Pets

The Theo World planet of Biota where Fin Fin dwells.

The Teo World jungle. Is this what digital biota worlds in the Internet will look like?

Plant Biota on the Internet

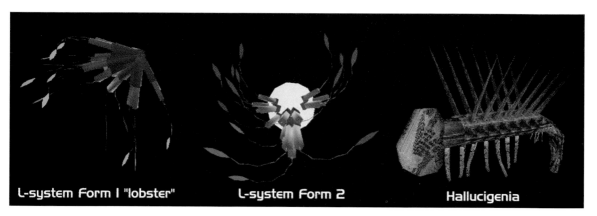

Synthetic Organism models created by Biota.org.

Nerve Garden One growing on the Internet, July 1996. In this garden, seeds in the form of
L-systems are sent through the Internet to grow the plants locally on your computer, saving
precious bandwidth. The plants become "smarter" and live within their own ecosystem.

Generative Art and Architecture

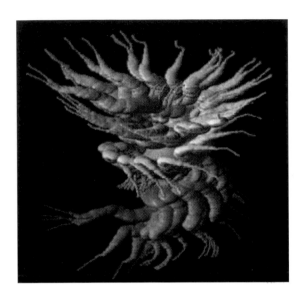

Darrel Anderson's generative organic artwork *Footless.* These sculptures should make avatar cyberspace worlds much better to look at. Avatar breeders are not far behind!

Eric Bucci's generative virtual architecture. This was created by a phenotypic genetic algorithm which goes through multiple generations, each of which are tested for fitness. This kind of generative form will allow a rich and interesting 3D cyberspace to be visited in the future.

William Latham's organic sculpture from the Virtual Garden.

Hot Sites in VP Land

Hot Spots

Because VP can use the whole World Wide Web as its chat space, there are many, many places you can go with VP. The following table lists some of the hottest spots in the VP Web cosmos.

Official pages

http://www.vplaces.com/vpnet/index.html
The Virtual Places home page.

http://www.vplaces.com/vpnet/schedule.html
The VP Events page.

http://www.vpchat.com
The VPchat.com home page.

http://www.ubique.co.il
The Ubique home page (the company that created Virtual Places).

http://talk.excite.com/
Talk! at Excite (a VP-powered chat site).

http://members.aol.com/avfactory/amazing.htm
The Amazing VP Everything Page.

VP apartments and towns

http://www.cyberclay.com/webtown/
Webtown@VP, where you can get your own Web page apartment for VP.

http://freeweb.nethead.co.uk/Devalin/Webtown/news.htm
Webtown News.

http://www.restaurantcity.com/
CyberSurfer Studios offering the VP apartments in Webtown at Restaurant City & Web Towers.

Avatar galleries and builders

http://www.vplaces.com/vpnet/support/support2.html
A listing of galleries in VP.

http://www.cris.com/~lophy/avatars.htm
A great collection of Anime Avatars.

http://members.aol.com/vphostjen/index.htm

Tori's Virtual Places Hut, featuring an impressive avatar selection.

http://www.execpc.com/~heiniken/avatars.html

Heineken's Homebrewed Avatars (another great avatar gallery).

http://www.csnsys.com/lundberg/trans.htm

The Spaceport VP transporter which includes avatars.

http://www.nfx.com/vp/vp_welcome.html

The nFX page which enables Virtual Places users to use the nFX Cartoon-O-Matic to create a personalized avatar.

VP spaces

The following Web sites are beautiful backdrops set up only for a special event in VP.

http://trureality.com/vp-chap.htm

The Tru Realities VP Wedding Chapel.

http://trureality.com/vp-mnlt.htm

A moonlit scene for romantic avatars.

http://members.aol.com/stustc/index.htm

Stu's Tent City, which has a great links page and plenty of VP chat room backdrops.

http://www.geocities.com/Heartland/9364/A-I.htm

Anjel and Inkee's Front Porch (a nice scene).

http://www.geocities.com/Heartland/3973/100acre.html

The 100-Acre Chat Room (a great setting).

http://www.cyberclay.com/webtown/opera/opera.htm

d'Angelou's Opera house.

http://www.pwrtc.com/~hawk/autochat/autochat.html

Auto Garage, the latest in automotive technology.

http://www.alb.de/home/silo/

Wiz Raven's Realm.

General VP pages

http://www.meson.com/~vega/index.html

The Virtual Hangout and VPlace (a fantastic source of information and resources about VP).

Links pages to other VP sites

http://members.aol.com/stustc/vplinks/vplinks.htm

Stu's VP Links (in Webtown).

Digi's Diary: For You Adults, Virtual Theaters for Our Comic Relief

Digi's Diary

DigiGardener, the big talk show host baby!

Just like in your America Online chat rooms, Virtual Places is bringing the concept of a chat auditorium to you. When I was writing this chapter, this feature was just about to be launched. I stumbled into an empty auditorium with a few avatars sitting around in the plush seats of the front row saying, "so what are we going to see?" I, being the extrovert that I sometimes am, jumped onto the stage to play Johnny Carson (boy, am I showing my age) in a kind of avatar Tonight Show. A few jokers jumped onto the stage with me, the cool baby, and we improvised. Hey, isn't that what virtual theater is all about, anyway? Vaudeville probably started with a few jokers playing around in an empty music hall.

Put on a show, play around, go wild, express yourself, fall over a few times, do a little shtik, get tragic, let it all hang out! Dr. Seuss, author of children's books, described adults as "obsolete children." Maybe we adults (or overly serious kids . . . I know, I was one) can loosen up a bit in these virtual worlds. If we can't play, we can't be creative or enjoy life. Avatar living may be one of the only places you can really escape to play.

I picture thousands of white collar employees in their cubicles sneaking into their favorite virtual world when the boss isn't around. Maybe one day you'll meet the cartoon character, Dilbert in a virtual world. Dilbert as an avatar, what a concept! The content of Dilbert comic strips and all of the characters (the consultant Dogbert; Ratbert, the bumbling boss; the evil human resources manager, Catbert) are a kind of theater of the absurd for the modern office worker. Thousands of e-mails pour into Scott Adams' mailbox (Dilbert's creator) from white collar workers everywhere. Scott then fishes out the best humor and story ideas and puts them into strips. In a sense, Dilbert is a true avatar virtual world. The comic strip lives of Dilbert and all the other characters are driven through e-mail by the real lives of thousands of office workers.

So, go back to that cubicle armed with the knowledge that life itself is a theater of the absurd. The next time you jack in to a virtual world, this is a great way to approach it. After all, most of the citizens of these worlds are kids who know how to be absurd, and who keep saying, "get a life."

A course in crazy

Forgot how to get crazy? Pick up a copy of Scoop Nisker's *Crazy Wisdom,* and learn the wisdom of the fool. (Nisker, Wes "Scoop," Crazy Wisdom, 1990. Berkeley: Ten Speed Press. ISBN: 0-89815-350-6) Yes, Scoop is Wes' nickname!

Nisker can answer your question: "how do I behave in avatar cyberspace?" with some pretty crazy wisdom. It is, after all, a crazy place, somewhere between a dream and a hallucination. Good advice from Nisker might be to not take yourself so seriously during your digital and personal brief allotment of time on this planet.

Black Sun
Passport

©aptain Digi, our fearless crew, and you, most honored passenger, have become seasoned veterans of virtual space. We have visited many worlds and survived to tell the tale. Along the way, we had heard of great new worlds built by the guild of VRML, the VeRMiLlions. Seeking these worlds, we set course for the great Star Gate to the worlds of the Black Sun. As the Star Gate comes up on our viewing screens, we maneuver the good ship *Avatar* close to the gate. A strange dark portal glowing with a black light beckons us to look inside. Join us in our first adventure in the home worlds of the guild of the VeRMiLlions, built by the followers of the Black Sun.

Your Guide to
Black Sun Passport

WORLD GUIDE

WORLD SKILL LEVEL	Advanced
BUILDING CAPABILITY	Yes, add your own VRML worlds
SYSTEM REQUIREMENTS	Windows 95
AVATAR CREATION CAPABILITY	Yes, build them in VRML
DEPTH	3D
SOUND SUPPORT	Netscape CoolTalk person-to-person voice

MINIMUM MACHINE

OPERATING SYSTEM	Windows 95, NT, Netscape 3.0, or Internet Explorer 3.01 required
COMPUTER	Pentium-based PC; 256-color video supporting VGA
RESOURCES	32MB RAM; up to 30MB free disk space depending on plug-ins loaded; sound card with speakers and microphone for optional voice support
CONNECTION	PPP dial-up to the Internet at 14.4 kbps; 28.8 kbps is recommended

Black Sun's Passport: Through the Star Gate

The Plaza welcome area shown in the Passport browser.

Black Sun Interactive (named after that famous club in Neal Stephenson's novel, *Snow Crash*) brought us the very first virtual worlds with avatars based on the *Virtual Reality Modeling Language* (VRML). Their first world, called PointWorld, was accessible through a program called CyberGate, a stand-alone program. This chapter will take you on a tour of Black Sun's worlds with their latest software, called Passport, the successor to CyberGate. The preceeding figure shows Passport running inside Netscape Navigator 3.0 or Microsoft Internet Explorer 3.01, and avatars inside the Plaza world (hey, watch out for that flying cow, you guys!).

One of the greatest features of Black Sun's VRML universe is that you can build your own world and your own avatars in it! This chapter is your passport to adventure in VRML worlds.

Installing

Installing Passport

Passport requires a pretty loaded PC, and you must have at least an intermediate level of understanding of how to download and install plug-ins for your Web browser. Passport is not for the Net-timid.

You must have Netscape Navigator 3.0 or Microsoft Internet Explorer 3.01 or higher installed before you can install Passport. Passport runs as a series of plug-ins and Java applications inside either of these Web browsers. In addition, you must install a VRML plug-in for these Web browsers (Live3D, Intervista's WorldView Cosmo Player for Netscape 3.0, or Internet Explorer 3.01 are recommended). You can download a VRML 3D plug-in along with your Web browser (both Netscape and Microsoft offer these as options).

What do I need to use Passport?

To run Passport and visit all of Black Sun's worlds, you need a Pentium-based PC running Windows 95 or NT, and a direct connection to the Internet. You can't use Passport through on-line services such as America Online, CompuServe, or Prodigy unless they support direct Internet access through the 32-bit *Winsock*. (Short for Windows Sockets, Winsock is a standard interface for Microsoft Windows applications and the Internet.) For example, you can use Passport through the Microsoft Network or CompuServe 3.0, as they do provide this service. If you can run Netscape 3.0 or Internet Explorer 3.01, you can install and use Passport.

The best option is to be directly connected to the Internet by dial-up PPP connection with at least a 14.4 kbps connection (28.8 kbps is recommended). If you are at work, or a place where you have a PC on the Internet full-time (such as a university or college), you can also use Passport. Connecting from work might require you to check on your *firewall* restrictions. (See, "Firewalls and proxies," in Appendix B for more information.)

Getting started and a few disclaimers

Passport is easy to install if you have Netscape 3.0 or Internet Explorer 3.01 (or higher) already set up. Another plus is that Passport is free to use (you have to accept the terms of your free license during installation). You are not charged for the time you spend chatting and exploring in Passport, but you could be charged for the hours you are online from your *Internet service provider (ISP)*. Check with your ISP on monthly free hours and rates. If you are paying toll charges on your telephone line to dial into your Internet service provider, you could be billed for the hours your line is used for the Internet. Check with your phone company and try to get a flat rate for this line.

More about the companion CD software

Passport is constantly evolving, and may have changed since this chapter was written. I placed the very latest version of Passport on your book CD, and it may be somewhat different from what is described here. These differences will be minor, however, and this chapter will still be a great guide to Passport. If you see new features or changes, and you want more of an explanation, you should check for information under the Help menu in Passport.

Similarly, if you download an upgrade from the Internet, or a whole new version of Passport, it may look somewhat different from what I describe here. To download an upgrade, or a completely new version of Passport from the Internet, follow the instructions under, "Installing or upgrading Passport from the Internet," later in this chapter.

Virtually up-to-date

Help

As a special service for readers of *Avatars!*, I have a home page on the World Wide Web devoted to keeping you up-to-date on your favorite worlds. Find news about software updates, social events held within these virtual worlds, and brand new worlds you might want to try at http://www.digitalspace.com/ avatars. Bookmark it!

If you have questions or problems

If you have questions or problems installing or running Passport, consult the "Black Sun Passport FAQ," on the companion Web site to this book. If this does not help you, check the Black Sun home page at **http://www.blacksun.com**, and its special Passport support page at **http://ww3.blacksun.com/sales/support/index.html**, for help with common problems. To contact the Black Sun Passport team directly with your suggestions, bug reports, or comments, fill out the feedback form at **http://home .blacksun.com/beta/spr.nsf/spr?OpenForm**. Sending e-mail to **support@blacksun.com** is also a good way to get help.

I appreciate your feedback on *Avatars!* but I don't have the resources to provide technical support. I would be happy to hear about your experiences with Passport. Contact us through the *Avatars!* book Web site at **http://www.digitalspace.com/avatars**.

Macintosh, UNIX, and OS/2 versions

At this writing, there are no versions of the Passport client program for the Macintosh, UNIX, or OS/2. Check the Black Sun and *Avatars!* book Web pages for updates on new versions which might support these platforms. At the time of this writing, Black Sun told me that a Macintosh version was in the works. You also may be able to run Passport using a Windows 95 emulation system on non-Windows machines. Note that if you are considering hosting a Black Sun community server, this software runs on various UNIX systems and Windows NT.

Do you have a previous version of Passport, CyberHub, or CyberGate installed?

If you have previously installed Passport, or the older CyberHub or CyberGate software, I recommend that you first remove it. To do this, go to the Windows 95 control panel and double-click on Add/Remove Programs. Scroll down to the listing for CyberHub or CyberGate, highlight it, and click on the Add/Remove button to delete it from the system. You can also delete these programs by removing the Black Sun folder. Note that CyberHub (and Passport) are stored in the Plug-ins folder under your Netscape or Internet Explorer folders, so you will have to look there to delete these resources. Passport also creates a folder called java\classes\blacksun which must also be deleted.

Installing Passport from your Avatars! CD

If you have a CD-ROM drive on your PC, you can install Passport directly from the book CD. If you don't have a CD-ROM drive, skip to the section, "Installing or upgrading Passport from the Internet." In "The Book CD-ROM" chapter, I provide a step-by-step example of how to install from the CD-ROM. I suggest you refer to this chapter, and follow the same steps for Passport. Once the installation program on your CD-ROM has started, you can go to the section, "Running the installation," later in this chapter.

Note that on other parts of the CD, Web pages are links to sites for Black Sun Passport and other virtual worlds, including the home page for *Avatars!* at **http://www .digitalspace.com/avatars**. If you are online while you run the CD, you can click on these links and explore the universe of virtual worlds on the Internet.

Installing or upgrading Passport from the Internet

If you want the very latest version of Passport, or were informed that you had to upgrade the version found on your *Avatars!* CD, then you must download files from the Internet. If you haven't done this before, don't panic; it is easier than you might think! Just follow these steps:

❶ Connect to the Internet (dial up with your modem and make sure your Internet connection is active).

❷ Start your Web browser, such as Netscape or Internet Explorer.

❸ In the top of the browser window, you will see a text box where you can enter text. Click in this area, delete the text inside, type **http://www.blacksun.com**, and press Enter. After a few moments, the home page for Black Sun should appear. If nothing comes up for a long time, check to see that you are online.

If the Black Sun page is not available for some reason, try entering the location for the *Avatars!* home page, which is **http://www.digitalspace.com/avatars**. This page may contain more up-to-date links for Black Sun and Passport.

❹ Once you are at the Black Sun home page, follow the instructions for downloading or upgrading Passport. At one point, you will click on a link and be prompted for a place to save a file. In response to the dialogue box, click Save to Disk (Netscape), or Save As (Internet Explorer), and save the file to a folder on your hard disk (or save it on your desktop). You should choose a folder where you will remember to find the new file, and note the name of the file. You can use the folder that your Web browser gives you, or move back up and select another. I put all downloaded files in a folder I call \download.

❺ Wait patiently. You can do other work offline, but be careful not to interfere with the connection. Try not to do more on-line work (such as Web surfing) on the Internet while the download is progressing, and if you are using your regular telephone line for your modem, don't make a call.

❻ The Passport download is just over 1MB in size. After the download is finished (about 20 minutes for a 28.8 kbps connection, and about 40 minutes for a 14.4 kbps connection), open the folder into which the file was downloaded and double-click on it to start the installation. Now proceed to the section, "Running the installation."

Running the installation

Whether you are running the installation from the CD-ROM, or from the file you downloaded from the Internet, use this section to guide you through the installation. Note that if you downloaded Passport from the Internet, the installation process may have changed. If this has happened, refer to instructions on the Black Sun Web site.

❶ You must have Netscape 3.0 (or higher) or Internet Explorer 3.01 (or higher) installed before you can install Passport. In addition, you must install a VRML plug-in for either of these Web browsers (Live3D for Netscape or Cosmo Player for Internet Explorer are recommended). You can download a VRML 3D plug-in along with your Web browser (both Netscape and Internet Explorer offer these as options).

➋ You must close the Web browser before you can install Passport. You can use Alt+Tab, or click on the task bar to switch to your Web browser, and close it before continuing.

➌ After you have downloaded the software, close the Web browser and go to the folder (or desktop) location where you saved the file. Black Sun Passport is packaged as a compressed file, which is a self-contained installer. Double-click on that file (it should be named ppxxx.exe, in which the xxx represent version numbers), which will launch an extractor application to decompress the file. If you are installing from the CD-ROM, you need only click on the installer to start Passport. The extractor will extract files and then start the Passport installer program.

➍ The installer setup program will run and prompt you at each step. Accept the license agreement terms, if you agree, and accept the folder into which Passport will be installed (or enter your own path). The default folder is \blacksun\passport. You should make a note of the path to the folder where Passport is installed.

➎ You will be prompted for the folder into which Passport plug-ins for Netscape or Internet Explorer will be installed. Check to see that the path given is for the desired version of your Web browser, and then continue.

➏ The installer will prompt you for a program folder name in which to store the references to Passport; accept this.

➐ The installation should be successful if you have enough disk space (you need about 5MB free).

➑ When the installation is complete, you will be prompted to place a shortcut to Passport on your desktop; do this.

➒ At the very end of the installation, you will be given the option to read the release notes (a good idea) and to start Passport. If you are eager, you can start Passport right away (remember, you must be online). I always come back a little later and start it from the new shortcut on my desktop, or from the Start menu entry.

Finding the installed software

The installation program should have created a shortcut to the new Passport virtual world software on your desktop, and also a program folder entry in your Start menu. If you cannot find the new software, you can open My Computer and the C: drive to search for a folder named BlackSun in which you should find the Passport application.

Cleaning up after installation

If you copied the Passport installation program file onto your desktop, into a folder, or downloaded it from the Internet, you can delete it after the installation is complete. It should have a name like ppxxx.exe (in which xxx represent version numbers). On the other hand, I keep the original installer around just in case I have to reinstall it. Of course, you also have the CD with the original installers, so you do not need to take up valuable hard disk space with them.

Stepping Through the Star Gate

Starting your journey

The first step in your journey is to double-click on the shortcut to Black Sun Passport (or use the Start menu entry). This will start your Web browser, and bring you to the entry page for the worlds. On this page, you can enter your avatar name, click on another link to select your avatar, and then select the link to enter some of the worlds. Note also that you can opt to use Passport to display only 2D worlds (Web sites with only the text chat displayed). I will focus on 3D worlds in this chapter.

The avatar selection page is a fun and easy place to test whether your 3D browser plug-in is working. Clicking on an avatar will bring the VRML file into a window frame. You can use the controls for the 3D plug-in to rotate the avatar and have a good look before you pick it. There are also buttons under the avatar for gestures. If your avatar has gestures, this will show you what they look like. Clicking on the Save button under the avatar will select it as your representation. You must then return to the entry page (press the back button), and then select, Visit Our Worlds.

Note that VRML exists in two versions, 1.0 and 2.0. VRML 2.0 has a lot more features, and is starting to get more popular. Black Sun is starting to offer VRML 2.0 avatars. I chose to stick with the original VRML 1.0 avatars for this chapter, but you should feel free to explore VRML 2.0 avatars and worlds.

Selecting an avatar for Passport.

Into the worlds

After selecting an avatar and user name, click on Visit Our Worlds, and you will enter the Passport Entry Plaza world, your starting point in the universe of Black Sun VRML worlds. The following figure shows the Plaza with a couple of avatars having a conversation.

Passport is organized as a series of frames within the Netscape window. In fact, Passport is composed of plug-ins and Java applications running all at the same time within Netscape or Internet Explorer. With Passport, you don't need a separate application. Visiting worlds is as easy as pointing your Web browser to Web pages which are designed to work with Passport. The actual world, shown in the main window, is displayed with a VRML plug-in such as Netscape's Live3D or Silicon Graphics' Cosmo Player. The other frames provide all the controls you need to interact with other people in their own VRML avatars.

The main window (called the World Frame) shows the world, along with the navigation controls of the VRML browser plug-in (as in the following figure, Cosmo Player from SGI). The interfaces on the left allow you to move between private and public chat lines, and to reach other services such as the avatar selection Web page. Clicking on Scenes will bring you a list of VRML worlds that you can visit, and Cards brings up your business card. Black Sun borrowed this concept from Neal Stephenson's novel, *Snow Crash*. You can exchange cards with any user you meet, and build a collection of cards. The bottom frame shows the chat areas and a list of users (by their chosen names) who are currently in the Plaza area. You can send text messages to users, open a private chat, or even start CoolTalk or Microsoft NetMeeting for voice conversations.

You really need a powerful machine to run Passport, and I recommend a minimum of 32MB of RAM and plenty of free disk space. Sometimes Passport and all of its VRML and Java just gets tangled up, and sometimes you will have to shut down your Web browser and start again. Be patient, as Passport, like all virtual worlds, is a work in progress.

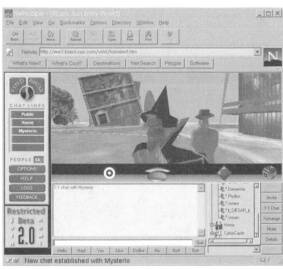

Passport in full operation, complete with avatars.

A closer look at the Passport interface

The Controls Frame

The Controls Frame, on the upper left, displays the controls for the Passport client functions. Clicking on the icons will change the work frame (on the bottom of the window), and let you access chat lines, scenes, cards, help, and other features.

The Controls Frame allows you to control everything in Passport.

Find list

The Find button calls up a list of all the VRML scenes (worlds) served by the current Passport program. Clicking on a scene will bring up the number of avatars in each world. Often, the more people in the world, the more interesting the world (or the people). If you click on a scene and then press the button, Go to Scene, you will load a new world. This new world may have its own set of connected scenes. In this way, the Black Sun universe of worlds goes on and on. Note that you can also list the top ten scenes by user population, and list all the users in all the scenes who can be reached from within the world you are currently visiting. People finders are very important tools in virtual worlds.

You can use the Worldwide Search function to find users in various virtual worlds. Just type in their user name. You can enter the asterisk (*) symbol to "find any user

The scene finder lists other Black Sun VRML worlds that you can visit.

matching this combination." For example, entering a* will find anyone whose user name begins with an A. Just entering * by itself will find all the users in the worlds listed in the Find directory. This user search function is very handy for finding where your friends might be in the various worlds at any given time.

Avatars list

Selecting the Avatar button allows you to take another look at the avatar that you are using. You can try out the gestures and even select a new avatar. This is kind of like going backstage between scenes to change costumes.

Chat lines

Clicking on the Public Chat line will change the work frame to show you all the chat that is going on in the current world, and list everyone who is in the scene (as shown

Opening the Public Chat line shows all the chat, and lists all the people, in the world.

in the following figure). In public chat, anything you type is "heard" by everyone else in the current world. The Home Chat line is a private party line for friends. Additionally, there are up to three one-on-one chat lines that you can set up. A red bar to the left of the list of chat lines indicates new activity on that line. Like a snoopy old-time telephone operator, you can monitor up to five simultaneous chat lines!

People

Clicking on People (which lists the total number of people in the current scene) will list all the people in the work frame.

Options

The Passport client has a number of options you can adjust to your own preferences, including personal preferences, font sizes, and firewall access settings. See the section, "Fine-Tuning Your World," later in this chapter for more details about options.

Help

Selecting Help will open your Web browser and display the Black Sun help documents for Passport.

Logs

Public and private chat sessions can be logged. Black Sun has implemented these logs as streams flowing into Web pages. Very cool! Passport automatically keeps transcripts of all your chat sessions in chat log files (the default directory for these is \blacksun\passport\chatlog). These files can be accessed at any time directly from the chat controls, or since they are plain text files, they can be loaded into Microsoft WordPad or any other ASCII editor or word processor. This feature could make Passport an excellent tool for remote business meetings or interviews.

Optional controls: World builders can add their own controls for additional features. This is an advanced topic for those hosting their own community servers. (See the Black Sun Interactive home page at **http://www.blacksun.com** for more information on controls).

Getting around with Passport

Right-clicking on the mouse brings up the controls for the VRML plug-in. One of the most important items on these pop-up menus is Viewpoints. Viewpoints are like camera locations in the scene. As you can see in the following figure, there are quite a few viewpoints defined for this scene, and we are currently in the one called Overhead, which places us over the entry Plaza. Viewpoints are a handy way to move to the hot spots of the world (as defined by the world's builders). You can also roll through these viewpoints by pressing Ctrl+Right Arrow. Viewpoints are a feature of any VRML world.

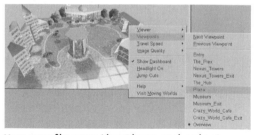

You can fly over the Plaza and select Viewpoints.

Basic navigation—it's not easy, folks!

You can navigate by pressing the left mouse button and rolling forward or backward. To navigate with the mouse, you will have to master the *dashboard* controls of the VRML plug-in you selected to run with Passport. The dashboard is the set of icons on the bottom of the 3D world window. Chances are if you click and hold your mouse button, and move it on top of these control icons, you will move in the world (or move the world). Every interface is different, and I recommend trying them all out to learn their tricks.

VRML plug-ins were built to look at simple 3D models, not to navigate in a large virtual world, so the navigation in Passport is difficult. Every VRML-based world (such as OZ, Sony's community place browser, and others) has navigation problems. I hope that the makers of these worlds will soon learn how to make navigation as fast and easy as it is in 3D games like *Doom* or *Descent*. Black Sun has tried to make navigation possible through keyboard keys. This is definitely a better way to move, although it is still like swimming through a bowl of porridge.

Keyboard and mouse navigation controls

Arrow keys: Pressing the arrow keys on your keyboard will move you in the corresponding direction in the world. Make sure that you've clicked the mouse in the frame in which the world is displayed, or your keyboard keys will not move you.

Ctrl+Arrow: Pressing Right Arrow while Ctrl is held down will take you to the next viewpoint. Press it again to move to the next viewpoint, and so forth. Correspondingly, pressing Left Arrow while Ctrl is held down, moves you backwards in the viewpoint sequences.

Mouse buttons: You can use the right mouse button to spin around the world. Just click while holding the right mouse button, and the world will spin. Holding down Ctrl while dragging the mouse with the left mouse button held down will allow you to slide in any direction.

Learn to fly: You can fly up over the scene by pressing Ctrl on your keyboard, and then pressing and holding down the left mouse button as you roll the mouse forward (away from you). This will cause you to rise up. To sink back down, do the same thing, only move the mouse towards you.

Navigation bar and shortcuts: To display the navigation bar (sometimes called the dashboard) on your screen, right-click, and choose Options ➪ Navigation Bar.

Traveling from one world to another

A number of worlds are accessible through the Passport client. You can list these worlds by using the Find List technique (described earlier in this chapter) or by finding a *teleport* to another world and double-clicking on it. You will see an example of teleporting in the section, "Tours of Passport Worlds," later in this chapter.

Let's Chat

The mysterious Mysterio

I had just entered the Entry Plaza, and kept seeing this mysterious character called Mysterio. I clicked on his avatar name in the work frame and then selected the 1:1 Chat button to send him a page. When you receive a page, you can hear a telephone ringing (if you have a sound card and your speakers are turned on), and you will be presented with a dialogue box saying, "xxxx would like to chat with you," where xxxx is the avatar nickname of the person calling. Mysterio accepted my offer to chat, so a new window opened in the work frame, and we got started. Chatting is easy; you just type into the text entry area below the chat window in the work frame, and press Enter to send the message.

The following figure shows my chat with Mysterio. His conversation sounded suspiciously like that of a *bot* (an automatic piece of software with no person behind it). He kept saying, "I did not understand your comment," while talking about riddles. Often, when you see long-winded talk like that coming at you quickly, you have a bot on your hands.

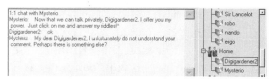

Chatting with Mysterio.

I decided to find out more about this Mysterio riddle bot, so I selected his avatar name from the list on the right side of the work frame, and pushed the Xchange button to offer a card exchange. Passport supports technology which allows public, business, and private cards that you can fill out for yourself and then exchange with others. As in real life, you can build quite a collection of cards. You can find your card, and your collection, by clicking on an icon called CyberCards at the bottom of the list of people and chat lines, on the right side of your work frame. (This is called the Participant list. You can see an example of the Participant list in the previous figure showing the one-on-one chat with Mysterio.)

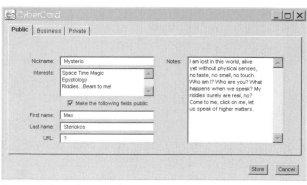

Mysterio's CyberCard.

Mysterio agreed to exchange cards, and his appeared in my collection.

Clicking on it brought it up on the screen, as seen in the previous figure. From his card, Mysterio seemed like a well-informed riddlemaker. I decided to invite Mysterio to join my Home Chat line, so I clicked on his avatar name in the Participant list and pressed the Invite button. Now, Mysterio is a member of my permanent private chat group, and has an entry under my Home Chat Line icon. Mysterio had asked persistently that I follow him and click on him to enter a riddle game, which I did. And like magic, a miniature Web page appeared in the work frame offering to let me play the Keys of Mysterio riddle game. So that's how bots operate!

More about communicating in Passport

Passport supports three types of chat: private (described in the previous example), public (a free-for-all), and group chat lines (these can be moderated discussions on specific topics). You can access all the chat lines by clicking on Chat Lines in the control frame on the upper left-hand side of the window.

Note that you can also see chat entirely as HTML Web pages by pressing Logs on the controls frame on the left-hand side of the window. This may be an easier way to chat, especially if your computer is on a slow connection, or the 3D scene is just too slow. More information about chat logs and 2D chat can be found in, "A closer look at the Passport interface," earlier in this chapter.

Beam me to you, Scotty

Use Beam to move your avatar toward a person in a scene. To do this, just click on their avatar name in the Participants list and then press the Beam button. You will travel until you are facing that person's avatar. Quickly type "Hi," or something to let them know of your good intentions.

Mute and give me a break

The Mute button will turn off the chat (from your viewpoint only) from a particular person who you find irritating. Their avatar will even disappear! Use Mute as a last resort, as it is a pretty severe measure in a social virtual world.

Start button and chatting with a CoolTalk voice

The Start button will start a selected tool. The Passport client provides an interface for a variety of extensions, such as voice chat, and a virtual whiteboard. The list of installed tools is available immediately to the left of the Start button. CoolTalk is distributed with Netscape Navigator 3.0, so that users of this browser will have CoolTalk installed automatically. Try clicking on an avatar name in the Participants list, then select CoolTalk from the list, and press the Start button. If the user you are trying to reach has CoolTalk, a microphone, and speakers, you can talk to that person in your own voice. Of course, it is a good idea to text chat with a person first to see if they can run CoolTalk.

Chat gestures

Your avatar may have a whole range of gestures. A row of buttons underneath the chat area lists the gestures you can make. Clicking on these buttons will create a gesture in the world by your avatar, and send a text version of that gesture into the chat area. If you want to see what your gestures look like, simply go to the avatar gallery by clicking on the Avatar button on the control frame in the upper left-hand corner of the window. In the gallery, you can look at your own avatar in the mirror and pick the gestures.

Clicking on the Avatar gesture buttons results in these chat lines.

Creating a CyberCard and changing your nickname

It's easier to "break the ice" with fellow chatters if you have your own CyberCard. To fill in your own CyberCard, scroll down to the CyberCard icon in the Participants list and open up your own card. You can fill it out when it appears in the work frame, and press the Store button to save it. There are three separate cards to fill out for the different aspects of your personality and activities. They include the following:

Public Card: This is your own on-line advertisement, consisting of the nickname by which you want to be known, and a few lines that you want to be associated with your avatar. You can also choose to publish your real name (i.e., the one that is associated with your personal and business cards).

Business Card: This is information about your profession.

Personal (Private) Card: This tells where you live and/or play.

The CyberCards that you exchange with other visitors to the Passport client are stored in a local database archive (its default location is \blacksun\passportclient\cards), which you can manage from this panel.

Note that in this release of the Passport client, your whole set of CyberCards is exchanged at once: if you give someone your business card, they get your personal card as well (unless you leave that blank!). In the future, you will be able to distribute these and other customizable cards selectively.

Meet the Natives

Tours of Passport Worlds

The Octagon is a floating pavilion, which is a gateway to many other worlds. I visited it in search of a guide to take me around the Black Sun universe.

Kerri takes me to PointWorld

I establish a good connection with Kerri.

Kerri, a medieval damsel avatar, was my guide for the day. As I was dressed as a dashing medieval bard, we were a great match!

Kerri is from Illinois, and is an old hand at the Black Sun landscape. I wanted to know where the most action was, and she said it was in PointWorld, the oldest and still most frequented spot hosted by Black Sun.

Kerri helped me navigate down into the center of the Octagon, where there were doors to many worlds. Navigation in Passport is based on the VRML plug-in browsers, which were not originally built with virtual worlds in mind. Getting around can be awkward, and I found it very hard to follow Kerri. I even shot past her and outside of the Octagon once. I hope that the navigation will improve, and become as easy as it is in game worlds such as *Doom,* or the original Worlds Chat.

We found a doorway to PointWorld (actually, a brick wall), and by holding my mouse over it, I saw that I could enter PointWorld here. Clicking on this wall started to load PointWorld, and we soon found ourselves there.

Kerri shows me the door to the old PointWorld.

PointWorld is a cool digital plain with a lot of objects that link to other worlds. I thanked Kerri, and she left me to tour around on my own. I invited her to join the friends list in my Home Chat line so that I could chat with her if I ever found her online again.

I'm with Kerri in PointWorld.

Emperor P'ter and his New Year's bash

The true power of Black Sun's approach is apparent when you see the large number of worlds built by users. This open approach even allows users to design their own avatars. One example is a 13-year-old called Emperor P'ter, whom I met in his world on New Year's Eve of 1996. Since I was pretty much stuck writing this book (even on New Year's Eve!), I decided to see what was going on online. Emperor P'ter had been wandering in the heavily populated Entry Plaza recruiting people to come to his world at the stroke of midnight (in

various time zones). Emperor P'ter had built his own world out of VRML 1.0, and had made his own avatar (which looked like a flaming king about to run you through). In the world, he had set a table with champagne and glasses and a clock that actually told real time (see the following figure). He attracted a whole stream of guests, offering them champagne, and pointing them to the clock. As he was explaining, someone had come in disguised as a table . . . "his av is a table thing." If you want to be a spy in a virtual world, just come in looking like the furniture!

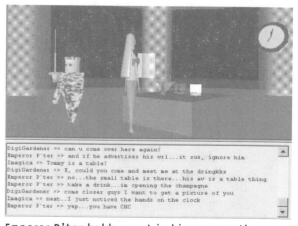

Emperor P'ter holds court in his own castle.

Meet Passport Citizens!

The design and content of worlds are only interesting for a limited period of time. After that, it is the *people* who make a world worth revisiting. Emperor P'ter's simple world attracted a big crowd because he had designed a clock which would count down the New Year, and he had gone out and found people to share this experience.

The Chicago Five

The Chicago Five (pictured in the follow-ing figure) are Dave Maloney (nicknamed Guy) and his wife Debbie, nicknamed Gal, and their friends WildBill, Pegasus, and Jedi (their avatar nicknames). They are posing in front of the Planetarium in Chicago where they all journeyed to meet *in the flesh* after knowing each other only as avatars in Black Sun worlds. Their sto-ries, which are recounted below, are about human contact through the new medium of digital space, and how new

The Chicago Black Sun Five pose at the Adler Planetarium.

friendships can blossom. You can find the full story of all members of the Chicago Five on the companion book Web site under the Black Sun link.

Guy, avatar ring leader of the Chicago Five, and Gal

by David Maloney (a.k.a. Guy)

"'Hello World!' Those were the first words I typed into the keyboard. Before me on my computer screen was a world totally new to me, and unlike anything I had ever seen before on the World Wide Web. A 3D world filled with color and light that I could walk and fly through in real time.

I had been rummaging around on the Internet since November 1995, and had seen my share of Web sites and chat rooms. In early March of 1996, I was pag-ing through a copy of *Computer Graphics World* magazine, and came across a small article announcing that a company called Black Sun Interactive had released a product called CyberGate. Reading that it was a beta version of a multi-user virtual reality chat room really did not mean much to me, until I went to their Web site, downloaded the program, and installed it on my computer. I soon understood what they meant.

Black Sun is a virtual space that allows people to communicate and interact from anywhere in the world as if they were in the same room. I could *see* other people that were also logged into the world that I was inhabiting, and commu-nicate with them through a chat box below the 3D window. They appeared in the form of avatars, 3D shapes that could move and fly just as I could. Black Sun had provided an avatar room filled with interesting and bizarre creatures that would allow you to change how you appeared to others simply by clicking on the avatar you wanted. At first, all we could say to each other was, 'This is incredible!' and, 'When did you find this?'

It was Black Sun Avatar #12 that I first crawled inside to inhabit the 3D spaces, and took the nickname of Guy. To this day, I am not sure why I took this name, except that Avatar #12 was a kind of generic-looking robotic shape, and I felt that I would start out simple and hopefully transform over time as I learned more about these virtual worlds. I soon felt at home there, and started to investigate this world. I was in the main meeting room called PointWorld, which had links to many other 3D spaces, some of which linked to Web sites.

Although this new approach to surfing the Web was interesting, it was the interaction with the people in these worlds that really caught my interest. I spent the next couple of months popping in as time allowed, and I began to learn more and more about some of the people who kept returning. Slowly, I began to think of some of these people as true friends that I saw almost daily, much more often than I was able to see good friends in the real world. An incredible dynamic was being created here: People linked through worlds alone, and who never actually met.

What made the conversation so dynamic was the diversity of the people there. There were housewives, computer system managers, Web developers, graphic designers, programmers, kids in high school, just to name a few. All connected through one thing: words. And it was through these words that we got to know each other. Not by how we looked, or how we were dressed, or where we lived, or even the expression on our faces—just words. Some of the conversations that took place were incredible. Subjects ranged from books, movies, new hardware, new software, to a new *Baywatch* episode. I guess we could get blamed for abusing this great new technology, but we also used this place to amuse and delight each other with our wit (or lack of it) and humor after a hard day at work, school, or home.

My wife, Debbie, soon became interested in these strange shapes moving across the screen, and was wondering why I was sometimes laughing hysterically at the computer. After she began to see some of these shapes start to emerge as real characters and real people, she decided to beam in and join our little community. Guy and Gal soon became part of the virtual landscape of PointWorld and beyond, sometimes causing friendly races to the computer terminal after work, as only one person could log in at a time.

As with any community, there can be problems. And we had our share in cyberspace. Because we were using only typed words to communicate, there was always the chance to misinterpret what someone said. This caused problems more than once. We had to learn to be careful of what we said. As Black Sun states on their site: 'Don't forget that there is a living, breathing, thinking, feeling person on the other side of that computer screen communicating through their keyboard, just as you are.'

As with any chat room, there is always the problem of people who enter only to cause trouble and ruin the experience for others. We came to call these people 'rudies,' not to be confused with newbies, who were new arrivals, and had not yet learned all the rules associated with these VR spaces. We even had set up meetings to discuss the behavior of these people and how to deal with them. These meetings were not pretty, as this was a divisive issue. Some believed that it was an issue of free speech, while others believed that the rooms should be patrolled for such people, and their right to be there revoked. Black Sun eventually created an elegant solution to this problem by installing an Ignore button into a new release of their software. This allowed those who did not want to hear someone to block them out, while others would not have this censorship forced on them. Peace reigned again in cyberspace . . . for the time being.

Avatars made by Guy, Gal, and Pegasus of the Chicago Five.

One of the most fascinating things for me was to first learn that we could create our own avatars. My first project was to create custom avatars for Guy and Gal. I had experience working with computer models in the engineering field that I work in, so I began to investigate VRML, and how to create for it. It wasn't long before we were using the avatars shown here. Gal also took on the alter-ego of the evil penguin, Feathers MacGraw, from the British claymation movies, *Wallace & Grommet* by Nick Park. I would change my avatar depending on the location from which I was logging in. Currently, I have over 80 different avatars posted on my Web site for use by the community. (see Guy's site at **http://www.execpc.com/~dmaloney/wrls.html**). I always thought that everyone should be able to have their own individual avatar.

Another great feature of the Black Sun browser is that, as well as adding your own avatars, you can also build your own worlds for yourself and others to inhabit. Black Sun supplies information on how to make them multi-user. Besides the Black Sun home page, another great place for information about world building can be found at Gerry's Inner Sanctum at **http://www2.magmacom.com/~gerryp/howtowrl.html**.

As I write this, we are planning the one-year anniversary party for PointWorld. As part of the celebration, we are going to try to set a record for the number of people in a Black Sun world at one time. The unofficial record is 44, I believe. We tried once before, and made it up to around 36 avatars in one world, but I know we can make it up to 50. (See Guy's Pile-in report at **http://www.execpc. com/~dmaloney/pilein/**.

Last summer, several of the regulars had an opportunity to actually meet for the first time. The meeting place was in Chicago, where some lived, but others traveled all the way from North Carolina. One even rode his motorcycle all the way from New Jersey to be there. I think we were all a little nervous meeting for the first time, but it did not take long for us all to get talking, just as we did in Black Sun worlds. We are also planning to make this a yearly meeting out in the real world, each year adding new people that we have met.

Won't you join us?'

Guy

Don't forget to see the full story of the Chicago Five on the companion book Web site at **http://www.digitalspace.com/avatars/chicago.htm**.

Netiquette in Passport Worlds

Following are some guidelines from the good folks at Black Sun about building a civil cybersociety.

If someone is bothering you

If someone is offending you in any way, you have the option of ignoring them. This means you will no longer see their avatar or any of the text they may write. To do this, highlight the offending party's name on the list of people and click on the Mute button. Use Mute as a last resort. Imagine how uncomfortable it would be if someone suddenly refused to acknowledge that you even existed!

Lurk before you leap

This is one of the few times virtual voyeurism is okay and actually encouraged. Listen in on what others are chatting about to get a general sense of how the regulars act. Once you understand a little of the lingo and tempo and topics, go ahead and participate.

Introduce yourself

In real life, it can be daunting to go up to a group of people you don't know and say "Hi," but in avatar cyberspace that's the best way to get started. You'll find that the people are happy to greet you (even if you are a newbie) and show you around.

Remember the human element

This is the Internet's (and life's) golden rule: Do unto others as you would have them do unto you. Imagine how you'd feel if you were in the other person's shoes. Stand up for yourself, but try not to hurt people's feelings. Don't forget that *there is a living, breathing, thinking, feeling person on the other side of that computer screen communicating through their keyboard, just as you are.*

Think before you speak

Avatar cyberspace is a community, and like every community, it has members of all ages, including minors. With this in mind, please try to refrain from obscene or offensive language. If you wouldn't say it in front of your mom, boss, or child, don't say it here. One of the joys of the Internet is that you can express yourself freely, explore strange new worlds, and boldly go where you've never gone before, but this should not be at the expense of the other community members' sensibilities.

Be careful when using sarcasm and humor

When you communicate electronically, often all you see is text on a computer screen. You don't have the opportunity to use facial expressions, gestures, and tone of voice to communicate your meaning; words are all you have, so be as clear as possible.

General communication tips

DON'T SHOUT! Typing in all capitals is the equivalent of yelling, so typing in mixed case is a softer touch.

Fine-Tuning Your World

The Options panel (which comes up when you press Options on the control frame) is a tabbed dialogue with settings for fonts, preferences, and firewalls. The About tab gives you the version of Passport. I describe some of the Options panel settings in this section.

Preferences tab

The Preferences settings include the following:

Show Information Messages For: Enables you to set up how long you are willing to wait for an answer, specifying your patience in seconds.

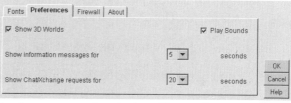

Preferences are located on the Options panel.

Show Chat/Xchange Requests For: Enables you to set up how long you are willing to wait for a response to a chat request or exchange of cards.

Show 3D Worlds: Enables you to shut off the 3D world and just chat.

Play Sounds: Enables you to turn off all Passport sounds.

Fonts tab

The text appearing in the work frame is under Java control, and is not directly affected by your Windows Font preferences. You must specify the font size for chat transcripts, avatar lists, and other parts of the interface independently from Window's settings.

Firewall tab

The Firewall options allow you to set up Passport to work through a firewall and proxy server.

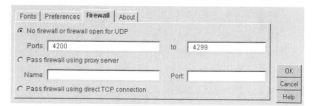

Configure Firewall settings from the Options panel.

About tab

Here you will find information about the version of Passport client you are using. The version number, its date of release, and copyright information are available here.

Building Your Own World and Avatars

Building Your Own Worlds

The first step in building your VRML world for Passport is to learn a 3D authoring tool. You could use a tool such as Pioneer from Caligari (**http://www.caligari.com**), Virtual Home Space Builder from Paragraph International (**http://www.paragraph.com**), or a simple text editor (if you really want to type VRML code in directly). More information about tools you can use to build worlds and avatars is contained in the "Build Your Own World, Design Your Own Avatar" chapter.

Briefly, a VRML world consists of the following design parts:

- A geometry (made up of polygons) and appearance (colors, textures) that make up a world

- Positions of camera viewpoints

- Lighting for the world

- Optimizations to make the world load faster over the Internet

Describing all the details of building your own VRML worlds for Passport would go way beyond the scope of this chapter. I advise you to look at the great, up-to-date documentation on this subject at **http://ww3.blacksun.com/buildertips/worldtips.htm**, for a guide to building Passport worlds.

Roll your own avatar

You can create your own avatar in Black Sun's world! This involves the creation of a VRML (Virtual Reality Modeling Language) 1.0 or VRML 2.0 file. See the section, "Hot Worlds in the Passport Universe," later in this chapter for Web sites in which Black Sun users describe how they built VRML worlds and avatars. There are even collections of custom avatars you can choose from on these sites. If you ask nicely, one of these users might very well build you a custom-tailored avatar! The section, "Can I build and use my own customized avatar?" in the Frequently Asked Questions section of the companion Web site, gives you more details. Note that this is definitely a job for the technically inclined! The "Build Your Own World, Design Your Own Avatar" chapter also covers some avatar building tools and techniques which might be a little bit easier for the rest of us!

Tool integration

The capabilities of Passport client may be extended by integrating tools which provide audio, video, teleconferencing, and whiteboard capabilities in real time. Examples of tools that are integrated into Passport are the conferencing utilities CoolTalk (included with Netscape 3.0), and Microsoft's NetMeeting. Electronic whiteboards can also be integrated into Passport. A whiteboard allows multiple users teleconferencing at their own computers to draw and write comments on the same document. I recommend that you check Black Sun's home page for more information on tool integration. The day when virtual worlds are used for serious business applications may be coming.

Hot Worlds in the Passport Universe

Official Web sites from Black Sun

http://www.blacksun.com/
The Black Sun home page.

Hot Spots

http://ww3.blacksun.com/cool/gallery/index.html
The avatar gallery.

http://ww3.blacksun.com/cool/builders/index.html
Companies and individuals who are building worlds.

http://ww3.blacksun.com/cool/guide/index.html
The Worlds Travel Guide.

Some Individual User's Sites and Worlds

http://www.execpc.com/~dmaloney/wrls.html
David Maloney's (Guy) site has dozens of avatars and worlds built in VRML and running in Passport.

http://www.bluenet.net/after5/flamingo/flamingowrl.html
Pam Miller's (Imagica) Flamingo World, and other worlds she has made.

http://www.bluenet.net/after5/fct.htm
Find the Flamingo City Times.

http://www2.magmacom.com/~gerryp/howtowrl.html
A great place to find information about world building can be found at Gerry Paquette's (Prince Charming) Inner Sanctum.

http://www2.magmacom.com/~gerryp/howtoav.html
Gerry's information on avatar creation.

Digi's Diary: Why Virtual Worlds are not Virtual Reality on the internet

Digi's Diary

Sometimes I hear people referring to virtual worlds as "virtual reality," and I feel duty-bound to say "not!" There are several reasons why. I can go on and on about how virtual worlds are a new form of human contact—not an artificial reality, but as real as talking on the telephone. But the best way to explain the difference is to tell a story.

Almost 100 years ago, Thomas Edison was perfecting his film cameras and manufacturing a box that came to be called a Nickelodeon. The Nickelodeon was set up at fairs or popular street corners, and for a nickel, people could step up to it, bend over, and peer in to witness a short film loop. These machines created a sensation for awhile, and were making Edison and others the first returns from their enormous investment in developing the movie camera and film. With the Nickelodeon, you got an immersive, private experience of a short, flickering film. Quite a dazzling experience for the turn of the century, but it left some dizzy. Moreover, women did not like the idea of men being free to stare at them while they were bent over the box.

One day, the key engineer who had built Edison's film camera (and who has received virtually no credit), came into the great inventor's office and proposed that he could build a projector that would place the image on a large white screen. He went on to say that they could rent a theater or music hall and charge admission, and audiences could share the experience in large numbers. Edison was furious and threw the engineer out of his office, claiming that such a move was ludicrous and would undercut sales of their Nickelodeon machines.

That engineer eventually left the Edison laboratories, formed his own company, built the projector, and opened one of the first cinemas. At the same time, the Lumiere brothers in France were creating wildly popular cinema experiences.

In the early 1990s, a new kind of Nickelodeon was invented, called the immersive virtual reality (VR) system. Most of us have seen it—the head-mounted display and data glove. Many of you have probably tried it, as there are a few of these systems at arcades, cybercafes, and even some home units. I have stepped into VR systems of all types, although most of them made me very queasy or even nauseated. It is not an experience I have rushed back to.

Meanwhile, by early 1995, after years of hearing about VR as the next big thing, quietly onto the Net emerged the medium of virtual worlds. Instead of a solitary experience requiring special equipment, virtual worlds allowed thousands of people viewing a shared virtual world on their common computer screens to be immersed in a common story. Like watching a good film, or reading a book, you can immerse yourself in a social avatar setting, and really feel as if you are inside the story. Virtual worlds step beyond cinema in that the story unfolding on the screen is written, directed, and acted by the citizens in that world. Players in the virtual world can even design the stage sets and props (as in Passport, AlphaWorld, or the Palace).

Maybe it is just Digi's own personal preferences showing here, but I am so relieved that the future may not bring us hundreds of thousands of people walking around wearing funny goggles, totally isolated from the people around them. Hey, with walkmans, cars, and our dangerous and unfriendly cities, we are already isolated enough! Just imagine if the only way to play in virtual worlds was with all that strange gear: the Kindrick baby Mark (who you met in the "OnLive! Traveler" chapter) would never have been able to get up out of his crib and get into the OnLive! Traveler world all by himself. When we all have wall-sized computer/TV/communicator screens, after the turn of the century, virtual worlds will really seem like places we can step into. Perhaps those old VR head mounted displays will turn out to be useful for some high-powered training or entertainment, but I expect that we will see many of them find their final homes in museum display cases.

ComicChat

COMIC COLONY

RANCID LOVE
STARRING

DigiGrdr as XENO

Bill_Gates as DAN

Ⓨou and the crew of the good ship *Avatar* are about to visit a world where your role in a living comic strip will put you inside a drama of tragicomic proportions with other users from around the world. Audition all the would-be stars in your cybernautic craft and beam them over to the Comic Colony!

Your Guide to Comic Chat

WORLD GUIDE

WORLD SKILL LEVEL	Beginner
BUILDING CAPABILITY	No
SYSTEM REQUIREMENTS	Windows 95, Windows NT
AVATAR CREATION CAPABILITY	No; user can select gestures
DEPTH	2D
SOUND SUPPORT	No; text chat

MINIMUM MACHINE

OPERATING SYSTEM	Windows 95; Windows NT 4.0
COMPUTER	486DX 66 MHz PC; 256-color VGA monitor
RESOURCES	8MB RAM; 6MB free disk space
CONNECTION	Dial-up to the Internet at 9,600 bps

Comic Chat for the Comic Artist in All of Us

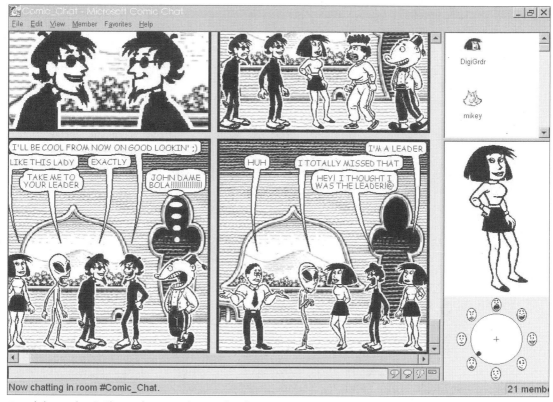

A quick peek at the goings on in Comic Chat.

Were you an artist for your school newspaper? Were you the one the teacher caught doodling all over your math notes? Did the arrival of the Sunday color funnies set your heart aflutter? If this is you, then Microsoft Comic Chat is going to be one fun frolic!

What happens in Comic Chat? You play a character in a comic strip. You are logged into Comic Chat at the same time as others who are playing in their characters. Everything you do as your character (chat, express an emotion, have a thought) is expressed in a panel within an ongoing comic storyboard. The more chat, the more panels generated by Comic Chat. Since it is all very familiar and looks appealing, Comic Chat is like a form of improvised theater in which anyone can participate.

When you finish chatting, you can scroll back and review all the zany conversations you had. You can even print the comic strip and stick it on your refrigerator or pin it up in your cubicle (Dilbert, watch out!).

Installing

Installing Comic Chat

What do I need for Comic Chat?

All you need to run Comic Chat is a reasonably fast PC running Windows 95 or NT 4.0 and a direct connection to the Internet by dial-up on a 9,600 bps modem or faster. You can use Comic Chat through on-line services such as America Online, CompuServe, or Prodigy, if they support direct Internet access through the 32-bit Winsock (the tool Windows uses to communicate with the Internet). For example, you can use Comic Chat through AOL for Windows 95, Microsoft Network, or CompuServe 3.0, which provide this service. For more information on configuring your on-line service to run Comic Chat, see "Setting up Your On-line Service to Connect Directly with the Internet," in Appendix B. If you have further problems, contact your on-line service for help.

If you are at work, or a place where you have a PC on the Internet full time (such as a university or college), you can also use Comic Chat. Connecting from work might require you to check on your *firewall* restrictions (see "Firewalls and proxies," in Appendix B). The recommended minimum machine listed at the beginning of this chapter is the system you should have to run Comic Chat.

Getting started and a few disclaimers

Comic Chat is easy to set up, and it's even easier to jump right in and join the social scene. Best of all, Comic Chat is free to use. As in other virtual worlds, you have to accept the terms of your free license during installation. You are not charged for the time you spend in Comic Chat, but you could be charged for the hours you use from your Internet service provider (ISP) or on-line service. Check with your ISP or on-line service for their monthly free hours and rates . . . Comic Chat can be addicting!

Version 1.1 of Comic Chat is described in this chapter. However, Comic Chat may have evolved since this chapter was written, so after you download Comic Chat from the Internet, it may look somewhat different from what I describe here.

Help

Virtually up-to-date

As a special service for readers of *Avatars!*, I have a home page on the World Wide Web devoted to keeping you up-to-date on your favorite worlds. Find news about software updates, social events held within these virtual worlds, and brand new worlds you might want to try at http://www.digitalspace.com/avatars. Bookmark it!

If you have questions or problems

If you have questions or problems installing or running Comic Chat, I suggest you consult the "Comic Chat FAQ," on the book companion Web site. If you need further assistance, check the Comic Chat page at **http://www.microsoft.com/ie/chat/** for help on more detailed questions. The Comic Chat readme page is also useful. Feel free to contact the Comic Chat team directly at **comichat@microsoft.com** with your technical questions, bug reports, or comments.

I can't provide you technical support for Comic Chat (please contact Microsoft for that). I would be happy to hear about your experiences with Comic Chat, or your comments about this book. Contact us through the *Avatars!* book Web site at **http://www.digitalspace.com/avatars**.

Don't forget to read the manual!

Another good source for information on how to use Comic Chat is the on-line help pages. Just select the Help menu, or press F1 while using Comic Chat, and use the table of contents or index to find the topic you are looking for.

Macintosh, UNIX, and OS/2 versions

At this writing, there are no versions of Comic Chat for the Macintosh, UNIX, or OS/2. Check the Microsoft and *Avatars!* Web pages for updates on new versions which might support these platforms. You may also be able to run Comic Chat using a Windows emulation system on non-Windows platforms. Comic Chat should run under some versions of Windows NT. Check on the Comic Chat home page for information.

Installing or upgrading Comic Chat from the Internet

Comic Chat is not provided on the book CD-ROM, so you must obtain it by downloading the program from the Internet. If you haven't done this before, don't panic, it is easier than you might think!

❶ Connect to the Internet (dial up with your modem and make sure your Internet connection is active).

❷ Start your Web browser, such as Netscape or Internet Explorer.

❸ In the top of the browser window, you will see a text box where you can enter text.

❹ Click in this box, delete the text inside it, type in **http://www.microsoft.com/ie/chat/**, and press the Enter key.

❺ After a few moments, the home page for Microsoft Comic Chat should appear. If it does not after a long wait, check to see that you are actually online.

❻ If the Microsoft page is not available for some reason, try entering the location for the *Avatars!* home page, which is **http://www.digitalspace.com/avatars**. This page may contain more up-to-date links for Comic Chat.

❼ Once you are at the Comic Chat home page, follow the instructions for downloading or upgrading. At one point, you will click on a link for downloading the file.

❽ A few seconds after clicking on the link, you will be presented with a dialogue box. Click Save File (Netscape) or Save As (Internet Explorer) to download the file to disk (or you can save it on your desktop).

❾ You will be prompted to choose a folder in which to save the downloaded file. Note where you chose to save the file and the name of the file itself. You can use the folder designated by your Web browser or select another. I put all downloaded files in a folder which I call \download.

❿ Wait patiently, this download is not large (about 1.1MB). It should only take about 15 to 30 minutes, depending on the speed of your connection. While waiting, you can run other programs, but be careful about interfering with the connection. (Try not to do more work on the Internet while the download is progressing, and if you are using your regular telephone line for your modem, don't make calls.) If you have a call-waiting feature, you may want to turn it off before beginning the download. If someone calls, this could interrupt your download.

Installing Comic Chat

Installing Comic Chat is easy, just follow these simple steps. Note that since you downloaded Comic Chat from the Internet, the installation process may have changed. If this has happened, refer to the instructions on the Microsoft Comic Chat Web site.

❶ It is a good idea to close other programs before you continue with the installation. You can do this by clicking on the running application icons on the task bar and then closing them. You can also use Alt+Tab to go to other running applications even when the installer is waiting for your input and you cannot see the task bar. Simply hold down Alt while pressing Tab and select the icon representing your running application. You should leave your Internet connection running.

❷ To start the installation, find the Comic Chat installer program you downloaded and double-click on that file.

❸ You will be prompted to accept the terms of a license agreement; read them and accept the terms.

❹ The Comic Chat installer program will run and install all the files you need for Comic Chat. The program will tell you when the installation is complete.

❺ Comic Chat is installed into the folder called Cchat inside another folder called Program Files which you will find on your hard disk. Inside the Cchat folder you will find the Comic Chat program.

❻ If you would like to create a shortcut to Comic Chat on your desktop, with your right mouse button held down, drag and drop the Comic Chat program icon onto your Windows 95 desktop and select Create Shortcut(s) Here. You can also find Comic Chat on your Start menu.

❼ I recommend that you do the following cleanup of files before you start getting absorbed in Comic Chat. After this, you will be ready to get started.

Cleaning up after installing

You can delete the Comic Chat installer program after the installation is complete. It should be in the folder you downloaded into it. You can keep the original installer around just in case you have to reinstall it but you can delete it to save hard disk space. Be careful you don't delete the Comic Chat program.

Creating a shortcut to Comic Chat

You may want to create a shortcut to Comic Chat on your desktop. Open \program files\cchat or the folder you selected for Comic Chat, and find the file called chat.exe.With the right mouse button down, drag and drop it onto the desktop, selecting Create shortcut(s) here . . . when prompted by the pop-up menu.

First Steps

Teleporting into Toon Town

Starting up Comic Chat

Before you start Comic Chat, you should connect to the Internet (dial up with your modem or make sure your Internet connection is active). If you can get to Web pages with your Web browser, you are probably online. Once you are online, you can start Comic Chat by double-clicking on a shortcut or by choosing Start ⇨ Programs ⇨ Microsoft Comic Chat.

When Comic Chat first starts up, it presents you with the Connect dialogue box (see the following figure). The first time in, you should leave everything as Microsoft has set it. For your reference, the following is a set of options and what they mean:

Favorites: This option allows you to jump directly to a chat room which you have marked as a favorite. See the description of "Favorites," later in this chapter.

Server: This is the address of the Internet Relay Chat (IRC) server.

Port: This is the port number of the IRC server (for Microsoft, the default is 6667).

Go to chat room: This is the *channel name* of chat rooms within a given IRC server. Channel names always start with the # symbol.

Show all available chat rooms: This option requests a list of all servers and channels available to Comic Chat, allowing you to select a room from a wider menu.

You are in!

You can tell that Comic Chat is trying to connect by watching for the messages at the bottom of the application window. If the server is unavailable or too busy, you will be told, and given the option to try again. I can get on most of the time, but sometimes I have to come back later when the Internet (and Comic Chat) is not so busy. If Comic Chat tells you, Now chatting in room # ..., with the name of the room you selected ... you are in!

Practicing on your own

If you want to practice on your own, or if you are not able to connect yet, you can try Comic Chat in *single-user mode*, where you are the only character around. Practicing in single-user mode is also fun, and will give you a chance to learn how to express yourself through text chat and emotional body moves. To run in single-user mode, just start Comic Chat without your Internet connection active, and Comic Chat will let you play all by yourself.

Connecting to other IRC chat rooms

If you want to connect to another IRC (Internet relay chat) server somewhere on the Internet, just enter the server address, port number, and channel name into the Connect dialogue box. Microsoft's basic Comic Chat IRC channel is **Comicsrv1.Microsoft.Com, 6667, #Comic_Chat**. Note that these names are not case sensitive. Microsoft is supporting the channels listed in the following table. Comic Chat can be used to put a really expressive face on dusty, old IRC! For a definition of the terms server address, port number, and channel name, see the glossary in the back of this book.

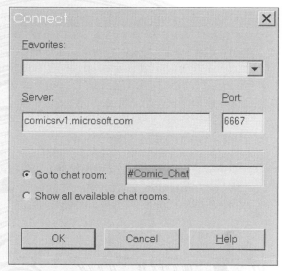

Use the Connect dialogue to open a new connection to Comic Chat.

Chat channels available in Comic Chat

SERVER ADDRESS	PORT NUMBER	CHANNEL NAME	WHAT GOES ON?
Comicsrv1.microsoft.com	6667	#Comic_Chat	Basic Comic Chat town square
comicsrv1.microsoft.com	6667	#Comic_Help	Help with Comic Chat
comicsrv1.microsoft.com	6667	#Newbies	Discussions for new users
comicsrv1.microsoft.com	6667	#Pet_Chat	Talk about your pet!
Comicsrv1.microsoft.com	6667	#Sports_Chat	Sports addicts!
Comicsrv2.microsoft.com	6667	#Family_Chat	Family matters
comicsrv2.microsoft.com	6667	#Internet_Chat	About the Net
comicsrv2.microsoft.com	6667	#Politics_Chat	Pundits on the political scene
comicsrv2.microsoft.com	6667	#Singles_Chat	Singles mixer

The stage is set

Remember, this is real life—well, bits of life. The drama that unfolds is never predictable; there is no plot, and rarely any conclusion. You might think: "how boring!" But wait . . . you must keep the play going: the audience may be just your cartoon compatriots, or maybe one of the characters in the plot will grow to become your long-awaited soul mate (either virtually or actually). The digital drama is yours to deliver!

Curtains up on the show

In the upper left-hand corner of the following figure, you can see the cast of characters, or *playbill,* in which you are one player. Comic Chat has chosen the name Rancid Love for this session (meaning that it will be a tragicomic drama?). You have now joined an ongoing conversation. Each of the people in this conversation has

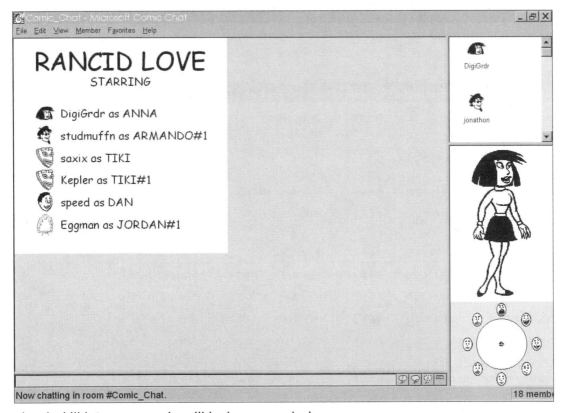

The Playbill lets you see who will be in your comic drama.

chosen an avatar, called a *character* in Comic Chat. This is a rotating cast; the next time you stop in, chances are there will be a completely different set of people playing a different set of characters. Sometimes there are *regulars,* who visit Comic Chat all the time, and may informally become *hosts.* Players have their own nicknames, chosen when they first entered Comic Chat, followed by the name of their character (in UPPERCASE). You are automatically given a default character (sometimes called a *dummy* or *dummytar*), which you can easily change later. Go to the section, "Fine-Tuning Your World," to learn how to change your character.

The cast members

Running down the list, the other characters include a player called *studmuffn* (with a name like that, perhaps one to watch out for) who has chosen the ARMANDO avatar. There are two other people (with nicknames *saxix* and *Kepler*) playing as TIKI avatars, *speed* playing a fairly neutral looking DAN and, possibly a humorous type named *eggman*, playing as a JORDAN.

I am playing as an ANNA, using my virtual world name DigiGrdr, short for DigiGardener, ever the digital naturalist, turning over the fertilizer in the virtual worlds social scenes. Many people choose different names and personae in each world, which hopefully would not give them a multiple personality disorder! I choose to remain consistent as DigiGardener in all the virtual worlds. This helps people recognize me, and I establish more of a distinguished presence.

Express Yourself!

Meet the Natives

The member list, or cast of characters in this room, is listed on the upper-right of the preceding figure. You can choose a character from this list to find out about that person. You can also use the member list to talk directly to, or ignore, someone (more about this later). Below the member list is your character, in its current body and emotional posture. Under your character, you will find the emotion wheel, a delightful feature of Comic Chat, which allows you to change your character's emotional state.

We all know that cartoon characters can be very expressive. This is why they make such great avatars! Comic Chat cartoonist, Jim Woodring, has done a great job of giving us characters in many poses and emotional states. To make ANNA laugh outrageously or be very annoyed, just click and slide the black dot around the wheel. In the next cartoon panel where ANNA talks, this will be her body language. This feature can be used to great effect, as you shall see.

With the emotion wheel, happy days are here again.

Sometimes stronger emotions are in order.

You can choose from the following eight different emotions for your character:

- Angry
- Bored
- Coy
- Happy
- Laughing
- Sad
- Scared
- Shouting

Combine the emotion with the words: ANNA says "Outta here!"

The closer to the outer edge of the wheel you move the dot, the more extreme the emotion; the closer to the center, the more moderate. Note that not all characters are designed to display the full range of emotions.

When you chat, your character is painted into the next panel in the comic strip. ANNA will be placed into the scene with the other characters who have recently chatted. The following figure shows ANNA who has just said: "Outta here!" and assumed an appropriate posture.

Your moods match your words

Through another great trick, Comic Chat will automatically match your gestures and mood depending on what you say in your chat. Word choices and some punctuation (!) will trigger a new position on the emotion wheel, unless you already have chosen the next gesture. The following table lists some of the automatic word/gesture matches.

Words and symbols and their automatic gestures

WORDS OR SYMBOLS	GESTURES THEY GENERATE
I	Makes your character gesture to itself
You	Points your character's arm and hand
:) or :-)	Makes your character smile
:(or :-(	Makes your character frown
;-)	Makes your character wink or act flirtatiously
LOL (Laughing out Loud) or ROTFL (Rolling on the Floor Laughing)	Makes your character laugh
Typing in ALL CAPS	Makes your character shout
Hello, hi, bye	Makes your character wave

Getting a word in edgewise

Getting heard is no problem here! You may have noticed the long white strip with four buttons on the bottom right-hand side of the Comic Chat window. This is the chat entry area. If you type into this area and hit Enter, your words appear in a bubble over your character's head. The following figure shows some text I entered in response to a remark ANNA did not appreciate too much.

Type into the chat entry area
to add your two bits!

A comic panel displaying what you type in a cartoon bubble.

And the figure to the left shows how ANNA is seen speaking . . .

And so it goes; the strip is cranked out, one panel at a time. The following figure illustrates just how interesting (or inane) the conversation can get.

A typical Comic Chat conversation.

Confusing threads

All text chat environments have problems when there are many distinct conversations going on at once. These distinct conversations are often called *threads*. On top of all this, there can be delays of up to 10 seconds before the text you type is seen by other people. It is like everyone in Mission Control trying to talk to a group of astronauts on the moon through one radio link . . . confusing!

For example, in the preceding figure, there are several conversations going on. I have put the identifiable threads together so you can make sense of it:

Thread One:
Suave dude in beret in the first panel: "Any cute women here now?"
Suave dude then asks: "Nikki you cute (meaning *are you cute?*)"
Nikki as ANNA eventually answers: "Hey you, watch it! We don't like the way this conversation is going!"

Thread Two:

Newbie Alien in the second panel: "I'm new here."

Nice guy in the fourth panel: "That's nice . . . " (Note that he uses an ellipsis ". . ." to indicate that there is more to come.)

Newbie Alien making a joke in the fifth panel: "I saw myself on the Weekly World News the other day."

Thread Three:

Laughing Alien in the third panel: "Did you see Ajax play tonight in Amsterdam?"

New woman character in the seventh panel: "No, but I used Ajax in my toilet!!"

With threads, sometimes your conversations can be out of sync. For example, you can ask a question and be asked a question, and answer the other person's question and get the answer to your question, all out of order. The first rule of chat Netiquette is, *be patient, and if you are uncertain, ask again.* I have seen people take great offense when they have misinterpreted something out of order, for example:

Me: "Are you a veteran here?"

Other person: "Yes, is the world running slowly today?"

Other person: "Am I boring you?"

Me: "Yes."

Other person: "I am sorry about that . . . good-bye!"

If an area is just too full of people to be able to converse, you have several options:

1. Suggest to your conversation partner that you both move to another, less crowded chat room or area.

2. Set up a private chat with someone by using *whisper* commands (described later in this chapter).

3. Use the ignore feature (described later) to screen out other people's conversations, leaving only the people you wish to hear. Note that using the ignore feature can be misinterpreted, as people who may want to talk to you will get no answer, and might deduce that you are ignoring them!

4. Conversation in Comic Chat may sometimes seem quite random until you put the threads together. Scrolling back up through the panels of the comic strip is a very useful way to find these threads.

That's a take!

The ability to scroll back up and see what was said earlier in the conversation is an excellent feature. The history of all conversations in the chat room since your arrival is automatically recorded. You can also save the chat in comic strip form! You can create an album of your own personal comic strips (ranking right up there with the home movies), to be reloaded and read, or shared with friends any time. I have found myself rolling over jokes I missed in the heat of the drama. When they become part of a living and breathing comic strip, people say the funniest things. You can save and print your own private funny papers on your laser or ink jet printer and stick it on the refrigerator. Your friends (your kids, your parents?) won't believe it was you in there!

Bear in mind that people are people, and sometimes can say very embarrassing or offensive things, so be sure to check over what every character says before you pin it up at the laundromat!

Words, words, words

In Comic Chat, you are not just limited to spoken words and body lingo, you have the other types of communication familiar to us from the funnies: thought clouds;

Use the chat option buttons to say, think, whisper, or declare an action.

whisperings of sweet nothings; and action captions. Pressing the buttons shown in the following figure will send your next text chat into the scene as a thought, whisper, or action caption. You can also press the keystrokes shown in the following table to produce the same effect as pushing the buttons.

Communication keystrokes

ACTION	KEYSTROKE
Say	Enter or Ctrl+Y
Think	Ctrl+T
Whisper	Ctrl+W
Action Caption	Ctrl+I

Sending private messages by whispering

If you want to send a message to be heard only by a particular character, select that person from the member list, found in the upper right-hand corner. Then enter your text and press the whisper button (or press Ctrl+W) to send it to that person only. Note that the other forms of communication— thoughts, action captions, and normal speech—can be seen by everyone.

As you can see in the following figure, I (as the Alien) am trying out the thought clouds and whispering, which confuses the other character. She asks in a normal voice, "Yeah, why?" I respond with an action caption which can be seen by everyone: "DIGIGRDR: Well, hello," and then explain to her that I am just testing the different ways to communicate. The action caption would typically be used to make a general statement about a scene, such as Dick Tracy calling headquarters.

You can use action captions to narrate your own actions. Captions will always begin with the name of the person who wrote the caption. If I wrote a caption, it might come out looking like: "DIGIGRDR seeks someone to share an intelligent conversation." The Action command automatically inserts your character's name; you don't have to type it.

Trying out all the communication options.

Speaking in Web-ese

Another cool trick in Comic Chat is to include a Web page URL in your text chat. It is shown as a link that anyone can click on, starting their Web browsers, and automatically bringing up that Web page. So, I could say, "Hey, take a look at my cool Web page at **http://www.biota.org**," and the other Comic Chat players could immediately click on that link in my character's speech bubble and bring up the page. Note that you must include the "http://" for Comic Chat to know that it is a Web link. Also note that Comic Chat can actually run inside Microsoft Explorer 3.0.

Fine-Tuning Your World

Comic Chat has several useful options you can access by choosing View ⇨ Options. The most common option is to change your character. The dialogue box in the following figure displays an array of characters from which to choose. You can even use the built-in emotion wheel to try out each character in all its different stances.

Another option is typing in personal information. You can give your real name (if you choose), your nickname (your name in the world), and a brief description of yourself. Many Comic Chat citizens forget to fill out their personal information. In the singles area, it is especially important to have *something* there, and to check what other people write about themselves.

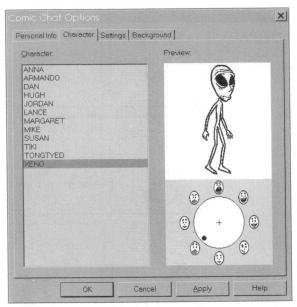

Change your character to Xeno the ET using the Options dialogue.

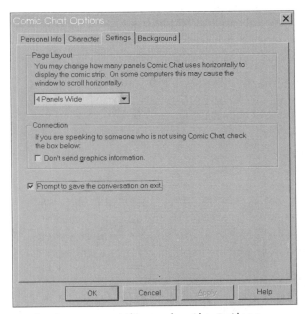

Customize your settings using the Options dialogue.

In their profiles, people have the opportunity to express their true selves or their fantasy selves, so don't take everything at face value (just like in the real world).

Another very important set of options can be found under Settings. Comic Chat normally paints only two comic strip panels across. If there are a lot of people talking, the panels can flash by so fast that you miss threads of conversations. If you set Page Layout to 4 Panels Wide or greater, you will get a better overview at the expense of graphical detail.

Other settings include Connection, which allows you to turn off the graphical information going out from Comic Chat's IRC server. This is important if you are chatting with someone who is just running IRC without Comic Chat. This will save that person from having to see a whole lot of graphics control gibberish. The last option turns on or off the prompt you get when closing Comic Chat, which asks if you want to save your last conversation.

See the Help file in Comic Chat, or visit the Microsoft Comic Chat Web at **http://www.microsoft.com/ie/comichat/** for more detailed information about using Comic Chat with IRC.

A final option allows you to change the background against which all the characters are painted. This changes the background just for you, not the other users.

Comic Chat keyboard shortcuts

Comic Chat has a whole set of keyboard shortcuts which are very handy to use (see following table), especially to keep up with a fast-paced conversation.

Keyboard shortcuts

Key Combination	Action
Ctrl+A	Selects all text in Compose window
Ctrl+C	Copies selected text from Compose window to the Clipboard
Ctrl+D	Deletes selected text from the Compose window
Ctrl+N	Closes the current chat session and opens a new connection
Ctrl+O	Opens a file
Ctrl+P	Prints a file
Ctrl+S	Saves a file
Ctrl+V	Pastes the Clipboard contents into the Compose window
Ctrl+X	Cuts the selected text to the Clipboard
Ctrl+Z	Reverses the most recent action in the Compose window (Undo)

The Comic Cosmos: Stories from the CyberFunnies

Brother Bill, can you spare a dime?

I was browsing through the list of active chat rooms one day (choose View ⇨ Chat Room List) when I spied a discussion on Windows hosted by none other than Bill Gates! My heart skipped a beat as I teleported, or clicked into that room. Gullible me; as I arrived as alien XENO (this might be how Bill sees most users), I found that I was all alone with Bill (at least at first). I was so excited! Maybe I could convince Bill to buy 100,000 copies of my book for his home library, which I am sure is larger than my house.

Bill (playing a DAN) looked like Bill, so I grabbed my opportunity. I could just picture Bill in his corner office up in Redmond munching a sandwich and killing time on Comic Chat. The conversation was captured just for you, in the following figure.

I met Bill Gates in Comic Chat?!

Imagine how I felt when my Bill Gates meeting-of-a-lifetime started to smell of week-old Pacific Northwest salmon, as it became clear I had unmasked an impostor. My greatest career break . . . blown!

An impostor is unmasked!

Superman—jerk of the day

On another bright and early morning on Comic Chat (you really *must* think I am crazy!), ANNA ran into a character called *Superman*. Suspect from the beginning, Superman proved to be both a poser and provocateur extraordinaire. Conver-sation was moving right along as I was helping two *newbies*, or new users, who are portrayed as aliens in the following figure. Then, in came Superman, entering from stage left.

As you can see next, Superman started to monopolize the conversation . . .

Using the iconic member list to find out who Superman is.

So I tried to find out who this character was by selecting him from the member list . . .

Superman is getting obnoxious!

. . . and I found out he had not entered a profile in his personal information!

Who is this Superman? Oops, no profile!

The power to ignore

Member

Get Profile

Ignore

Use Member Options to find out who someone is, or to ignore them.

So, my only option left was to *ignore* him, which I did by choosing Member ⇨ Ignore. Now, I no longer have to see this person's character or what they have been spouting out. This type of *banishment* is controversial, but often useful in virtual worlds. You can also Ignore someone by right-clicking with your mouse over the top of their character in the Member List area, in the upper right-hand corner of the Comic Chat screen. See "Netiquette and Community Hosting," on the book companion Web site, for tips on of how to behave in virtual worlds.

To quickly find out a character's chosen name, just hold your mouse over that character until you see their *badge* appear, as in the following figure. You can also right-click on a character inside the comic strip panels and get the same menu as you would by right-clicking on them in the member list. So, you can right-click on a character in a panel and ignore them, or select Get Info on them.

Hold your mouse over a character to find out who is speaking

Hot Spots in Comic Chat

Hot Spots

If you had a particularly good time in a Comic Chat room, you can save it as a favorite by choosing Favorites ⇨ Add to Favorites. You then can open the favorite area later with Favorites ⇨ Open Favorites, or stow your favorite room right on your desktop by choosing File ⇨ Create Shortcut. When connecting to Comic Chat in the future, your favorites are now easily accessible. Favorite is one of my favorite features! Note that Comic Chat always brings you back into the chat area where you were during your last session.

Hot Comic Chat home pages

Note that some of the following Web page links may have changed, or the Web pages may have been discontinued. Consult your *Avatars!* book home page at **http://www.digitalspace.com/avatars** for a more up-to-date list of links.

Official pages

http://www.microsoft.com/ie/chat
The Comic Chat Home Page.

Press blab about Comic Chat

http://www.startelegram.com:80/archives/07141996.arc/news/opinions/starcol/wow.htm
A Comic Chat review.

http://www.usyd.edu.au/~mwoodman/spunk/woodring.html
An interview with Comic Chat cartoonist Jim Woodring.

http://register.cnet.com/Content/Reviews/Hands/082096/comic.html
A review of Comic Chat in C|Net.

Unofficial pages

http://www.iol.ie:80/chat/index.html
Ireland On-Line's Chat Centre Comic Chat Page—the gift of the gab.

http://www.cyberway.com.sg/irc.html
CyberWay's IRC pages featuring Comic Chat.

http://www.davecentral.com/irc.html
Davecentral's IRC Universe.

http://www.ozbiz.com.au:80/comicch.htm
OzBiz Comic Chat.

Digi's Diary: Toons Teach Us How

Digi's Diary

Hey, did you know how many people are working on getting your face onto the Internet? There are scanners costing half a million dollars that can scan your head all the way around and make a three-dimensional model. Researchers are putting little detectors on your cheeks and eyebrows to send your expressions over the Internet, and *move* a dummy computer model at the other end. You can even look into a TV camera to capture your own facial expresssions and transfer these expressions through the Internet to drive an animated rubber puppet face on the other end.

Why go to all this trouble? Cartoons have been used to communicate expressive feelings for about as long as humans could start doodling on cave walls. Back in my halcyon days, I was a cartoonist for local newspapers in my town. At school I also participated in producing a weekly teacher caricature which was posted near the school office (until one time it got a little too expressive for one particular teacher). With just a few strokes of the pen, I could create a face and body that would express any kind of emotion or action. So why do we need to do all this work to put our real faces on the Internet? The answer is right in front of you. We do not have to wait around for the virtual reality types to get that perfect human online (and sell us those funny glasses, too). We can start expressing ourselves today through avatars. And why not? Who wants every wrinkle and wobble to be seen by the whole world? Besides, it is much more fun to live in the fantasy of a big masquerade party.

So, the long and the short of it is that the toons have a lot to teach us about how to make and move avatars. Jim Woodring, the comic artist who designed the Comic Chat world and avatars, shows us all that toons can do the job. If you are interested in cartooning and can see how great it is for avatar cyberspace, read *Understanding Comics* by Scott McCloud, which is listed in the bibliography at the end of this book. Go toons!

OZ Virtual

JOURNEY TO THE DARK STAR

FILE DESTINATIONS COMMUNICATION HELP

The good ship *Avatar* is caught up in the whorls of a dark gaseous cloud in deepest, coldest space. As we penetrate this icy zone, we spot a distant dark star on our viewing screens. Scanning our charts, it is clear that we have found the mysterious world of OZ, a realm of truly cool beauty. This is a newborn world in digital space, and we will be among the first outsiders to set foot on it.

Your Guide to
OZ Virtual

WORLD GUIDE

WORLD SKILL LEVEL	Advanced
BUILDING CAPABILITY	No
SYSTEM REQUIREMENTS	Windows 95/NT
AVATAR CREATION CAPABILITY Customizable from given set	
DEPTH	3D
SOUND SUPPORT Music, sound effects, optional voice chat	

MINIMUM MACHINE

OPERATING SYSTEM	Windows 95
COMPUTER 90MHz Pentium PC; 16-bit color video or higher	
RESOURCES 16MB RAM; 5 to 10MB free disk space including ActiveX; 16-bit sound card (optional) for music and sound effects; microphone (optional) for voice chat	
CONNECTION Dial-up to the Internet at 28.8 kbps	

OZ Virtual: Journey to the Dark Star

The creators of OZ Virtual come from Iceland, which they describe as, "a volcanic island inhabited by a small, strong-minded population which lives on fishing and speaks the oldest language in Europe." In the midst of glaciers and very dark winters, the Icelanders have maintained a strong sense of cultural heritage, and quickly embraced new technology such as the Internet. OZ Interactive Inc. was founded by some young and ambitious Icelanders who have now stormed into California and onto the Internet with their own VRML (Virtual Reality Modeling Language) entertainment system, complete with customizable avatars, performance animation, music, and beautifully designed spaces. OZONE, OZ's new 3D entertainment community, is one of the newest worlds in the avatar cosmos, so you and I will become some of the earliest explorers there.

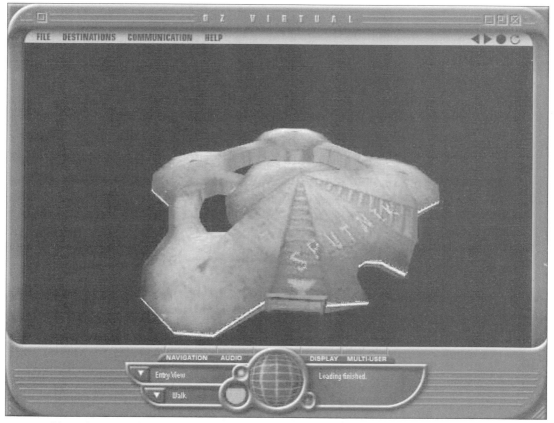

Approaching the Sputnik Space Station in OZ.

Installing

Installing OZ Virtual

What do I need to use OZ Virtual?

To use OZ Virtual, you need a PC with a Pentium processor of at least 90MHz. You must run Windows 95 or NT 4.0. A sound card and speakers will also let you experience the high-quality music in OZ worlds. A microphone will let you enjoy voice chat with other avatars. OZ takes up at least 20MB of disk space (OZ Virtual is about 4.5MB; ActiveX, DirectSound, and Java Virtual Machine will take up the rest, but users of Microsoft Internet Explorer will already have ActiveX and Java Virtual Machine). Note also that you will consume more disk space as you travel and download new OZ VRML worlds from the Internet.

Software and connection requirements

The OZ Virtual client software is all you need. This software communicates with an OZ server network, allowing you to explore worlds with other people. OZ worlds can be visited alone, but it is much more fun if you are in the world with other (human) avatars.

OZ Virtual requires Microsoft ActiveX and Java Virtual Machine, and automatically gets these components for you. If you run into any problems, or would like to install the components yourself, you can download ActiveX directly from **http://www.oz .com/ov/download/ActiveX.exe**, or find all the components on Microsoft's home page at **http://www.microsoft.com**.

You may also choose to download Microsoft DirectX, which supports 3D sound (DirectSound) in OZ worlds. This is optional. It can be found at **http://www.microsoft .com/directx/resources/downloads/directx.exe**.

If you would like to download all the OZ Worlds to your PC (this will decrease loading time), you can get them from the directory at **http://www.oz.com/zipvrml**.

In general, if you can use Netscape, you should be able to use OZ. You can't use OZ through Windows-based on-line services such as America Online, CompuServe, the Microsoft Network, or Prodigy, unless they support direct Internet access through the 32-bit *Winsock*. (Short for Windows Sockets, Winsock is a standard interface for Microsoft Windows applications and the Internet. Winsocks allow communication between Windows Web browsers, e-mail clients, IRC clients, or any other Windows Winsock applications and the TCP/IP.) See, "Setting up your on-line service to connect directly with the Internet," in Appendix B of this book. If you have further problems, contact your on-line service for help.

Getting started and a few disclaimers

OZ Virtual is free to use (you have to accept the terms of your free license during installation). You are not charged for the time you spend exploring or interacting in OZ worlds, but you could be charged for the hours you are online from your *Internet service provider (ISP)*. Check with your ISP on monthly free hours and rates. Of course, you should remember that you are also charged by your telephone company for using the phone line.

More about the companion CD software

OZ Virtual is constantly evolving, and may have changed since this chapter was written. I placed the very latest version of OZ Virtual on your book CD, and it may be somewhat different from what is described here. These differences will not be major, and this chapter will still be a great guide to OZ worlds. If you see new features or changes, you should check for information under the Help menu in OZ Virtual.

Virtually up-to-date

Help

As a special service for readers of *Avatars!*, I have a home page on the World Wide Web devoted to keeping you up-to-date on your favorite worlds. Find news about software updates, social events held within these virtual worlds, and brand new worlds you might want to try at **http://www.digitalspace.com/avatars**. Bookmark it!

If you have questions or problems

If you have questions or problems installing or running OZ Virtual, consult OZ Virtual Frequently Asked Questions (FAQ)," on the companion Web site to this book. If this does not help you, check the excellent OZ Web site at **http://www.oz.com**, and especially the support pages at **http://www.oz.com/ov/support/main_index.html**. These contain on-line manuals, FAQs, and technical support pages. Reporting a bug to OZ Interactive is simple. Simply fill out the bug report form on the Web site, or send an e-mail to OZ Virtual user support at **virtualbeta@oz.is**.

I appreciate your feedback on *Avatars!*, but I don't have the resources to provide technical support. I would be happy to hear about your experiences in OZ Virtual. Contact us through the *Avatars!* book Web site at **http://www.digitalspace.com/avatars**.

Macintosh, UNIX, and OS/2 versions

At this writing, there are no versions of the OZ Virtual client program for the Macintosh, UNIX, or OS/2. Check the OZ and *Avatars!* book Web pages for updates on new versions which might support these platforms. You also may be able to run the OZ Virtual client using a Windows emulation system on non-Windows machines. Note that if you are considering hosting a complete OZ world, the server software runs on Windows NT and Windows 95.

Installing OZ Virtual from your Avatars! CD

If you have a CD-ROM drive on your PC, you can install OZ Virtual directly from the book CD-ROM. If you don't have a CD-ROM drive, skip to the following section, "Installing or upgrading OZ Virtual from the Internet." In "The Book CD-ROM" chapter, I provide a step-by-step example of how to install any virtual worlds software from the CD-ROM. I suggest you refer to this chapter and follow the same steps for OZ Virtual. Once the installation program on your CD-ROM has started, you can go to the section, "Running the installation," in this chapter.

Installing or upgrading OZ Virtual from the Internet

If you want the very latest version of OZ Virtual, or were informed that you had to upgrade the version found on your *Avatars!* CD, then you must download files from the Internet.

If you don't have any versions of OZ Virtual on your system, you need to download the initial program from the Internet. When you start the program, it will prompt you to download all the components you will need (the rest of OZ Virtual, ActiveX, DirectSound, Java Virtual Machine). If you haven't done this before, don't panic; it is easier than you might think!

❶ Connect to the Internet (dial up with your modem, or make sure your Internet connection is active).

❷ Start your Web browser, such as Netscape Navigator or Microsoft Internet Explorer.

❸ In the top of the browser window, you will see a text box called Location, where you can enter text. Click in this area, delete the text inside, type http://www.oz.com, and press Enter. After a few moments, the home page for OZ Interactive should appear. If nothing comes up for a long time, check to see that you are online. If the OZ Interactive home page is not available for some reason, try entering the location for the *Avatars!* Web site, which is http://www.digitalspace.com/avatars. This page may contain more up-to-date links for OZ Interactive.

❹ Once you are at the OZ Interactive home page, follow the instructions for downloading or upgrading the OZ Virtual software. At one point, you will click on a link and be prompted for a place to save a file. In the dialogue box, click

Save to Disk (Netscape) or Save As (Internet Explorer), and save the file to a folder or a place on your desktop. You must choose a folder where you will remember to find the new file, and note the name of the file. You can use the folder that your Web browser gives you or move back up and select another. I put all downloaded files in a folder I call \download. Wait patiently while the download progresses (about 200KB). You can work in other applications, but be careful not to interfere with the connection. Try not to do more on-line work (such as Web surfing) while the download is progressing, and if you are using your regular telephone line for the modem, don't make a call.

❺ After the download is finished (less than a minute for a 28.8 kbps connection, and about a minute for a 14.4 kbps connection), open the folder into which the file was downloaded and double-click on the file (which should be named ozvirtual.exe) to start the installation. Go to the next section, "Running the installation."

Running the installation

Whether you are running the installation from the CD-ROM, or from the file you downloaded from the Internet, use this section to guide you through the installation. Note that if you downloaded OZ Virtual from the Internet, the installation process may have changed. If it has, refer to the instructions on the OZ Virtual Web site.

❶ The installer setup program will run and prompt you at each step. First, read and accept the license agreement terms.

❷ You will be prompted for the folder into which you will install OZ Virtual. The default folder is \program files\oz interactive\oz virtual. You can change this or accept the default (recommended).

❸ You will be prompted to download and install the components of OZ Virtual from the Internet. This process (performed by the OZ Installation Gizmo) will obtain the needed components and updates for OZ Virtual. As these components are about 5MB to 10MB in size, this will take some time. I downloaded OZ Virtual in 30 minutes on a 28.8 kbps modem. The other components (ActiveX, DirectSound, and Java Virtual Machine) would have taken another 30 minutes, but since I had Internet Explorer 3.0 installed, I already had most of these components. The OZ Installation Gizmo is smart enough to sense what you already have, and will not download it again.

❹ After all the components are downloaded, the installation will commence. If you have enough disk space, and all other necessary components are present, the installation should complete normally.

Files created by the installation

A shortcut to OZ Virtual will be placed on your desktop. All other files created by the installer should be found in the folder called \program files\oz interactive\oz virtual.

Cleaning up after installation

If you downloaded the OZ Virtual installation file from the Internet, you can delete it after the installation is complete. Do not delete the OZ Virtual program in \program files\oz interactive\oz virtual by mistake, as this is your running version.

First Steps

Entering the OZ Universe

Once you have finished downloading and installing OZ Virtual, ActiveX, and DirectX (optional), you should be ready to start up the OZ Virtual client software. First, make sure you are connected to the Internet. If you can run your browser and surf Web pages, you are surely connected. Double-click on the shortcut on your desktop. If you cannot find an icon for OZ Virtual on your desktop, search for it in the folder \program files\oz interactive\oz virtual\program (it should be called ozvirtual.exe).

Connecting to the server.

The OZ Virtual program will then start and attempt to connect to an OZ server. You should see a message in the lower right-hand corner of the OZ Virtual window, like the one shown in the adjacent figure. This could take some time (a minute or two). OZ Virtual may come back and inform you that the server is unavailable, in which case I recommend that you try again later. You may also receive a message that OZ Virtual needs an update. OZ Virtual can update itself over the Internet. I recommend that you opt to receive the update.

If all goes well, OZ Virtual will connect to the server and download the information for its VRML (Virtual Reality Modeling Language) entry world. Before long, you should begin to see scenes like the ones above, as you are taken on a journey into the first of OZ's exciting worlds. You can see our spacecraft approaching the OZONE space station and then landing inside.

Inside the OZONE.

Docking at the Dark Star

The following figure shows my avatar inside the OZONE. I like the little green man (what better choice in these alien worlds?). I am also walking around in an out-of-body view. I'll talk more about selecting your own avatar and entering this view later in this chapter.

To give yourself a good lay of the land, I recommend choosing OZ Destinations from the Destinations menu. This will give you a Web page map of the OZONE areas. In the following figures, you can see these maps shown inside the OZ Virtual client software. If you have Internet Explorer 3.0 installed, then Web pages will appear inside your OZ Virtual program window (as an ActiveX control). If you use another Web browser, OZ Virtual will launch that browser to show these special Web-based maps.

Me and my avatar in the OZONE.

A Web-based map of the OZONE.

You can click on these maps (on the text labels which lead to areas on the maps), and you will go directly to the selected part of the OZONE. I tried Soundroom, and my avatar traveled to a room where I could hear high-quality music. OZ is known for both quality of the sound and the body animation of its avatars. In fact, two of the founders of OZ were nightclub owners and promoters in Iceland when they conceived of the company. As a result, OZ worlds have the feel of a club environment. OZ Interactive often demonstrates its worlds at live events, such as trade shows, where a performer in a full body suit is "wired up" to the avatar in the virtual world. Every move the performer makes is mirrored by the avatar. This is called *motion capture,* and it gives avatars very lifelike moves. Many of the avatar movements in OZ worlds were made by capturing the motion of a live performance artist. (See "Digi's Diary," at the end of this chapter, for more details.)

Sailing through OZ space

Now that we are on board the OZ space station, let's learn how to move around. OZ has a variety of ways to move, either by keyboard or mouse.

Mouse navigation

You can start by holding down your left mouse button and moving the mouse. OZ worlds have a kind of motion physics whereby the more you push forward the faster you go, up to a kind of terminal velocity (maximum speed). You can hold down the right mouse button to decelerate, or both buttons at once to stop. If you move the mouse with the right button held down, you will slow down and eventually move backward. Holding down Shift while moving with the mouse will rocket you along at twice the normal terminal velocity. Dragging your mouse around to the right or left will steer you around. Holding down Control or Alt will move your avatar to either side in a sliding motion called *translation.* The physics of OZ worlds also gives you friction, so you will eventually stop moving if you stop using the mouse. The mouse movement options are listed in the following table.

Mouse navigation controls

MOUSE BUTTON AND KEYBOARD COMBINATIONS	ACTION
Left button	Accelerate
Right button	Decelerate
Both buttons	Stop
Drag right/left	Turn right/left (Yaw)
Drag forward/backward	Lean forward/backward (Pitch)
Ctrl+Drag right/left	Lean sideways (Roll)
Alt+Drag right/left	Translation left/right
Alt+Drag up/down	Translation up/down

Keyboard navigation

Keyboard navigation, often more convenient to use than the mouse, is a mirror of the mouse navigation. The Up arrow key accelerates you forward, while the Down arrow key slows you down and moves you backward. Holding down the up and down arrow keys at the same time will stop you in your tracks, and pressing the arrow keys and Shift at the same time will move you at twice the normal maximum or terminal velocity. Holding Alt and Control down at the same time as the arrow keys, gives you various tilting, rolling, or translation (sliding) motions. The keyboard movement options are listed in the following table.

Keyboard navigation controls

KEYBOARD KEY	ACTION
Up arrow	Accelerate
Down arrow	Decelerate
Up/Down simultaneously	Stop
Shift+Up or Down arrow	Double terminal velocity
Ctrl+Up or Down arrow	Lean forward or backward (Pitch)
Ctrl+Right or Left arrow	Lean sideways (Roll)
Ctrl+Up or Down arrow	Tilt up or down
Ctrl+Right or Left arrow	Roll clockwise or counterclockwise
Alt+Right or Left arrow	Translation left or right
Alt+Up or Down arrow	Translation up or down

Flying versus walking

The walking mode automatically takes effect when you are affected by gravity. You can turn off gravity and enter a flying mode. In the walking mode you are "stuck" to the floor and therefore unable to move up or down.

Turn off gravity by selecting the area marked Navigation from the dashboard of controls at the bottom of the OZ Virtual window. A pop-up menu will appear, and you can turn automatic gravity on or off. To fly off the ground, turn automatic gravity off and then hold down Ctrl while pressing Up arrow. You will tilt up. You can then fly above the ground.

With automatic gravity on, you would automatically snap back to the floor (as though you were wearing gravity boots) after you reached a certain height. With no

Use the navigation pop-up menu to turn gravity and collision detection on or off.

gravity, you would just sail up and out of the room. If collision detection is on, you will hit the ceiling (or wall or floor) and travel no further. If it is off, you will pass through any surface and continue on into the OZ cosmos. It is quite easy to get lost if you have collision detection off.

Driving through OZ with the dashboard

The dashboard, shown in the following figure, has other features to aid you in navigation. One of the most important is found just below the Navigation pop-up menu. It is a set of viewpoints, kind of like fixed camera positions in the world. In the previous figure, entry view is listed. Clicking on this control allows you to pop back to your starting place (called the entry view). This is very handy if you get lost by turning off collision detection and fly out of the world!

Other parts of the dashboard allow you to control how fast you can travel. By selecting the control just below the viewpoints (entry view, as shown in the preceding figure), you can switch your travel speed from normal to slow or fast. Also on the dashboard are four circular indicators. The large central one is a kind of rolling marble called the trackball. Clicking on the trackball with your left mouse button allows you to roll the world around. Clicking on it with the right button will put you outside of your avatar's body. The little green light to the lower right of the trackball indicates when you are out of body or back in first-person point of view. The figure earlier in this chapter showing my little green man was an example of an out-of-body view. I prefer traveling in OZ out of body as it allows me to see my avatar's gestures (see more on this later). Note that if you press the letters Z or X while in out-of-body mode, you will move closer in or farther out of your avatar. To go back inside the body of your avatar, just right-click on the trackball or select the small green light on the lower right side of the trackball.

The little light to the upper left of the trackball allows you to turn a headlight on or off. This headlight feature is useful for brightening dark areas you may enter. The larger round indicator below the headlight control is a kind of progress indicator. When it is rolling around, something is being loaded.

Elsewhere on the dashboard are areas where messages are displayed (to the right of the trackball), as well as pop-up menus for Audio, Display, and Multi-user options.

The remaining dashboard options are described in a later section of this chapter entitled, "Fine-Tuning Your World."

The OZ Virtual dashboard.

Travels Through OZ

Meet the Natives

Exploring the OZONE

OZ has created some of the best-looking worlds ever built using VRML (Virtual Reality Modeling Language). OZ artists are real masters in light, texture, and mood. High-quality sound and music also fills OZ worlds. The OZONE is the best OZ world yet, and it is the world you enter first when you start OZ Virtual. Earlier in this chapter, in the section, "Docking at the Dark Star," I began to explore the OZONE. In this section, I will tell you a little more about this large, futuristic virtual world.

What can you do in the OZONE? This world features virtual reality music concerts, nightclubs, multi-user games, and music listening areas. OZ will be hosting live music and performance avatar events in the OZONE, so watch for announcements on the home page at **http://www.oz.com**.

OZONE is a spaceship floating in 3D cyberspace with the following virtual entertainment areas to explore:

- The *Centrum* is the public commons of the community, and is a meeting place for people (or their avatars) on their way to music events, games, or nightclubs in other parts of the world.

- The *Club* features events such as motion-captured concerts presented by OZ, and other entertainment providers. The performer appears in real-time as an avatar on the club stage, while the concerts are broadcast using streaming audio.

- The *Arcade* is a VRML game room created by OZ, featuring multi-user games such as chess, Reversi, and backgammon. More games will be provided in this space soon including action multi-player adventures.

- The *Soundroom* is an environment filled with spatialized (sound cast into space) sound surprises and vocal delights. As the Soundroom is empty of all visual stimuli, it's a cool place for visitors to hang out and rest their eyes while exploring with their ears.

Other OZ Worlds

OZONE is not the only OZ world out there. There are many others, each with different themes. You can visit these OZ worlds by following the instructions in the section, "Hot OZ Worlds," later in this chapter.

Docking with Sputnik Space Station in OZ.

OZ has created space stations like Sputnik and Orion. I navigated my avatar into Sputnik (see the preceding figure), and then went on to explore Orion, where I met

my date (a guide from OZ) to go dancing in the disco. Disco did not die in Iceland, so it is introduced in the virtual worlds, complete with real avatar dancing moves and CD quality sound. The following figure shows me on the disco floor with my date . . . move that avatar!

Boogie on down at the Orion Station Disco.

Exploring the Kidscape world with.

My date then took me to the bright and cheery Kidscape world which features a Farmer John type of setting. When you get close to the cows in this world they start mooing. Ditto for the farmhouse cat. The cat is a type of automatic avatar in a virtual world I like to call a *biot,* that is, it is like a robot trying to be like something from biology. Biots, like bots (faithful agents at your service), pay attention to you. Another class of thing in virtual worlds, which I term *biota,* is one more step removed; they are artificial life forms in virtual worlds which may or may not pay you any heed. Farmer John needs a nice tall crop of biota corn in his fields! See the chapter, "Bots, Biota, and Virtual Pets," for more on this.

The community

OZ is a relatively new world, so at the time I wrote this chapter, there was no strongly developed community. I did meet some interesting characters on The Street, one of the oldest OZ worlds. By the time you read this book, there should be many more people in the world.

Meeting and chatting with the natives

The OZ chat manager window.

To chat, you must start the chat manager from the Communication menu. If the chat manager is able to connect to a chat server (it sometimes cannot, so keep retrying), then it should come up with a window like the one in the following figure. As you can see, there are two groups of people present; all (including everyone in this OZ world at the time), and a separate chat group called, Hello, please join. You can create your own chat groups and name them anything you like.

The chat interface is pretty simple, with the nicknames of the people listed in front of the chat they type in the Submit area. You must press the

Submit button or Enter on your keyboard to send chat into the chat stream. The following figure shows the live chat for the group called "hello . . . ."

The OZ chat interface.

Private chat

To request a private chat session with another user, select the icon for the person in the chat manager window, press the right mouse button, and select Request Private Chat from the pop-up menu. When you request a private chat, the other user will be notified of the request for chat. To accept the chat request and establish a chat session, the other person must double-click on your icon or right-click and select Answer Chat Request in the pop-up menu.

Group chat

To use group chat, you can either join an existing group, or create a new one. To create a chat group, simply right-click in the chat manager window (not on a user), and choose New Group from the pop-up menu. You will then be prompted to enter the name of the group, and if the name is accepted, a group chat window will open, with you as the only group member. Other people can join the group by right-clicking on the group icon in the chat manager and selecting Join Group. To leave a group text chat, just close the chat window.

More about chat: Who is in my space?

If you turn off Auto Answer Chat in the Multi-user menu on the OZ Virtual dashboard, you can force another user to specifically get your approval to open a private chat. If you are being bothered by someone, you can right-click on their avatar and ignore them, which will thereafter screen out all their chat.

Another tip: you can launch a chat session in a separate window by choosing Tear Off from the Split menu in the chat manager.

Audio chat

OZ Virtual supports audio chat (which you can use only if your PC has a sound card, speakers, and a microphone). Microsoft DirectSound 3.0 must be installed to have the full-duplex audio chat functionality. The DirectSound 3.0 drivers for full-duplex are only available for Windows 95, and can be found on the Microsoft Web site at **http://www.microsoft.com**. If the person with whom you want to audio chat has an older version of DirectSound, you will not hear their voice. They could hear your voice if you have DirectSound 3.0 installed.

To request an audio chat with another user, choose the icon for the person in the chat manager, press the right mouse button, and choose Request Audio Chat in the pop-up menu. When you request an audio chat, the icon for the person will get a phone hook (shown in the chat manager window) and the other user will be notified of your request. To accept an audio chat request and establish an audio session, the user must choose the icon for the person requesting the chat, press the right mouse button, and choose Answer Audio Chat in the pop-up menu. When an audio chat session has been established, a pop-up window appears with a volume control for the audio session.

To end an audio chat, either close the dialogue, or select the icon for the person with whom you are chatting, press the right mouse button, and select Close Audio Chat in the right button pop-up menu.

Buttons and controls

The OZ Virtual window controls.

In the top right corner of the OZ Virtual window there are several buttons. This section describes what these buttons do. Most controls on the main window have a tool tip (a short help description which pops up beside the control when you move your mouse over it).

Window control buttons

The button at the top left corner of the main window (not shown in the preceding figure), blacks out the background and removes any distracting items. Clicking it again brings the background back. The remaining buttons perform the same actions as the window controls in your computer's operating system: they minimize or maximize the window, and close the application.

News of the world

The first button will launch a Web page (inside OZ Virtual, if you have Internet Explorer 3.0; outside in your Web browser, if not) with the latest news of the world.

Move quickly between worlds or scenes

The next four buttons control scene loading. These are like the forward and backward buttons in your Web browser. The first button moves back a scene (the last world you loaded). The second button moves forward to the next scene you had previously loaded. The last two buttons on the right will stop loading a world or reload a world.

Advanced OZ

Avatar motions (gestures)

The OZ Avatar Motions (gestures) palette.

If you are in out-of-body mode, it is fun to watch your avatar boogie along with gestures. Gestures are called *motions* in OZ, and they allow you to put on quite a performance for other users in OZ worlds. Selecting Motions from the Communication menu will bring up the Motions palette (shown in the following figure). Motions are custom designed for each avatar, and not all the same motions are available for every avatar. You can make your avatar move by choosing from this palette or by pressing the keyboard function keys listed in the following table. The Avatar Editor (also available under the Communication menu) also allows you to preview motions.

Avatar gestures and their keyboard keys

KEY	MOTION
F1	Walk (go back to normal motion)
F2	Fly
F3	Wave ("Greetings earthling!")
F4	Silly jive
F5	Cossack dance
F6	Splits
F7	Ballerina
F8	Funky step*
F9	Punch*

*Note: May not work for all avatar types.

The Avatar Editor

One of the most powerful (and coolest) features of OZ Virtual is the Avatar Editor. Found under the Communication menu (or by pressing Ctrl+A), the editor allows you to select your avatar, its pieces, change its color and scaling, and preview its motions (gestures). The following figure shows how to select Bzingo, the little green man avatar. You can navigate by holding down your left mouse button in the window on the left where Bzingo is displayed to get a closer look at him.

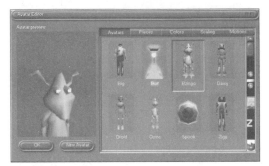

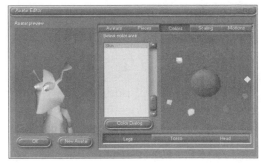

Selecting the little green man named Bzingo in the OZ Avatar Editor.

Changing Bzingo's colors in the OZ Avatar Editor.

I used the Color Property page in OZ to change the colors on my avatar (as shown in the figure on the right). I then stretched him out a bit on the Scaling Property page in the editor.

Making a new avatar

You can create more avatars by pushing the New button in the Avatars mode of the editor. Select an avatar type from the drop-down menu and name it. The new avatar will be a copy of an existing form that you can now shape and color differently. To delete an avatar, right-click on it and select Delete from the pop-up menu. The following sections list the Avatar Editor specifics.

Avatar pieces

Some avatars allow you to select different pieces for the avatar's body—different heads, for example. The pieces property page in the Avatar Editor displays all available pieces and allows you to select the desired piece from a list. A detailed view of the piece appears in the window on the right, and you can zoom, rotate, and move the light the same way as in the left window.

The buttons at the bottom of the pieces property page allow you to select a particular part of the avatar. For humanoid avatars, for example, there are Torso, Head, and Feet buttons. If you select the Torso button, for example, you can choose from the variety of different torsos in the piece list.

Avatar colors

In the color property page, you can change the color of an avatar or one of its pieces by clicking and dragging the small spheres in the color selector in the right window, or by pushing the Color Dialogue button to select a color directly.

Avatar scaling

After selecting a viewpoint with the Front, Side, Rear, or Top radio buttons, you can then enlarge and shrink a piece by clicking the horizontal and vertical plus (+) and minus (-) buttons. You can reset the scaling by pressing the middle button. You can also change the size by clicking and dragging the mouse over the right window. Use scaling to make avatars that are skinny or fat.

Avatar motions

This page doesn't actually change anything; it's just used to preview an avatar's (or its pieces') motions. You can select a motion from the list and watch it play. Start and stop it with the Start button, and change the speed of the motion with the slider.

OZ's Mascot avatar: Avatars don't look this good . . . yet!

Building your own world in OZ

OZ Virtual will read any VRML 1.0 and 2.0 file on the Web and make it a multi-user world. You can then call up your friends, and have them meet you in your own *homeworld!* In the version of OZ Virtual described in this book, you cannot import your own avatars into OZ Virtual. OZ has plans to provide content developers with tools that allow for custom avatar creation and insertion into OZ Virtual. Check OZ Interactive's home page at **http://www.oz.com** for details on importing your own VRML homeworlds into OZ.

Fine-Tuning Your World

Setting up your avatar's cybercards

To find your cybercard, choose User Card from the Communication menu. You will be presented with a dialogue box like the one shown in the adjacent figure. You can enter your real name, location, change your nickname, reveal your e-mail address, and then choose to reveal this card to others. You can exchange these cards by clicking on someone's avatar nickname in the chat manager window.

Set up a personal cybercard for your avatar.

Other dashboard options

The dashboard (the area at the bottom of the OZ Virtual screen) has some additional controls that I did not discuss earlier. The Audio pop-up has controls to turn sound on or off, and to adjust its volume. The following table shows several Display pop-up options.

Display pop-up options

OPTION	ACTION
Light intensity	Adjust light intensity (most people prefer it set to maximum)
Smooth shading	Smooth shading on/off
Lit textures	If on, light intensity affects texture maps
Display while loading	If set, the world is displayed while it is loaded
Double faces	Double face rendering on/off

In general, if the Display options are all off, your worlds will display faster. The multi-user pop-up lets you define your nickname in the world. The multi-user pop-up menu on the dashboard allows you to set up some key multi-user options.

Multi-user pop-up options

OPTION	ACTION
Multi-user enabled	Turns multi-user on or off. If off, OZ Virtual will not attempt to connect to a server when it loads a world.
Auto answer chat	If you turn this option off, it will simply present a dialogue box asking you whether you want to respond. If this is on, your chat and other users' chat is automatically mixed in the chat area.
Nickname	Your nickname in the multi-user world

Hot Spots

Hot OZ Worlds

In addition to OZONE (the world you enter when you start OZ Virtual), there are other OZ worlds. The following table lists the other OZ worlds. See the color section of this book for OZ scenes of hot dance clubs and the streets of the OZiverse.

Hot OZ worlds

WORLD	URL
Orion	http://www.oz.com/VRML/orion/orion.wrz
OZ Kids Exterior	http://www.oz.com/VRML/ozkids/exterior.wrz
OZ Kids Interior	http://www.oz.com/VRML/ozkids/interior.wrz

OZ Records	http://www.oz.com/VRML/ozrecords/ozrecords.wrz
Space Chat	http://www.oz.com/VRML/spacechat/spacechat.wrz
Sputnik	http://www.oz.com/VRML/sputnik/sputnik.wrz
Square	http://www.oz.com/VRML/square/square.wrz
Stage	http://www.oz.com/VRML/stage/stage.wrz
The Street (the original OZ world)	http://www.oz.com/VRML/street/street.wrz
The Nightclub	http://www.oz.com/VRML/nightclu/nightclu.wrz
Nightclub Light	http://www.oz.com/VRML/nightcno/nightcno.wrz

Opening a world

OZ Virtual supports VRML 1.0 and 2.0 files as input. You can either use the Open File dialogue to load scenes from a local disk, or Open Location to load from servers on the Internet. Find these choices under the File menu. For the worlds listed above, you must use Open Location and enter the URL. The client uses the HTTP (Web protocol) to locate files over the network. The world files can be either in pure ASCII form or compressed using GNU gzip or UNIX compression. The ASCII files have the standard extension .wrl, but the compressed ones have either a .gz or .wrz extension.

More about OZ worlds

When connected to an OZ server, each OZ Virtual client registers a world name with the server for the 3D world being loaded. If the VRML file contains a *world name node* specifying the name of the 3D world, the world name is used to identify the world. This is true for most of the OZ worlds. If no world name node is present in the VRML file, the URL is used to identify the world. When a world has been loaded from a local disk, its URL is comprised of file/drive/path/filename.

All OZ Virtual clients having the same 3D world identity registered with an OZ Server are in the same world. You can only see other avatars located in the same world as you. For example, if there is no node name in the VRML file, square.wrz, then two OZ Virtual clients are in the same world if they both loaded it from their local disk as \worlds\square.wrz, or if they both loaded it using HTTP from **http://www.oz.com/vrml/square/square.wrz**.

Digi's Diary

Digi's Diary: The Magical Combination of the Physical and the Virtual

Over the past year, as an observer and sometime participant in many virtual worlds, I have often had the most fun when someone rigged a setup where you could really mix together the experience of virtual worlds with the real physical world. After all, how much fun can this be if it is just you sitting there avataring alone for hours on end?

It all started innocently enough. I was presenting at a conference in Nice, France. It was the end of May 1995, and a group of us (including the translators from the conference) were trying to find something stimulating to do. I asked if there was any sort of cybercafé in the city. I know what you are thinking: here they are, on the French Riviera, in one of the most beautiful cities on Earth, and they are pining to spend just a few more hours in front of a cathode ray tube. Well, you have to know that my compatriots were all *from* Nice (or at least France), and cyberthings counted as welcome relief from too much high culture. They said, "but of course, La Douche a l'etage" (translated: the bathroom (or shower?) on the second floor . . . what a name for a joint!). La Douche turned out to be the first cybercafé on the Cote d'Azure, and only the second in all of France.

So off we trucked through the winding labyrinth of the old city, and found the place in a marketplace by the Mediterranean. After a few quick words with the harried-looking owner, he allowed us upstairs where there were a few PCs embedded in definitively French aluminum sculptured cases. Jacked into the Internet, I decided to do something avant garde. I downloaded Worlds Chat, then just over 30 days old, and installed it on three machines.

My compatriots immediately started using this strange new world, sailing around the space station together, and trying to find other French speakers. It turned out they found quite a few, including someone in Australia whose grandmother, 100 years old, lived in Nice. I proceeded to install Worlds Chat on the one remaining PC downstairs by the bar, and then retired to have a much-deserved aperitif.

While engrossed in the subtleties of French liqueur, I didn't notice a whole cohort of French teenagers who had occupied the area around the downstairs PC. A roar of laughter erupted from the group crowded around the PC, and I thought, "no one could find the Web that funny," and took myself and my drink over to them. It turned out that these teenagers had wandered in asking, "we want to talk to people on the Internet," to which the owner just pointed to the PC. They had started Worlds Chat by random chance, chosen the sexiest avatar in the gallery, and had started chatting up a set of French speakers aboard the station. It turned out that those French speakers were my male compatriots upstairs who thought they had a really hot avatar affair going. When one of them came downstairs for a drink, the ruse was exposed, much to the embarrassment of the upstairs crowd and the humor of the teenagers.

What I realized that night was that the mixture of people in a shared social place, reaching out through this new realm of digital space to interact with other people, was a really magical formula. If you could also allow people in their avatar world to get a glimpse of the physical world, this would complete the loop.

For the next couple of years, projects within and outside my organization (the Contact Consortium) sought to experiment with this physical and virtual mixing of people and avatar-people. The Sherwood Forest Towne construction days in AlphaWorld (starting in March 1996) were always done with a group having a big all-day party, and crowding around two or three PCs, taking shifts hosting and building on the site.

Next, we experimented with large screen projection of avatar worlds during a kind of Space Bridge in Florence Italy, in June of 1996. Avatars hanging (3 feet tall) above a glass virtual university campus were projected on large screens with simultaneous live video between the Lower Fortress in Florence, Italy and the American University at Sophia-Antipolis in Nice, France. Avatars spoke in French, English, and Italian and came into the event from all over the world. Even though they could not see the audience (we assured them they would be seen by 300 Italian press and digital media professionals); they took us on faith and exclaimed "Ciao, Italia!" See a glimpse of the Florence experience at **http://www.ccon.org/theU/protos.html**.

We continued the experiment with the Digital Mixer, our first avatar teleport, on July 13, 1996. For this we held a large (50-plus people) physical party at the beautiful hilltop home of my friends here in Boulder Creek California. We packed in a half dozen computers and, working with Match.com (a very successful Web-based matchmaking service), we hosted a singles party simultaneously in three virtual worlds: The Palace, PointWorld, and AlphaWorld. Hundreds of avatars crowded into the spaces, trampling on the flower garden in AlphaWorld, and forcing at least one eviction. The Palace party turned into a hat-giving competition. A famous Boulder Creek poet read a new poem, "I saw the strangest thing today," in a virtual redwood grove in Sherwood Towne, attracting crowds of poetry-spouting avatars. The Digital Mixer can be seen at **http://www.ccon.org/events/mixup1.html**.

The Digital Mixer was quite an event, and we learned a lot about doing a physical/virtual event. We learned that a certain magical transfer of excitement and energy can flow between a physical gathering and gatherings in virtual space. One set of Sherwood builders was hard at work for over 11 hours on a Saturday. Try Web surfing for 11 hours!

At the Earth to Avatars conference in October 1996, we featured the Voce, a live exercise blending the collective voice of a group in song (a musical rendition of the seven Chakras of the body from eastern mysticism) into a single avatar in OnLive! Traveler's Utopia world. Other avatars in the space (appropriately, a Stonehenge world) joined in with their songs from all over the world. See photos of the Voce exercise at **http://www.ccon.org/conf96r/gallery.html**.

The next Cyberphysical event was held in January 1997, at the 9th Digital Be-In, a huge party and digital cultural venue organized annually to coincide with the Macworld Expo in San Francisco. Be-In originator, Michael Gosney, invited us to include an avatar teleport. We set up an area full of computers where people could sit down and connect with others in avatar worlds. In a large dance floor several hundred people participated in a huge Voce experience with the avatars projected on 60-foot screens around the crowd. I wound through the crowd explaining to people that the 15-foot-high lip synching avatar head on the wall was *us* (or at least our collective voice) and they were amazed! See the Be-In avatar teleport at **http://www.digitalspace.com/bein/index.html**.

OZ Virtual brings the mixture of physical and virtual to a new level. The OZ company crew will often connect a performer in a body suit to one of their avatars and present dance and performance art in their world, all while other avatars watch and join in online. OZ has an in-house band, and produces its own music (including live performances) for the world. OZ hosts large parties and live demos at trade shows that draw big crowds who wonder about all those shapes on the screen.

All of this is very exciting and suggests to me that the true power of the virtual world medium is simply that it provides people with a new way to be together.

Icelandic pop diva, Moa, in a motion capture suit running dance partner Punk Avatar (right).

Brave New Worlds

A NEVER ENDING MISSION

In our long mission we have touched down on many worlds and fraternized with all different sorts of natives. You might be wondering, *what more could there be?* New virtual worlds are appearing on the Internet all the time. It seems as though everyone has a unique approach to building this next form of cyberspace. You could see it as an "ecosystem of worlds" where a kind of Darwinian natural selection will determine the types of worlds we will inhabit in the future. What makes a world fit for survival, the number of people who visit it, or the goods sold there? No one seems to know the answer to this question just yet. I take up the question of what makes a world worth revisiting in the chapter, "Build Your Own World, Design Your Own Avatar," later in this book.

In this chapter you'll get a look at a dozen or so new worlds which had not been out there long enough (at least when this chapter was written) to develop a large community of regular users. You will also be introduced to *near-avatar worlds*, which include worlds that you can only visit alone.

Your Guide to Brave New Worlds

Brave New Worlds Background

With these *brave new worlds* appearing all the time, you could make a career of just exploring them. In fact, I have received e-mails from people who start out by introducing themselves "hi, I am so-and-so in this world and such-and-such in this world and whozit in this other world . . . " giving a whole new meaning to the term *multiple personality*. I don't know how these brave new citizens can exist as different personas in so many worlds and still keep track of it all!

So where do these worlds all come from? Most of them are built by companies. Some world providers are large, like Microsoft, Intel, and NTT, and others are small, hopeful startups like Electric Communities and Atomic3D. Soon, tools from these and other companies will allow regular Internet users to build their own *homeworlds* to go along with their home pages. When this happens, there will be far too many worlds to visit or to write about in one book!

So let us now embark on our multi-year mission to explore brave new worlds. Of course one "Internet year" goes by in an instant, so don't panic about being lost out in deep digital space forever! There is a lot of exciting *terra virtual* out there, so let's get started.

Sony's Community Place Browser

Sony Corporation's various divisions, including Sony Research Laboratories in Japan and Sony Pictures Image Works (SPIW) in California, have been working on computer spaces to support what they call "virtual society." The latest incarnation of this work is Sony's Community Place Browser (CPB). Sorry for all the new acronyms; to people like me it is just an impulse, so please excuse us! Sony's challenge with CPB was to implement a full version of the second release of the Virtual Reality Modeling Language (VRML 2.0) complete with behaviors (i.e., things move) driven by the Internet programming language Java.

With CPB you can explore some of the best VRML worlds inhabited by avatars. CPB is already being used to build large public multi-user spaces, as you shall see later in this section.

Virtual Society on the Web

Sony states that the goal of the Virtual Society project is to create *a seamless integration of real society and electronic society, another kind of* community, *a virtual* society that's fun, fast, and free. To make your place in virtual society, download the Community Place Browser (CPB) from Sony Pictures Imageworks' site at **http://vs.spiw.com/vs/**. This is a small and simple application (although the download is over 5MB) which can run as a plug-in to Netscape or stand-alone. If you are running it stand-alone, you can try the built-in voice chat.

Avatars in the Sony ChatRoom.

The interface

The MultiUser Window and its emoticon gestures.

From the preceding figure you can see CPB in action, with a few avatars there (these were SPIW employees there to give me a tour).

Text chat is shown above avatar heads in a translucent bar, a nice touch allowing you to look through someone else's chat to read another conversation. The main chat interface is a window which pops up by the browser window. The adjacent figure shows the MultiUser Window. When you click on the row of emoticons (smiley faces) CPB will send funny sounds into the world and make your avatar gesture for everyone to see. In the text chat itself, all the avatar aliases (names people chose) are shown in color along with the chat, making it easy to trace conversational threads. Note that you have to click between the chat window and the browser to go from moving to talking. It is my hope that Sony will improve this. Well designed worlds allow you to walk while you type.

The speaker/microphone icon combination at the bottom of the MultiUser Window are controls enabling the use of your PC's microphone to speak to other people in the world. My microphone was gray, despite efforts to get sound working. I could not talk and the only thing I heard were the sound gestures emanating from my PC's speakers every time someone pressed one of the smiley faces (whoop dee-doo!).

I expect you will be able to get sound working and try it out. Voice done well gives you a great sense of "presence" in the world. With voice, you can communicate a wider bandwidth of human emotion and culture (you don't need those smiley emoticons so much).

CPB has support of VRML 2.0 behaviors, which are implemented not only in the worlds but in the avatar editor. As the following image shows, I found an undulating ceiling sculpture which was activated by the proximity of another avatar. The addition of Java into the equation means that simple animations like this can grow to become very entertaining, including sound, textures, and more shape shifting.

Navigation is somewhat tricky in CPB worlds. Holding the mouse button down and moving your mouse is one awkward way to move. Keyboard cursor keys can also control movement and a series of simple icons on the right and bottom sides of the browser window allow you to initiate some common motions like floating or turning around. Related to navigation is *collision detection*. Some objects you collide with, while others you pass right through. This is a source of confusion in all VRML environments and leads to frightening experiences like being buried in walls or falling out of the world.

VRML Moves!

The worlds

The initial Sony world looks a little bit plastic but this is just a basic VRML space. CPB can load in a variety of VRML 2.0 worlds and models so you can use it to build your own world (see the chapter, "Build Your Own World, Design Your Own Avatar").

Some beautiful worlds built for The Mirror project (in conjunction with the BBC television programme, The Net) by British Telecom and partners showed what could be done with the Sony tools. I recommend visiting **http://www.bbc.co.uk/the_mirror/** to find out more about what went on in The Mirror when it was online between January 13 and February 28, 1996. See more on The Mirror in the section, "Worlds that Were," later in this chapter.

The Honjo Jidai Mura and Sapari Park worlds were built using CPB for Japanese speaking users. Honjo Jidai Mura is a model of an old Japanese city built showing how it looked about 200 years ago. It was captured from old Nishiki-e (Japanese polychrome woodblock prints of the Ukiyo-e). You can visit Honjo Jidai Mura through the English Web site at **http://gcoj.com/english/index.html**.

Sapari Park is a fun relaxation and play zone (in Japanese only) and can be found at **http://pc.sony.co.jp/sapari/index.htm**.

The community

As CPB worlds are pretty new, the community is still evolving. And as I don't speak Japanese, I could not do much reporting on the Honjo Jidai Mura and Sapari Park worlds, which are very active places. Keep a close eye on Virtual Society on the Web as this exciting new social technology continues to evolve.

Virtual Society Homepage (mostly in Japanese) is at **http://vs.sony.co.jp**.

Find VRML Models for use in constructing VRML 2.0 worlds for Community Places and other browsers at **http://www.ocnus.com/models/models.html**.

Pueblo: Gateway to the MUD-verse

Pueblo is an interesting hybrid of 3D VRML worlds and text-based MUD and MOO communities. *MUD* stands for Multi User Domain and MUDs have been used for almost 20 years to link people together in virtual worlds described completely in text. *MOOs* are MUDs constructed out of pieces called *objects* making them somewhat more flexible than MUDs. There are many other variants of MUDs, including LPmuds, DikuMuds, TinyMuds, MUSHs, MUQs, and more.

There are hundreds of MUDs and MOOs where people battle dragons and each other inside imaginary dungeons or live in space colonies in simulations of some future civilization. Pueblo, like SenseMedia's The Sprawl (described later in this chapter), allows users of MUDs and MOOs to offer a 3D virtual world and avatars to their communities. Pueblo was developed by Chaco Communications which recently merged with another firm to form a new company called LikeMinds. As Pueblo is so widely used, LikeMinds will support Pueblo or will be finding a user group that will continue to maintain it, so you should still find it online when this book is published.

Download the Pueblo Browser from Chaco's home page at **http://www.chaco.com**. Visit the LikeMinds home page for news of Pueblo and their other products at **http://www.likeminds.com/**.

The browser

A crash course in MUDding

MUDs and MOOs both use a text chat interface to the Internet called *Telnet*. Pueblo integrates a Telnet program with a three-dimensional world. It helps to be familiar with MUD style interfaces (there are a few basic commands to learn). Being a true newbie MUDder, it took me a while to figure these out. With Pueblo, the top part of the program window gives you links to select a world. Once you have selected your MUD or MOO world, the Telnet program opens and presents you with a login screen. Each MUD or MOO has a different login procedure. Usually you can log in as a "guest." In some worlds you must define a character. Each character has a name and all kinds of properties and objects like clothing, swords, spells, keys, and a defined profession or social status. In these worlds, users called *gods* or *wizards* often have great power in the world.

The imaginary "rooms" in MUDs and MOOs can be built by users (sometimes only by wizards) entering commands to "create" new virtual terra firma. To travel through one of these worlds, you enter commands that take you through doors from room to room (or out the window, or any other direction the room lists for you). You can talk with other people by text chatting. MUDs and MOOs are often full of "bots," software robots that will perform services for you. You can instruct bots to do tasks like buying and selling objects or keeping a record of every person who enters a room.

As you can see, there is so much to MUDding that I cannot possibly cover it all here. There are many excellent books on the subject, including *Playing MUDs on the Internet* by Rawn Shah and James Romine (New York: John Wiley and Sons, 1995, ISBN: 0-471-11633-5) and Michael Powers' *How to Program Virtual Communities, Attract New Web Visitors and Get Them to Stay* (New York: Ziff-Davis Press, ISBN: 1-562-76522-1). These books will show you how to interact in these worlds and set up and manage your own MUD-based communities.

Another variant on the MUD is called a *MUSH*. The following figure shows the basic introductory Pueblo MUSH with its VRML avatar selection room. Here I can click on avatars, navigate with my mouse, and enter commands in the Telnet window to move around in the world. You can build a VRML 1.0 world and connect it to the text-based MUD within Pueblo. This world will come up, complete with avatars, when Pueblo logs users on to the MUD. Pueblo worlds also support a wide array of streaming media like music and sound files.

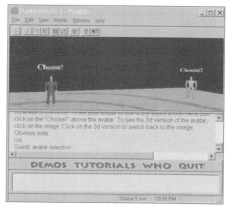

Pueblo MUSH running with avatar selection gallery.

The worlds of Pueblo

Pueblo's worlds are defined by the text-based MUD communities that run underneath the 3D interfaces. These worlds may be only text-based but are certainly not shallow social environments. Many MUDs and MOOs have years of history and hundreds or thousands of dedicated users who have formed complex social organizations and built large virtual spaces. LambdaMOO, run for years by Pavel Curtis at

Xerox PARC, often had several hundred users logged in at the same time and even experienced a mutiny against the hierarchy of community operators. DragonMUD, run by Jopsy (his world name) has experienced an excommunication in its order of wizards. My character was killed within minutes of entering DragonMUD, showing just how green I am on this side of the tracks in virtual community.

NAU's SolSys Sim

Bar scene shot from VRML-enhanced Pueblo World.

On the positive side, I successfully served as Odiyah, the bartender in the Low Earth Orbit space station in Professor Reed Riner's Solar System Simulation (SolSys Sim), a widely acclaimed MUD used in several universities to teach students the art and science of community. This MUD has been running out of Northern Arizona University since 1989 and has served a whole generation of students in anthropology and engineering with a rich experience of virtual community. Find a Web site for SolSys Sim at **http://www.nau.edu/anthro/solsys/**. The preceding figure shows a bar scene from a Pueblo world. This reminds me a little of my bar in SolSys Sim.

Some innovative Pueblo communities

Many groups of MUD users and some private companies have aligned their communities around Pueblo. One such company is MetaPlay (**http://www.metaplay.com/**) which hosts improvisational "Simprov" events in their Pueblo enhanced worlds. A particularly popular world is Mom's Truck Stop, which comes complete with sassy waitress avatars. For a story about Mom's see Stephen Brewer's HomePC feature article at **http://techweb.cmp.com/hpc/mar97/33chat05.htm**.

At Star Base Cube (**http://www.cube3.com**), a 3D *Star Trek* environment is being built for users in Trekkie avatars to re-enact their favorite *Star Trek* episodes.

SenseMedia's The Sprawl: Pan Pacific Worlds

From deep in the Santa Cruz Mountains and spreading out across the Pacific Rim comes this little known but fascinating group collaborative project. Modeled loosely on Gibson's *Sprawl* in *Neuromancer*, Sensemedia's Sprawl is a series of several dozen servers in a scaleable, hubless network located mostly in the U.S. and Japan.

A lot of hard work by SenseMedia's two principals and volunteers has layered 3D VRML 1.0 virtual worlds (VRML 2.0 by the time you read this book) on top of a Lambda MOO server (ChibaMOO).

The interface

The following figure shows the VooDo client open within Netscape 3.0 with a second Netscape window on the right hand side for locations and a frame below for text and command entry. You navigate using your mouse or keyboard commands in the main window and type MOO instructions or text chat into the entry area at the bottom of the browser. It helps to be MOO-literate although there is a help system available. The interface is complex but easy once you have mastered some basic commands.

One of the most powerful features is the ability to create your own VRML "rooms" with a simple MOO command. The following figure shows an overview of the Sprawl where the buildings on this digital plain represent VRML areas on different servers. This kind of virtual world is called hubless, which means that there is no central server and the overview of the world must be pulled together for display in real time (it can be slow).

I created and entered a room "digigarden" in The Sprawl with these two commands:

@dig digigarden
@go #1935

VooDo browser

SenseMedia's VooDo browser can be accessed through Netscape 3.0 on a PC (Win95/NT) or a Power Macintosh (3D virtual worlds come to the Mac!). You must first download and install any capable VRML 1.0C or higher browser plug-in (Live3D, WorldView, or Cosmo Player are recommended) and then contact SenseMedia for an account at http://www.sensemedia.net/ or by emailing info@sensemedia.net.

To find a plug-in, visit one of the following sites and download and install the plug-in for Navigator or Internet Explorer:

For Live3D from Netscape:
http://www.netscape.com/comprod/products/navigator/live3d/

For WorldView from Intervista:
http://www.intervista.com

For Cosmo Player from Silicon Graphics: http://vrml.sgi.com

To try The Sprawl go to http://www.sensemedia.net/voodo and log in as "guest" with no password; you can look around.

SenseMedia's VooDo Browser interface.

Communicating with an avatar in a home-built Biota Sprawl VRML 1.0 room.

which made a room on a server in Honolulu assigned the unique ID 1935. I then was able to plaster a texture map onto the walls of my room. The SenseMedia people imported some of our infamous "biota" VRML (see the chapter in this book called "Life in Digital Space") and placed it into the room (shown in the adjacent figure). Would building VRML areas into other VRML multi-user worlds be so easy!

Here I am visiting my completed room with Irradiate, an avatar from the SenseMedia team, to talk over this first ever biota area in a VRML world. Hundreds of other rooms have been created, even full art galleries, including one of the work of photographer Daniel Leighton.

The worlds

The SenseMedia world, being a community creation, has a wide variety of styles and quality of content. From simple rooms like the one I constructed to Stonehenge monuments (every world seems to have its Stonehenge!) to large auditoriums for concerts, the Sprawl seems to have never ending content. If you are using the Sprawl with the Live3D 1.0 plug-in on the Windows platform, you can view animations. In some versions, your avatar is merely a placeholder, announcing your presence in a room. This environment is really centered on the MOO dialogue and command structure and this is where a great deal of interface and attention is focused.

Note that you can use the Sprawl with Chaco's Pueblo (also discussed in this chapter). Avatars move in the Pueblo enhanced version. For a preview of Sprawl worlds and good screen shots, see **http://www.picosof.com/sprawl/**.

The community

I was not able to talk to more than a few people in the Sprawl on my guided tours but I did get a sense that this is a truly dedicated "homebrew" VRML community, adept in stepping around the glitches and creating innovative fixes to keep the world going. The Sprawl reminds me of Terra Vista, another grassroots project in VRML community building (see **http://www.terravista.org**).

Kayla Block and Samuel Latt Epstein (developers of the Sprawl) tell me that they have about 3,500 people who log in at least once every 3 months across 5 nodes located in Fujisawa, Japan; Hokkaido, Japan; Sydney, Australia; and Honolulu, Hawaii. They say that the average number of people logged in at any one time across nodes is 50–70.

A sense of the SenseMedia community can be gained by visiting their white papers collection at **http://sensemedia.net/papers**.

Intel's IDMOO Experiments

Intel Architecture Labs up in Hillsboro, Oregon have brought us *IDMOO* (Intel Distributed MOO). These are a series of experimental text and voice chat supported VRML and Java avatar worlds. We will look at two very different worlds: IDMOO 1 and 2.

Download the various IDMOO Browsers from Intel's site at http://connectedpc.com/iaweb/idmoo/.

IDMOO 1 interface

As the following figure shows, we are in a kind of pavilion with other avatars. I was engaged in both text and voice chat (note the highlighted speaking man icon) with a gentleman from Montreal named Rocky. The sound was clear when it came in but rather difficult to tell when you should speak or hold. As you can see from the text, Rocky was having a hard time also. This points out the value of having more than one mode of communication!

Another feature of the IDMOO 1 is the Views Window (on the right) with its avatar mannequin and "pegs." I had selected the peg on the lower left and changed my view from my own eyes so that I could see myself from the side and Rocky (facing me). Clicking on the mannequin will bring the view back into my own eyes.

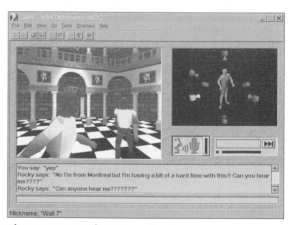

The IDMOO 1.0 browser client.

Download IDMOO and try out some of the basic technologies and tricks, including:

- Personally created VRML avatars and rooms (you can link in your own VRML 1.0 worlds)

- Queued audio and text chat

- Multiple views of the virtual environment

- URL-based browsing of Intel Distributed MOO servers worldwide

The world and the community

I have not done much exploring beyond the pavilion, but I am told that there are quite a few worlds ported together through Intel's IDMOO servers. The times I have been in IDMOO, I have met one or two people, all using the default "dummytar"

Custom avatars built by IDMOO citizenry.

avatar you saw in the first image in this section. This avatar looks just like the dummytar in AlphaWorld (maybe there is a universal dummytar?). Even though its name contains the word MOO (meaning MUD-multi user domain, Object Oriented), IDMOO is not based on an actual MOO (as are Pueblo and The Sprawl). The adjacent figure shows custom avatars built by users.

A sneak preview of IDMOO 2

Intel gave me a sneak preview of their next experimental world, IDMOO 2. This world is the first virtual world written entirely in Java and loads its two dimensional worlds dynamically from the Web. The first world built with IDMOO 2 is a fish tank full of simulated fish with realistic swimming behaviors. Some of the fish are avatars, which means people are driving them. Other creatures, such as the shark in the adjacent figure is a *biot*, an autonomous agent acting like a piece of biology. The shark can eat fish

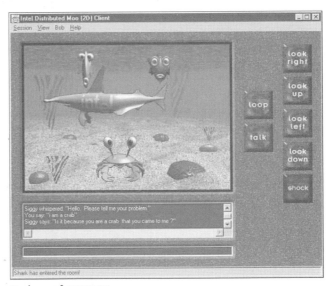

A view of IDMOO2.

(but not user-embodied avatar fish). In this world, you can clone fish and watch them being eaten by the shark. Users can communicate through the fish tank with text chat. You can download IDMOO 2.0 from **http://labtoys.hbtn.portland.or.us/ Idm20Worlds/docs/public/**. This Web site also contains a great deal of information about how to make Java-based virtual worlds. Both IDMOO 1 and 2 run on PCs with Windows 95.

Microsoft V-Chat: Frantic Antics

Microsoft brought us Comic Chat, described in an earlier chapter in this book; Microsoft has now created V-Chat, a multi-dimensional world full of avatars with expressive personalities and a powerful will to chat. V-Chat debuted in early 1996 on the Microsoft Network (where it is still available). More recently, V-Chat appeared on the open Internet in version 1.1. If you are an MSN member or have a general Internet account and a Windows 95 PC (486 or above), you can join the antics in V-Chat.

The interface

The interface of Microsoft's V-Chat is very clean and easy to operate. The big window shows my own point of view of several avatars meeting in the Compass (the world everyone goes into first). Text chat can be entered into an area below this and sent with various types of delivery: normal, thought balloons, exclamation, or whisper. This is very similar to Comic Chat which was also produced by Microsoft. Threads of text chat flow through the window above the world view area. On the right hand side are listed participants in this particular world. You can see DigiGardener (me) in the list and just below the list of people you can see how my avatar looks. Mr. Dredd, in this case. In the world you can actually see another dreadlock guy who looks like me.

V-Chat showing avatars in conversation in the Compass world.

Sources for V-Chat

To learn all about V-Chat for the Internet, visit the home page at http://vchat1.microsoft.com/. (To find V-Chat on MSN, search for the keyword "chat"). Download the open Internet V-Chat from the V-Chat install page at http://vchat1.microsoft.com/install/default.htm and enter the V-Chat worlds from http://vchat1.microsoft.com/chat/default.htm (you must download and install these worlds individually before you can enter them). Note also that you must have DirectX installed before you can use V-Chat. DirectX is available from the V-Chat install page listed above.

There is an avatar gallery for V-Chat at http://vchat1.microsoft.com/avatars/default.htm and an Avatar Wizard which allows you to create personalized avatars available from the same Web page. You can then use those avatars privately or publish them on a web server so that other V-Chat users can use them.

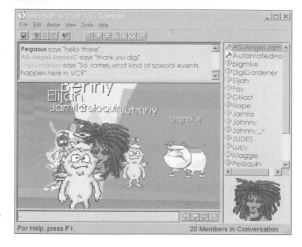

Hello, host JamesC, how are the avatars behaving today?

As well as a healthy set of avatar participants, you can see AS-Angel-JamesC and AutomatedHost in the following figure. AutomatedHost is just a bot representing the room manager. AutomatedHost gives you periodic updates on activities in the world and does housekeeping. AS-Angel-JamesC is the name of a real human host (JamesC) who happens to be online at the moment. To go to JamesC (or any other avatar user) just right click on their name in the list and select Find. V-Chat will then pilot you over in front of the avatar attached to that name.

Gestures, a great part of V-Chat, can be applied to your avatar by clicking on the buttons at the top of the window or selecting them from the Avatar menu.

The worlds

V-Chat features many worlds, called *environments*. Some environments are two dimensional (such as Bugworld, shown below) and some are 3D. Each world has its own particular set of avatars. The Compass

Hey babies, V-Chat avatar gestures are sure expressive!

environment (shown earlier in this section), where everyone enters for the first time, is a 3D plateau surrounded by teeth-like mountains. You can navigate around the worlds by either holding down the left mouse button or by using the cursor keys. Holding down the Ctrl key while moving forward or backwards will cause you to rise or fall.

The current list of V-Chat environments are listed at **http://vchat1 .microsoft.com/chat/default.htm**. Note that you must download and install these worlds individually before you

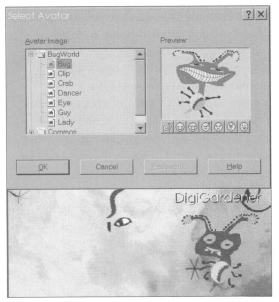

Bugworld showing the Avatar Selector and what the Happy state of my bug avatar looks like.

can enter them. I list these worlds in the following table. Note that there will probably be more worlds available by the time you read this book.

V-Chat Community Spaces

WORLD ENVIRONMENT	DESCRIPTION	APPROXIMATE SIZE OF DOWNLOAD
Compass #1	A general chat area	Included when you download the V-Chat 1.1
Compass #2	Another general chat area	Included when you download the V-Chat 1.1
Practice Area	A place to meet other newbies	200KB
Table Top	A chat area that looks like a kitchen table	350KB
Fishbowl	A general chat area inside a fish bowl	400KB
Lodge	A very popular country lodge chat zone	1000KB
Bugworld	A 2D chat world. You can see yourself in the environment!	800KB
Lunar Islands	A gathering place for teens	450KB
Red Den	A great place to meet other singles	650KB

Build your own V-Chat world

The V-Chat Building Kit, which enables you to create custom V-Chat environments, is currently only available to forum managers and content providers who have a relationship with Microsoft. If you are interested in creating a V-Chat space, contact Kelvin Chan at kelvinc@microsoft.com.

The community

Being a newbie in V-Chat, I really did not get the sense for the community that has formed there. However, JamesC, the first host that I met, pointed me to his web page at **http://www.tex-is.net/users/jamesc/james.htm**. JamesC described himself in this way:

Well a little about myself. I'm a retired construction supervisor. I retired after I had major back surgery. I'm currently an angel host on MSN Vchat1.1, which is a lot of fun.

Judging by how many people were in V-Chat when I visited, I would say that this brave new world has quite a future ahead of it!

NTT's InterSpace: Your Face in Cyberspace!

NTT Human Interface Labs (an in-house laboratory for NTT, a part of Nippon Telegraph and Telephone, Japan's national telephone company) has created InterSpace, a truly brave new world complete with avatars having video faces. This means if you have one of the popular QuickCams (those little "eyeball" cameras), your very own face will be painted on your avatar! On top of this, they support voice and text chat, so you can have a thrilling experience of almost really being there inside cyberspace.

Getting the InterSpace Experience

InterSpace is available as a free download from NTT Software. InterSpace requires at least a Pentium 133 MHz PC running Windows 95 and a 28.8 kbps modem connection. If you have a sound card, speakers, and microphone you will be able to talk to and hear other people in their InterSpace avatars. A video capture device like a Connectix Color QuickCam (see http://www.connectix.com) will enable you to get your own face in cyberspace. Note that you can also use InterSpace with just text chat and don't need the microphone or video capture device.

To get InterSpace go to http://www.ntts.com/interspace/ and fill in the forms to create your account, download the software, install it, and start InterSpace VR Browser (isc95.exe) at which point you will have to enter the login ID and password you were emailed. The main entry world (at least when this chapter was written) is the virtual Palo Alto. To get to it, enter its world locator at vccp://is0.ntts.com/pa_downtown. If you have questions or problems, see the InterSpace FAQ (Frequently Asked Questions) at http://www.nttsoft.com/interspace/faq.html.

The interface

As you can see from the following figure, InterSpace is a 3D world where the avatars look a little bit like kiosks. The interface to the world is a simple window with a 3D frame and optional text chat window (not shown here). The radar map on the right shows where other people are relative to you. My real face would be showing (instead of the smiley) except that I don't have a video capture device. I can see the other users of InterSpace painted every second or so on the front of their avatars.

I am actually looking into their offices (the folks shown here are all NTT Software employees). Also on the right side of the screen are the audio controls. I do have a microphone so I am connected to the others and can speak to them.

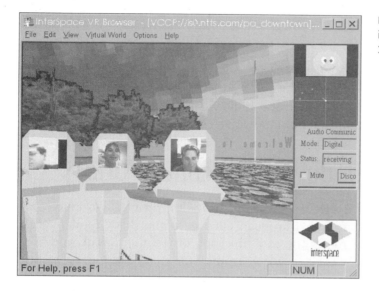

Meeting a group of friends in NTT Software's InterSpace interface.

I really didn't like the smiley face so, to place a still image of myself on my avatar, I went to a dialogue (shown in the following figure) where I can bring in a still frame Windows BMP image of myself (80 pixels wide by 60 pixels tall). I could also tie in my video capture system (Color QuickCam) when I get one.

Plastering my beautiful mug on my avatar.

The worlds

InterSpace uses the Sense8 3D worlds format (see **http://www.sense8.com**). NTT and others have constructed a number of different worlds, including the virtual Palo Alto, a cybercampus, and shopping and gaming worlds.

InterSpace also runs over ISDN, a higher speed connection which will give you much better voice and music and faster video updating on the avatars. One world to visit at higher speeds is the Virtual Tower Records store. While in the store, you can play albums through a virtual jukebox, view streams of videos, jump through tubes to get to other floors, and actually order music CDs from a linked Web site.

In some environments, you can use a plain old analog telephone line and set up InterSpace to actually dial your telephone and connect you into a conference. Of course, you need two telephone lines, one for your modem and one for the phone (but hey, NTT *is* a telephone company)!

The community

I was fortunate enough to be one of the first people to user InterSpace through the Internet while composing this chapter. As this is a new world, the community is only beginning to develop. With the live video and audio working so well on a normal 28.8 bps modem, I expect to see quite a lot of innovative events evolve in InterSpace.

La Deuxième Monde (the Second World)

At the time this chapter was written, Deuxième Monde was available as a free service to residents of France for a limited time only. You definitely must be able to speak (or at least read and type) French to participate in this world. If you want to enter la vie virtuelle (the virtual life) with a French twist, visit the Deuxième Monde Web site at http://www.2nd-world.fr/. There you will find instructions to order the CD-ROM necessary for entry into the world. Note that at the time of the writing of this book, the CD cost 349 French Francs (60-70 dollars).

La Deuxième Monde is the third virtual world to come from a European culture. While Black Sun's worlds reflect the cool precision of German design and OZ's worlds revolve around dark, remote space station worlds like their far-out Icelandic home, France's Deuxième Monde (which means Second World) embodies Gallic character and fashion to the hilt.

The interface

The interface to La Deuxième Monde is typical of many text-chat avatar virtual worlds. In the main window is a view of the world and other avatars. Below that is a text chat area showing threaded discussions and system messages. On the right side is a window showing an overhead view of where you are in the virtual Paris. Few virtual worlds try to recreate actual physical cities but Deuxième Monde recreates portions of several French cities including an elaborate Paris. The virtual Paris comes complete with areas dedicated to Trocadèro, Père-Lachaise, Rue de Rivoli, Pyramide du Louvre, République, and le Sacré-Cœur. Choosing real cities can provide a context, as many of the "citoyens" (citizens) already have knowledge of Paris, and therefore, a starting point for discussions.

The La Deuxième Monde interface showing le Sacré-Cœur, text chat, and an overhead view of Paris.

The avatar editor in Deuxième Monde is quite sophisticated, allowing you to choose characters from different races in a bank of 20 body models, to select clothing, hair style, and color, and to define an identity. As you can see in the preceding figure, the avatar even looks pretty French, a refreshing change from just fish or penguins!

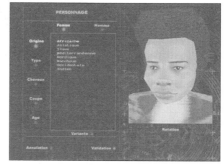

The Avatars Editor.

The world and the community

From the surrounding figures, you can see avatars mixing in Paris street scenes. Several thousand people use Deuxième Monde and much has happened there that I, as a non-participant and a poor speaker of French, cannot report on. From the Web page it looks as if a lively debate on the politics of virtual communities has started within a city radio station and a community newspaper (**http://www.2ndworld.fr/journal/journal.htm**). They also talk about games, events, services, and shopping being tried in the world.

Avatars congregating in Deuxième Monde.

A familiar Parisienne scene inside Deuxième Monde.

History of the project

The project was created by Alain Lediberder, president of Canal + Multimedia (a division of a private French television station) starting in the fall of 1994. Philippe Ulrich and many others were involved in the genesis and building of the project, which found its original roots in MUDs (Multi User Domains) and in discussions at the famous Xerox Palo Alto Research Center.

For France, Deuxième Monde is a big step up from Minitel, the aging national teletext system.

Near-Avatar Worlds

There is a whole slew of virtual worlds on the Internet that you can cruise through alone. In these worlds, you could be joined by helper bots or virtual critters. Of course in 3D games like Doom, there were always other competitors or monsters you had to battle. None of these things can be called an avatar because they are not operated by a person. Nonetheless, roaming virtual worlds alone can still be fun.

SuperScape's Viscape

SuperScape, a British company with offices near my home in Northern California, has created a very large set of single user spaces called the "Virtual World Wide Web" (or VWWW). SuperScape had a fast 3D browser years before VRML, the emerging industry standard. The key to access VWWW is Viscape, SuperScape's 3D browser. If you have a Windows 95, Windows 3.1, or Windows NT PC you can download Viscape from **http://www.superscape.com/**. You need to have a Web browser (either Internet Explorer 3.01 or Netscape Navigator 3.0) to run Viscape.

After installing Viscape, you can start visiting VWWW by pointing your Web browser to **http://vwww.com/**. Viscape will load as a plug-in to your browser and set you down in SuperCity, the hub of the VWWW.

The following figure shows a scene from the SuperCity entry plaza. The person you see walking is not an avatar, so don't be tricked and try to follow and talk to her! SuperScape worlds often have bots or simulations of living things (biots) moving around to give the worlds some life they lack by being single user. Navigating in Viscape is difficult in that you have to move by holding the left mouse button down over the arrow controls at the bottom of the window. You cannot use your normal keyboard keys to move. This will definitely limit the time you spend in VWWW. Viscape is a very fast browser and the worlds created for Viscape are small as 3D worlds go. Every time you click on a doorway or other entrance to a new world, Viscape will spend some seconds or minutes downloading the new world.

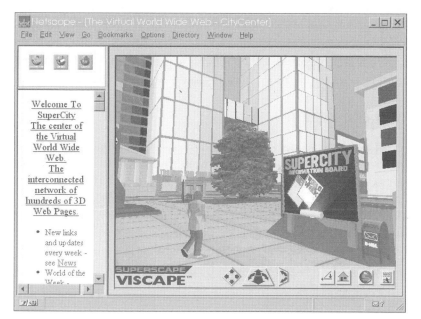

Viscape Browser in the Entry Plaza of SuperCity.

Places to go in VWWW

There are over 150 3D areas joined together in VWWW. The most popular areas are the amusement arcade (with virtual darts and virtual pool), the art gallery featuring mathematical art, the simulation area with training applications, and Cool Street, containing a Blues Bar and the Virtropolis experience.

Meeting a butterfly bot person in SuperScape's VWWW worlds.

Multi-user under SuperScape

Cruising around SuperCity can be cool but you will soon wish there is someone to talk to. The good news is that SuperScape recently teamed up with Black Sun Interactive (described in the "Black Sun Passport" chapter) to produce multi-user virtual worlds. This was a newly formed partnership and I have not had a chance to see how the worlds work.

Other SuperScape projects

SuperScape has been busy and creative over the past decade, creating virtual training environments, virtual railway carriage design worlds, 3D shopping malls, and even working with a group called Terraformers to build a virtual cemetary called Tombtown (**http://www.tombtown.com/**). SuperScape has built a business on these kind of simulations. You can imagine the value of training someone on a simulation of an expensive machine used in manufacturing. A company certainly cannot afford to take the real machine offline to train workers. Using a simulation is the next best thing. Flight simulators have been used for years to do the same thing.

Atomic3D's Neutron and Proton

A new phenomenon has just started peeking over the wall of Web pages: *the three dimensional episodic performance dramas* (that's a mouthful!). What could be more different from sterile Web documents than a cartoon performance that jumps out at you complete with coy characters hamming it up in their own voices? Well, a company called Nucleus Interactive from Los Angeles has created Atomic3D to bring this vision into reality with near-avatar casts played by a special piece of software called Neutron. You can try it out by downloading the Neutron animation viewer from the Atomic3D home page at **http://www.atomic3d.com/**. Neutron will play on a Windows 95 PC (sorry, no Mac version yet, but keep checking their Web site).

You play Atomic3D performance animation episodes through the Internet just like a Web browser. To view and play Atomic3D sites, you should have a connection to the Internet or be using 32-bit AOL for Windows 95.

When you play an Atomic3D episode, you can click on cues and drive the drama. To see the Atomic3D signature character Stanley and his girlfriend from a scene in their episodic drama, "A Deeper Place," see the color section of this book. These dramas can be played off the Atomic3D Animation Theater at **http://www.atomic3d.com/theatre.html**. Some of these worlds and all the sound associated with them can be quite big, so you must be patient while they download. I term these kind of worlds "near-avatar" as there are no real people in these scenes, only *bot actors*. In the chapter on Biota, you can see more examples of bot actors (such as Floops, a bot created completely with VRML).

Proton Pro

Once you get hooked on Neutron shows, Nucleus Interactive will sell you a CD-ROM with a development tool called Proton Pro. With Proton Pro you can compose your very own performance pieces, complete with virtual worlds containing characters having their own voices, special animations, and sound effects. In the scene shown in the following figure, I am setting up a stage show with three performers and a bulging brain. Working with my neighbor, Allan Lundell, we recorded our own sound (which you can see in the oscilloscope-like reading across the bottom) and connected the voice to the scene. I then tied the sound of hands clapping directly to the brain, which expanded and contracted with the level of applause (talk about an overblown ego!). Next, we went on to animate the parrot, the girl, and the man. In the end, we produced a little stage play that we could run from a link on our Web pages.

When you are ready to play Atomic3D episodes from your Web page, you will need to contact Nucleus Interactive to get their Electron license. Performance art comes to the Internet; can live avatar episodes starring *you* be far behind?

Using the Proton Pro authoring tool to create Atomic3D cartoon episodes.

Worlds that Were

As virtual worlds are born so do they die. Some worlds have been long running early experiments that have ended their life cycle. Habitat was such a world. Other worlds were purposely built for one event and then taken down. Earlier in this book, I described some of these event worlds. One such world was The Mirror world built for British Telecom in support of a BBC TV Series early in 1997. Van Gogh TV's Worlds Within was constructed just for the 1996 Olympic Arts Festival and is detailed in Appendix A: "Projects, Groups, Events, Philosophers, News, and Predecessors in Avatar Cyberspace." Both Habitat and The Mirror are also described in Appendix A: "Advanced Course (Avatar University)."

Digi's Diary: The Really Big App

Digi's Diary

"**The Movie Star Quadrant is easier to look at. Actors love to come here because in The Black Sun, they always look as good as they do in the movies. And unlike a bar or club in Reality, they can get into this place without physically having to leave their mansion, hotel suite, ski lodge, private airline cabin, or whatever. They can strut their stuff and visit with their friends without any exposure to kidnappers, paparazzi, script-flingers, assassins, ex-spouses, autograph brokers, process servers, psycho fans, marriage proposals, or gossip columnists.**"

—Neal Stephenson, *Snow Crash*

Can you imagine being a cast member in a *Star Trek* episode, or playing the sleuth in an Agatha Christie novel? Well, this may not be as far-fetched as you think! What if the home entertainment center morphs into a kind of "home Holodeck"? The Holodeck was a creation of the *Star Trek: The Next Generation* TV series. In the series, crew members aboard the Enterprise could walk into a special room and be carried into a virtual world directly piped into the neural centers of their brain. The Holodeck could simulate feeling from shapes so crew members could even engage in sword fights.

The Home Holodeck

The Holodeck idea is not new. Science fiction author Ray Bradbury described it all almost a half century ago in his short story, *The Veldt,* part of a published collection called *The Illustrated Man*. In *The Veldt,* a room in the family home could simulate any environment, complete with visuals, temperature, touch, and sound. Kids in a hypothetical 21st Century family built a model of an African veldt in this room. A veldt is a dry savanna plain full of animals, both hunting and hunted. In the story, the veldt was just a little too real. Luring their parents into the "simulation" room, where the lions were really very hungry, the youngsters solved their parental control problem once and for all.

A sort of Home Holodeck could be a reality by the early 21st Century and here is how it could work:

- The family rec room is now morphed into an all encompassing entertainment pod with 3D stereo sound and walls, ceiling and floor completely enveloped in a wrap-around pixel screen projector.

- The friendly 1000MHz family PC sits in this room connected to the Internet by good old slow phone lines at 56K bps or perhaps with a newfangled high speed ADSL, cable modem or satellite uplink.

- Virtual worlds are piped through the Internet into the PC and out into the room projector where they are painted in glorious 3D all around you.

- Voices, music, and atmospheric sounds emanate from speakers hidden in the walls.

- Sensors know where you are in the room and can track your every movement. The more expensive Holodecks can even track your facial expressions with invisible laser tracer beams.

- On the walls you see fantastic scenes of worlds and your own avatar is projected in glorious photo-realism or total fantasy construction into those worlds.

- Other people's avatars or live disembodied video floats on the walls of the Holodeck or jumps right out at you if you are wearing stereovision glasses.

- For the true VR-nauts, a rocker chair with hydrolics gives you experiences of motion and haptic feedback suits provide that all-around body grip.

Avvywood: Hollywood meets Avatar Virtual Worlds

So what would you do in the Holodeck? One of the big activities would be to enter into inhabited movies, books, or TV shows. You could be a role player, bystander, extra, or even a star. But who else would star in these worlds? Well, if Hollywood gets into the act, plenty of people you know very well (if the money is right). In the mean time, thousands or hundreds of thousands of ordinary people at home will create and star in the dramas. They might even go far beyond the imagination of the best writers and directors.

That might well happen, but the fictional worlds created by Hollywood have become a big part of millions of people's daily lives. Even today, avid fans in Agatha Christie mystery clubs and devoted Trekkies at conventions already cast themselves and act out roles in simulated dramas. Meanwhile, virtual worlds on the Internet are now inhabited by over 400,000 users playing ad-hoc roles as avatars. A few of these early worlds are taking on Hollywood themes. Will the inevitable joining of Hollywood and Avatar Cyberspace be a marriage made in heaven? Or will the new medium of virtual worlds emerge separate and distinct from the old "push" providers of our media experiences? I suspect that there will be a lucrative mixing of Hollywood and Avatars to create a concoction called Avvywood. I also expect that parts of this new cyberspace will be more exciting and stranger than could have ever been imagined or created by an old line media studio. For a sneak preview of Avvywood, see Alex Lightman's HollyWorlds at **http://www.hollyworlds.com**.

GamingWorlds
AVATARS AT PLAY

The good ship *Avatar* is going into hyperdrive and entering a wormhole into a whole new quadrant of cyberspace: the gaming worlds. In this zone, the action is fast and furious. War bird ships come out and blast us, we beam down to planets full of medieval castles, lords, and dragons and get lost forever in endless board gaming halls. These worlds are full of real people like you and me having fun with their avatars at play.

Your Guide to Gaming Worlds

Introduction

Until now, you have been adventuring inside virtual worlds where what goes on is almost all communication and creation. A world like AlphaWorld did not have a whole lot of structure to start with; it emerged as things got built and people became known as local heroes or villains. In gaming worlds, a great deal of structure is put there ahead of time by the developers of the world. The world may include pre-designed quests; have defined roles like wizards, magicians, or warriors; and have lots of rules to keep everyone in the game. Gaming worlds almost always have elements of risk: You can lose and get knocked out of the game, or have to backtrack through levels. And gaming worlds which enable you to play other real people online often have a social life, too. Whether it is the medieval avatar party scene in The Realm, Quake, or War Birds, videogames have grown up and are hosting their own forms of virtual community.

A taxonomy of gaming worlds

On-line multi-player gaming worlds come in all flavors and at all prices. Some are free to use, some you can use for a trial period, and others offer an hourly, monthly, or yearly subscription fee. Most of the gaming worlds described in this chapter are available as free or limited-use demonstration downloads. You should check the terms of use for each world as you go in. And as these worlds can be quite addicting, it is a good idea to keep one eye on your piggy bank.

What kinds of game planets are out there? There is a whole Darwinian natural selection going on with games competing to be the king of the jungle in their classes. The following table gives you an overview of the gaming worlds genre.

Social Gaming Worlds

Social gaming worlds are full of avatars who are less intent on killing each other than having fun together. In these worlds, people can communicate and form associations, often called *guilds*. There is usually a virtual economy of objects and plenty to discover on quests. In this section, I describe a couple of social gaming worlds, including Meridian 59, The Realm, and the upcoming CyberPark.

Meridian 59

Meridian 59 is a warriors, monsters, and sorcerers medieval role playing game. Some people describe it as a MUD (Multi User Dungeon) with a 3D interface and role

The world of gaming worlds

Social Gaming Worlds
These games give you plenty of reason and time to communicate with your fellow players. Meridian 59, The Realm, and Ultima Online are just a few of these socially-oriented quest and action adventure games. Guilds are often formed in these worlds.

Nonsocial Competitive Gaming Worlds
This type of game (i.e., Quake or Duke Nukem 3D) doesn't have a whole lot of room for social interaction during the game. Let's face it, if your goal is to kill your opponent's character, you are not going to stop and talk to them. On the other hand, users often form off-game associations, such as Clans (see "Quake clans," later in this chapter).

Multi-Player Sim Worlds
These include worlds such as War Birds and race car driving games, which place you in well crafted competitive simulations. In the cockpit of a World War II Spitfire or in the driver's seat of an Indy race car, you can converse with your team or squadron members and race or battle other players.

Constructivist Sim Worlds
These worlds, such as Active Worlds, allow you to create shared spaces and define rules about them. Sim City 2000 is a good example of this kind of world in which you design a whole city, complete with economic structures.

Board, Card, and Strategy Game Worlds
Good old favorites like backgammon, bridge, scrabble, chess, Monopoly, and Risk are easily transposed to the Internet, and sites like Internet Gaming Zone give you plenty of choices.

playing characters. Life in Meridian 59 starts out in the tavern shown in the following figure. Once you find the locked door (with only a few clues from the bartender) you can enter the larger environs of the city of TOS.

In Meridian 59, unlike purely social/creative avatar worlds, the main activity is player combat. You start by choosing among skills (I recommend you select the "slash" skill immediately), and after you begin playing, you decide your alignment: good, neutral, or evil. Chat is supported so you can communicate with other players. After players become strong competitors, able to defeat most of the monsters in the game, they join or form guilds (there are several dozen) which then engage in guild politics including rivalries and blood-feuds.

Social interaction is important in Meridian 59, not only to be able to join a guild, but also to progress in the game. If you are killed by another player or an ogre, your friends can pick up your avatar's belongings and return them to you when you re-enter re-incarnated. There is an entire economy of objects, from spells to weapons, and plenty of NPC's (non-player character bots) to sell or buy these things.

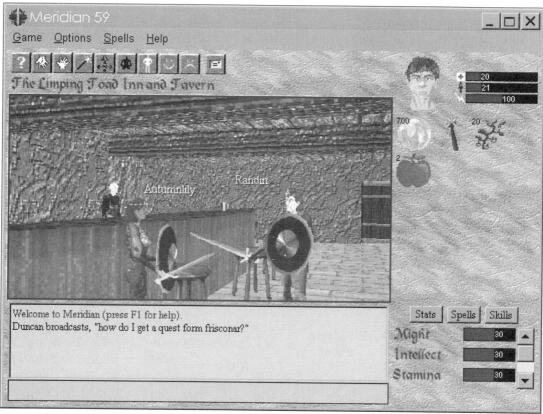

The Limping Toad Inn and Tavern in Meridian 59.

Pitfalls

You can't build in Meridian 59, but many guilds have assigned areas. New users should be careful about entering a guild area (doorways will have markings, or your *guardian angel* NPG might warn you that she cannot protect you in there). Guilds have been known to murder newbie users on sight. Newbies are advised to fight often and kill a lot of giant rats and baby spiders to build your strength and earn hit points. Mutant ants or trolls are too powerful, so turn and run from them! Like all Internet-based multi-user games, Meridian 59 suffers from *Net latency*. This means that while you are swinging your sword, the packets of data that communicate with the other player may be waiting in a queue somewhere behind someone's e-mail or big file download. This can make for frustrating combat and your character may meet its end at the hand of an extra network hop.

Key Meridian 59 Web sites

Meridian 59 is available from the 3DO Company at **http://www.3d0.com**. The Meridian 59 home page is at **http://meridian.3do.com/meridian/**. Meridian 59 comes on a CD-ROM that is sold in many computer stores or can be ordered from 3DO or its retailers for about $40. The software requires a Windows 95 PC and a dial-up connection to the Internet. Meridian 59 has a 30-day free trial and then a monthly charge of about $11 for unlimited play.

The great Meridian 59 bible can be found at **http://www.wolsi.com/~orbs/meridian/** and the registry of guilds is at **http://www.wolsi.com/~orbs/meridian/guilds.htm**. These pages contain resources and links to most Meridian 59 citizen player pages.

The Realm

Another medieval fantasy RPG (role playing game) world beckons. The Realm is an avatar gaming world that works in two-and-a-half dimensions much like WorldsAway (described in an earlier chapter in this book). You enter The Realm as a warrior, thief, wizard, or footloose adventurer, and earn skill levels based on your success in the virtual economy, or in battling other players or monsters. The following figure shows a fight between two players just ending, with one having lost all his possessions (including his clothes!) while an ogre lurks in the background. Other players are standing around in their avatars waiting to pick up property left behind by the loser, or are just chatting with each other.

Avatars in The Realm engaged in battle (or waiting for the spoils).

There is a vibrant economy of objects, with bot street vendors selling black trousers for exorbitant sums. As a Realm citizen you have a private home with a password protected door and strongbox for your avatar stuff. You can opt not to fight with other players and stick with monster matches. The more of these poor critters you kill, the better your armor and spells. You can even take dead monsters' spare change. But beware, bending down to pick some poor defeated soul's pocket automatically turns on your player's fighting signal, so that his or her friends can come after you with a vengeance.

People of The Realm

You can go on quests in The Realm either alone or with a team of friends to fight ogres, solve puzzles, or find treasure. While on the road, beware of the colored Ratlings, who are really dangerous dudes! If you like your group, you might consider forming a guild. To find other Realmers and guilds, check out the large number of individual users pages and guild pages linked at **http://www.realmserver.com/links.html**.

How to get The Realm

The Realm is available in a limited-use demonstration version from Sierra's Realm home page at **http://www.realmserver.com/**. The full CD-ROM version costs about $50 through stores or by ordering through Sierra Online's home page at **http://www.sierra.com**. To run The Realm, you need a 486 PC with 8MB RAM, 16MB disk space, SVGA, 2X CD-ROM drive, Windows 3.1, and an Internet connection (sound card is optional).

CyberPark

CyberPark is a new 3D role playing avatar gaming world that will be launched by WorldPlay Entertainment in late 1997. CyberPark is a cityscape with great articulated avatars, text chat, sponsored gaming tournaments, social cafes, and a virtual economy. Watch for CyberPark at **http://www.inngames.com/**.

Action Adventure Worlds

One step beyond social gaming worlds come the action adventure worlds. Combat, adventure, and distant journeys are the main themes here. In this section, I describe two such worlds: Ultima Online and Diablo.

Ultima Online

Origin's Ultima Online (UO) comes from a long lineage of role playing games: the Ultima series. Like many other RPGs, UO is medieval-fantasy-based and supports battles with other players, perilous quests, and chat in a tavern. UO has a functioning virtual ecology which drives monsters to search for food when it becomes scarce. There is also an economic system which allows you to run businesses such as taverns. You can buy a building, furnish it, manufacture a large supply of food, and then open for business.

UO is a large world built on an overhead-view 3D operational model similar to the bird's-eye view in Active Worlds (the techies call this an *isometric three-quarter view*). You always see your character and the others players and terrain immediately around you. The following figure shows a typical UO scene, where our character (in the center) is surrounded by hostile men with swords and winged creatures: it's not our day!

UO distinguishes itself with its skill system. You can study skills from a teacher (a non-player character bot, or another real person player). The longer you study and

Our heroes in Ultima Online surrounded by foes at a waterfall.

practice a skill, the better your character will perform that skill. There are skills for attack, defense, spells, and artisan workmanship. The challenge in UO is that there are so many skills one could master that skills already mastered—but not used—begin to decrease. Mastering and maintaining UO's skills will keep you on your toes.

Like other gaming worlds, UO allows and encourages the formation of guilds. UO also allows pets on the premises! You can own almost any animal, name it, and train it. Training dogs is easy; keeping a dragon as a pet is a much trickier endeavor.

How to get Ultima Online

Find Origin's Ultima Online at **http://www.owo.com**. Currently, Ultima Online is in beta test (as of the writing of this chapter). By the time you receive this book, Ultima Online may be a released product. This game needs a pretty hefty PC: a Pentium 133 with Windows 95, 16MB RAM, and DirectX installed. You must have at least a 14.4 bps dial-up connection to the Internet to play.

Diablo

Like Ultima Online (described earlier), Diablo is a fantasy overhead view 3D combat world. Diablo has a more diabolical heart in its 16 levels of dark dungeons, catacombs, and intriguing plots spelled out in mystical books. Characters move fluidly and die in gruesome realism.

A trio of adventurers face off against the Skeleton King and his undead warriors.

To run Diablo, you need a Windows 95/NT 4.0 machine with 16MB RAM and DirectX installed. At the time of this writing, a Macintosh version was in the works. Check Blizzard Entertainment's home page at **http://www.blizzard.com/** for information and to download a free demonstration version (warning: the demonstration version is a whopping 50MB). Internet play is supported through Mpath's Mplayer software available free from **http://www.mpath.com** or Battle Net at **http://www.battle.net/**.

Multi-Player Sims

It's time to move beyond medieval fantasy to the more hard core world of simulation games. These games seek to emulate real world situations, from flight simulators to battle tanks, Indy 500 races to the creation of virtual cities. In this section, I describe a couple of examples. I encourage you to check out Gamecenter.com's extensive reviews of Sim games at **http://www.gamecenter.com/Reviews/sims.html**.

War Birds

War Birds is a World War II combat flight simulator. You can join a squadron and engage in real-time dogfights with other teams from all over the Internet. You might tangle with a British Ace in a Spitfire or duel with a squadron of Japanese A6M Zeros. You can engage in historically accurate campaigns and use real flight test data. Want to rewrite history? Re-enact the attack on Pearl Harbor as though the U.S. pilots were actually in the air that fateful morning!

War Birds is a cockpit-view, six-degrees-of-freedom flight simulator. Find War Birds at iMagic Online's home page at **http://www.icigames.com/**. To use War Birds, you must have a Win95 Pentium PC (Macintosh version is being built) with DirectX installed.

X-Wing vs. TIE Fighter

Lucas Arts has provided *Star Wars* fans—young and old—with a dream come true: X-Wing vs. TIE Fighter (XWvTF). With XWvTF, you can engage in sorties and inter-planetary dogfights with up to eight other Internet users in their own ships. Battle can also be engaged with non-human software operators of Empire or Rebel Alliance ships. These bot ships are often every bit as tough as those with human pilots. There are plenty of single-player missions you can go on to hone your skills before joining a squadron in the Imperial Fleet or the rag tag rebel guerrilla crews.

Order the CD-ROM ($50) or download a mission demonstration version for Windows 95 Pentium PCs from LucasArts at **http://www.lucasarts.com/**.

Twitch and Shout:
Shoot 'Em Up at the Old Avatar Corral

Twitch games are fast moving shoot-'em-up worlds in which players battle each other and an assortment of nasty characters, scoring points and building up armor and ever more powerful weapons. In this section, I describe two front runners in this category: Quake and Duke Nukem 3D. Get your twitching finger on that trigger!

Quake

Quake is the eagerly awaited successor to Doom, that high speed shoot-'em-up 3D wonder of 1994. Like Doom, Quake is played through first-person view and in glori-ously fast 3D. The big difference with Quake is that the monsters and fighters you are stalking and eliminating are other real people playing against you through the Internet. Up to 16 combatants can be running around in a particular Quake server (this event is known as a *deathmatch*). The usual assortment of grunts and ogres are also present, making for complete gore and mayhem. Dead avatar players and kill bots look all the same.

One of the key goals in Quake is to acquire the largest totable weapon possible. Weapons range from the wimpy axe all the way through various shotguns to the super nailgun, rocket launcher, and ultimate thunderbolt. When you pull the trigger, the gun takes some time to come up and fire, giving Quake extra time to overcome that bothersome network latency. As you play Quake, you pick up new weapons, ammunition, health kits, and other objects. If you are killed during the game, you retain ownership of most of these items.

Quake clans

Another part of the Quake culture are *clans*. These are like the guilds in medieval fantasy worlds, such as The Realm. With names like The Unholy Alliance, Terminal Gibbage, and the Widow Makers, you can imagine that these "social" organizations are out there to protect each other while blasting away at their declared enemies. For the low-down on Quake clan society, visit Will Bryant's super Quake Clanring at **http://www.mpog.com/clanring/**.

Another very powerful feature of Quake is that you can build your own Quake worlds (called *levels,* from their dungeon metaphor). There are several Quake level editors on the market, many of them shareware. THRED is one of these and can be found at **http://www.visi.com/~jlowell/thred/**.

How to get Quake

ID Software provides a shareware version of Quake from their Web site at **http://www.idsoftware.com**. You can also purchase a registered version of Quake from retail stores almost anywhere. To run Quake you need a Pentium-based PC with 8MB RAM, and 30MB of disk space. Major sound cards are supported for some pretty gory sound effects.

Duke Nukem 3D

A hot contender with Quake is Duke Nukem 3D ("Duke"), another "twitch" game full of human and non-human combatants. In Duke, murderous aliens have landed in a futuristic (i.e., wasted) Los Angeles and human beings are now on the endangered species list. Duke has 28 levels, including a space station and moonbase.

Created by 3D Realms Entertainment and published by G.T. Interactive, find Duke at the official Duke Nukem 3D home page at **http://duke.gtinteractive.com/**. Duke can be downloaded in a shareware version or purchased in fully licensed form. It can run on a 486/33 machine with DOS or any Windows PC supporting a DOS application.

Let's Deal! Board Games Gone Virtual

Old fashioned board and card games are a natural for play over the Internet, and just about every game you can think of is being played out there in cyberspace right now. In this section, I describe a couple including Hoyle Internet Blackjack and Risk, and point you to some sources for many more.

Hoyle Internet Blackjack

The Sierra Internet Gaming System provides dozens of networked multi-player games. One I liked in the board game genre was Hoyle Internet Blackjack. As you can see in the following figure, you sit your player avatar around the blackjack board, the

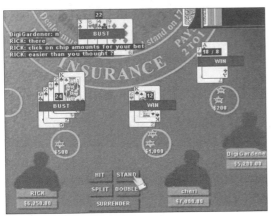

Playing Hoyle Internet Blackjack.

dealer deals, and you play. Not being an experienced player myself, you can see my paltry winnings in the figure. No real money is exchanging hands, but some small Caribbean islands are working on real Internet gambling. An artificial intelligence player called Howie will replace any player who leaves a game. In addition, tournaments can be hosted, which begs the question: Could whole teams of Howies play each other? Hoyle Blackjack is available for Windows by order from Sierra's home page ($15) at **http://www.sierra.com**.

Risk

One of my old favorites, Risk, is now available for play over the Internet. You can match wits with other Internet "generals" with world conquest on their minds. Networking is provided by Mpath's MPlayer system. Risk must be purchased on CD. See information about it and other games, including Scrabble, Monopoly, Trivial Pursuit, and Battleship, on Hasbro's home page at **http://www.hasbro.com/**.

Internet Gaming Zone

Microsoft's Internet Gaming Zone ("the Zone") provides dozens of games, from bridge to chess to golf. Most are free of charge and many are designed for play over the Internet. A unique feature of the Zone is *ZoneMatch lobbies,* which allow players to find each other easily on the Internet and start a game. Enter the zone at **http://beta.zone.com/asp/default.asp**.

Hot Sites and Tools for Gaming Worlds

Hot Spots

http://www.gamecenter.com
Gamecenter.com features terrific news, reviews, and insights into the gaming world industry as well as demonstration versions of games.

http://www.happypuppy.com/
Happy Puppy is another great source of links to games.

http://www.gamesdomain.co.uk/
Games Domain from the UK has mirrors all over Europe, Russia, and South Africa.

http://gamespot.com/
GameSpot is a truly great site for demonstrations and reviews of all the games you can think of.

http://www.outland.com/
Outland features multi-player gaming for the Mac.

http://www.virtus.com
The Virtus 3D Quake level editing system which provides real-time, 3D visualization, and drag-and-drop interfaces to build your own Quake worlds.

http://www.ten.net/
Total Entertainment Network provides networking services to play dozens of games over the Internet.

http://www.mplayer.com
Mpath interactive provides MPlayer for multi-user gameplay.

http://www.dwango.com/enter.html
Dwango is a networked "gaming village" which offers servers providing low latency networked access to a large number of games.

http://www.idsnet.com/ids/cave2/cave.html
The Cave of Madness is an experiment in gaming in VRML.

http://www.newfire.com/
NewFire provides fast VRML browsers that enable VRML worlds to be built for bona fide action and simulation games.

Life in Digital Space

BOTS, BIOTA, AND VIRTUAL PETS

Ⓢomething powerful is emerging in cyberspace: life! How could this happen? Well, consider the Internet itself. Since its birth, the Internet has been a lot like a great mass of tubing. You often see terms like *pipe* and *socket* and *port* describing the plumbing which carries data streams through the Net.

All those streams are pooling into a common digital ocean. That ocean contains a wonderful variety of objects, some of which can recombine and replicate to make new objects. And there you have it, the old primordial soup recipe for life! One of the richest soups will be avatar virtual worlds, full of structures, behaviors, and above all, people. People will be a tremendous catalyst in the mix, building and tearing down structures, creating software robots, playing games, and tweaking the genetic codes of artificial life forms growing inside virtual worlds. We have already seen the explosion which can occur in cyberspace with the growth of the World Wide Web. Well, just wait and see what will happen inside virtual worlds!

Your Guide to
Life in Digital Space

Agents, Daemons, Bots, Biots, Biota —Where Did This All Come From?

"People are moving out of the way; something big and inexorable is plunging through the crowd, shoving avatars this way and that. Only one thing has the ability to shove people around like that inside The Black Sun, and that's a bouncer daemon."

—Neal Stephenson, *Snow Crash*

What are avatars and where did all this come from? Stories were told around campfires thousands of years ago, just as they are today. Only back then, that was the only form of evening entertainment and they really knew how to tell a story. Complete with dancing, drumming, masks, and costumes, members of those old communities donned other personae and acted out fables from the overworld, the afterworld, and other features of the local mythology. Cave paintings also showed fanciful representations of the community and its world. Stories told in front of these vivid action-filled paintings must have had the power to totally immerse listeners. So how are avatars and virtual worlds connected to this? You could look at it as a neo-digital cave culture. Just picture millions of us sitting in front of our glowing screens (largely at nighttime) all reaching out to paint on our shared digital cave walls.

Daemons in the night

In all of those ancient campfire stories the most terrifying and intriguing character of all was the disembodied spirit. As the tellers described it, these spirits could inhabit any person or object, giving voices to stones and causing trees to walk. The ogre, the monster, the demon all sprung from fearsome living creatures that threatened human lives. The difference was that these creatures were creations of the human imagination and all embodied human attributes: a human body, a crafty mind, the voice of a man or woman. These creatures were all morphs of people.

When people started to build machines that had some attributes of living things, such as mechanical power or logical processes, all of their beliefs in spirits and monsters began to transfer to these machines. Our fascination with Frankenstein and his progeny continues today and underlies the fields of robotics, artificial intelligence, and artificial life. The unique environment of virtual worlds will allow us to visually embody little experimental Frankensteins in the form of software agents, robots, daemons, biots, and biota.

Avatars in Prague: A personal story

From 1990 to 1994 I had the great fortune to frequently visit and then to live in Prague, a beautiful city in the then newly "liberated" central Europe. Prague, the capital of Czechoslovakia (which later became the Czech Republic), had ended up on the Soviet side of the so-called "iron curtain" after the end of World War II. For forty years, Prague had existed in a time warp under an intensely autocratic communist dictatorship (with the exception of the famous Prague Spring which lead to an invasion in 1968). I went there to help set up a software laboratory for my company and ended up joining the community. I became part of the faculty of Charles University, learned to speak some Czech, helped create a salon for artists and musicians, and generally had a great time.

Prague and Prague Castle—a spiritual home of automata and birthplace of the Robot.

As I studied the history and culture of the region of Bohemia and Moravia, which make up most of the Czech Republic, I got a glimpse into some of the origins of the concept of avatars. I was surprised to learn that the term *robot* was coined by a Czech playwright, Karel Capek, earlier in this century. Playwright Capek's 1923 work was called "R.U.R., Rossum's Universal Robots" (robot derived from *rabotai,* the Czech word for work).

The Czechs—Sudeten Germans and Jews—and built a rich culture and a prosperous industrial society in Bohemia-Moravia that gave us articulated body armor, elaborate locks, and guns, including the pistol (which is another Czech word). Prague is a city of spires and clocks, including an elaborate astronomical clock with figures that march out of trap doors on the hour. About 500 years ago, King Rudolph II decided to fund a group of alchemists and even built a street full of tiny houses for them inside the walls of Prague Castle. Under the protection and funding of the king, these secretive alchemists were charged with a mystical mission: to animate matter, to give life to dead material and take a step toward creating *homunculi,* or artificial men.

Elsewhere in the culture and myths of Bohemia lie legends that speak of a great fascination with the

The Old Jewish cemetery in Prague, mythical birthplace of the Golem man/robot.

automaton, or artificial being. One of the most well known is that of the Golem, a giant clay creature called forth by Rabbi Loew of Prague to protect the Jewish community from the consequences of an accusation of a blood libel. He arose out of the 900-year-old Jewish cemetery (shown in the preceding figure). You can find one version of the story of the Golem, as told in the on-line interview piece, "Adam, Golem, Robot—A Dialogue between Ken Goldberg and Ovid Jacob," at **http://www.cyborganic.com/People/ovid/agr.html**. The following is an excerpt:

> Rabbi Loew asks the creature to fetch water from the well. The Rabbi goes upstairs to sleep and awakens to discover that the entire house is filled with water! The Golem continues dutifully fetching water until the Rabbi tricks it into leaning close enough that the Rabbi can erase the first letter inscribed on its forehead, thus changing Emet (Truth, or Life) to Met (Death), whereupon the Golem turns into a lifeless mass of clay which crushes the Rabbi to death. Again, harsh consequences for the creator. As a Computer Scientist I note that the rabbi's fatal error was to forget to specify what we call a "termination condition.." The Golem went into an infinite loop due to a programming error!

Ken Goldberg goes on to conclude:

> Prometheus, Icarus, Faust, the Sorcerer's Apprentice, Frankenstein, the Hasidic tale of the Golem. The archetype generally describes a human who creates a creature that comes to life. Initially the creator takes great pride and delight in the creature, until at some point the creature takes a life of its own and runs amok, and in the end the creator pays the consequences for this act of hubris. The event wherein the creator loses control of the creature is a necessary step toward the development of the creature.

Prague is a beautiful city, full of castles and ancient bridges, spires and labyrinthine streets; catacomb-like pubs; and pristine gothic and baroque squares and avenues. Prague seems like a virtual world itself. When I lived there, I heard older Sudeten Germans describe it as a true "Wunderland." From the Golem to the agents and informants of past puppet regimes to the Byzantine mask that Czechs wear to hide and preserve an inner life, in Prague, avatars walk the streets.

Modern-day puppeteers on the Charles Bridge in Prague.

So perhaps avatars, agents, bots, and biota are just the latest digital alchemists' work in the long quest to create the *homunculi*. Originally the term avatar came from Hindu mythology and is the name for the temporary body that a god inhabits while visiting Earth. We may not be able to imbue gods in our avatars but it will be interesting to see how much of ourselves we can slip into their virtual sleeves.

Are we all puppets in some way? Are we all not avatars?

A Parade of Bots

From an interview with Sherry Turkle (**http://hpcc920.external.hp.com/Ebusiness/ january/main1.html**).

> *"I was in this online environment one time, and I kept hearing about this character named Dr. Sherry. Well, this Dr. Sherry administered questionnaires. Dr. Sherry interviewed people about their lives in this online environment—but I wasn't Dr. Sherry.*
>
> *However, many people assumed, not unreasonably, that I was this person. I didn't know what to do. So I began looking into the activities of Dr. Sherry, and I found that she was in this online environment all the time. Dr. Sherry would be there at 3 a.m.; she would be there at 6 a.m., and she would be there at 5 p.m.*
>
> *It finally dawned on me that this person might not be a person at all. She might be a bot that was programmed to interview people about their online experiences. It was an astounding moment: I meet my double and it could be an artificial being.*
>
> *So I think that bots are a wake-up call that we're getting to the point where some of the entities we interact with online may in fact be machines. It makes us reflect on what it is to be intelligent and what it is to be alive."*

Bots, bots, bots, they are popping up everywhere. In the Jetsons cartoons of our youth (or at least mine) there were all sorts of helper robots. They would serve you dinner, drive you places, and carry your bad news to the boss. Well, it turned out that the household robot was a little bit harder to build than everyone thought. But take heart, for the bots are finally here for you! A *bot* is like an avatar, except that no person inhabits it; it's just a piece of automated software. It may come as no surprise that bots have been living in computers in various forms for a long time.

Agents: Much touted ancestors of bots

Back in the early days of Unix and the Internet, tiny pieces of software called *daemons* were created to do a lot of nasty little background tasks, like killing off errant programs and bouncing misaddressed e-mail. In recent years, there has been a lot of attention focused on *intelligent agents,* or software with a little more personality and brains than daemons. Proponents are really convinced that intelligent agents will become the universal tools to simplify our ever more complex lives. Agents will do all your bill paying, help our kids with their homework, and even book our funerals and manage our living trusts when we die. The Pharaoh's dream of immortality will come true as our agent successors accumulate enough wealth to clone us anew.

The Internet is full of bugs!

Agent evangelists tell us that the era of the agent is already here. They point to the Internet and say that it is crawling with them: "spiders" or "webcrawlers" are constantly visiting Web pages and gobbling up juicy tidbits we may want to search for later on. "Search agent: *crawl my website!*" is a cry heard across the Net by people desperate for more visitors to their beloved home pages. It turns out that a great proportion of the "hits" or visits to home pages are actually search agents. With the new agent-centric Java language, more agents are on their way to make the Internet an even more complicated place. Who knows, there may be a need for agent hunters to cull the teeming agent population.

There is a bot in your virtual community

Agents long ago became a part of the furniture in virtual communities. In fact, it was inside chat based communities built using IRC (Internet Relay Chat) and MUDs (Multi-User Domains) that the word *bot* was first used to describe a software agent that interacts with the citizens of a virtual community.

There are some great taxonomies of bots on the Net. If you want to investigate further, check out the Bot Spot at **http://www.botspot.com/**. In addition, bot historian, Kenneth Lonseth, developed this comprehensive description and links page about all the various species of bots at **http://www.mindspring.com/~lonseth/alife/bots/bots.htm**. Ken has kindly agreed to describe for us his view of bots and chatterbots including the famous great ancestor bot, Eliza:

> "*Bots are software programs that reside on the Net responding to communications protocols and users. Some perform maintenance tasks and gather information, while others are meant to disrupt online communications or just be plain annoying.*
>
> *The first acknowledged bot was Eliza, made by MIT professor Joseph Weizenbaum in the mid 60s. Eliza is a psychotherapist of sorts, annoyingly dodging questions with questions of her own. Eliza is also the first chatterbot: a bot meant to interact with humans. She looks for certain key words and responds according to her programmed algorithm. Eliza is painfully simple compared to modern chatterbots, and her limitations are quickly revealed during a short dialog. These days it's common for chatterbots to employ a host of 'tricks' to help simulate human responses. They also store conversations to build up databases for future use.*"

An actual rendition of Eliza can be downloaded and talked to at the Simon Laven Page at **http://www.student.toplinks.com/hp/sjlaven/eliza.htm**.

Ken goes on to describe the thriving ecosystem of bots in MUDs and IRC:

"MUDs are considered the first breeding ground for bots. Online multi-user games are sprinkled with automated scripts designed to respond to user interaction. In the late 80s Michael Mauldin created the Mass-Neotek bots for TinyMUD at Carnegie Mellon University. These bots can register who are present, and make sure the users are abiding by MUDs rules. Newt is a bot of the Maas-Neotek family and resides within DragonMud. Newt can relay messages and keep track of your e-mail and homepage. He also tracks all players and objects within the MUD and can record all conversations up to a set memory limit. Most MUD bots or 'mobiles' are not as sophisticated as Newt. They are just simple scripts designed to react when a user enters a certain area.

Multi-user domains are not considered a vibrant ecosystem for bots because of the many flavors of MUDs. With MOOs, MUCs, and MUSHes the bots are confined to separate corners of the Internet universe, each programmed on a different variety of language.

IRC has the most thriving online bot community. With thousands of different people interacting, clashing, and chatting it's no wonder bots are deployed into the pool in drones. Most bots are made to hold ops on a channel or guard against hostile takeovers. There is an ongoing war between hostile bot users and channel operators. Of a less violent nature are the variety of gamebots and chatterbots that offer a little challenge and simple interaction. #Riskybus is a gamebot that gives Jeopardy style questions to users. It keeps the score of all users and even has some chat abilities.

Eggdrop is one of the most powerful and long lasting bots on IRC. It has many advanced features that help you protect a channel or even save it for you while logged off. Eggdrop has also the ability to link to other bots to form a pseudo-IRC called Botnets. The Botnet development has spurred a new line of "Limbo Bots" that never join IRC but only connect to Botnets.

Bots are banned from most servers because they are generally a nuisance. In most cases unauthorized bot deployment will get you K-lined or kicked off the server.

IRC bots live a firefly existence, with continuos changes. Most don't last for more than a few weeks. Entire generations are wiped out with new IRC server upgrades, and when bot rules of conduct are introduced.

They're here...

Emerging from the agents craze and the bot ecologies we should see some pretty interesting bots walking around in our local virtual worlds. I personally hope we get bots as smart as the house robots on the Jetsons. In fact, bots are already appearing in avatar cyberspace even as you read this! Lets meet one of the first of these nefarious characters: Floops.

Floops is a creation of Protozoa (**http://www.protozoa.com**). He was created to star in a string of regular short performances at the big Silicon Graphics VRML Web site (**http://vrml.sgi.com**). Floops has lifelike body moves and a great voice (provided by a human actor). Floops is a bot with a human personality. His gestures were made by capturing a real actor's motions in a body suit. This is called *motion capture* and is used in many Hollywood films to make synthetic actors move around in believable fashion. All of this is called *performance* or *character animation* and seeks to achieve what the experts are calling *suspension of disbelief*. Your disbelief has been suspended if just for an instant you forget that you are just looking at computer models and start to immerse yourself in the story unfolding on the screen.

Protozoa has a fascinating history of its own. Using their custom built *ALIVE!* animation software, the folks at Protozoa created the *Moxy* character, a virtual host for the Cartoon Network. Short scenes starring Moxy would be created every week so that he always had fresh shtick to serve to the masses of cartoonaholics. An actor in a body suit would walk Moxy around and do his gestures while a comedian would read Moxy's lines. Moxy's scenes would be made in real time driven by these performance artists and prepared to go on the air within minutes. See more about Moxy and Protozoa's other projects at **http://www.protozoa.com/alive/index.html**.

There's no reason why the nightly news couldn't be presented to us by some future Floops. With the voice processing and lip synchronization from Onlive Traveler and a good VRML toolkit, any ten-year-old wired genius with a PC, microphone, and modem could run her own TV network. Hey, why wait for years to see video through the Internet?

Episodic avactors

Let's take a closer look at Floops, an *avactor* bot who stars in one- to two-minute episodes produced twice a week. This reminds me of those film shorts from about a century ago, which were all about one to eight minutes long. It is hard for us to believe now that people would line up at a nickelodeon box just to peer in and see a three-minute film loop. It will amuse our kids when they picture us sitting on our 28.8 bps modems, waiting for a half hour to "experience" a VRML episodic cartoon. But hey, you have to start somewhere.

Here we can see Floops after we started the episode. He is watching us through the tube of our computer display, gesticulating for us to "do something." Floops comes with his own voice, as recorded by a voice-over artist and replayed in time with Floops' body moves. The Floops follies are a little interactive in that you can click on things and Floops will notice. In the following figure, Floops is desperately trying to get us to click on the dish on his right. If you finally click on the dish, a fish is ejected into the air and swims (or flies) off. End of episode.

Was it worth the three-minute wait for the download? Maybe. Bot performance worlds like Floops or Atomic 3D's Neutron (see the chapter, "Brave New Worlds") will get better and better when the models of the characters can be downloaded only once and the only thing that will need to stream in will be their gestures and voices. Downloading all the props, avatars, and sequences of body moves to begin with will decrease the time necessary to play every episode. This is how Active Worlds and many of the other virtual worlds work today and part of the reason we have avatar cyberspace years before everyone thought it would be possible. Of course, more interaction with the bots in episodes should make them more interesting and less like the familiar old couch potato "push it down my throat" TV.

Find more VRML episodic cartoons at Mediadome's Driftwood at **http://www .mediadome.com/Webisodes/Protozoa/Fun/**.

Floops says, "click on that dish!"   Bingo! You get a fish.

Bots: Coming to a world near you

Of course, we have yet to see something as sophisticated and well crafted as Floops inside an inhabited virtual world interacting with real people. But bots are already making their appearance. Most worlds already have simple agents or daemons, like the building inspector in AlphaWorld that watches to make sure you are not encroaching on someone else's property. Way back in the summer of 1995, a hacker calling himself Cure95 inserted two bots into Worlds Chat. This fascinating event is described in the section, "A Brief History of Worlds Chat," in the chapter on Worlds Chat earlier in this book.

Black Sun introduced bots into Passport in the spring of 1997. You can see one described in the section, "The Mysterious Mysterio," in the Black Sun Passport chapter. Bots in the Palace have been seen sporting a *Star Trek* "Borg" eyepiece. I have often wondered whether or not bots should tell avatars that they are not people. I know that bots running in text-based MOO communities have carried on conversations with people for hours, convincing them that they were other users.

This all harkens back to the Eliza program described earlier in this chapter and the famous "Turing Test" of machine intelligence devised in the 1940s in which a person at a keyboard would chat at the computer with a real person and with a computer to see if they could differentiate between what was real chat and what was generated by the computer. It is all pretty silly when you get right down to it, but people seem to thrive on tricking each other. It seems to me that a good way to indicate that an avatar is actually a bot would be to give it something like a Borg eyepiece, say, a monocle. If the avatar is not human-looking, you could still find a place to hang the monocle and its chain. If perchance the bot was temporarily being driven by a person, the monocle could be temporarily placed in the bot's shirt pocket.

Why do we need bots?

In an otherwise empty, lonely virtual space, a bot can be a great trigger for conversation and can keep the attention of new users just long enough for others to join in. Onlive implemented bots to do just this in their ABC Monday Night Football world. In this world, the "tackle dummies" were bots that would play audio files when you got near them. These audio attention getters would usually be a sports trivia question related to the football game happening on TV at the same time (and streaming into the world). You could then try to answer the questions.

Good "welcome" or "greeter" bots should give newly arrived users a sense of belonging and a feeling of being included. These avatar citizens are more likely to stay longer and return in areas where they are not accosted by pushy "salesbots."

I played a bartender named Odiyah in the Low Earth Orbit station in the MUD called SolSys Sim for a while, and so I can appreciate well designed "cybartender" bots found in worlds like Onlive Traveler and Extempo's Spence's Bar.

Of course, bots could do other jobs in virtual worlds. One idea I have had for a while is for a community service bot that could roam the giant AlphaWorld cityscape looking for "parking lots." Parking lots are big pieces of virtual land covered over by some overzealous citizen who then does nothing with all that acreage. These bots could identify this gratuitously grabbed land, determine who the neighbors are, call a hearing on the land, and then auction it off to citizens willing to do something creative with it.

Virtual Pets

How can we think of virtual worlds without having our most beloved companions there—our pets? Remember the movie *Planet of the Apes* where the people traveled through time to some future where apes ruled and thought of us Homo Saps as just great pets? The power of pets cannot be underestimated in their power to affect our everyday lives. When we start to tend litters of virtual pets living in our digital cityscapes, they may evolve so much that we will end up on the other end of the leash! You don't have to worry about that yet, so let's enter the world of v-pets.

Cyberlife's creatures

Creatures from Cyberlife in the United Kingdom takes the v-pet phenomenon to new heights. Steve Grand, Creatures' inventor, worked for years to give these critters dramatic lives as they hatch from eggs, learn how to eat, communicate, survive illness and attacks, breed, and die all within ten to 15 hours.

To run Creatures you have to have a Macintosh running System 7 or later, or a minimum 75 MHz Pentium PC running Windows 95 with a sound card. You also must purchase the CD-ROM, which should be available from most computer stores. You can get a preview of Creatures by visiting Cyberlife's home page at **http://www.cyberlife.co.uk**.

I spent hours using Creatures and hatched three individuals (called Norns) from their eggs. The following figure shows my starter set of six eggs which came on a floppy disk with the CD-ROM. My creatures are unique and would have different behaviors from any other Creature on the planet. After breeding, these Creatures can inherit traits and mutate to yield yet more unique generations. Cyberlife tells me there is no end to this and that they have seen some pretty strange creatures emerge. You can package up these "eggs" and send them through the Internet to other Creatures users.

Teaching the first Norn to eat was a pretty easy task. I was picking up carrots, pots of honey, and other things and dropping them in front of the Norn, when suddenly, I heard the Norn slurp down the honey. Norns have digestive systems, brains full of neural networks, and complex physical and mental health patterns. Norns can expire if they don't learn how to eat, or can become sick from bacteria which are inherent in their world. Cyberlife told me about a family in Australia which called them in a panic. Their Norn was not eating or responding and was in danger of dying on the spot. A hasty e-mail later and Steve Grand was looking at the wiring in the sick Norn's brain. He discovered that through a mutation, this Norn had no sight or hearing and so it could not learn how to eat. A quick bit of neural network surgery later and the Norn was back in Australia leading a normal, if short, ten-hour life.

Norn eggs ready for hatching.

Training Norns to eat can sometimes be a futile task when they are obsessed with each other!

If you can coax your Creatures to enter a teleporter, they will be transported to a special computer learning center (shown here) where you can prompt them to learn words. I finally did get my Norns to say other words than "goo." Their voices are quite endearing and provide the best indication of how they are doing, so make sure your speakers are turned on when you run Creatures. FinFin, which we will look at next, is a v-pet to which you can actually talk back.

Teaching Norns to say something other than "Goo."

Fujitsu Interactive's FinFin and TEO World

In 1996, Fujitsu Interactive (working with inventors Macoto Tezca in Japan) introduced a virtual world called TEO (The Other Earth) which features a fantastic forested planet full of creatures, all living on a CD-ROM. TEO world may be a hint at the worlds and creatures to come to the Internet. Of course, you can also combine a CD-ROM with the Internet by delivering all the art and software on the CD-ROM and then sending only changes to the world and interaction through the Internet. This is known as the *hybrid* approach and should become a common way of delivering a great experience that is also shared with other people (the CD-ROM in this book is an early hybrid and hopefully will save you a lot of downloading). One day, who knows, maybe TEO world could become a giant connected biosphere.

FinFin and some of his friends.

The TEO world CD-ROM is available from most computer stores. More information on TEO can be found at **http://www.teo-world.com/**. You need a minimum Pentium 75MHz PC with a CD-ROM and a sound card. The PC must also be running Windows 95 on 16MB of memory to experience TEO.

The main critter inside TEO is a little fellow named FinFin. FinFin is a sort of half dolphin-half bird with quite a personality. The creators of FinFin describe his (or is it a her?) species in this way:

"Initially a mammal that lived in the sea (comparable to a dolphin on Earth), it adapted to the land and then took to the skies. It doesn't form packs like dolphins, but moves around alone. It is very curious by nature and playful. It will "sing" (the mode of communication believed to be indigenous to the FinFin species) songs for you and even perform acrobatics for you. Smaller than a dolphin, it is about as large as a cat."

FinFin spends his days much like your pet or you would: wandering around aimlessly, singing, flying, sleeping, or eating something called Elmo fruit or Tsubu seeds. Interacting with FinFin is a new experience. You do not have to hammer away at the old keyboard or mouse, but instead you can use a domed device called the *comlink antenna* (see following figure). By speaking into the antenna (it has a microphone) you can address your FinFin virtual pet. By waving your hands in front of the antenna you can signal FinFin visually. Over time you can learn what kinds of things FinFin will respond positively to and what actions will cause him to fly away in a fluster. You can even try whistling (there is a special whistle provided), playing an instrument, or even cranking up the stereo (which will probably drive FinFin off over the horizon). FinFin will adjust to you over time and will remember previous experiences. Remember when you closed the door on your pet's tail or paw? Well, I did and my pet cat held her paw up in the air every time she waited by that door from that time forward, for *12* years!

The world, the background

Japan has a fascination with "artificial life" (as witnessed by the current Tamagotchi craze—those little portable devices with a pixel creature painted on a tiny screen). Read about them at **http://www.bandai.com/tamagotchi. html**. So it is not surprising that FinFin should come from Japan. A lot of home grown Japanese technology embodies FinFin and TEO, including recognition and learning engines, fast computer graphics, and lifelike character animation and sound generation. The folks behind all this have been working since 1989, creating various creatures from jellyfish to sharks which would recognize gestures or voice.

The dome antenna device for communicating with FinFin.

Other TEO creatures

A wide variety of other creatures inhabit TEO world along with FinFin. None of them will respond to you like FinFin. I guess you could say that FinFin is the only sentient race on TEO. Other TEO creatures are described at **http://www.teo-world.com/teo_hp_sw_e/Animal/frame.html**.

Waving and talking to FinFin through the dome.

PF Magic's Dogz, Catz, and other Web pets

In the mid 90s, the famous "Bad Dog" screen saver from Berkeley Systems' "After Dark" series of screen savers featured a pretty ingenious prototype v-pet that would take over your desktop, sniff around the windows and your trash can, and create havoc with your screen by tearing holes on the desktop.

PF Magic has taken all this a step further and brought us a whole litter of virtual pets (or *petz,* as they call them) on the Internet. You can download "adoption kits" for Catz and Dogz from their Web site and immediately play with your digital critters. Once you bond with your critters (or they bond with you?) you might be so inclined to get out that credit card and adopt the fully featured pet. I went for the adoption kits to find out and downloaded both Catz and Dogz from PF Magic's home page at **http://www.pfmagic.com/**.

It's rainin' Catz and Dogz!

I played with both Catz and Dogz for a couple of hours and took snapshots with the conveniently provided "pet cam," and then put my favorite photos together into the following figure. These petz do everything from responding to being scratched with your mouse cursor, to chasing you around (the screen) and playing with balls, mice,

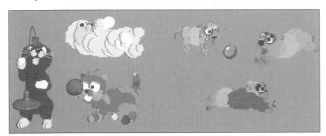

A wild selection of Catz and Dogz on the loose.

and other toys. More goodies come when you adopt. If you buy the full version of Catz, you get to use the infamous water sprayer bottle which you can use to show your v-cat who is really the boss. I don't know if they provide Kitty Litter or pooper scoopers to clean up after your petz.

Oddbalz—now that's more my style

Oddballz are a third kind of petz from PF Magic, which can mutate and be trained to perform tricks. You can even craft and exchange your own oddbalz with other v-pet breeders. PF Magic describes these creatures as the wackiest of their stable of "digital life."

More virtual pets on the way

In this section, I've shown you just a tiny sampling of the virtual pets coming to a Web page or a virtual world near you. When I was finishing this chapter I heard rumors of v-pets projects being started inside several of the avatar worlds. With Oddbalz, we see the beginnings of a pet making toolkit. Another great example is Awesome Animated Monster Maker from ImaginEngine Corp. Check out their mini Monster Maker character builder kit at **http://www.imaginengine.com/**.

Will v-pets be the true beginnings of artificial life on the Net? Silly as they may seem sometimes, these spunky chunks of software face the toughest of survival tasks: they have to satisfy human desires and keep our attention. They also are free to wander inside our virtual cities, knocking over our garbage cans, and poking their noses into everything. Like trying to design a rover that will travel on its own on the Martian surface, v-pets also face a great unknown. Put in a genetics system to allow them to breed and pass on traits, and you could be faced with a bona fide artificial life colony on your hands.

From Internet Worms to feral Creatures?

It wasn't so many years ago that Robert Morris created the famous "Internet Worm" that brought down thousands of servers. Will v-pets go feral and rampage across the Internet? When a million ten-year-olds become genetic or neural hackers, creating and exchanging critters, they may set off the proverbial "Cambrian Explosion" of forms of *digital biota*. Will the Internet be overrun with these *biota*, consuming all the servers, and sucking in all the bandwidth? I don't think so, as most v-pets or other biota need to exist in carefully crafted environments, like the Creatures universe. It is an interesting possibility, however.

We Are Not Alone: Artificial Life Growing on the Internet

Living things are so key to the inspiration of our language, philosophy, science, art and very thought patterns that they were bound to be represented in cyberspace. We are part of the Earth's biosphere, so by putting ourselves into cyberspace as avatars, we are introducing a small representation of the Earth's biota into digital space. But what happens when we introduce a little more of that biota? In this section, I will review some of the forms of digital biota emerging in cyberspace. Much of these biota are actually pretty simple mathematical rule sets that mimic living processes. But perhaps *real life* is just a matter of the scale of complexity. As these simple forms grow into more complex systems feeding off computer resources and our attention spans, perhaps we will some day see something really "alive" and really digital. In this section, I discuss several life simulator systems, such as Mathematical Life Models and Synthetic Ecosystems.

Mathematical Life Models

John Conway's Game of Life

The Game of Life was invented by John Conway back in the 1960s and has been described and implemented thousands of times since. Billions and billions of iterations of Conway's Life have been played in the past three decades, even hosting competitions to generate familiar patterns like spaceships. The recent arrival of the Java programming language on the World Wide Web has lead to an entire ecosystem of approaches to Conway's Life—all playable with a Java enabled Web browser. The following description of Conway's Game of Life rules is courtesy Paul Callahan (whose great Web pages on Conway's Life are also listed at the end of this section).

The rules

The game is played on a field of cells, each of which has eight neighbors (adjacent cells). A cell is either occupied (by an organism) or not. The rules for deriving a generation from the previous one include the following:

1. Death: If an occupied cell has 0, 1, 4, 5, 6, 7, or 8 occupied neighbors, the organism dies (0, 1: of loneliness; 4 thru 8: of overcrowding).

2. Survival: If an occupied cell has two or three neighbors, the organism survives to the next generation.

3. Birth: If an unoccupied cell has three occupied neighbors, it becomes occupied.

See Paul's Pages full of Conway's A-Life at **http://www.cs.jhu.edu/~callahan/lifepage.html** and Alan Hensel's fast and powerful Life Java applet at **http://users.vnet.net/alanh/life/**.

Self-reproducing Cellular Automata loops

In the same vein as Conway's Game of Life, are a whole slew of *Cellular Automata* (CA) programs available through the Web. The one shown in the following figure is by Chris Osborn of Softrise Limited. It is a configurable CA program written in Java and runs inside your Web browser (Netscape Navigator 3.01 or Internet Explorer 3.0). Like Conway's Game of Life, cellular automata are like tiny organisms that check the state of adjacent cells (or pixels, in this case) to decide whether to grow there.

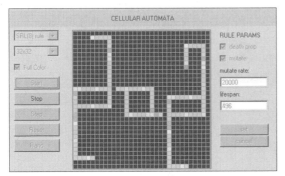

Cellular Automata growin' on the Web.

The CAs shown here remind me of Chris Langton's first "Artificial Life" programs he created 15 years ago on an old Apple II computer. See Steven Levy's book, *Artificial Life,* listed in the Bibliography, for a great description of the beginnings of the A-Life movement. Drive the cellular automata loops yourself at **http://ourworld. compuserve.com/homepages/cdosborn/**.

Robert Silverman's Live Artificial Life Page

Robert Silverman has pulled together a first class set of Mathematical Life Models on his home page at **http://alife.fusebox.com/cb/alife.html**. This is a very complete compendium of running demonstrations, including Swarm (see following figure), which allows you to select the number and size of critters that attempt to find each other and swarm together and fly off. Planet Wa-Tor, another Silverman simulation, pits rabidly hungry sharks against rapidly reproducing fish. Schools of green fish soon give way to marauding sharks which then starve and the fish return. These kind of sustainable cycles are common in on-line A-life ecosystems which can literally go on forever.

A composite of Swarm images from Live Artificial Life Page.

Craig Reynolds' Boids

Craig Reynolds has been fascinated with coordinated animal motion such as bird flocks and fish schools. Since 1986 he has been creating models of this behavior in software he calls *Boids*. Boids has been used as an inspiration and starting point for lifelike special effects, particularly the bat swarms in the feature motion pictures *Batman Returns* and *Cliffhanger,* as well as the wildebeest stampede in *The Lion King.*

In his on-line Boids simulation, the following three simple rules drive the behavior of each individual in the flock:

- Steer to avoid getting too close to neighbors

- Steer to keep towards the direction of the flock

- Steer to stay near the average position of a neighbor

See how Boids runs with these simple rules and read about the theory and thinking behind it at **http://hmt.com/cwr/boids.html**.

Neural networks

Many Artificial Life researchers, especially those concerned with learning and adaptation, endow their organisms with a neural network which serves as an artificial brain. Neural networks can function as learning algorithms and may be trained. A typical task of neural networks is to recognize and correlate images such as human handwriting.

A neural network is composed of a collection of input-output devices, called *neurons,* which are organized into a well-connected network. In this network, there is an input layer which receives sensory input, a number of hidden layers which perform computations, and an output layer through which the results of these computations are reported. Neural networks can be trained by adjusting the strengths of the connections between neurons (so that they can carry different levels of signal or symbols).

The Nerves project described in the section, "The Synthetic Ecosystems of Biota.org," later in this chapter, is an effort to provide neural networks for virtual worlds and avatars. Neural networks are also used in the PolyWorld system described in the next section.

Synthetic Ecosystems: The Virtual Terrarium

Synthetic ecosystems are where mathematical life models like those described in the previous section are put to the test in a large scale. Imagine thousands or millions of simple forms based on cellular automata or neural networks going at it in a shared virtual world full of food, predators, and other hazards. Also imagine that these forms mate and mutate, like creatures in a real-world colony. You will then have what we call a virtual terrarium (or aquarium, for that matter). Next I describe two such terraria. A third terrarium, Nerve Garden, is described in the next section, "The Synthetic Ecosystems of Biota.org."

Tom Ray's Tierra

The Tierra Synthetic Life program, developed by Tom Ray and the Artificial Life Monitor (ALmond) program by Marc Cygnus, simulates creatures in digital primordial soup. Tierra is run inside a *virtual computer* in order to protect the real computers it is running on from a hypothetical infection. The ecosystem of Tierra is a memory space filled by strings representing *genomes* (a kind of virtual DNA), which seek to copy themselves, mutating in the process. The following figure shows a view of this space, with each creature represented as a colored bar. In this scene, immune hosts are engaged in a battle with parasites, driving them into the top of the memory space.

Tom Ray has been working to run Tierra on thousands of machines throughout the Internet, creating a "digital biodiversity preserve." The goal of this preserve is to create a large environment for digital biota to evolve into diverse and complex forms. Recently Tierra has also been represented in 3D using VRML. Find the Tierra home page at **http://www.hip.atr.co.jp/~ray/tierra/tierra.html** and the VRML versions of Tierra at **http://www.construct. net/tierra/**.

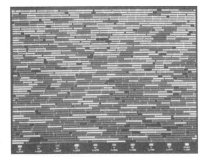

Tierra in the ALmond interface.

PolyWorld

Larry Yaeger of Apple Computer developed PolyWorld, a fully featured synthetic ecosystem in the early 1990s which is today still one of the most compelling examples of this medium. PolyWorld was featured along with Tierra in Steven Levy's book *Artificial Life*. A description of Larry's work follows:

> "PolyWorld is a computational ecology that I developed to explore issues in Artificial Life. Simulated organisms reproduce sexually, fight and kill and eat each other, eat the food that grows throughout the world, and either develop successful strategies for survival or die. An organism's entire behavioral suite (move, turn, attack, eat, mate, light) is controlled by its neural network 'brain.' Each brain's architecture—its neural wiring diagram—is determined from its genetic code, in terms of number, size, and composition of neural clusters (excitatory and inhibitory neurons) and the types of connections between those clusters (connection density and topological mapping). Synaptic efficacy is modulated via Hebbian learning, so,

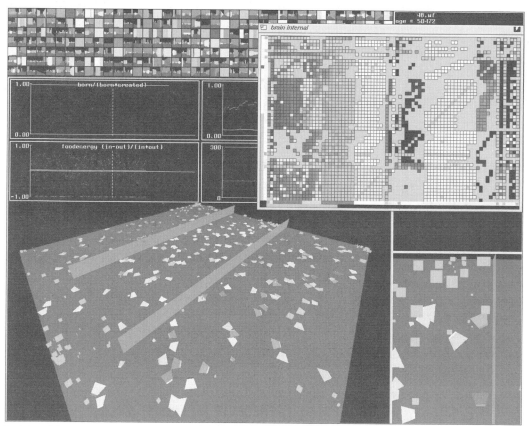

PolyWorld.

in principle, the organisms have the ability to learn during the course of their life-times. The organisms perceive their world through a sense of vision, provided by a computer graphic rendering of the world from each organism's point of view. The organisms' physiologies are also encoded genetically, so both brain and body, and thus all components of behavior, evolve over multiple generations. A variety of 'species,' with varying individual and group survival strategies have emerged in various simulations, displaying such complex ethological behaviors as swarming/flocking, foraging, and attack avoidance."

You can download and try the PolyWorld Artificial Life System and Computational Ecology at **http://pobox.com/~larryy/polyworld.html**. You must have a Silicon Graphics workstation to run PolyWorld in its original form, though a pointer to an early version of a Macintosh port is provided on Larry's Web site. Source code and executables are provided.

Will avatars venture here?

Both Tierra and PolyWorld would probably be very confusing places for human beings to venture. This is the realm of basic high speed and highly complex life processes. Future immersive video games may entice avatars into such worlds, where you are playing the role of mutator or mutated. More exciting is the prospect that these synthetic ecosystems could provide the very backbone of virtual worlds. Please find more on this in the section, "The Synthetic Ecosystems of Biota.org," later in this chapter.

More live links

There is so much A-Life to explore on the Internet. The links in the following table provide a few more peeks.

A-Life list

http://k2.scl.cwru.edu/~gaunt/java/SeaMonkeys/SeaMonkeys.html
Sea Monkeys features a fluid drag and semi-realistic physics system containing 30 sea monkey models moving about with random motion.

http://tdg.linst.ac.uk/technosphere/index.html
Create your own beastie and follow its life cycle at Technosphere.

http://www.concentric.net/~srooke/references.html
Steven Rooke provides one of the best reference sections to the people, ideas and further reading in the area of Artificial Life and Digital Biota.

http://morganmedia.com/m2/shock.html
Morgan Media's Fish Tank; you must have a Macromedia Shockwave plug-in installed in your Web browser to see this. Clicking on models of fish sends them into the tank. Some fish are carnivorous, and they eat the other fish. This is a very simple simulated "ecosystem" that gives you a quick experience through the Web of something biologically inspired.

http://alife.santafe.edu/alife/
Artificial Life Online, from the Santa Fe Institute, is the Web companion to MIT's Artificial Life Journal. This extensive site lists events, publications and hordes of artificial life software for the Mac, PC and Unix.

http://www.csad.coventry.ac.uk/~mep/amoebic.lifeforms/start.htm
Amoebic Lifeforms are Shockwave simulations.

http://www.mathcs.sjsu.edu/faculty/rucker/boppers.htm
Rudy Rucker's Boppers is an inspired genetic algorithm system.

http://alifegarden.com/
Alife Garden, from Japan, allows you to pick an organism and mutate it on a Web page without special software other than your Web browser.

http://hmt.com/cwr/alife.html
Craig Reynolds' Artificial Life Links.

http://www.wi.LeidenUniv.nl/home/mvdweg/alife.html
Marco Maddenings Artificial Life Page is a great and updated links page.

http://www.cs.utoronto.ca/~dt/
University of Toronto Computer Scientist, Demetri Terzopoulos, has researched and published just about every topic in computer modeling, simulation, artificial life (including artificial fishes!).

http://www.krl.caltech.edu/~brown/alife/
A Web site supporting the Artificial Life newsgroups comp.ai.genetic and comp.ai.alife.

http://www.biota.org/conf97/ksims.html
Karl Sims' fabulous evolving block creatures.

The Synthetic Ecosystems of Biota.org

Biota.org is an organization that found its roots at the Fourth Foresight Conference on Nanotechnology in the Fall of 1995. At this conference, I was exhibiting a special piece of software I had designed over the previous year or two. The software was called Amoeba and its purpose was to simulate the lowest levels of control in biological systems: tubes and the things that flow in them. When you really look at it, tubes, flows, and places where flows accumulate, make up just about every living thing. From your stomach to your blood vessels to the neurons in your brain, everything seems to come down to channels and flows. For the conference, I had reworked Amoeba to show the flows of individual molecules in a simulated molecular manufacturing system. At the same show, a fellow named Todd Goldenbaum was demonstrating a series of VRML models of hypothesized nanotechnology machines.

It didn't take long for Todd and I to strike up a conversation and before long we were asking ourselves: Couldn't these flows inside the Amoeba software be used to animate these VRML models? Couldn't Amoeba become a sort of *nervous system* for VRML? And so the Nerves project was born. Todd and I knew that in order to make compelling virtual worlds there had to be believable lifelike behavior in them. Nerves and VRML seemed like a good way to go.

Nerves begets Biota.org

By the spring of 1996, the Nerves team had grown and was considering some way to introduce Nerves into the emerging VRML 2.0 standard. In July of 1996, I was up on a mountaintop in British Columbia and conceived of a new organization called Biota. Biota would extend beyond the Nerves concept and create a forum for any kind of biological simulation in virtual worlds. When I returned to California, a special meeting was called and we created the new organization, calling it Biota.org, with its own Web site (**http://www.biota.org**). Biota.org held its first conference program at Earth to Avatars on October 27, 1996 and attracted more members, who begun to call each other *Biotians*.

Nerve Garden: The genesis of L-systems in virtual worlds

An Airhorse creature generated from an L-system.

Biota.org began to grow rapidly, and was soon invited to present at several conferences and participate in educational grants. Biota.org became a Special Interest Group of the Contact Consortium and a Working Group of the VRML Consortium in early 1997. Biota was invited to participate at SIGGRAPH 1997, a major computer graphics conference to display the original Nerve Garden, first developed under the Nerves group in mid-1996. The goal of Nerve Garden is to create a virtual world into which users can "grow" simulated VRML plants.

The adjacent figure shows a "creature" generated from an L-system. An L-system is a set of mathematical rules that involve the rewriting of strings of symbols that grow and

Flight of the bumblebee over Nerve Garden Island.

change until at some point you decide to attach shapes to the symbols. These strings can thereby generate beautiful branching structures like the Airhorse.

Nerve Garden was being built as I wrote this chapter so I can show you only a glimpse of what it may be like. The preceding figure shows the second prototype Nerve Garden running. You can choose a plant and germinate it in a Java program. Once grown, the plant is then placed on an island. You can ride on the back of an insect (like the bee shown here) and tour the island, visiting your plant. Nerves operates like a drip irrigation system, with tokens flowing to either stimulate or inhibit plant growth.

Why not grow your worlds?

For some time, creators of virtual worlds had been complaining about how difficult it was to build good looking models for their worlds. They were crafting these models by hand, one polygon at a time. With L-systems and other *generative methods* objects and whole worlds could be grown from a simple rule set. In the Extreme Cyber Edge (discussed later in this chapter) you can see an example of generative architecture. Landscapes have been created from fractal algorithms for years. A company called Construct Internet Design (**http://www.construct.net**) even created an *avatar breeder* to create compelling avatars through mutation. As you can see in the section, "The Organic Artists," later in this chapter, there is a whole movement behind *generative arts*. Believe it or not, there is even a *generative music* movement.

Doing cyberspace right: To abstract and serve

With all these generative methods, it should be possible to pack the description of a complete world into a set of generative rules. The resulting rule set would be a kind of *abstraction* and a natural *compression* of the world. In nature, eggs and seeds and the very DNA in cells are abstracted representations of living organisms. It turns out that it is a lot easier to deliver the parts of a virtual world through the thin pipes of the Internet in their abstracted form than in full final geometry. Sending big fully finished VRML worlds through 28.8 bps modems is about as smart as an architect building complete houses and then shipping them to their construction site. Houses are built by shipping the *plans* to the construction site and then building the house out of individual parts.

Members of the Biota.org group identified that a fatal flaw in VRML was that it did not support some form of abstraction, instead forcing designers to ship finished copies of their worlds through the Internet. Biota.org set out to apply its knowledge of generative methods, background in Nerves, and understanding of how other abstracted worlds like AlphaWorld functioned to bring both abstraction and *streaming* to VRML worlds. The first project was Nerve Garden. In the garden, only the L-system *seeds* of the plants along with their current *growth state* needs to be sent through the Internet. Each user's garden can be grown locally on their own computer once the seeds and other data arrive. Benefits of this method are that large gardens can be served through slow modems and the gardens can grow only as complex as the user's computers can bear. And like AlphaWorld, traveling through a huge jungle of VRML will be possible as seeds and growth state are streamed in as you move forward through the forest. If all of this works, Nerve Garden should be compelling proof of a smarter way to make virtual worlds, and quite possibly the key that unlocks the doors to the "new cyberspace."

Become a Biotian!

Visit the Biota.org home page at **http://www.biota.org** and try out Nerve Garden, join the mailing discussion list, or become a Biotian yourself and participate in projects. Biota.org hosted its first ever conference in August of 1997 up in the Canadian Rockies where we trekked to the Burgess Shale, a 530-million-year-old fossil bed full of weird creatures of the Cambrian. We sat down for discussions with paleontologists and computer scientists and considered the use of virtual worlds to both model living systems and the future of artificial life in cyberspace. For a bit more of my own personal vision on this, see "Digi's Diary: Let Life Out (Or In)," at the end of this chapter. The color section in this book features more synthetic organisms from Biota.org.

The Organic Artists

Organic artists represent a vital new movement in the visual arts and music. Recognizing the beauty in natural forms (as have all artists down the ages), these artists seek to plumb the basic generative rules behind forms in nature. Armed with tools like genetic algorithms, L-systems, neural networks and automata, these artists can use these tools both as a painter's palette and sculptor's tool to create stunning organic art.

What role will organic artists play in the digital biota movement and the emergence of the new cyberspace? Darwin's system of natural selection will apply to biota in cyberspace as it does to life forms in the world of atoms. If it is survival of the fittest, then what defines fitness in a digital ecosystem? Given that a digital lifespace is very much an artificial world, inseparable (for the moment) from the millions of users that feed and maintain it, the success of digital biota will be closely tied to how users value their presence. If a representative form of digital biota (a *biote*) grabs our attention and encourages us to make a copy and forward it to our friends (or enemies), then it would be reproductively fit. If an organic artist crafts a biote that is aesthetically pleasing or performs wondrous feats of animation, then the artist has served as successful midwife. Organic artists as a whole will help beautify and interpret all forms of the emerging inhabited cyberspace and we will owe a great deal to their talents.

The grand masters

The artists featured here take much of their inspiration from grand masters who came before them. Perhaps the original digital generative artist is Benoit Mandelbrot, who in the early 1980s created a branch of mathematics called Fractal Geometry. Fractal algorithms are a cornerstone of the organic art movement and frequently used in virtual worlds. Thousands of Web sites cover the work of Mandelbrot and the field of fractals. Searching the Web for either of these words will bring up these sites.

While visiting the Santa Fe Institute in August of 1994, I was rendered speechless by Karl Sims' creatures. The Santa Fe folks had just installed software called Mosaic and they were browsing this newfangled thing called the World Wide Web and found Sims' first Web page. They were playing movie sequences of Sims' creatures, which were built out of blocks and exhibited lifelike swimming, flying, and walking behavior. Sims was a chief scientist at Thinking Machines in Cambridge, Massachusetts and used of one of their powerful multi-processor Connection Machines to create moving creatures within worlds having the physics of wind, gravity, and friction. You too can play the original MPEG movies of some of Karl Sims' Virtual Creatures at **http://www.biota.org/conf97/ksims.html**. Sims created plenty of other "evolutionary art," which you can search for on the Web.

Organic art gallery

The following gallery shows the works of four organic artists: William Latham, Charles Ostman, Darrel Anderson, and Steven Rooke. There are perhaps dozens or even hundreds more organic artists. For more images of organic artists visit the home page of Biota.org at **http://www.biota.org** and links of the companion book Web site at **http://www.digitalspace.com/avatars**. Following the gallery I include short descriptions of the featured artists.

Gallery of Organic Arts

Organic Art from the Virtual Garden by William Latham et al.

Charles Ostman's nano-life synthetic sentient starburst.

Ear Shell, by Darrel Anderson.

In The Beginning, by Steven Rooke.

The Organic Sculpture of William Latham

Starting out at the Royal College of Arts in London and then working at the IBM Scientific Centre in Winchester, U.K., artist William Latham developed what he called his "evolutionary tree of forms." Beginning from a fascination with horns, Latham worked with a number of people to customize a solid modeling software package to bring this tree of forms into reality.

Latham's style is inspired by stalactites, the art of the Baroque period, Rene Magritte, and science fiction films, such as *Aliens*. Latham and his colleagues have produced some of the most stunning organic sculpture I have ever seen. One sample from the Virtual Garden is shown in the gallery.

Today, with their software tools in hand, artists using Computer Artworks products generate thousands of pieces through the random mutations of the basic genetic generative codes. In this way, a generative artist becomes a creative gardener, selecting pleasing forms to propagate and mutate further.

Download organic art screen savers and purchase virtual gardens and art mutators on CD-ROM from Computer Artworks. Find the Computer Artworks home page at **http://www.artworks.co.uk**.

The NanoWorlds of Charles Ostman

Charles Ostman is a real wonder of a "Professional Synergist" from Berkeley, California. Ostman brings his years of experience in building successively smaller and more complex electronics at Lawrence Berkeley Labs and intense interest in Nanotechnology to bear through his organic art vision. Ostman's works seek to give us a reflection from a future "virtual terraform" inhabited by "synthetic sentients." Ostman sees a time in the future when Nanotechnology (the ability to make things one atom at a time) renders all current economic systems obsolete and transforms human lifestyles and our very perception of reality.

The basic inspirational building blocks of Ostman's art include molecular machines, self assembling "nano lego" components, nanobots and nanocritters, pseudo proteins, quasi-viral components, "artificial" organisms, and ubiquitous nano "foglettes." Visit Charles Ostman's Web site at **http://www.biota.org/ostman/charles1.htm**.

Darrel Anderson's GroBot

GroBot is software being developed by artist Darrel Anderson to give kids a fast, fun, intuitive 3D drawing environment that has a distinctive biological feel. GroBot will allow kids to explore the synergy between art and science. Anderson's entire project owes a lot to Seymour Papert's programming language for kids called LOGO and Papert's ideas about learning and thinking. Kids will be able to enter LOGO-like commands and employ recursion, proximity, touch, relative direction, attraction, repulsion, gravity, and other useful behaviors to starter shapes such as blobs or cells.

Anderson's mission to bring organic art to kids is noble and very important for the development of biota in virtual worlds. After all, kids will be the main genetic hackers and organic artists shaping the new 3D cyberspace landscape!

Steven Rooke: Evolutionary Artist

Steven Rooke describes himself as an "evolutionary artist" who selectively breeds images from a primordial soup of virtual DNA. Rooke was inspired in a tradition started by evolutionary art pioneer Karl Sims (mentioned earlier in this section). Rooke does large runs (creative variations) of images, selects some for particular aesthetic fitness, and then commands the population to spawn again. Reproduction is accomplished by "sexual mixing" of virtual genes mostly from the fittest parents, accompanied by occasional random mutation. Particularly fit individuals survive intact and generate a whole new mosaic of images.

Rooke terminates image evolution (a mass extinction except for certain genes preserved in digital amber) and then begins a lengthy process of fine-tuning the colors and regions. Most images saved during the genetic run do not survive this further selection during post-production. The final images are output to IRIS prints or are used for filming on a film recorder.

You can find the Evolutionary Art of Steven Rooke at **http://www.concentric.net/~srooke/** and one of the best reference sections to the people, ideas, and further reading in this area of digital biota at **http://www.concentric.net/~srooke/references.html**.

Extreme Cyber Edge

Genetic algorithms and the evolution of virtual spaces

As you saw in the previous section, organic artists using generative methods are able to create wonderfully interesting virtual worlds and creatures in them. Biota.org's Nerve Garden illustrated how to populate a virtual world with simulated plants. Why then could you not generate a whole virtual world, making 3D structures on-the-fly? Well, you can! One example of this is Eric Bucci's work at the University of Texas at Austin. Working with Professors Marcos Novak and Michael Benedikt, he has generated a large array of virtual architecture, an example of which you can see in the color section of the book. Michael Benedikt's seminal book, *Cyberspace, First Steps,* (see the Bibliography) mentions generative architecture, notably Marcos Novak's "Liquid Architectures in Cyberspace." Eric was completing his masters degree and sent us this description of his work on the "embryology of virtual spaces":

> *"The recent emergence of virtual environments as a realm of architectural design and inquiry precipitates questions regarding design philosophies in virtual versus physical environments. The search for valid architectures of Cyberspace will become increasingly important as the technology which allows its existence becomes more pervasive."*

Visit The University of Texas' School of Architecture home page at **http://mather.ar .utexas.edu**.

Digi's Diary: Let Life Out (Or In)!

Digi's Diary

So why would life want to squeeze through the cracks into digital space, anyway? Well, for billions of years life has struggled to build up complex bodies and ecosystems only to have them destroyed by one mass extinction after another. Whether it is an asteroid, overheated volcanoes, or overly successful members of Earth's biota (i.e., us), mass extinctions nullify most progress of an ecosystem. Some argue that mass extinctions are a kind of spring cleaning that opens up new opportunities for evolution.

However one looks at it, the inevitable and final mass extinction is on its way. Far in the future when the sun's hydrogen fuel is spent and it enters its red giant stage, our puny Earth will be consumed as an afterthought. So ultimately all this experimentation, striving, living, and dying is going to come to an end, without much of a trace left behind. This destiny is assured if Earth's life remains pinned down by gravity onto this one planet. Surprisingly, the digital realm gives life some properties it could use to escape this ultimate extinction. For one, life represented purely as information structures can recombine and reproduce much more rapidly than its molecule-based forebears. Another point is that digital life forms would not be tied to the supply of atoms or have to compete with the body plans and survival strategies that occupy all the current niches in the physical world.

Another potent property of life in the virtual is that it can travel through free space or conduits such as wires or optical fibers at the speed of light. Aim a laser at just the right spot on the moon and it will bounce off a corner reflector left by an Apollo crew back in the 1970s. If you packaged up your artificial life as a datastream you could laser it on a neat round trip to and from the lunar surface. Well, you might say, that hardly counts as sending life to the moon, if there is nothing to receive and keep it there. Yes, I would agree, but I would counter that the manned Apollo lunar landings themselves did a similar kind of bio-reflection. They used enormously costly and cumbersome vehicles to send men there only to return them back to the Earth.

Galileo's new brain

The only examples of working off-planet receivers are unmanned planetary probes like Galileo. Galileo is a large robot spacecraft now orbiting the Jupiter system. Just after its launch from Earth, Galileo had an unfortunate accident with its main antenna, which failed to open. Mission controllers had to decide whether to scrap the mission or work out a fix. Galileo had one remaining functional antenna, known as a low gain antenna, through which all communications with Earth now had to pass at an excruciatingly low bit rate (far slower than your modem). Mission planners decided to rewrite a great deal of the software that controlled Galileo's primitive vision, communications, and other sensing systems. Uploading this software took days but after it was completed, Galileo had a new brain. As you read this, Galileo is now carrying out its mission to peer down at the moons of Jupiter, and study the giant planet and its electromagnetic field and rings. Galileo sees in a series of "jailbars" which allows mission controllers to quickly scan a scene and tightly focus the camera on features they find interesting. Galileo also compresses its data much more than its original programs were designed to do, as this technology improved so much in the few years since Galileo was launched. In a strange way, a little piece of the mechanism of Earth's life forms was transmitted out the Jovian system and stuck.

Of course, the software running inside Galileo will itself be turned off when the spacecraft reaches the end of its life. This software and its host, Galileo, both lack the ability to reproduce and carry on. One could imagine some far future date when such vehicles and the protoplasm of software and data within them have the ability to use local resources and add on to the vehicle. This type of craft, which would undoubtedly look radically different than anything we might conceive of today, might employ nanotechnology to stream in molecules and weave or extrude new structures.

What would a nano-biota craft make? I think that a kind of artificial lichens may be a good bet. On Earth, lichens colonize the barest rock and live by virtue of colonies of sunlight absorbing bacteria which give them their basic energy source. The lichens also use acids to break down the rock and prepare the ground for other life forms to follow. A sort of nano-lichen engineered to live on the surface of asteroids or comets or any small particle floating in the Solar System would absorb unending solar radiation and grow its own RAM. These lichens would bud spores with multi-million year lifespans which can colonize other asteroids or drift into other star systems.

A little help from our friends

So why is he so down on humans, you might be asking? I think the human race might find their destiny in space but I don't think that human beings will sail forth on Star Trek-like ships any time soon. These ships, with their nineteenth century pipes and valves will be prone to failure. As can be seen by Apollo 13, the space shuttle Challenger, space station Mir, and any number of space systems, conditions beyond the biosphere are harsh and system failures over time are highly likely and often fatal to a crew of biologics like us. So what do we need to settle the Solar System? Perhaps a little help from our friends.

Some argue that Earth's atmosphere and oceans were processed by early single celled life forms which made them habitable by later more complex life. Could not digital/nano-life forms prepare the infrastructure that would allow humans to safely and cost effectively settle other parts of the Solar System? Could these life forms crack oxygen and other gasses from the lunar regolith, could they grow energy generation matrices? Perhaps this type of life form would serve needs inside the Earth's biosphere, helping to clean up pollution and generate food to allow us to free up agricultural land. Of course nano-biologics, as you might call them, could also colonize the our own world to the detriment of us and our brethren here. Don't panic, though, I think we might have a few decades to use our computer spaces to evolve some forms in simulation before we can fabricate them in atoms.

So where is this "digital life" now?

All of this seems far off in the future, so what is happening *today*? We have all heard of computer software viruses and the debates over whether or not they constitute "real life" or not. Experiments like Tom Ray's Tierra (**http://www.hip.atr.co.jp/~ray/tierra/tierra.html**) seems like a convincing lifelike ecosystem. A million ten-year-olds with genetic hacking tools may ignite a "digital Cambrian explosion." One of the goals of the Biota Nerve Garden project, described earlier in this chapter, is to allow ten-year-olds to hack L-systems and grow their own plants in virtual worlds.

Of course, the digital primordial soup is a fragile and ephemeral space and relatively tiny compared with the Earth's ancient oceans. But as far as the properties afforded life by digital representation, human beings, acting as surrogates, may be providing life its one best chance to break the bonds of Earthly limitations. Perhaps as we perpetrate our own mass extinction, we can open this new niche, and let life in (or out, depending on how you look at it).

What does this have to do with avatars?

After all this you might be asking: so grass will grow in virtual worlds and force all of us avatars to mow the lawn every week, so what's the big deal? Well, life is made interesting not only by the people and buildings surrounding us but also by living things. In modern day life it is sometimes easy to forget that the Earth is inhabited by a rich biota. We will only really miss it when it is gone, it seems. So digital life in virtual worlds will make them richer and more interesting places. Maybe face to face with a strange and evolving biota on our computer screens will remind us how fascinating and precious life in the real Earth really is.

The virtual E.T.

Some people claim that we won't have to wait for UFOs to land to meet aliens; we will meet them as a form of digital biota on our computer screens! Do I think we will soon see the virtual E.T.? Well, years ago scientists thought that we could create artificial intelligence through software. It turned out to be a lot harder than anyone thought, as we had no good working definition for intelligence or even for thought processes. My own humble opinion is that we will see something undeniably alive in digital form some time early in the next century. I suspect that it will look a lot like a virtual *slime mold*. A slime mold is a fascinating form of life in that individual cells come together to form a single colonial organism for a while before reverting back to individual cells. Slime molds could be a great model for net-based life forms as the layout of servers and the pipes between them maps well into an organism made of distributed parts that come together at points. Search agents traversing the Internet today and creating central indeces seem to suggest that this form is possible.

Digital biota should provide us all a great deal of entertainment and a chance to learn about the rules guiding living things. It will be a long time before some fully evolved form walks out of the Net and onto the surface of some distant world. If nothing else, this vision might provide us at least one answer to the question: Why are we doing this?

Build Your Own World
Design Your Own Avatar

Just about everyone who journeys into virtual worlds asks the same question: How can I build my own world and design my own avatar? Well, new tools just made available and included in this book make it possible. In this chapter, I give you plenty of guidelines to build virtual worlds and some tips about developing a strong community within them.

You may have already built your own home page on the World Wide Web and probably know how this can help show the world your creative side and your interests. Well, building a *home world* in virtual world cyberspace is more work, but it is that much more rewarding an experience.

Your Guide to
Building Your Own World

Introduction: Designing Worlds People will Visit Often

Designing, building, and managing virtual worlds and the communities that emerge within them has got to be one of the most challenging tasks in computers and the Internet. You might think that building and maintaining a Web site is hard enough, but you must realize that a Web site is just one small aspect of a virtual world. So before rushing off to design your own virtual city like some eager postwar land developer, let us ask some of the hard questions.

Why do you want to build a world?

Everyone seems to have their own reasons for building a virtual world that can host avatar visitors. I know someone who has the vision of building vineyards and giving wine lessons in a kind of virtual Napa Valley. Another person told me that their dream is to use virtual worlds to create shared spiritual experiences. A Hollywood producer told me recently that he is developing virtual worlds so that big name stars can simultaneously reach a large Internet and TV audience as "avastars." You can see from the previous chapters in this book that there are about as many ways to use avatars and their worlds as there are users of those worlds. To aid you in your decision making process, I provide the following checklist of hard world builder's questions.

A checklist of world builder's questions

Before you put in all the work to design a world of your own, you might want to ask the following questions:

- What is the purpose of your world: to teach, entertain, do business, experiment, or to express your own creativity?

- How will you design your world to attract visitors and keep them coming back?

- What will be your overall themes and activities for this world: communicating, learning, working, creating, or gaming?

- Will your world support avatars, and will it be single-user or will it use some other method for people to share the same space?

- How will you promote your world, and what is your target audience?

- How will you document your world, its history, its community members and activities, and will you design a Web site?

- How will you nurture and manage the communities that will emerge in your world?

- Will you allow visitors to make their own permanent mark on the world, such as building or posting notices?

- Will you provide a set of avatars for people to use and customize or will you allow them to build their own avatar?

- Will you charge people to use the world, and how will you keep your project afloat financially?

- What technologies will you use: 2D or 3D scenes, text or voice chat, will your world have avatars, bot and biota, will your world be preloaded or stream-in, will you use standard protocols and formats like VRML or invent your own?

You might notice above that I listed the real technology decisions last. The technology choices should be made only after the other questions have been addressed. We can become blinded by "cool" technology and want to build things with it for its own sake. All through this book you have been visiting worlds that were successful for many different reasons. Some worlds had large numbers of users without using cool 3D technology (e.g., The Palace) while others looked and sounded really good in 3D but had only a few visitors (like OZ Virtual). This goes to show that a virtual world does not need to be built out of the latest cool technologies to successfully attract users.

Your community plan

Your plan for nurturing and managing your community is perhaps the most important factor influencing the success of your virtual world. The preceding chapters in this book are full of numerous examples of what keeps citizens coming back to a virtual world. These chapters should give you a primer in virtual community design and hosting. For a more in-depth treatment of virtual worlds and community hosting, I recommend you take our on-line "Advanced Course at Avatar University," found at **http://www.digitalspace.com/avatars**. Pay special attention to the section, "Netiquette and Community Hosting."

World and avatar designers

In this chapter, I introduce you to virtual world and avatar building. This topic area is so huge that it could take up far more than one chapter (it probably needs several more books). In addition, world building tools and methods are changing just about as fast as the avatar social scene. To address these two problems, we have included extensive resources on building worlds and designing avatars on the companion book Web site. I recommend looking at the following for more background:

"The same social mores that exist in the real world persist in cyberspace! That all the pathologies present in the real world are present in cyberspace by virtue of the fact that we are the agents of the pathologies! And when I say "we," I mean the part of us that can squeeze through the keyhole into cyberspace. That's the very interesting point, that cyberspace, I call it the mirror of the third eye, because boy does it show us what you really are! Because if you look in there, and you see dragons and demons and devils, then I know what you are full of, because what you are doing is you are seeing yourself.

—Mark Pesce, cyberspace visionary and co-creator of VRML
Florence Italy, June 1996

- The companion book Web site at **http://www.digitalspace.com/avatars** provides a continuing source of ideas, links, and examples of virtual worlds in action, and contains a great "Advanced Course at Avatar University," complete with a "History of the Virtual Worlds Medium, the Underlying Technologies," "Netiquette and Community Hosting Guide," and "Applications of Virtual Worlds in the Home, Classroom, and at Work."

- Appendix A: "Projects, Groups, Events, Philosophers, News, and Predecessors in Avatar Cyberspace," gives you some idea of what other people are doing with virtual worlds.

- The Bibliography of recommended reading in this book and on the companion Web site provides excellent sources to literature on building virtual worlds and hosting communities.

What is the "killer application" of virtual worlds?

Everyone is fond of asking: What is the killer application of virtual worlds that will make people want to visit? Well, what makes any place worth visiting? One answer might seem obvious: Places full of people are often visited. You visit a place mostly because of your affinity with the people and by the quality of the interactions you experience there. Other places are visited because they are not full of people. We go to the woods or hike into the back country of the Sierra because there is life there other than human life. A third kind of place we visit because there are things there (not living, but perhaps once living), such as grocery stores, malls, or cemeteries. There are some people who detest visiting places of things, but would certainly visit places of people. So, the upshot is that different kinds of people will visit different kinds of virtual spaces.

What does all this mean for the designers of successful 3D environments? It probably means that the 3D cybermalls will be soon boarded up if you design them to be navigated alone. It means also that we ought to pay close attention to how people interact in groups (a hard pill to swallow for computer geeks like me, but easier for creative social folks).

Several of the virtual worlds documented in this book attract repeat visitors because they enable people to communicate or play with other people, or to leave their creative mark on the world. Perhaps there really is no "killer application" of virtual worlds, and perhaps like any other new medium that people use to interact, virtual worlds are on a long development curve to becoming an indispensable tool. Telephones were few and far between in the early days and people had a hard time justifying why you would use one instead of just sending a letter or dictating a telegram. It was only after decades of development of infrastructure and the emergence of new generations that would accept a "telephone culture" that the lowly telephone became completely intertwined with our daily lives. And yet a significant part of humanity has yet to make a telephone call. Recent statistics show no more than one percent of the world's population has regular access to any kind of computer connected to the Internet.

Build a better avatar mouse trap

All these sobering facts seem to tell us that the use of virtual worlds as a part of our daily lives is quite a long way off and that we have a lot of experimenting to do before that time. This is why you, dear reader, are such an important part of this new medium. Because you have got this far you probably have what it takes to build some of your own worlds and push the medium a few steps forward. Like an inventor tinkering in his or her workshop, you could come up with a few key new pieces that will make a big difference down the road. So go out and build that better avatar mouse trap!

World Building Tools

There are many tools you can use to build virtual worlds. Because virtual worlds are created differently for each of the different virtual worlds programs, you may have to use different tools to create worlds for each of these environments.

As you have seen earlier in the chapter on AlphaWorld and other Active Worlds, some worlds allow you to build right inside them. AlphaWorld works on the Leggo metaphor, allowing you to fit a set of 3D objects together. This method has been quite successful for the Active Worlds universe. WorldsAway lets you customize your avatar and personal spaces using prebuilt components. In worlds like the Palace or Virtual Places, the world is represented as a 2D image or Web site backdrop. These worlds can be built using standard image editors or HTML Web page building tools.

For worlds like Onlive Traveler, OZ Virtual, Black Sun Passport, and others, you must use a separate *authoring* program to build a virtual scene and then connect this scene into the world. In this section, I discuss a few of these VRML authoring programs, including Internet3D Space Builder, which is provided on the book CD-ROM. Note that making VRML worlds for *multi-user* or avatar supported environments can require a few extra steps over plain old surfing VRML scenes alone.

The table on the following page lists many of the multi-user virtual worlds we have talked about in this book and the associated tools used to create new worlds or design avatars.

ParaGraph International's Internet3D Space Builder

As you can see from the following figure, ParaGraph International's Internet3D Space Builder (ISB) is a sophisticated modeling program. Models or whole virtual worlds built in VRML 2.0 can be brought into ISB. Older D96, and Virtual Home Space Builder .MUS files can also be imported. A wide range of editing operations can then be carried out on models and then whole virtual world scenes can be constructed. Models and world scenes can be saved as VRML 2.0 files in compressed format (GZIP) or uncompressed format (.WRL). You can also "publish" your worlds by exporting the geometry and all images, movies, and other resources into a common folder. You can find ISB on the book CD-ROM.

What is included on the CD-ROM

The version of ISB on the book CD-ROM is a restricted version, meaning that you can't build a scene (a world) with more than 1,400 faces, seven textures, two pictures, two movies, and two Web address references (URLs). Even though it is restricted, you can still use this version of ISB to build some pretty nice worlds and then export them to VRML. If you really get into world building, you should purchase a full unrestricted version of ISB, which costs less than $100. To find out how you can order ISB, or where you might find it in your local computer store, call ParaGraph at (408) 364-7700, or send them email at **info@paragraph.com**, or visit their home page at **http://www.paragraph.com/**.

Tools of the trade

Virtual world environment	Tools used to create a world	Tools used to design avatars
Worlds Chat	No public tools available; Worlds Inc. can make custom worlds	Users have created avatars using their own 'hacks' see "Creating Your Own Avatar and Other Activities," in the chapter on Worlds Chat
The Palace	Tools come with the Palace server to make your own Palace site. Palace worlds are GIF images with selectable hot spots.	The Palace has a built-in avatar builder. You can also use Sven Technologies' AvatarMaker (described later in this chapter) to export Palace avatars
Active Worlds	You can build in the common AlphaWorld space using the selection of "Leggo" objects. Circle of Fire offers world servers for sale, in which case you can create your own world and its avatars.	There is no avatar maker included, but if you become a caretaker of your own world, you can design your own avatar using tools like LifeForms from Credo Interactive
WorldsAway	You can change your own areas in the world using pre-built objects. Fujitsu Software offers WorldsAway worlds and servers for sale and will also work with you to design your own world.	There is no avatar maker available, but you can customize your avatar with available body parts
Onlive Traveler	Onlive Technologies can provide a space authoring building kit. Any program exporting VRML 2.0 can also be used to create worlds for Traveler.	The Traveler Avatar Authoring Kit uses 3D Studio Max and you need a special design license to publish them. You have to be quite skillful at building Traveler avatars, which must be crafted by hand to coordinate with the voice/lip synching.
Virtual Places	Web pages are the backdrop for worlds	Avatars can be imported as images fitting certain dimensions
Black Sun Passport	Worlds can be built from VRML 1.0 and 2.0 files using any 3D authoring tools, such as ParaGraph's Internet3D Space Builder, described later in this chapter	Avatars can be made using any VRML exporting avatar authoring kit, such as Sven Technologies' AvatarMaker
Comic Chat	Proprietary tools	Proprietary tools
OZ Virtual	Worlds can be built from VRML 1.0 and 2.0 files using any 3D VRML authoring tool	Avatars must be constructed by OZ designers
Sony Community Place Browser	Worlds can be built from VRML 1.0 and 2.0 files using any 3D VRML authoring tools	Avatars are built from VRML components
SenseMedia's Sprawl	Worlds can be built from VRML 1.0 and 2.0 files using any 3D VRML authoring tools	Avatars are built from VRML components
Microsoft V-Chat	A world authoring kit is available to qualified partners of Microsoft	Avatars can be made and imported by users of the authoring kit
NTT's Interspace	Spaces are built by NTT or its partners for clients using tools such as Sense8's World Up	Avatars must be built by design partners for NTT
Sierra's The Realm	Proprietary tools	Proprietary tools
3DO's Meridian 59	Proprietary tools	Proprietary tools
ID's Quake	A Quake Level Builder is distributed as shareware. Other companies, such as Virtus, also offer Quake builders.	Avatars can be built within the Quake authoring system
Ultima	Proprietary tools	Proprietary tools

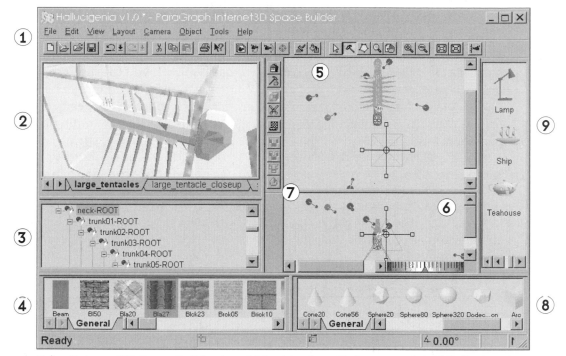

Using Internet3D Space Builder to add texture to a Biota.org model of Hallucigenia.

Reviewing the interface

(1) Briefly, across the top are menus and a toolbar. The toolbar contains shortcuts to many items, including camera position, flood filling with textures and cut, copy, and paste procedures.

(2) The Perspective View Window enables you to navigate the current camera around the scene and select from the viewpoints or cameras listed as tabs below the perspective view.

(3) Scene Tree Window, representing the objects in the scene graph and the scene objects hierarchy.

(4) Using the Texture Gallery, you can drag and drop any texture onto the model in the Perspective View Window and it will be applied to the face you select.

(5) The Top View Window enables you to perform various editing operations. The preceding figure shows a wire framed version of the model from above. Cameras are indicated as small stick-ball figures.

(6) The Front View Window provides the same set of cameras, except that they give you front views.

(7) Collectively, the top and front view windows are called the Plan Window.

⑧ From the Shape Gallery, you can drag and drop any shape into the Plan Window and it will become part of the scene.

⑨ The Object Gallery contains objects that are fully formed models, complete with color and textures. They are more than just basic shapes; you can also drag and drop these into the Plan or Perspective Windows to place them into the scene. The Movie Gallery contains movies that are repeating loops of images that play on a surface. You can also drag and drop these onto any surface in the plan or perspective windows.

Integrating the VRML output between other authoring programs

The following figure shows a model of an avatar made with Sven Technologies' AvatarMaker (see the section on AvatarMaker, later in this chapter) brought into ISB for further touch-up. Using several tools to develop one world is a common approach and almost a necessity. No one tool does it all.

Other products from ParaGraph

An avatar made with AvatarMaker that was brought into Internet3D Space Builder.

ParaGraph also provides more products to support you in your world building adventures. Some of these are available for free trial downloads. A quick summary of these products follows:

• Virtual Home Space Builder: an earlier ParaGraph program used for simpler VRML 1.0 worlds. Available in a demonstration version for download at ParaGraph's home page.

- Internet3D Avatar Animator: no details were available when this chapter was written; check the ParaGraph home page.

- Internet3D Font Magic is a VRML 2.0 tool used to create 3D interactive text logos for Web sites, and sign-boards for virtual spaces, all using any True Type font.

Silicon Graphics' Cosmo Worlds

Cosmo Worlds (**http://cosmo.sgi.com/**) is one of the most powerful VRML authoring systems available. Cosmo Worlds currently runs on Silicon Graphics workstations under their flavor of UNIX called IRIX. SGI tells me that Cosmo Worlds will be available for Windows NT, further widening its audience.

AutoDesk's 3D Studio MAX

AutoDesk, makers of AutoCAD (**http://www.autodesk.com/**), have brought 3D Studio Max and Character Studio to the virtual worlds authoring scene. See 3D Studio Max and other products from Kinetix at **http://ktx.com/3dsmax/**. 3D Studio MAX is used extensively to create VRML worlds, and is the primary authoring tool for Onlive Traveler worlds and avatars.

Other world building software

See "Links to World Building and Avatar Designing Resources," at the end of this chapter, for extensive links to more world building software.

Avatar Designers and Methods

"It's ironic that Juanita has come into this place in a low-tech, black-and-white avatar. She was the one who figured out a way to make avatars show something close to real emotion...they all came to the realization that what made this place a success was not the collision-avoidance algorithms or the bouncer daemons or any of that other stuff. It was Juanita's faces."

—Neal Stephenson, *Snow Crash*

In this section, I cover two Avatar character designer software applications which are included on the book CD-ROM. I also discuss avatar creation methods from Live Picture and RealSpace.

Sven Technologies' AvatarMaker

AvatarMaker runs on Windows 95 or Windows NT and allows you to make a 3D avatar of yourself without having to know about 3D technology. You can use AvatarMaker's FaceMapper tool to take a scanned photograph of yourself and wrap it around a frame to create your avatar head. With the BodyBuilder tool you can sculpt and animate your avatar body and place it into a number of different poses. Next, you can clothe your avatar in the Wardrobe area of AvatarMaker using a variety of textured clothing options. The PropShop allows you to add props to your avatar, such as hairstyles, hats, or even a bicycle!

When you are happy with your avatar, you can use the Teleport tool to export it to a number of formats, including VRML 1.0 or 2.0 (for use in Black Sun's Passport, or other VRML worlds), as a 2D Palace avatar or as an image or movie (.AVI) file. To integrate your avatar into a Black Sun Passport world, you should check the Cybersockets documentation on the Black Sun Web site at **http://www.blacksun.com/ products/csockets/doc/index.html**. Note that the integration of avatars into multi-user VRML environments is still a process best left to the technically literate. When using AvatarMaker to make an avatar for the Palace, you should realize that your model will be exported as a small flat image. This image can then be imported into the Palace. You should not be too concerned with 3D detail in your avatar model as much of it will be lost when it is made into the small image.

You can install AvatarMaker from the book CD-ROM or download a newer demo version from Sven's Web site.

Sven Technologies' AvatarMaker.

3D Planet's 3D Assistant Internet Utilities

The good folks at 3D Planet, a Los Angeles-based software company, have been kind enough to provide us with 3D Assistant Internet Utilities, a great avatar design kit which can produce a texture-mapped 3D VRML avatar. Future versions available from their Web site (**http://www.3dplanet.com**) will allow you to design whole avatar bodies and to export 3D Assistants. 3D Assistants are bot avatars which can float on top of your desktop or Internet sites, popping up when people visit your Web page. This is an exciting new technology that makes "agent" software (used for searching or storing your preferences) more usable by embodying it with a more human interface.

Find 3D Assistant and Sven Technologies' AvatarMaker in the "Build Worlds, Design Avatars" section on the CD-ROM. Both of these programs are designed for Windows 95 and NT. Good help files are available in the software and on both the 3D Planet and Sven Technologies home pages.

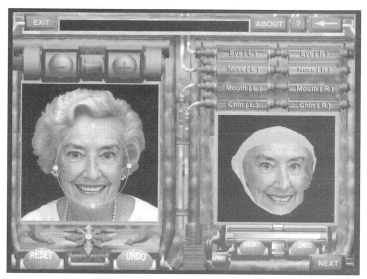

3DCreate in action.

Live Picture FlashPix Avatar and RealSpace World Technologies

Live Picture (**http://www.livepicture.com**) has developed a whole series of avatar and world creation technologies based on the concept of *photorealism*. Photorealism means that you use real pictures of the world to create the backdrops or textures of a world. This is becoming much more important in virtual worlds and avatar design. A Phototextured avatar is one made by wrapping images of real peoples' faces or bodies around the frame of an avatar. You saw this in action in the previous sections on AvatarMaker and 3DCreate.

Live Picture has developed a whole range of technologies to bring photorealism to virtual worlds. Chief among these is the RealSpace image server using a technology called FlashPix. You may notice when you get really close to avatars or objects in virtual worlds that you can start seeing the individual colored rectangles that make up the textures on their surfaces. This is called *pixellation* and FlashPix solves this problem by serving you increasingly detailed images as you get closer to an object, or zoom in on a picture.

Modeling Scott's hut in Antarctica

A company called RealSpace, Inc. (which recently merged with Live Picture) developed a technology called RealVR Traveler, which allows beautiful wrap-around phototextured scenes to be delivered over the Internet. Members of the RealSpace team originally developed Apple's QuickTime VR, in which you could present a cylinder or sphere of pixels that represents a view of the world from one spot. Combining FlashPix with this, you can travel closer to the walls of this sphere and see more details. Recently, Live Picture placed VRML objects inside RealSpace worlds with FlashPix and build a model of the adventurer Scott's hut in Antarctica. You could navigate through realistic scenes of this hut and go up to the biscuit tins on the table. Both FlashPix and RealSpace promise great contributions toward making virtual worlds look richer and more realistic.

Putting it all together on an avatar

On the turnstile, creating
advanced avatars with Live Picture.

I was involved in a series of experiments sponsored by Live Picture and performed by Peter Hughes, an expert in the creation of photorealistic scenes and avatars. Peter set up a turnstile at the home of my neighbors Alan Lundell and Sun McNamee, and for several hours he used this contraption to create some pretty advanced avatars. He would start by having someone rotate a live model for an avatar, in this case, Wendy Sue Noah (shown in the adjacent figure). To make a great looking avatar, the proper lighting and reflections from her clothing had to be achieved.

Peter took dozens of still pictures with high speed film and then scanned them in and stitched them together. He also mastered the technique of taking photographs of faces with closer and closer focus on the eyes. This was done for the FlashPix image enhancement. The closer you got to someone's avatar's eye the more detail you would see. My ugly mug was used for

The author in a
FlashPix Avatar.

the first phototextured and FlashPixed avatar faces ever made. As you can see in the previous figure, the results are interesting if not flattering. I can turn this model of me ·and zoom in getting whole new levels of details (down to every pore).

Other world building and avatar creation tools

The tools and techniques described here represent only a small fraction of the ways you can make avatars. The movie business has used methods for capturing virtual actors for more than 20 years. Hollywood studios have been scanning in actors in 3D, capturing their motion, and creating virtual doubles or principal stars for many films and TV shows. This field is sometimes called *performance animation*. I expect that performance animation and Hollywood will contribute a great deal to the technologies underlying avatars in the next few years. See "Links to World Building and Avatar Designing Resources," later in this chapter, for more resources on world building and avatar creation.

VRML worlds

The best way to learn how to build worlds is, of course, to go and visit a few. If you are going to use VRML to build 3D worlds, the best way to explore other VRML worlds is to download and install a VRML plug-in to your Web browser and then visit Web sites hosting these worlds. Be sure to use a VRML 2.0 browser for VRML 2.0 worlds. The old VRML 1.0 standard is still used. If you make a VRML world, you can plug it into avatar environments like Black Sun's Passport and Onlive Traveler, or you can link them to Web pages to be browsed (visited alone).

The Experts Speak on Avatar Design

As you contemplate how best to design effective avatars and the worlds they live in, you might be concluding that this is a very big design challenge. Whole new fields are emerging around the representation of human identity in cyberspace. From anthropologists to character animators, psychologists to fashion designers, everyone seems to have something to contribute to this new medium. In August of 1997, a major panel and special interest group on avatars as a new design medium was held at the annual SIGGRAPH conference. Experts in this new field gathered, presented their views, and engaged in lively discussion with the audience. You can find an on-line version of this discussion hosted by SIGGRAPH at **http://www.ccon.org/sig97/index.htm**. After SIGGRAPH, I collected together a set of short writings from some of these presenters and added a couple more avatar visionaries for good measure. If you are a budding avatar worlds designer, these folks provide valuable information for you.

The experts

Steve DiPaola leads a team of artists, architects, UI designers, and musicians in designing and developing 3D Avatars and virtual spaces at Onlive! Technologies, the creators of the Traveler voice-supported virtual world.

Reid Hoffman was director of technology and responsible for several major releases of Fujitsu Software's WorldsAway. He is currently starting his own company specializing in on-line relationships.

Moses Ma is an Internet and computer gaming visionary and was the originator of the Universal Avatars specification with IBM. He recently became co-author of the Open Community VRML multi-user specification proposal with Mitsubishi Electronics.

Mitra is a true pioneer of virtual world cyberspace, as one of the key developers of VRML and the original designer of Moving Worlds, which became VRML 2.0. Mitra has worked on multi-user products at Worlds, Inc. and ParaGraph International. He heads up his own consulting company.

Ioannis Paniaras is a fashion designer who recently completed his graduate research at the Media Lab of the University of Art and Design, Helsinki UIAH, Finland. Ioannis is designing virtual communities and studying avatar fashion trends and their influence on social life in cyberspace.

Kirk Parsons is a developer of avatar authoring software at his company, Attic Graphics, and has served as an avatar technologist for a number of companies including Black Sun Interactive, Extempo Systems, and Circle of Fire Studios.

Bernie Roehl is a software developer based at the University of Waterloo in Ontario, Canada. Bernie has written several books and dozens of articles on virtual worlds and currently chairs the Virtual Humans Architecture Group and the Humanoid Animation Working Group of the VRML Consortium.

My two bits: The emergence of a new design medium

Who do you want to be today? As thousands of Internet users begin new lives as avatars in virtual worlds, a new design industry is being born. Avatars and the worlds they live in comprise a vast new design medium attracting a wide range of professionals including: anthropologists, 3D and multimedia designers, character animators, musicians, voice and facial expression specialists, performance artists, architects, business workgroup and workflow experts, and educators involved in distance learning. In addition, avatar standards efforts such as Living Worlds, Universal Avatars, and Open Community have been initiated.

Issue areas

The design of multi-user graphical virtual environments is one of the most challenging new areas in computer science and consumer on-line services. Virtual worlds supporting tens of thousands of users in simultaneous communication and in which they can build their own spaces and shape their own faces represents a truly great achievement.

Despite all that wonderful technology, the number one question asked by users entering these virtual environments is: *how can I design my own avatar?* The success or failure of these worlds can hinge on avatar design issues. Basic design decisions often involve trade-offs: in the initial technology choices (2D versus 3D, polygonal versus photorealistic), in the methods of communication (text versus voice, gesture versus facial animation) and in the use of standards (VRML versus proprietary 3D, IRC versus custom communication backbones). The most difficult design criteria to pin down are aesthetic: what makes one person like or identify with their avatar can often be very personal and subjective.

Steve DiPaola

I believe in design approaches which rely heavily on techniques to make users feel that they are *really interacting in the virtual space*. These techniques include: 3D attenuated voice and sound, 3D navigation, an immersive first-person user interface, individualized 3D head avatars with emotions and lip synchronization, and good 3D space design. Our team at Onlive! Technologies transposed this experience to consumer based PC platforms connected to the Internet at dial-up speeds. The design approach to avatar cyberspace that I use is born of experience trying to emulate natural social paradigms and attempts to provide immersion in a 3D visual and sound landscape. The following three design criteria are, I believe, key to the creation of experiences in virtual worlds in which users *suspend their disbelief*, and get lost in a kind of *virtual cocktail party* experience.

Does community come from communication? I hold that the structural process of a community and socialization—real or virtual—is communication, and that the most natural human form of communication is verbal. Therefore, 3D spatial multi-participant voice with distance attenuation and stereo positioning is the best tool for the development of virtual cocktail parties and virtual communities alike.

You are your avatar, but can we use just heads? A fundamental goal of avatar cyberspace is to bind the Real Person at their computer *with* their avatar in cyberspace. Given the finite CPU/polygon/bandwidth resources, we need to invest in the most natural form of socialization first: face to face. I believe that the body (hand gestures, body language) is secondary for human communication and can be added later.

A final design issue: physically based spiral of infinite betterment. Given the natural emulation goal, one might assume that the natural design choice is to strive to make things more and more realistic. I don't believe this is so. A major truth in computer graphics and simulation (especially for facial modeling) is the more realistic you make something, the more open to criticism it is for not being realistic enough. So I believe we should emulate a *realistic look* just enough to achieve recognition of familiarness. I believe that *just good enough for all practical purposes* is good enough.

Onlive Traveler, on which Steve worked, is described in this book and on the Web at **http://www.onlive.com/**.

Reid Hoffman

At first blush, virtual communities seem like a novel invention. Cohabiting a virtual space with other real people—what a concept! What are these chat rooms, these virtual worlds, these simulated social realities? Are they games? Are they real places? Are they a new form of life? These questions seem natural. Therefore, these apparently new virtual communities seem strange, even alien, to everyday experience. With this alien strangeness, it appears that perhaps only social outcasts will grace these communities, that these new worlds will only exist in the shadow of everyday life.

I have news. You have been living in virtual communities for years. Telephones, fax machines, postal mail, and other media, have created a living, breathing, virtual community around us as we slept. A telephone number is an address in virtual space. A voice is an avatar, the electronic representation of a person. Even so, not all avatars represent real people! Sometimes, the result of surfing a dialtone results in a synthetic voice—fully interactive, but only partially real. Virtual communities are already mainstream.

The novelty, the strangeness, arises from two sources: the casual social environment and the visual look. As recently as two years ago, all mainstream virtual communities involved *directed* communication. Each real-time, interactive communication was directed to specific individuals. Sure, a teleconference might involve an unusually large number of people or an unfamiliar person, but a person did not stumble accidentally into a teleconference. Suddenly, virtual communities include casual social environments. It is no surprise that chat rooms have become the pick-up bars of the '90s.

The other important evolution of virtual communities is the new visual overlay. Virtual communities now have visual substance. People generally apply the rule, "if I can see it, it is real." Correspondingly, suddenly, on the basis of this rule, visual communities leap from the electronic wires to a comfortable spot in the living room.

These two new capacities will drastically increase peoples' participation in virtual communities, and thereby increase the belief in their reality. Eventually, real virtual communities will be virtually real communities. Virtually speaking, the only real difference will be their location in cyberspace.

See Reid's WorldsAway projects (**http://www.worldsaway.com/**) and his current work at **http://www.relationships.com/**.

Moses Ma

I am part of several efforts to develop and promote a standard set of formats, protocols, and design methodologies for avatars. Until now, avatars have been system and browser dependent, which meant that an avatar created for one virtual world wasn't necessarily compatible with other worlds. A number of people in the VRML business have put together a proposal, called Universal Avatars, which details a way to standardize what avatars are and do.

By using this proposed standard, avatars will be able to move from one world to another, keeping the same appearance and behavior. This means that users will be able to recognize other users' avatars that they met in other worlds. And their avatars will have individualized automatic actions, moods, and even pets. And they'll be able to tell how their friends, from around the world, are feeling today, just by the look on their avatar's faces.

The latest draft of our proposal now deals with a variety of issues, which begin with 3D models and behaviors, but now ventures forth to discuss other important issues, such as persistent identity, interworld communications, database concerns, and support for additional emerging standards such as T-120, H-323, and Versit. We believe that this is an early basis for an emerging "operating system" for socialization.

Why have avatar stardards? It would be useful to have a standardized avatar representation for the purpose of visiting all virtual worlds with a user's preferred avatar representation and openly tendered identity profile. This has many benefits, including the reduction of the workload on the user, the standardization of global search for other people through their public avatar presentation, and the ability to create new business opportunities for VR vendors. The Universal Avatar system, if adopted, could have a fundamental impact on the design of avatars in the medium of virtual worlds on the Internet.

Learn more about what Moses does at **http://www.i-game.com/**.

Mitra

The area of multi-user virtual worlds is progressing on two parallel and equally important fronts: content (what avatars looks like, how they behave, and so on) and technical (how virtual worlds work under the covers). I say parallel and equally important, because in the rapidly changing world, we see two feedback loops. In the first, the technical possibilities and potential drives what the content authors create. In the other feedback loop, the content authors' experiences (and frustrations) with the technology drive the next technical steps. Personally, I sit firmly on the technical side of the equation, having designed the architecture behind two pioneering systems: Worlds Chat, the first consumer multi-user 3D chat system, and People Space, Japan's first 3D avatar virtual world (see the People Space home page at **http://www.people.or.jp/peoplespace/** and the birth of People Space at **http://www.people .or.jp/my/psn.htm**. Note that these pages are in Japanese).

Both these worlds were built by single companies: Worlds Inc., and ParaGraph. Within these companies were network engineers designing the networking architecture, client designers building the application, and authors building the content for both the world and the avatars which would populate it. Both these architectures were subsequently used for other projects, but the architectures show a common limitation in that the creativity cannot be used in other worlds (i.e., avatars from one world are not supported in other worlds). As we've seen in the 2D World Wide Web, the space only really takes off when large numbers of very creative people can each work on one part of the puzzle, knowing that whatever they build will work with the parts of the puzzle being solved by other people. The key enabling technological element for this is standards.

Living Worlds is an attempt to address this, to provide the technical framework within which people can work on different parts of the puzzle. In a Living Worlds system, network engineers, avatar authors, world authors, and authoring tool builders can all work independently. Ideally you or I will be able, for example, to buy an authoring tool from Attic (Kirk Parson's company), use it to build an avatar, animate this avatar with an animation tool from someone else (i.e., downloading funky new dance behaviors from OZ), and then use that avatar in a world built with SGI's world building tool. Once we can build an avatar that can be used across all worlds, we'll spend a lot more of our time, energy, and money on the avatar knowing it'll have maximum exposure.

I believe this is the future which will drive 3D multi-user worlds to a place where they become the new cyberspace.

Visit Mitra Internet Consulting at **http://earth.path.net/mitra**.

Ioannis Paniaras

As an artist, designer, and researcher in CMC (computer mediated communication), I focus on issues related to the aesthetics, design, visual management of avatars, and their identity within the community. For any designer of avatars, I pose the following provocative questions:

- What is a virtual persona, and how does one design for and manage a virtual persona?

- How do the aesthetics and the visual appearance of an avatar contribute to the instructional and entertainment aspects of virtual life and communication in the virtual community?

- How does the design of the avatar influence the identity and the perception of the self in real life?

- What is an ideal interface for human contact?

This medium is not well understood, but it has demonstrated the power to defragment solid, singular identity (the modern notion of identity) and sustain the emergence of a plethora of virtual identities. Avatars are a key part of the visual and behavioral grammar of emerging cultures in virtual communities. By analyzing the design structure of the avatar we can help understand directions in which we might be heading in human contact. I challenge avatar designers to create new visions for avatar mediated communication by first starting with a solid understanding of human behavior.

View Ioannis' work at **http://www.uiah.fi/~paniaras/**.

Kirk Parsons

I have developed a profession in which I am able focus on avatar representation issues, including avatar animation. I always work with the primary goal of relating the key technical trade-offs to avatar authoring possibilities. The underlying technology always affects an artist's choices in the design process. Important elements of that underlying technology include:

- Expressiveness in avatars: how is it achieved?

- Suspension of disbelief: how is this accomplished?

- Avatar animation: morph based versus keyframed versus real-time motion technologies

- Artificial intelligence: what role does it play in avatars?

I believe that any designer of avatars must have a solid understanding of underlying technologies, not only to enable them to function within narrow bandwidth constraints, but also to create effective and aesthetically pleasing designs. The use of photorealism to reduce polygon count, texture mapping and morphing to create facial expression, and other "tricks" must be in the designer's grab bag of techniques.

Bernie Roehl

Because I come from a strong virtual reality background, I have insight into the activities of various standards groups (Living Worlds and the Virtual Humans Architecture Group) which are relevant to our efforts at avatar standards definition and avatar design. I feel it's important that we acknowledge the need to create expressive and communicative avatars within the constraints imposed by bandwidth, latency, and rendering performance. My own personal feeling is that the key issues in the emergent field of avatar design include the following:

- Defining standards that enable the creation of interoperable avatars

- Creating tools that allow users to create their own avatars

- Providing avatars with as much expressive power as possible, using voice, gestures, and facial expressions

- Finding effective methods for integrating speech, expression, and movement

- Resolving issues surrounding identity and the ownership of one's virtual self

Visit with Bernie Roehl (**http://sunee.uwaterloo.ca/~broehl/bernie.html**) and see the VRML Humanoid Animation Working Group's Web pages at **http://ece.uwaterloo.ca/~h-nim/**.

Hot Spots

Links to World Building and Avatar Designing Resources

There are a large number of tools out there on the Internet for building worlds and designing avatars. The following table lists links where free software is freely available for download for a trial period.

3D world authoring tools

http://www.paragraph.com
ParaGraph International's Virtual Home Space Builder and Internet3D Space Builder.

http://cosmo.sgi.com/
Silicon Graphic's Cosmo VRML 2.0 authoring system.

http://vrml.sgi.com
Silicon Graphics VRML worlds page containing many great examples, including Floops, described earlier in this book.

http://www.tgs.com
TGS 3Space Publisher.

http://www.ids-net.com/
Integrated Data Systems page featuring a powerful VRML authoring system called V∑Realm Builder 2.0.

http://www.vream.com/
VREAM Inc. page featuring a complete authoring system for VRML 2.0 called VRCreator, as well as a VRML plug-in called WIRL.

http://www.virtus.com
Virtus 3D WebSite Builder and other 3D tools.

http://www.caligari.com
Caligari page featuring their latest product, Truespace.

http://www.sense8.com/
Sense8 corporation provides a set of powerful source code libraries called WorldToolKit and a 3D authoring system based on them called World Up. World Up supports a wide variety of file formats including VRML, 3D Studio, and AutoCAD.

http://www.superscape.com
SuperScape, a company that has been around for more than a decade, produces 3D browsers and tools, including VRT, a 3D authoring system.

http://www.radiance.com
Radiance International offers a VRML 2.0 authoring system for Windows 95 and NT called Ez3d VRML Author.

http://www.metacreations.com/
MetaCreations, maker of wonderful image enhancement tools, is starting to get into avatar character and world authoring.

VRML browsers

http://cosmo.sgi.com

SGI Cosmo Player is a great VRML plug-in for your Netscape Navigator 3.0 or Microsoft Internet Explorer 3.0 Web browser. Note that Cosmo player may come bundled with Netscape Communicator.

http://cosmo.sgi.com

Live3D is a Netscape VRML browser that is being integrated with Cosmo Player.

http://www.intervista.com

Intervista WorldView is one of the most powerful and easy to user VRML 2.0 plug-in browsers available. With great Java support, the External Authoring Interface, and fast VRML rendering, WorldView is becoming a browser of choice for developers.

http://www.newfire.com.

Newfire's Torch is a very fast VRML 2.0 player that is being developed for great 3D gameplay. These guys know how to make VRML fly!

http://www.spiw.com/

Sony's NPChooser enables you to switch between VRML plug-ins in Netscape Navigator (a very handy tool if you are going to use different browsers).

Avatar designing toolkits and avatar galleries

http://www.sven-tech.com

Sven Technologies' AvatarMaker is covered in this chapter and is included on the book CD-ROM. You can download more recent demonstrations from their page.

http://www.3dplanet.com

3D Planet provides 3Dcreate, an avatar designer that is part of its 3D Assistant. This program is included on the book CD-ROM and is downloadable from their page.

http://www.closerlook.com/avatar/

Closer Look Creative (http://www.closerlook.com/) has an Avatar Bazaar.

http://www.graphcomp.com/vrml

An extensive gallery of VRML avatars in Grafman's VR World Avatars.

Virtual world and community designers

http://www.naima.com/
Naima is a first rate team of virtual community designers that also helps craft the interfaces on virtual world software.

http://www.scamper.com/art/wc/wctour01.html
http://www.scamper.com/rezume/threedee.html
J. Robinson helped design Worlds Chat. See his description and tour of the project, and his art for the Worlds Chat CD.

http://www.aikiu.de/
Aiku is a German company providing services to build virtual communities.

http://www.zoecom.com/
Zoecom is a collaborative of new media artists with a specialty in creating imaginative and original 3D interfaces and environments for the on-line and video/film industries.

http://www.cube3.com/
Cubic Space, a New York City world builders productions group, created Starbase C3 for Black Sun Passport among other creative projects in VRML. They also support the New York VRML Special Interest Group.

http://www.hollyworlds.com
The first VRML avastars and movie worlds at Alex Lightman's Hollyworlds

Other tool makers and world technologists

http://www.www.livepicture.com
Live Picture and RealSpace (described in this chapter).

http://www.extempo.com/webBar/
Extempo Systems does "artificially intelligent" interactive bot character actors as seen in their world called Spence's Bar.

http://www.thinkfish.com/
ThinkFish has a great character authoring system which makes great "unrealistic" cartoon-like 3D characters.

The Companion Web Site

ENTER THE AVATAR TELEPORT

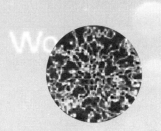

As a service to you honored readers of Avatars! we have built a colorful companion Web site. This Web site will give you updated information on the worlds featured in this book, let you know about happenings inside the worlds and about new worlds which have appeared since this book was written. You can go straight to the Companion Web site by pointing your Web browser to **http://www.digitalspace.com/avatars**. Bookmark this site and don't be afraid to share it with your friends—the more avatars the better!

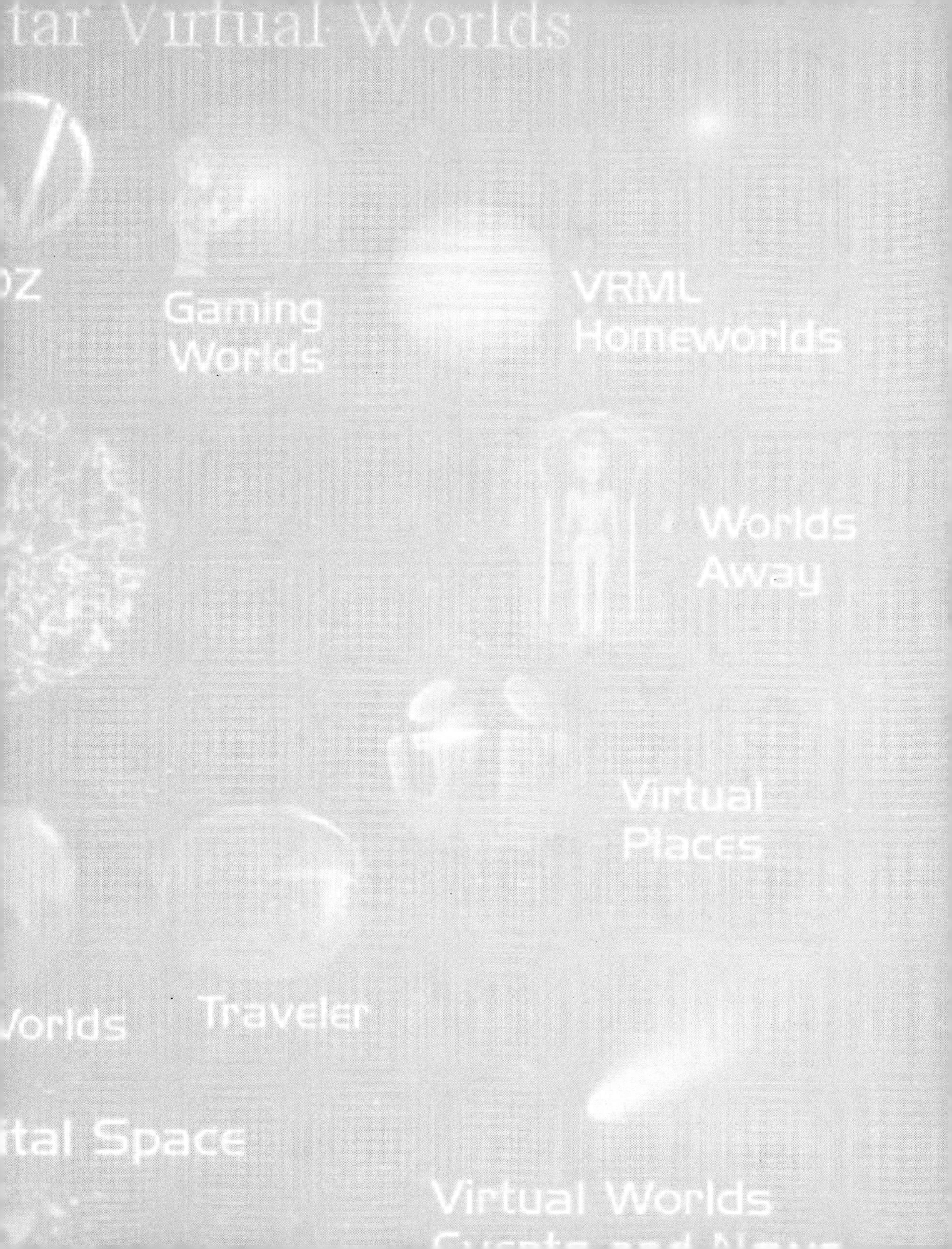

tar Virtual Worlds

OZ

Gaming
Worlds

VRML
Homeworlds

Worlds
Away

Virtual
Places

Vorlds   Traveler

ital Space

Virtual Worlds

BookWorld, a virtual bookstore constructed just for readers of *Avatars!*

A Tour of the Companion Web site, the Avatar Teleport

You can view the Avatar Teleport with any Web browser supporting tables. This includes Netscape 2.0 or higher, Microsoft Internet Explorer 2.0 or higher or other browsers such as America Online, Prodigy or CompuServe World Wide Web browsers. Point your Web browser to **http://www.digitalspace.com/avatars** and let's get started! Note that these Web pages may look slightly different by the time this book is in print. We are constantly updating them for your benefit. The basic format we will describe here will not change, however.

Your companion Web site is packed with resources about virtual worlds and the avatars that live in them. The following is a short list of what you will find there.

The Solar System of Virtual Worlds

World Guides: as you can see in the figure on page 456, a ring of digital planets sends you to custom pages for each virtual world described in Avatars! and new worlds that have come online since the book went into print. Each World Guide has preview images and news of the world, instructions for downloading it from the Internet, and copious links to Web sites by users of the world. Also included is a set of frequently asked questions (FAQs) for each world. If the software on your book CD-ROM is out of date or there is a problem installing or connecting to a particular world, just visit its World Guide for help.

Ordering more copies of Avatars! through its publisher, Peachpit Press: click on the glowing teleport in the center of the digital planets and go to the Avatars book ordering page. Tell your friends, give it as a gift to your cube-mate, or order a box of books for your class! You can also find Avatars through Amazon.com books, and in Borders Books and Music and fine bookstores everywhere.

World News and Hot Links: for each world and the whole virtual worlds industry is available here.

Build Worlds, Design Avatars: takes apprentice world builders to links for tools and techniques to build your own world and design your own virtual personae.

Life in Digital Space: takes you to key sites like Biota.org where you can witness the birth of artificial life inside the new virtual world cyberspace and even hatch or plant something of your own.

Extra Bonus Stuff

The Avatars! BookWorld: a virtual world has been constructed just for readers of *Avatars!* Come in and meet your author in his avatar DigiGardener and peruse a complete on-line bookstore with your friends. Find a teleport to the BookWorld on the companion Web site. The first Book World is brought to you through Active Worlds by Circle of Fire Studios (see **http://www.activeworlds.com** and Colors of Life at **http://www.colorsoflife.nl**).

Upcoming Events in Avatars Cyberspace: learn about upcoming lectures, conferences, user group meetings, or events inside virtual worlds. The author or his organization, the Contact Consortium, are always on the road talking about the new cyberspace.

A Complete Sample Chapter: The "Alphaworld and Active Worlds" chapter is featured here in all of its glory. Here you will find the complete Building 101 Guide and bonus images and links we could not fit into the book.

Take An Advanced Course at Avatar University: the Web site has links to a great set of on-line course notes for educators or eager students of the virtual. These notes contain a great Netiquette and Community Hosting Guide, Applications of Virtual Worlds in the Home, Classroom and at Work, the History of the Virtual Worlds Medium, and the Technology Underlying the Medium.

Extended Bibliography: these pages extend the bibliography in *Avatars!*

The Latest Glossary: including the full Glossary in the book, this indexed page contains some new words. Learn the Lingo of the new cyberspace and send us a new word or two.

Ways to Contact the Author with feedback: Bruce Damer and the whole Peachpit team would like to hear from you about your experience with *Avatars!* and welcome your suggestions for the next edition. Simply fill out the form on the Web site or e-mail us directly here at **avatars@digitalspace.com**.

About the Author: see what DigiGardener really looks like.

Avatars Art Gallery and Original Art from Roger Zuidema: see Roger Zuidema's famous Avatar Bar Scene from the book in our Avatars Art Gallery. As time goes on, we will add more avatar art into this gallery. Got a favorite screen shot? Designed a great avatar? Submit it for our gallery!

Avatars Link Bazaar and Broken Link Zone: got a link to share with the avatar users community? Then submit it to us and we will see if we can post it here or under the World Guides. If a link in the book or on the Web site does not work, let us know and we will try to post its new link. If it is truly a dead link, we will post it in the Broken Link Zone.

Join the Order of the Avatars User Group: sign up for our mailing list and talk to other Avatars like yourself! When you want to get serious about projects in virtual world cyberspace, you can join the Contact Consortium by visiting **http://www.ccon.org**.

News about upcoming new editions of Avatars!: we hope you will like the book so much that we will have to make another edition!

The Making of Avatars!: read about the unusual way this book was put together, from its development as a huge Web site to interviews inside virtual worlds.

Errata: if we goofed, can you forgive us? This section will have a complete listing (to the best of our knowledge) of errors in the book.

The Book
CD-ROM
YOUR KEY TO AVATAR CYBERSPACE

The World

The palace is a sprawling cosmos of chat. Against a variety of image backdrops, two dimensional avatars wander, talk and misbehave. Avatars range from the simple guest 'round heads' to elaborate displays of digital showmanship by veteran registered users. Build your own Palace area in a jiffy and host your own events.

What do I need?

Size of download: approx 2.5-4.0 Megs
Hard disk resources: approx 4.0-6.0 Megs
Platforms Supported: MacOS, Win 3.1 & 95
Setup: Simple, self installing file
Cost: Shareware guest version free! $25 US registration for cool features

The Palace

Chat Cosmos

Read about The Palace.

Go to The Palace page at the *Avatars!* Companion Web Site

Install me from the CD

Install me from the Internet

Go Back! To Avatar Teleport

Quit

The CD-ROM included with this book is your ticket to a journey into avatar cyberspace. The CD-ROM is packed with virtual world software that will allow you to connect with other people all over the world who are living and enjoying life as an avatar. The CD-ROM includes virtual world software, a guide to each world, sample chapters, and special sections of this book for reference when you are online or using Avatars! with students in the classroom. In this chapter, I help you understand how to use the CD-ROM and begin your exploration of avatar cyberspace.

Your Guide to the Book CD-ROM

"Avatars are not supposed to die. Not supposed to fall apart . . . The Graveyard Daemons will take the avatar to the Pyre, an eternal underground bonfire beneath the center of The Black Sun, and burn it. As soon as the flames consume the avatar, it will vanish from the Metaverse, and then its owner will be able to sign on as usual, creating a new avatar to run around in. But, hopefully, he will be more cautious and polite next time."

–Neal Stephenson, *Snow Crash*

What's on the CD-ROM

This quotation from *Snow Crash*, where the avatar for Da8id, hacker operator of the virtual Black Sun club, is expelled by bots from his own premises. Nothing like this can happen (yet) to your avatar in a virtual world, but as you enter worlds through this book's CD-ROM remember that you will be entering a community of living, breathing people. You will be warmly accepted or summarily rejected from each community depending on your behavior. There is nothing virtual about your interactions with these real people and the community you all create is no less real than many communities in the real world.

The book CD-ROM contains many useful resources to help make your exploration of avatar cyberspace easier. The CD-ROM includes the following:

1. **The Avatar Teleport:** a powerful interface to your CD-ROM which gives you information and links to each virtual world and the other resources on the CD-ROM. You must have Adobe Acrobat PDF Reader 3.0 installed to access this interface. The reader is provided free for you on the CD-ROM.

2. **Virtual world software for PCs and the Macintosh:** These are called "clients" and they are the special software you will need to connect to virtual worlds and interact with other people around the world. Because the client software is on your CD-ROM, you will not have to download it from the Internet, saving you a lot of time and trouble. Note that the client software for virtual worlds is changing all the time, and you may find that the software on the CD-ROM is out of date. To help you with this, we have included links to places on the World Wide Web where you can download the latest copies of the virtual worlds.

3. **Plenty of HTML (Web) documents:** We have included these documents so you can access them with an ordinary Web browser. The following documents are included:

- The complete HTML (Web) version of the book, totally linked together in bite sized pieces. There are hundreds of pages of text and pictures, including some bonus pictures and sections not contained in the print book. Throughout this giant CD-ROM based Web site, live links to on-line Web pages are embedded, so you can directly jump to these Web pages.

- A bonus HTML version of "An Advanced Course at Avatar University" is included here for easy use in classroom or seminar teaching about virtual worlds. This provides a powerful companion to the book when it is used in schools, colleges, and universities. The extended "Bibliography of Recommended Reading" and "Glossary of Terms" is also included on the CD-ROM for teachers and researchers.

- Links to the companion Web site are also sprinkled over the CD-ROM interface. These links will take you to home pages of virtual world providers and users.

What's not on the CD-ROM

Note that not all virtual worlds and other software covered in this book are included on the CD-ROM. Where we could not include the software, we have provided links to Web pages where you can either download it or find details to order it.

Getting Started

To make your life easier, we have provided a point-and-click interface to the resources on the CD-ROM. This interface is built with documents in Adobe's Acrobat PDF format. To use the interface you must install Acrobat Reader 3.0 for Windows or the Macintosh.

If you don't want to use this interface, you can access the files on the CD-ROM directly. If you prefer this method, skip to the section, "Directly Accessing the Files," later in this chapter.

Installing the Acrobat Reader

You will find the free Acrobat Reader installer program on the top level of the CD-ROM file structure. Simply put the CD-ROM into the CD-ROM drive, close the door, and double-click on the CD-ROM icon on your desktop to open it. On the Macintosh, it will appear as an icon on the desktop. In Windows 3.1, open the File Manager and you will be able to open the CD-ROM drive (sometimes listed as the D: or E: drive). On Windows 95 or NT, find the CD-ROM drive icon under My Computer, where it is sometimes called Audio CD.

When you have opened the CD-ROM drive, you should see several files. If you are using a Macintosh, you should find a program file called Reader 3.0.1 Installer. In Windows 3.1 it is called ar16e301.exe, and in Windows 95/NT, it is called ar32e301.exe. Double-click on it to start the installation process. Note that if you already have Acrobat Reader 3.0 installed, you don't need to do this step. The installation should proceed by asking you where you want to install the reader. It is a simple setup and should not take up much time or hard disk space.

A Quick Tour of the CD-ROM Interface

The front screen of the CD-ROM interface.

Once you have installed the Acrobat 3.0 Reader, you should be able to open the book interface. Simply open up the CD-ROM and double-click on the file named TheBook (in Windows 3.1 it might be called thebook.pdf). If you want to access the files directly without using the interface, you can open the folder called BookFiles and skip to the section "Directly Accessing the Files." The Acrobat Reader should start and bring up the front screen, which should be similar to the preceding figure. Note that if the image does not come up filling your whole screen, you can select View and then the option Full Screen to switch to full screen mode.

Launching Web sites and local Web pages from the CD-ROM interface

As you can see, the interface is very similar to the format of the companion book Web site. A solar system of digital planets rings a central teleport. If you click on the central teleporter, it will take you to the companion book Web site itself. For this to work, Acrobat Reader has to know where your Web browser program is. When you click on the teleporter link, you will be prompted to find your Web browser software. It is often in the folder Program Files (on Windows 95). You also have to be online for this to work. Once this is all set up, you will be able to click on links throughout the CD-ROM interface and launch Web pages.

Accessing the whole book on the CD-ROM

In a similar way, your Web browser will launch to show Web pages stored right on your CD-ROM. We have provided the entire book as a series of linked Web pages. Just click on the avatar icon labeled "This way to the book" and you will enter the BookWeb, which has the entire book in Web format, packed with images and more live links to the Internet. There are bonus resources like "An Advanced Course at Avatar University" as well as many images and text not included in the book. Note that there may be slight differences between the printed version of the book and its Web (HTML) version on the CD-ROM. Feel free to use this version of the book to teach your classes, do quick searches, or follow live Web links found in the print version.

The World Guides

The rest of the CD-ROM interface is pretty straightforward: click on a planet and you will be taken to a new interface screen, like the one shown in the following figure. This is a world guide, and each guide contains:

1. A description of the virtual world software that is available on the CD-ROM.

2. Links to the installers for the software for your operating system: MacOS, Windows 3.1, or Windows 95.

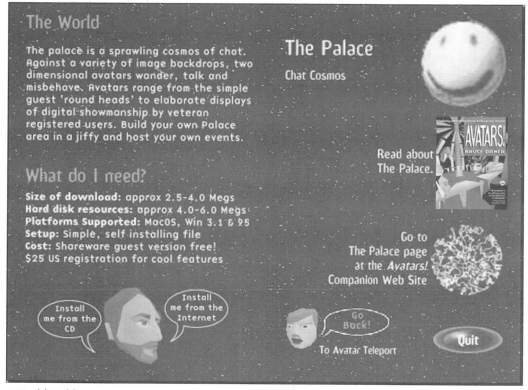

A World Guide screen.

3. Links to the home pages for the companies that provide the world.

4. Links to the pages on the companion book Web site for this world.

5. Links to the book chapter Web pages for this world which are stored locally on the CD-ROM.

6. A button to go back to the main screen.

7. A button to quit out of the CD-ROM interface.

Installing a world from the CD-ROM

Some virtual world programs are not stored on the CD-ROM, or there may not be a version for your computer's operating system. If this is the case, click on the Web link to the home page of the company that provides the world and download it directly from the Internet. If there is an installer available on the CD-ROM, click on its link to start it and return to the book chapter section on running the installation. You can then continue in that chapter to start using the virtual world. As each installer runs, you will be asked for a location to install the software to; select a folder on your hard disk (not on the CD-ROM).

If there is a problem running the installer or connecting with the virtual world (make sure you are online) you may have to download a brand new copy of the software. To do this, visit the home page of the company providing the world or the book companion Web site at **http://www.digitalspace.com/avatars**.

Finding the world and avatar creation tools

Click on "Build Worlds, Design Avatars" for the guide to installing Internet 3D Space Builder, AvatarMaker, and 3DAssistant. All of these programs require Windows 95 or NT.

The other links

"Virtual Worlds Links and News" will take you to the News section on the companion book Web site. Selecting DigiGardener's "Get the Book" will take you to the ordering page on the Web to order additional copies of Avatars! "Gaming Worlds" takes you to the Web page on the companion book Web site where links to gaming worlds can be found.

Directly Accessing the Files

If you have a problem with the Interface of the CD-ROM or would like to access the files directly, this section will help you understand the structure of folders and how to run the installers for virtual worlds directly from the CD-ROM.

Map of the folders on the CD-ROM and their contents

The resources on the CD-ROM are organized into folders. I have designed a tree of folders to keep everything organized. At the top of this tree is the root, where you will find the installers for the Acrobat Reader 3.0 and the inital interface screen document. Below the root, in other folders, you will find the virtual world software, HTML documents and other resources. To keep some resources separate, there are separate trees for different types of computer and operating system. The following is a map of folders on the CD-ROM:

root—contains the CD-ROM interface program and control files for edition and copyright. There is one top-level folder at the root called BookFiles which contains everything else. Here is a map of the folders under BookFiles:

- **pdfdocs**—contains the Adobe Acrobat PDF files used in the CD-ROM interface with the exception of the main screen, which is at the root.

- **htmldocs**—contains the HTML document resources, the entire book in HTML (Web) document format. This folder contains many sub-folders. The only file you really have to remember is the file Index.html. Opening this file will start your Web browser and allow you to access the rest of the book, including bonus sections like "An Advanced Course at Avatar University."

- **winworld**—contains virtual world client software and tools for use with Windows PCs. Each installer is contained in its own sub-folder.

  - **win31**—contains virtual world software for Windows 3.1 that will work with Windows 95 also*

    - **wchat**—software for Worlds Chat

    - **palace**—software for the Palace

    - **vp**—software for Virtual Places (several versions)

    - **wa**—software for WorldsAway

  - **win95**—contains virtual world software and tools that are specifically designed for Windows 95*

    - **aworld**—software for Active Worlds

    - **blacksun**—software for Black Sun Passport (several versions)

    - **oz**—software for OZ Virtual

    - **traveler**—software for Onlive Traveler

    - **vp**—software for Virtual Places (Windows 95, several versions)

    - **wa**—software for WorldsAway (Windows 95)

    - **3dspace**—Internet 3D Space Builder

    - **avmaker**—AvatarMaker

    - **3dassist**—3D Assistant Avatar Designer

  - **macworld**—contains virtual world client software for use with Macintosh or compatible computers

  - **palace**—software for the Palace

  - **vp**—software for Virtual Places

  - **wa**—software for WorldsAway

*Note that any virtual world software for Windows 3.1 should be able to run with Windows 95 (but not the other way around). Also note that Windows 3.1 and Windows 95 software may work under Windows NT.

From the preceding tree structure, you can open any of the folders and files. If you have a Web browser and Adobe Acrobat Reader installed, you will be able to open any HTML or Acrobat PDF document you find on the CD-ROM. Double-clicking on any installer software for a virtual world or tool will start the installation of that software. Make sure you don't try to start installing software for the wrong operating system (i.e., for Windows 95 programs if you are running Windows 3.1). As each installer runs, you will be asked for a location to install the software to; select a folder on your hard disk (not on the CD-ROM). You can return to the chapters in the book for each program and follow the installation instructions there.

If you are going to install this software more than once on different machines, you may want to make a copy of the installer file on your hard disk or server: drag and drop this file onto your desktop or into a folder you use for temporary work. Make sure you make a copy of the file, not just a shortcut. To do this, drag the file (with the left mouse button on the PC) and drop the file. On a PC running Windows 95, you will get a small pop-up menu. Select "Make A Copy Here," from this menu. To start the installer from your hard disk, double-click on the new icon.

Troubleshooting the CD-ROM

What if the CD-ROM spins or makes a funny sound in the drive when I click on the icon to access it but a window does not open?

You may have the CD-ROM in upside down or the CD-ROM may be dirty or defective. You have to place the CD-ROM in the drive with the shiny side down (and the label on top). If you think the CD-ROM is defective, hold it by the edges and look at the shiny side under a light. If you see scratches this could be causing the CD-ROM to fail to be read by the computer. If there are fingerprints, dust, or other particles on the shiny side of the CD-ROM, it may need cleaning. See your manuals that came with your CD-ROM drive for instructions on how to clean a disc. Try the CD-ROM again. If the problem persists, you may have to return the book to the store where you bought it and exchange it for another.

When I click on a virtual world installer to install the software, it crashes my computer or does not completely finish.

Check to see if you are installing software for the right computer and operating system. If you are running Windows 3.1, you cannot install software that is designed only for Windows 95 systems.

After I installed the software from the CD-ROM and tried to connect to the Internet, it reported "this software is out of date" or simply would not connect.

Check your Internet or on-line service connection and try again. If this problem persists, you should follow the link (included on the guide for that software on the CD-ROM) to the Web page for the company that provides the virtual world. You should check for any news about the virtual world (it may be discontinued or have a new version). Downloading and installing a new version directly from the Internet may solve the problem and allow you to connect. If you still cannot get the world to work, check the technical support pages on the Web for solutions. Some of the companies supplying these worlds may have an e-mail address or telephone number you can call for support.

Bibliography
of Recommended
Reading

This bibliography includes both fictional and non-fictional references for the student of virtual worlds. It is quite a varied selection, providing a kind of primer reading list. As there are precious few books about avatars (the one you are holding is one of the very first), the references listed below deal with general issues about life in cyberspace and our relationship with our own identity. The books listed below are written for a wide audience and will not scare you off with nerdy acronyms or programming languages. For your further investigation I have provided Web page URLs where you can find out more about the books and their authors.

There is a much more extensive bibliography listed on the companion Web site to this book at **http://www.digitalspace.com/avatars**. It is part of the "Advanced Course at Avatar University" and is also listed on its own. I will be updating the book Web site (and hopefully writing more books) to assist you as you get deeper into your study of this exciting new medium of human contact.

Short Bibliography of General Reading

Benedikt, Michael, ed. *Cyberspace: First Steps*. (Cambridge: MIT Press, 1991). The seminal classic work on the structure of cyberspace and the societies that could emerge within it. No traveler in digital realms should go forth without this one.

Gibson, William. *Neuromancer* (New York NY: Ace Books, 1984). ISBN: 0-441-56959-5 Almost ten years before *Snow Crash, Neuromancer* was the original avatar drama, kind of like the *Old Testament* for us converts. Note that William Gibson wrote this classic on a manual typewriter, having little personal experience with computers, so it is a pure creation of his imagination, unsullied by the limitations of working systems. Step into the light at William Gibson's yardshow at **http://www.idoru.com/** and visit an unofficial but very useful home page at **http://www-user.cibola.net/~michaela/gibson/**.

Haraway, Donna. *A Manifesto for Cyborgs: Science, Technology and Socialist Feminism in the 1980's* in Feminism/Postmodernism Linda Nicholson, Ed., (New York: Routledge, 1990), pp. 190-233. Haraway's modern interpretation of why she believes we all are becoming cyborgs. Also see Jenny Cool's essay on this title at **http://www.cyborganic.com/People/ovid/coolonharaway.html**.

Lem, Stanislaw. *Mortal Engines* (New York NY: First Harvest/HBJ, 1992). ISBN: 0-15-662161-4 Want to know what artificial intelligences and "bots" might be like in a future avatar cyberspace? Polish writer Stanislaw Lem wrote some of the best science fiction on this theme.

Levy, Steven. *Artificial Life* (New York NY: Pantheon, 1992). ISBN: 0-679-40774-X What will happen when life gets into avatar cyberspace? What will you think when you come to find your beautiful home on the digital range overgrown by a virtual form of kudzu? Avatar worlds may be the best place for digital biota to evolve. Steven Levy presents a very interesting history of the artificial life movement and its pioneers. Visit Steven Levy's home page at **http://mosaic.echonyc.com/~steven/**.

McCloud, Scott. *Understanding Comics* (New York NY: HarperCollins, 1993). ISBN: 0-06-097625-X Cartoons can tell us a lot about how to make avatars and their worlds. Scott McCloud will open your eyes to the power of cartoons to express ourselves in cyberspace. See the many faces of Scott McCloud at **http://www1.usa1.com/~aycrumba /zot/scott.html**, and an interview on the digital future of comics at **http://www.halcyon. com/fgraphic/Medium/cloud.html**.

McLuhan, Marshall. (publisher) Find Part I, Chapters 1-6 on the Web at **http://www .leland.stanford.edu/~xinwei/pub/img/media/McLuhan/UnderstandingMedia.html**.

Negroponte, Nicholas. *being digital* (New York: Knopf, 1995). ISBN: 0-679-43919-6 As the director of the MIT Media Laboratory, Dr. Negroponte has a first-hand look at where the digital revolution is taking us. Will we wear digital clothing? Will cyberspace emerge from our computers to surround us? Dr. Negroponte will open your mind to these questions. Tour the MIT Media Lab at **http://www.media.mit.edu/**.

Nisker, Wes "Scoop." *Crazy Wisdom* (Berkeley: Ten Speed Press, 1990). ISBN: 0-89815-350-6 Scoop Nisker doles out some pretty crazy wisdom while answering the question, "How do I behave in avatar cyberspace?" It is, after all, a crazy place, somewhere between a dream and a hallucination. Good advice from Nisker might be to not take yourself so seriously during your digital and personal brief allotment of time on this planet.

Pearce, Celia. *The Interactive Book: A Guide to the Interactive Revolution* (Indianapolis IN: Macmillan Technical Publishing, 1997). An overview covering interactivity in an historical and cultural context, tracing the history of interactive multimedia and design principles from the author's experience over the past 14 years.

Pesce, Mark. *VRML, Browsing and Building Cyberspace* (Indianapolis IN: New Riders, 1995). Read how the original visionary and co-creator of VRML (Virtual Reality Modeling Language) sees his invention being used to create a planetary management system. Visit Mark Pesce's home page at **http://www.hyperreal.com/~mpesce/**, and Read Mark's regular columns at **http://web1.zdnet.com/zdi/vrml/filters/columns.html**.

Powers, Michael. *How to Program Virtual Communities, Attract New Web Visitors and Get Them to Stay* (New York: Ziff-Davis Press, 1997) ISBN: 1-562-76522-1

A superb guide to building and running virtual communities, covering everything from text-based MUDs to 2D chat environments and virtual worlds. It provides informationt you need to start building virtual communities, structuring their activities, and managing their resultant societies and economies. Visit Michael's book companion Web page at **http://www.insideout.net/community**.

Rheingold, Howard. *The Virtual Community: Homesteading on the Electronic Frontier* (New York NY: HarperPerennial, 1993). The original source on virtual community. Howard Rheingold takes you on a tour of a wide range of virtual communities that came before the rise of avatar cyberspace. Look here for definitive coverage of The WELL. Experience Howard's brainstorms at **http://www.well.com/user/hlr/index.html**, and at Electric Minds home page at **http://www.minds.com**.

Stephenson, Neal. *Snow Crash* (New York NY: Bantam Spectra, 1992). ISBN: 0-553-56261-4 The Bible of the avatar cyberspace movement. If you haven't read it, you haven't seen the light, brother! You can find a compendium of Stephenson's on-line references at **http://www-user.cibola.net/~michaela/diamondage/stephen.htm**.

Stoll, Clifford: *Silicon Snake Oil* (New York NY: Doubleday, 1995). ISBN: 0-385-41993-7 Getting scared about where all this is taking us? Worried that avataring will remove us even further out of our real neighborhoods and ruin our kids' social and learning skills. The grand poo-bah of Internet luddites, Clifford Stoll really gives you something to think about! See Town Hall's pages on Clifford Stoll at **http://town.hall.org/university/security/stoll/cliff.html**, and his own (!) very simple home page at **http://www.OCF.Berkeley.EDU/~stoll/**.

Turkle, Sherry: *Life on the Screen: Identity in the Age of the Internet* (New York: Simon and Schuster, 1995). ISBN 0-684-80353-4 Professor Turkle has been studying and living life in virtual realms about as long as anyone. This very readable book complements her earlier work The Second Self. These books focus largely on MUDs, MOOs, and other text-based communities, but there is a great deal of relevance with regard to avatar cyberspace. Visit Professor Turkle's home page at **http://www.mit.edu:8001/people/sturkle/index.html**.

More Extensive Bibliography of Books, Papers, and Articles

Find a much more extensive and constantly updated bibliography on the book companion Web site at **http://www.digitalspace.com/avatars**.

Glossary
of Common Terms
Used in Virtual Worlds

Your Guide to
the Glossary

About the Glossary

The glossary of terms follows. Note that all words indicated bold can be found elsewhere in the glossary. Feel free to bounce your way around the glossary as it can be an education in avatar Cyberspace on its own! If you have seen a new word you think should be in this glossary, let us know by sending email through the avatars companion book Web site at http://www.digitalspace.com/avatars. Note also that as a service to the avatar community and educators using this book, a continuously updated version of this glossary is also posted on the companion Web site.

0-9

1D Shorthand for "one dimensional," which refers to virtual environments based on text interfaces. These include **MUDs** (Multi User Domains), chat rooms, **Internet Relay Chat (IRC)**, and others. This term does not indicate that discourse or the worlds described in text are at all limited, merely that interaction is focused primarily on the singularity of the text chat line.

2D Shorthand for "two dimensional," this refers to scenes that are flat, having width and height (represented by the x- and y-axes) but no depth (represented by the z-axis).

2 1/2 D This is shorthand for "two-and-a-half dimensions" which means that a scene appears flat but in fact has some ability to move avatars or objects "back" into a third dimension. WorldsAway from Fujitsu, and Sierra Online's Realm described in this book, are both examples of 2 1/2 D worlds.

3D Shorthand for "three dimensional," which indicates that a scene possesses three directions of possible motion: left and right (the x-axis), up and down (the y-axis) and into and out of the scene (the z-axis). The term "3D" can refer to a 2D image that has the appearance of depth. Of course 3D scenes displayed on a flat 2D computer monitor are only clever illusions, relying on our primate brains to perceive depth from perspective cues.

3D sound Sound that seems to emanate through a virtual world in three dimensions. For example, as you can experience in Onlive's Traveler (described earlier in this book), as you get closer to talking avatars, the volume of their voices increases. This is related also to stereo sound which gives you different sound out of your right- and left-hand speakers.

A

abstraction An abstract representation of the world. In virtual worlds, this might mean that instead of sending a scene of a world as fully described geometry, you would send the plans from which this scene can be made. This is like the difference between a whole building and an architect's plans for the building. Seeds and eggs in nature represent abstractions of the plants or animals to be. **Biota** often use abstractions (**L-systems, genetic programs**). Abstraction is one of the most powerful techniques and will be essential for the emergence of a large connected and inhabited virtual world cyberspace.

affordance A capability in a world. An object may have the affordance of being able to be moved; an avatar may have the affordance of being able to gesture.

agent Agents are chunks of software that have certain amount of freedom to move themselves around virtual spaces or computer networks on their own. The Internet is crawling with simple search agents which are constantly following Web links to build ever larger catalogs of Web pages. Agents are designed to serve the needs of users rather than to just exist on their own like **biota** or become destructive like **viruses.** Researchers in the field of agents are constantly debating when an agent is an agent or just an ordinary program. It seems that a program graduates to agenthood when it acts with the authority of the user and becomes autonomous, goal-oriented, collaborative, flexible, self-starting, communicative, adaptive, and mobile. Agents are close cousins of **bots** and are somewhat related to **virtual pets, daemons, biots, biota,** and **viruses.**

alias   A name a user chooses to associate with himself or herself within a text based or visual virtual world. Users often choose fanciful names that hide their real identity. This name is also called a **handle** or **nickname** and can be found on avatar **badges.**

alpha, alpha tester   An initial version of a new program which has been made available to a select group of brave and patient users (alpha testers). Saying "this software is very alpha" refers to software that has a large number of bugs or untested features. After alpha, software enters a larger **beta test** phase.

ambient sound   Sound that is played as a background to a virtual world. If this consists of cheesy **MIDI** tunes, it is often referred to as gratuitous **virtual elevator music.**

anchor   Also called a link, hyperlink, **URL,** or a **hot spot.** This is a location in a virtual world that can be clicked and will then bring up a page on the **World Wide Web** or move you to another scene within the world. This term also refers to a spot in the world where an object is to be placed (like the **Renderware** object anchor points in Active Worlds).

ancient, legend   These terms refer to a user in an avatar or text based world who has been around for a significant part of the time

the world or its community have been around. These users are usually proud of this fact and often have low **citizen numbers.** These users may have been involved in the fundamental building of the world or its community.

anonymity   A social property of a virtual world that guarantees that users can be anonymous. For example, using a **handle, nickname,** or **alias** instead of a real name guarantees a certain amount of anonymity. Users may not be anonymous to the people running the world, however, who have to maintain some means to contact their citizens.

application   Another name for a software program which does some greater task like word processing. Virtual world **clients** are often called applications.

application programming interface (API)   A method by which software can be joined together or extended. By using an API, one program can use services provided by another.

ARPAnet   A forerunner of the **Internet,** the Advanced Research Projects Agency network went into service in 1969–70.

artificial horizon   Like the little viewpoint rolling in the glass ball in most aircraft, the artificial horizon indicates where you are in space relative to the ground level. This interface is found in flight simulators and in the navigational controls of many virtual worlds and 3D browsers.

artificial intelligence (AI)   A general term for software and hardware systems that seek to mimic or extend higher order functions of the human mind, like cognition, vision, or locomotion. An AI is another term for a sophisticated **agent** or **bot** in an avatar world.

artificial life   Refers to a field of study that seeks to reproduce the complex worlds of simple living systems like bacterial colonies or the bloodstream. Chris Langton defines artificial life as "the study of artificial systems that exhibit behavior characteristics of natural living systems." Artificial life is an important progenitor of **biota** now appearing within virtual worlds.

aspect ratio   The physical proportions of the width of your screen to its height. Aspect ratios affect how images are displayed. The number of pixels that are shown across the width and height of your screen must be factored into aspect ratios. Square aspect ratios mean that an image will not be distorted when displayed on your screen.

av   An abbreviated form of the term avatar.

avatar teleport or **av port**   This is a central area where avatars can travel between worlds. Alternately, an avatar teleport refers to a room or large projection space where people represented as avatars can interact with a crowd of people in a real physical gathering. These are often called **cyberphysical events.**

avabuse   A user who verbally abuses another user with their avatar in a virtual world. This can take the form of offensive text chat, screaming, or loud music played in a voice and sound supported environment. Also see **avattack, boom boxer,** and **head banger.**

avacar   A vehicle used by a user to move their avatar some distance in a world. Also related to **teleport** and **portal.**

avactors   Real-life actors using avatars to address audiences in virtual worlds.

avaddiction   Addiction to life and interaction in avatar virtual worlds. Related to **chataholism.** Avaddicts often have one or more virtual worlds onscreen all day and will greet anyone who comes into their space.

avagenic   Photogenic as an avatar. This can mean that one's face or body makes a picturesque image to wrap around an avatar. This could also mean that one's avatar is so distinctive that people stop to gawk or take a screen shot picture. Avagenic avatars could be destined for **avastardom.**

avahunk   An avatar dressed up (or undressed) to look like a beefy hunk. Almost never representing the real person behind the avatar. Designed to kick sand in the face of 90-pound weakling avatars. See also **avatart.**

avamarks   Avatars which are copies of popular and fiercely defended trademarks, such as Disney or Star Trek characters. Avamarks will be marks for many a media company lawyer in the future. Expect to see blue suited lawyertars chasing avatars through worlds near you.

avapunks   Offensive avatars, also called **rudies,** who live to disturb and offend others sharing the same virtual world space. Teenage users are often the perpetrators, but not always.

avastar   An **avactor** who is a star in real life and dons an avatar to enter virtual worlds. Like the voices of famous people embodying characters on The Simpsons, or stars entering chat rooms on America Online, avastars are sure to make more than just cameo appearances in virtual worlds near you. This term was coined by Sun (Marian) McNamee.

avatainment   The use of avatars and virtual worlds to provide entertainment, as role playing, virtual theater, or other types of grand standing performances. See also **avvywood.**

avatar   Originally the term avatar came from Hindu mythology and is the name for the temporary body a god inhabits while visiting Earth. Avatar can also denote an embodiment or concrete manifestation of an abstract concept. The ancient Sanskrit term, avatara, meant "a passing down." Avatar was first coined for use in describing users' visual embodiment in cyberspace by Chip Morningstar in the early days of Habitat back in 1985. In text-based virtual communities, the term avatar is not used; users are identified instead by **handles, aliases,** or **nicknames.** Avatars are also called: characters, players, virtual actors, icons, or **virtual humans** in other virtual communities or gaming worlds.

avatar gallery A special virtual room, page, or selection menu which enables you to choose your avatar from a set of canned avatars. Custom-built avatars could also be shown here. First popularized in Worlds Chat in 1995.

avatart More common than **avahunks**, **avatarts** are scantily clad centerfold avatars, mostly scanned in from magazines and pasted onto 2D **postage stamp avatars.** Sometimes referred to as "those naked pix," avatarts are the source of more parental controls and an exodus of users to worlds where avatars are built from an approved set of body parts.

avattack Bodily attacks on your avatar carried out by other users by either passing their avatars back and forward through yours (if your avatar is transparent) or making body contact and bumping your avatar around (as in Onlive Traveler). Avattacks can also take the form of someone repeatedly placing their avatar overtop of yours in a 2D world or blocking your view in a 3D world. Related to **avabuse.**

avaway team A group of avatars who set out to explore areas of digital terra firma. An avatar gang that meets regularly. Taken from the *Star Trek Next Generation* series.

avizen A citizen of an avatar virtual world.

avvy, avvies Other nicknames for **avatar.**

Avvies, the Annual avatar awards at the Contact Consortium Avatars conference. Like the Oscars or Grammies, these awards give prizes for avatars in categories like best humanoid, most emotive, best gestures and animation, and most bang-for-the buck (smallest number of **polygons** used).

Avvywood The merging of Hollywood and avatar virtual worlds. Virtual worlds on the Internet are now inhabited by thousands of users playing ad-hoc roles, some of which are directly modeled on Hollywood themes. In a hypothetical Avvywood, millions would flock into virtual worlds to watch or role play in improvised episodes of their favorite film, TV show, or book. On rare occasions, big name talent will make cameo avastar appearances in the worlds.

B

backdrop An image used as a backdrop over top of which avatars float. This is common in the Palace and Virtual Places and other 2D avatar worlds.

badge A badge is a name tag on an avatar, with the **nickname** the user chose when they immigrated.

banishment A severe form of discipline for misbehaving users where the operator or caretaker of the world throws the miscreant out. See also **neutroning.** The user may or may not be able to log back in using the same identity. More minor forms of banishment include **ignoring.**

beta, beta tester, beta program Software in development which is beyond its initial alpha version. The select group of users who are trying this software are called beta testers in a beta program. Saying "boy, this software is really beta" refers to software that has a large number of bugs or untested features. When software completes its beta phase it is given a version number.

biota Biota is a variety of **artificial life** that populates virtual worlds. Biota are objects that have organic personalities resembling plants, insects, animals, or resembling forms of life outside of our everyday experience. Biota are characterized by the fact that they exist independently inside virtual environments and may or may not interact with users in the worlds. Biota spread, reproduce, mutate and die based on rules in the world and the properties of the biota. Many examples of biota are "hackable," meaning that users can open them up and redesign their basic operating codes. **L-systems** have made possible an early form of biota plants. **Genetic programs, neural networks,** and **complexity theory** are important technologies underlying biota. Biota may represent an entertaining or aesthetic addition to virtual worlds or a bona fide form of life expressing itself into a new medium.

biot A biot is similar to a **bot** or **agent** in a virtual world but has characteristics of a living thing. **Virtual pets** or the trusty dog in the virtual homestead that follows you is an example of a biot. Biots are not quite **biota** as they need interaction with users to stimulate their activities. Biots are not bots in that they could go rambling through their world on their own with no particular purpose.

biote An individual example of **biota.**

bird's eye view A viewpoint where you hover above your avatar. Sometimes called **god view.**

Black Sun The Black Sun is the club featured in Neal Stephenson's epic 1992 virtual world novel, *Snow Crash.*

body language Avatar gesture lingo which is an important part of communication in virtual worlds.

body parts Components or pieces which can be used to construct a whole avatar.

bookmark A Web page location (**URL**) which is remembered for later revisiting.

boom box, boom boxer Boom boxers are users in voice supported virtual worlds who crank up their stereos and waltz around inside virtual spaces with their microphones open, thereby disturbing everyone they come near.

borg, borgtar A borg is another name for a bot or agent in a virtual world. A borg has one difference in that it can sometimes be operated by a person, transforming (or borging) into an

avatar sometimes called a borgtar. Borgs are sometimes recognizable by the eyepiece around an eye, which looks like a monocle. Borgtars which have the monocle in their shirt pocket are currently inhabited. Borg comes from the popular Star Trek Next Generation series.

bot A bot (short for robot) finds its roots in **IRC** and **MUDs** and is a program that acts like a user in the chat space and often provides a useful service. Great bots of the past include NickServ, which prevented random IRC users from adopting nicks (**nicknames**) already used by others, and MsgServ; which allowed the packaging of messages to be delivered when the recipient signed on; and lastly, "annoybots," such as KissServ, which performed no useful function except to send gratuitous messages to other users.

The "Julia" **MUD** bot which was active in 1990–91, provided a remarkably impressive **Turing Test** experiment, able to pass as a real human user for as long as fifteen minutes of chat with other users. Bots are making their appearance in virtual worlds in the form of helper avatars like Mysterio in Black Sun or greeter bots elsewhere. Bots with more brains, acting like agents will soon be doing civic duty cleaning up vandalism in areas like AlphaWorld. Of course mistaking a bot for another human user can be an embarrassing experience, so watch for the telltale signs of a bot. Bots are related to **agents, biota,** and **virtual pets.**

BPS Bits Per Second, indicates the speed of your connection (usually through a modem).

browser A browser is a type of program which is able to bring up a certain class of information (like HTML Web documents or VRML 3D models) and allows you to manipulate them. A browser is a kind of **client** program and usually talks to a **server** to get its information. A browser is distinguished from a virtual world client program in that a browser is merely a viewer of information, not usually a communications medium.

bugs Errors in a program which might cause it to crash or behave unexpectedly.

building inspector A building inspector is a class of agent which watches building activities in a world and informs the user if he has done something unacceptable, such as pick an object that is not available for building or encroach on a neighbor's property.

bumper pool A game played where avatars can make body contact.

C

cache, caching A place on your hard disk where files are stored, sometimes temporarily. Many virtual worlds build caches of scenes, avatars, and other objects. These caches must be filled, cleaned out and checked every once in a while by the virtual worlds software. Caches speed up your experience in the world as the software running the world will take objects from your hard disk rather than downloading them from the Internet.

camera position A place where a **viewpoint** is set onto a scene. You can jump between camera positions to see the scene from different angles and with different lighting.

caretaker The operator of a given virtual world or area of a world.

channel A channel is a computer term for a pipe flowing with data. Programs can open channels to then exchange data one way (asynchronously) or two ways (bisynchronously). IRC (Internet Relay Chat) operates on a system of channels.

Character animation A field which seeks to generate cartoon or virtual human characters using digital tools, often for use in films or TV. Sometimes these virtual characters are given their body movements through **motion capture.**

Chat room This is a name for an area where text chat is entered and seen by all users as a scrolling list. Chat rooms are often set up around specific themes, like people in their 30s, or love and romance. Chat rooms don't look like rooms at all but like a teletype machine running in a window on your computer.

chataholism Addiction to chatting on the Internet, through virtual worlds, chat rooms, IRC, voice chat, or other channels to kill vast amounts of time in idle conversations with strangers. Chataholics in-avatar are often called **avaddicts.** Chataholism can lead to greatly emboldened communications skills for shy or overtly techie persons and can actually initiate or improve social skills in real life (RL).

chatiquette Proper etiquette while chatting online. An example of this is saying goodbye when you finish a conversation.

cheat A trick in a gaming world that allows you to get around the limitations of the game or gain a skill or knowledge nobody else has. Sometimes called a **hack.**

citizen number This is a number issued to a user upon immigration. Unlike the **immigration number** (which is usually used for database purposes), the citizen number is associated with the user's privileges and identity.

client A name for a software program that runs on your computer and talks to another piece of software called a server, which is somewhere out on the network. Most virtual worlds have their own custom client programs talking to servers.

client/server Network This is a network made up of **client** programs communicating with central **servers.**

cloning The replication of an avatar with all of its properties intact or the duplication of an entire virtual world. World cloning is often done when an area of the world gets beyond a certain population threshold. An identical copy of a room or series of rooms will then be cloned and a fresh set of users allowed in.

CMC Computer Mediate Communications is a field that studies and develops computers, software and networks to enable different kinds of person-to-person communications.

coders Another name for programmers.

collision detection A process inside virtual worlds where contact between objects is detected. If your avatar bangs into a wall and stops, it means that collision detection is active.

complexity theory A theory that posits that complex processes, systems, and structures can arise from a few simple rules. Related to biota and **artificial life,** it is a key foundation of research at the Santa Fe Institute.

compression The act of taking data and representing it in a compressed form, allowing faster transmission or less disk storage.

coordinate system This is a method of knowing where you are by using sets of numbers. For example, in AlphaWorld you can report your position using numbers like 105 North, 187 East, 1 Altitude, 180 Degrees Skew. By entering these numbers in a teleporter, you will be placed out at 1050 meters north, 1870 meters east, floating 10 meters above the ground, and facng south (0 skew is north).

CPU Central Processing Unit, your computer's "brain."

crash A term used to describe when your software fails and has to be shut down. This is also called dump or die or a number of other terms not to be repeated in polite company. Neal Stephenson's book, *Snow Crash*, referred to the ability of a **virus** program to crash people's lower brain functions and kill them.

CSCL Computer Supported Cooperative Learning is an area of study and product development which supports learning through software and networks. CSCL supports distance learning and helps set up virtual universities.

CSCW Computer Supported Cooperative Work is a field that seeks to foster collaborative work through computer and network technologies. Groupware is an example of software that comes out of the CSCW field.

cyberspace Cyberspace is a term coined by author William Gibson back in the early 1980s, but which was borrowed from Norbert Wiener's 1948 classic, *Cybernetics* (formed from the Greek term for steersman and reflecting the feedback mechanisms of ships). Appropriate to the navigation theme, a cybernaut is a person who boldly ventures forth to explore digital realms opening up in cyberspace.

cyberphysical event An event where avatar virtual worlds are projected near or around a group of people who are using the "virtual presence" of the users in-avatar to create a combined creative or party atmosphere. Sometimes called an **avatar teleport.**

D

daemon A program that runs in the background waiting for specific events to occur. For example, mail daemons lurk in wait of e-mails with malformed addresses to then hurl back at the sender.

dashboard Refers to a control surface usually placed across the bottom of the screen. Like a dashboard in a car, software dashboards help you navigate through three dimensional spaces. They can also look like controls in an airplane and feature such interesting navigational controls as an **artificial horizon.**

dial-up access Using your modem and a telephone line to get access to an on-line service as opposed to having a direct connection to a network which runs all the time.

dialogue box An interface control that enables you to select a series of settings. Dialogue boxes usually sport an OK and Cancel button.

Digerati Those people who consider themselves "in the know" regarding all things cyber. Also called "wired" people, they are eternally keyed into the latest technology and news of the digital world.

digital mixer A social event in a virtual world meant for singles—a kind of cocktail party for avatars. Internet dating services are driving the growth of **romance worlds.**

digital village An area of a virtual world constructed by a set of users to look like or act like a small community. Also called a virtual village, these areas usually stick to a common theme, like the Olde England of Sherwood Forest Town, a digital village in AlphaWorld.

digital space A general term describing parts of cyberspace, whether they be Web sites or virtual worlds.

Direct 3D A set of extensions from Microsoft that support the rendering of 3D scenes.

directional sound Sound that can seem to come from certain spots in a virtual space, not just emanating as uniform background sound.

DirectX Microsoft's extensions which support **3D sound,** among other things.

DNS Domain Name System. This is the system that links **domain names** to their respective IP (Internet Protocol) addresses for the Internet. The computers on the Internet know each other according to their IP addresses which are a series of numbers. You know these IP addresses by names like www.mydomain.com. DNS translates back and forth between these names and the numbers needed by the Internet.

domain name A domain name is assigned to a computer on a network as a way for it to be more easily identifiable to people using that network. The **DNS** is the database for the Internet that matches domain names to IP addresses. The domain name is used as part of a URL. When you enter the URL of a site you want to visit in your browser, the browser first makes a request to the DNS to get the proper **IP** address so it can find the computer you are looking for.

Doom A popular 3D shoot-'em-up game of the early 1990s which proved that you could do fast 3D with characters running around dungeon levels.

download The process by which you grab software or other things, like art, music, or Web pages, off the Internet. The opposite of **upload.**

drone Instance of a **shared object** replicating the state and behavior of a **pilot.**

dummytar A default avatar, or the avatar you are given when you first enter a world and before you have had a chance to select one of your own. Dummytars often look like storefront display dummies or crash dummies in automobile safety tests, hence the name. You are often assigned a dummytar when you first enter a new virtual world as a **newbie.**

E

emoticon A symbol created with text characters, like the smiley face :) to express emotion.

emotion or mood wheel or panel An interface which enables you to quickly set your avatar's mood by changing facial expression or body stance.

emotie A text symbol used to express emotion, like an **emoticon.**

entry chimes, doorbell A sound or text message used to announce the arrival of a person's avatar into an area of a virtual world.

entry view The viewpoint you get upon first entering a particular part of a virtual world, especially after just **teleporting.**

examiner mode   A mode allowing you to spin, zoom in on, or otherwise examine an object. Used in VRML browser interfaces.

exit gong   The sound effect or text generated when an avatar leaves an area or world. Related to entry chimes.

F

face/facet   A term for a face on a polygon or other shape in the geometry of a virtual object.

facial expressions   The set repertoire of emotions an avatar model can express.

FAQ, FAQ page   Frequently Asked Questions, usually of a technical or social nature.

farcaster door   Another term for **teleport**, a door that takes you into a new virtual world.

file   A collection of computer data, organized under a name. A file could contain music data just as easily as a software program.

firewall   An Internet security mechanism whereby a piece of software or hardware is checking all the sources and destinations of data packets and blocking those it feels are risky. Firewalls are often used by companies to keep unwanted traffic and visitors off their internal **intranets**.

first-person view   First-person view is your viewpoint as though you were inside your avatar, looking out through its eyes. In this view, you cannot see your avatar's own body. See also **bird's eye view** and **third-person view**.

flames   Seriously nasty, funny, or overtly descriptive messages, usually sent as e-mails or text chat to flood someone's account, related to **spamming**.

flat shading   Shading composed of flat colors with no textures or other surface effects.

flying   Taking your avatar up high above the virtual surface and soaring along; try it!

FTP   File Transfer Protocol, a mechanism to upload and download files over the Internet.

frame, frame rate   A frame is a distinct view of a 3D scene. As you move through a virtual world, you are seeing many frames of that world, creating the illusion in your mind that you are traveling through the world in three dimensions. Frame rate is the speed (in frames per second) that the **rendering** software can generate these distinct views.

friends and family space   A virtual world designed for meetings of friends and family. This space might have pictures, messages, voices, and anything else that represents aspects of your life to the world.

full duplex   Two channels allowing sending and receiving at the same time. In a full duplex voice system, you can be talking and hearing someone else all at once.

G

gateway   A set of servers or programs on servers that control access to files or services.

gender bending   The act of behaving like someone of the other sex. For example, wearing a male avatar when you are a woman is a common form of gender bending used to avoid male **avabuse**.

genetic programs   Small programs which may be based on strings of symbols that behave analogous to genes. These programs may compete in a common soup and reproduce and mutate their basic gene strings over time. Tom Ray's Tierra project is an example of a large-scale experiment in genetic programming. Genetic programming is an important component of **biota** found inside virtual worlds.

gesture   An expression which an avatar can give, using facial or body movement, a sound or text sequence, or special flags or graphics, like a waving hand symbol.

gesture pallet   An interface device allowing you to pick and send gestures out through your avatar. Related to **emotion** or **mood wheel.**

ghost mode, ghosting   A mode in which your avatar is **lurking** near others but not participating in the conversation. Sometimes your are depicted as hidden in a cloud or shown in a lurker list.

GNU gzip   A public form of compression (gzip) offered by the GNU free software foundation, whose members believe all software should be free.

god view   Like **bird's eye view**, seeing your avatar from above.

gravitated surface   A surface for which there is **gravity.**

gravity   The effect of gravity in a virtual world, sometimes created by making a surface sticky, holding your avatar down on it.

ground zero, gz   The default entry point into a virtual world.

group chat   Chat set up between a specific set of named users. This chat is usually private.

H

Habitat   The very first virtual world supporting avatars. Created by Chip Morningstar and F. Randall Farmer in the mid 1980s.

hack   A way found by devious users to get inside software and make it do things the designers did not intend.

handle   A name a user chooses to associate with himself or herself within a text based or visual virtual world. Users often choose fanciful names that hide their real identity. This name is also called an **alias** or **nickname** and can be found on avatar badges. Handle is a term often used in citizens band (CB) or HAM radio.

head banger   Avatars in a virtual world who travel around clubbing the heads of other avatars. This occurs in virtual worlds like Onlive Traveler, where avatars can make body contact.

home page   A particular top level page on the World Wide Web that leads to other related pages underneath it.

homeworld   A virtual world designed to act like a **home page.** This is a world in which you represent your personal or business to the world, and meet people. See also **friends and family space.**

Homo Virtualis   Another name for those of us caught up in communities and life in virtual space.

horizon   Some virtual worlds have a boundary beyond which there seems to be nothing until you approach it, whereupon more of the world streams in. This boundary is often called a horizon and these worlds are using something called proximity-based streaming.

host   A term for a designated person in a virtual world who is hosting an event or serving as an in-world helper. Hosts are also called acolytes.

hot spot   Also called a link, hyperlink, URL, or **anchor.** This is a location in a virtual world that can be clicked and will then bring up a page on the **World Wide Web** or move you to another scene within the world.

HTML   HyperText Markup Language, the language used to create pages on the **World Wide Web.**

HTTP   HyperText Transport Protocol, the way in which data is moved around the **World Wide Web.**

I

ID   Short for identity or identification.

idling   When an avatar is not speaking or doing anything else, it may be idling. The person inhabiting the avatar may be away from their computer temporarily.

ignoring   The act of blocking out communications with someone in a virtual world. This is usually a feature of the interface and is also called **muting.**

immigration number   This is a number issued to a user upon registering to use and enter a virtual world. This is usually used to index the user into the citizen database. There is often a related **citizen number** which is tied more closely to the user's identity.

in-avatar   The position of being inside your avatar. Someone might say "I met you in-avatar."

in-world   Similar to in-avatar, the act of being inside a virtual world: "I met her in-world."

Internet   The global connection of computer networks using a common protocol, **TCP/IP.**

Internet Relay Chat (IRC)   A mechanism to chat in **real time** through the Internet.

intranet   An internal company version of the Internet, usually protected by a **firewall** or other security mechanisms.

IP address   Internet Protocol address is a way to identify a machine or user on the Internet. IP addresses are made up of a series of numbers like 250.123.14.5 which are later assigned to a more human readable address like www.mydomain.com.

J

jacking in   The term from cyberpunk writers for connecting your awareness to a virtual world. In *Snow Crash*, Neal Stephenson's characters jacked in to the Metaverse, a large-scale digital planet and society.

Java   A programming language used ubiquitously across the Internet. Java is used as a kind of glue to tie programs together between clients and servers.

K

kewl   The universal term for ultra hip, extremely neat, or just plain cooool.

kill bot   A bot (automatic agent avatar) that is designed to kill avatars, objects, or processes in a world.

L

landscaper   A program, bot, or user that builds or decorates landscapes inside virtual worlds. Also see **shaper.**

latency   Delays in receiving data through the Internet, from your computer to a server to someone else's computer. Often manifests itself as delays in voice or text chat or very poor swordfighting in gaming worlds.

light source   An artificial light placed into a virtual world to cast light onto a scene. Shadows can also be produced in this way.

LOB   Level of Behavior, where an object in a virtual world can exhibit more or less behavior if you are closer or farther away from it.

LOD   Level of Detail, where more detail is stored and revealed for objects when they are closer to you than farther away. This is an important technique used to cut down on **rendering** times and increase **frame rate.** See also **LOB.**

L-systems   Mathematical formalisms based on the work of Aristide Lindenmayer which enable the generation of lifelike plants and other branching forms and patterns found in nature. L-systems are often used to generate **biota** in virtual worlds.

lurker, lurker list   The act of listening in on conversations but not participating. Also called **ghost mode** for avatars. If you are waiting outside a chat auditorium, you might be in the lurker list.

M

Mac OS   The operating system found on Macintosh computers.

matrix   Author William Gibson's term for a large virtual world in cyberspace.

MB or megabytes   A measure of data storage, the size of a hard disk file, or the amount of memory in your computer, roughly equivalent to one million bytes.

member list   A list of users of a virtual world which you want to keep in touch with or chat privately with. Also called a friends list.

metaverse   Author Neal Stephenson's term for a large virtual world in cyberspace.

MHz or megahertz   A measure of the clock rate of your computer's central processing unit (**CPU**) or of your microphone's gain level.

MIDI   A standard for representing music in a digital form.

models   A general term for any object—from a house to an avatar—in a virtual world.

modem   The piece of hardware you use to communicate with other computers on the Internet.

MPG   Multi Player Game.

motion capture   A method by which motions in real life are captured and used to drive animation, say, of a virtual human or other character. Body suits or batons are often used to digitize motion. Avatar gestures are often produced using motion capture systems, as in the OZ Virtual worlds.

MUD, MUCK, MOO, MUSH, MUQ   Common abbreviations for various flavors of the common MUD (Multi User Domain/Dungeon), a system of text chat and virtual world building created in 1979. There are now hundreds of MUD communities, many set up as role playing games.

multivar   An avatar used by more than one person. Like an avatar with a multiple personality disorder, you can be talking with the avatar and the person on the other end might suddenly change.

multi-user   A technology which supports avatars or some other representation of users in a shared world. Usually this implies that the users can also communicate in the world. Also called mutech or MU.

muting   The same as **ignoring**, the act of choosing to turn off communications with someone.

N

navatar   An avatar which has the ability or duty to take you on a tour through a virtual world.

Nerves   An open effort to provide a simple neural network plug-in and **Java** library to builders of virtual worlds. Nerves is designed to provide a basic "wiring" for avatar cyberspace, allowing you, for example, to turn on the lights in a virtual office space, gesture with your avatar, or grow and tend digital plants.

netiquette   The common term for etiquette on the Internet.

neural networks   Software that replicates the behavior of biological neural networks, carrying symbolic or numeric signals around pathways which sum and split the signals. Neural networks are used in pattern recognition and learning, and lie at the heart of behaviors of agents, bots, biota, and virtual pets. Neural networks are expected to provide a more fundamental "wiring" of virtual cyberspace in the near future (see **Nerves**).

neutroning   A form of **banishment** where, from the misbehaving citizen's perspective, all other avatars disappear and they are left to wander alone in the world. Neutroning was first done on July 13, 1996 in AlphaWorld.

newbie   A popular term for a new user of anything, including an avatar world. Newbies are often seen wearing **dummytars.**

nickname   A name a user chooses to associate himself or herself within a text based or visual virtual world. Users often choose fanciful names that hide their real identity. This name is also called an **alias** or **handle** and can be found on avatar **badges.**

node   A term for some junction or end point in a network. Your computer at home could be seen as a node of the Internet.

O

object   Another generic term for anything in cyberspace, from tables to daemon bots to avatars. Also see **model.**

operating system or OS   The big piece of software that runs your computer and allows other programs to work on the hardware.

P

page   A private message sent between two users in an avatar world. Sometimes called a **telegram.**

Pesce-isms   Terms or phrases attributed to or like those of Mark Pesce, the co-creator of **VRML.**

phone ring   A wake-up call (usually a sound) sent by one user of a virtual world to another. Sometimes goes along with an **instant message** or **page.**

pieces   Often referring to different body parts of avatars: torsos, heads, or arms.

ping   An Internet technique in which a short data burst is sent out to see if another machine on the Internet is able to respond. This term is being used more in social virtual worlds: "ping him to see if he is awake."

pitch   The act of rolling forward and backward; see **yaw** and **roll.**

pix   Short for pictures or images.

pixel   Picture Element, the colored dots that make up anything displayed on computer screens.

placemark   Like a bookmark for favorite Web pages, it is a remembered location in a virtual world. This location can be stored and retrieved for later revisiting.

playbill   A listing of characters who are participating in conversation or play-acting in a particular virtual world area.

plug-in   A piece of software that attaches to a larger program to enhance its capabilities. **VRML** often comes as a plug-in for a Web browser.

polygon   The basic building block of many 3D scenes. Polygons (often built up out of triangles) are fit together, lit, and texture mapped to build up **objects** such as trees and avatars.

polygon count   The number of polygons in a scene. Polygon budget refers to the number of polygons a designer is allowing a scene to have, which among other things, affects **frame rate.**

pop-up menu   A menu of choices that appears when you press the mouse button.

portal   Like a **teleport,** a means to jump a distance in or between worlds.

portal hum   The sound effects sometimes associated with portals or teleporters. The original *Star Trek* transporters had a very memorable portal hum.

port number An Internet mechanism identifying a point of access to read and write data to a server.

postage stamp avatars Avatars made of two-dimensional images pasted together. Commonly used in two-dimensional virtual worlds like the Palace or Virtual Places.

PPP Point-to-Point Protocol, the most common method used for those connecting to the Internet by modem.

production values A Hollywood term denoting the look of a movie or TV show. Great special effects equals high production values. Virtual worlds are often criticized for having low production values (although their users often don't think so).

progress bar A misnomer for progress, it refers to the small slowly moving meter that is displayed while downloading or rendering large objects. Often accompanied by the instructions "please wait."

properties An all encompassing term denoting the capabilities of an object. "That avatar has great props—you can smile, dance, and play the guitar."

protocol A general term meaning the rules or language controlling a dialogue. Protocols are usually necessary only between computers and diplomats.

proximity detection A mechanism to determine closeness or contact between objects in a virtual world. Proximity sensors are used to trigger actions, such as "bump that tree and the apple will fall on your avatar's head."

proxy An Internet term meaning that something is acting as an agent. Proxy servers are agents for servers.

pucking The act of using your mouse to move around in a virtual world. This often involves picking up and putting down your mouse repeatedly, similar to pushing a hockey puck around.

pulse Forcing a piece of software to send or reload data: "Pulse that world again, maybe I will see your changes."

R

real life (RL) People, objects, and places in the real, physical world. One's "day job" real existence.

real-time When things happen with a minimum of delay, you are said to be in a real-time situation. For example, if your chat is sent right away to someone else who can respond right away.

reboot The act of restarting your computer (or your life).

regions Regions are areas of a world which are immediately visible around the user.

reload Forcing software to go and get an object again, like reloading a Web page.

render The process of taking the description of a three-dimensional world and producing it in visual form. Often 3D scenes are rendered a frame at a time.

rendering artifacts Junk left over in a scene by the software that **rendered** it. It is not part of the scene.

Renderware A software package commonly used by developers of 3D virtual worlds to present their worlds and models to the users onscreen.

roll The motion of rolling around your axis; see **pitch** and **yaw**. This could also be understood as leaning sideways.

romance world A virtual world oriented toward singles or other people in search of romance. Often the place of virtual weddings and digital mixers.

robot The term robot was coined by a Czech playwright, Karel Capek, earlier in this century. Playwright Capek's 1923 work was called "R.U.R., Rossum's Universal Robots." Robot derived from rabotai, the Czech word for work. Also see **bot**.

RPG A Role Playing Game in which your character takes on a part in a larger drama. RPG environments are usually improvisational.

Rudie A nickname for a verbally abusive user of a social virtual world.

S

scene A set of **VRML** or other 3D format objects that are fit together to provide a coherent whole, such as a room, building, or forest.

screen left, screen right Similar to theatrical stage instructions like "exit stage left," a way to describe the movements of avatars into and out of a scene. These terms are applied to virtual worlds with **third-person point of view**.

screen shot or screen capture The act of taking a digital capture of what is on the screen or shown in the current window. This is done by pressing the Print Screen button on PCs or by pressing Command-Shift-3 on a Macintosh. This book contains screen shots as do many albums of virtual photojournalists.

script A set of instructions defining or controlling the behavior of an object or avatar in the world.

server A software system coordinating the experience of a virtual world as shown to one or more users through their client programs. Servers also coordinate communications between users, the positions of avatars, and changes to the world.

shadowing The act of stalking someone's avatar without communicating with them. This form of **avabuse** can freak people out.

shaper A program or interface tool that allows you to shape an object in a virtual world. Shapers can also be **bots** which can build to suit.

shared object An object in a scene whose state and behavior are synchronized across multiple clients. With shared objects, one user can make a change and the other users, no matter where they are in the world, will see that change.

single user mode The unfortunate occurrence when a server is not available and you are forced to enter a world offline as the sole inhabitant.

SLIP Another Internet communications protocol, also see **PPP**.

soft disconnect A situation in which you are disconnected from a world's server but the world continues to display on the screen. Often, the avatars stop moving or speaking. In a hard disconnect, you are notified of the problem and often your **client** software shuts down.

spam, spamming The act of flooding people's e-mail boxes with unwanted junk mail or offensive messages.

spoofing, to spoof Using software tricks to make someone else's avatar say things that the owner did not say.

streaming A method wherein parts of a larger virtual world, sound, or video segment, are sent so that you can start experiencing them before the entire file is downloaded.

suspension of disbelief An often used term in virtual worlds which means that you are "so into" your experience with other people on the screen that you stop being aware of all the technology and start believing your are "really there" with them.

T

TCP (TCP/IP) Terminal Control Protocol/Internet Protocol is the fundamental "language" allowing programs to send data on the Internet.

telegram A private message sent between two users in an avatar world. Also called a **page.**

Teleologist Someone who studies evidence of design in nature, or the use of design as an explanation of natural phenomenon.

teleport, teleporting A mechanism, often represented as a gateway or glowing doorway, by which people can move their avatars over a large distance inside a virtual world or jump between different worlds. Also called a **portal, farcaster door,** or **wormhole.**

Telnet An Internet tool used to remotely log into an account from any computer. Used for older text chat sessions and often supports **MUDs** and **MOOs.**

terminal velocity The maximum speed which you can make your avatar move through a virtual world without resorting to **teleportation.**

texture mapping The wrapping of images composed of **pixels** onto a geometric frame, often made out of **polygons.** This technique is used to make plain flat geometric shapes come alive.

third person point of view Third person view is a viewpoint allowing you to see your avatars and others from outside. Related to **bird's eye view.**

threads Lines of conversation between people. Threads are often intermingled in the scrolling text chat windows.

toad, to toad To permanently and totally exile a player from a **MUD.** A very serious action, which can only be done by a MUD wizard; often involves a lot of debate among the other characters first.

township A distinct neighborhood in a virtual world comprised of a larger city. Townships are usually associated with an association of builders and inhabitants.

trademark An infringement of an image or sound's trademark used to create an avatar. Also called **avamarks,** you might hear someone say "look at that *trademark* over there, the Michael Jackson."

transitive behaviors Actions made by one user or object that are expected to affect another user or object such as the ability of a person using an avatar to affect a common environment and be affected by it through text chat, body language, object manipulation.

Turing Test A test devised by Alan Turing in the 1940s as a measure of machine intelligence. In the Turing Test, a human subject would communicate with a computer and other human subject via teletype, not knowing which participants were computers or humans. If the human subject is unable to consistently determine between the human and computer conversants, then the computer (or its software, rather) passes the Turing Test. Text processing programs like Eliza from the 1960s, bots in IRC and MUDs, and virtual worlds in the '80s and '90s come close to passing the Turing Test.

U

UAE The feared Unrecoverable Application Error that occurs in Windows programs often resulting in a **crash.**

unghost To stop **lurking** and join a conversation.

UNIX An operating system commonly used to run **servers** on the Internet.

upload The process of moving data from your computer up to a place on the Internet, opposite from **download.**

URL Uniform Resource Locator, commonly referring to links to Web pages (the famous http://).

V

vending machine A mechanism in a virtual world allowing the purchase of objects or capabilities. These facilities can be manned by vendor bots. Also called vendos or vendroids.

vertex A coordinate joining two or more lines or planes in space.

viewpoint Like **camera position**, a place from which a certain view and lighting of a scene in a world is set.

virtual community A generic term classifying regular group communications through digital media. Virtual communities may form inside text chat rooms or avatar virtual worlds if people share enough common goals to keep coming back and continuing with their conversations or other shared activities.

virtual elevator music Background music of a cheesy nature usually composed in MIDI and sounding like very early synthesizer compositions set to Lawrence Welk.

virtual human Another term for an avatar, but much more broadly defining any representation of the human form in a digital medium. Character animation producing virtual actors for feature films or a digital representation of a human face for language instruction are both types of virtual humans. Virtual humans are often not embodied by real people, as opposed to avatars.

virtual photojournalist A person who enters virtual worlds and takes copious screen shots of avatars in action. Often hired to cover virtual wedding ceremonies.

virtual pets or v-pets Pieces of software that behave like pets. Your avatar could have a faithful dog that would chase you around and search out fire hydrants. These are also called **biots.**

virtual reality The term coined by Jaron Lanier in the 1980s to describe immersive digitally rendered visual experiences. Usually associated with goggles or head mounted displays. Virtual worlds are often called "virtual reality on the Internet," although they don't require the goggles.

virtual university A difficult term to define, it has been used most widely to describe distance education courses through e-mail or Web pages. Avatar virtual worlds are hosting more experimental virtual university projects, where students and instructors meet in the world.

virtual wedding A wedding ceremony held inside a virtual world. Sometimes representing weddings in real life (RL) but often bonding two people together who are not married in real life. A form of advanced cyber-friendship. Some virtual worlds have hundreds of these weddings per months. Related to virtual weddings are **digital mixer** singles events.

virtual world, worlds The generic and shortened form for navigable visual digital environments. These worlds can be inhabited by users represented as **avatars.**

virus A virus in the context of software is a small program that embeds itself into some part of a user's applications or operating system without the user's knowledge or permission. Viruses can make copies of themselves and spread from computer to computer via media like diskettes or by being carried through networks. Viruses are designed by programmers (often called hackers in this context) to cause benign or destructive effects in a large number of computers. Viruses can mutate and escape the detection of the many virus scanner programs designed to fight software viral plagues. Benign forms of viruses are related to biots, biota, agents, and virtual pets.

voice disguising In voice-supported virtual worlds, the ability to change the pitch and other properties of your own spoken voice as to sound different (to make a woman sound like a man, for example).

VRML   Virtual Reality Modeling Language, an animated 3D virtual environment specification developed and supported by a large number of companies and other organizations.

W

Web site   A set of HTML documents housed in a server which can be accessed with the HTTP protocol.

Windows 3.1, Windows 95, Windows NT The most common operating systems for personal computers.

wireframe   A way to view the elements of a 3D scene, showing only the edges, not the **faces, polygons,** or other shapes.

workspace, virtual workspaces   The concept of a shared virtual world being used as a collaborative environment to enable business.

worl   A common nickname for the VRML file extension ".wrl".

wormhole   Another term for **teleport,** a mechanism to take avatars from one place to another within a virtual world.

WWW   The World Wide Web or Web, a giant collection of documents based on the **HTML** language and which are accessed using the **HTTP** protocol. Sometimes mistakenly thought of as the whole Internet.

X

X Windows   A windowing interface system used on **UNIX** operating systems.

Y

yaw   Rotation from side to side. Also see **pitch** and **roll.**

Z

zine   An on-line magazine, usually represented as a Web site. Citizens of virtual worlds create many zines about their favorite worlds.

Emoticons and Social Acronyms (what does LOL mean?)

In this section, I list common emoticons and other social acronyms used in virtual worlds. Acronyms can be used to abbreviate when possible, but messages filled with acronyms can be confusing and annoying to the reader, so don't overuse them.

Emoticons and Emoties

The following tables list some of the common ways in which you can use simple text to express deeper emotions and more flamboyant speech in your daily conversations on the digital street.

Social emoticons (view sideways)

EMOTICON CHARACTERS	WHAT IT MEANS
;-)	Winking
:-)	Happy (smiling)
:-D	Very happy (laughing)
:-]	Silly grin
:-(	Sad
(:-(	Very unhappy
:-C	Shocked
:-0	Shocked even more
:-/	Uncommitted
:-|	No reaction or scowling
@>—>—	A rose, for you
:'-(	Crying
:-}	Wry
>:-(	Grimacing

Basic emoties

EMOTIE	WHAT IT MEANS
<smile>	Smile
<smirk>	Smirk
<grin> or <g>	Grin
<vbg>	Very big grin

Social acronyms

Social Acronyms are shorthand expressions for longer phrases. They are used extensively in text chat worlds, and the list keeps growing every day. The following are some of the more common social acronyms.

General-purpose shorthand

SHORTHAND PHRASE	WHAT IT MEANS
LOL, lol	Laughs out loud (lol = softer laugh)
ROFL	Rolls on floor laughing
IMHO	In my humble opinion
IMNSHO	In my not-so-humble opinion
Grrrrrr	Grrrrrr
BRB	Be right back
AFK	Away from keyboard
k	OK
Av	Avatar
hehehehehehehe	hee hee hee hee hee
WYSIWYG	What you see is what you get! (pronounced wizziwig)
nice 2cu	Nice to see you
RW or RL	Real world or real life
c u	See you
cu 8er	See you later

Flirtatious social acroynms

For more intimate shorthand communication, try the flirtatious social acronyms in the following table:

Flirtatious shorthand

SHORTHAND PHRASE	WHAT IT MEANS
ILY	I love you
LAFS	Love at first sight
LDR	Long distance relationship
LJBF	Let's just be friends
LO	Love (or lust) object
LTR	Long term relationship
MOTOS	Member of the opposite sex
MOTSS	Member of the same sex
NG	Nice guy
PDA	Public demonstration of affection
RI	Romantic interest
SNAG	Sensitive new-age guy
TL&EH	True love and eternal happiness
SO	Significant other
(X)SO	(Ex) significant other

Adding emphasis beyond emoticons

Note: in addition to emoticons, to add emphasis to what you are saying, you could SHOUT IN ALL CAPS or use *Asterisks* and _underscore characters_ to emphasize words or phrases. It is a good idea not to overuse these conventions, however.

Jargon Resources

I have tried to list all the terms I think you will find useful in your journeys through avatar worlds. However, there is a lot more jargon thrown about which will find its way into your on-line life. The following table lists Web sites that are useful resources for jargon you may encounter.

Jargon resources

http://www.bitech.com/jargon/cool
Cool Jargon of the Day site.

http://www.ccil.org/jargon/jargon.html
Jargon File is a great set of resources.

http://www.eps.mcgill.ca/~steeve/tnhd.html
Download the *New Hacker's Dictionary* at this site.

http://www.ccil.org/jargon/jargon_toc.html
The on-line version of the *New Hacker's Dictionary*.

http://www.denken.or.jp/cgi-bin/JARGON
A searchable jargon index.

http://www.huis.hiroshimau.ac.jp/Computer/Jargon/Jargon.html
A jargon file mirror in Japan.

http://www.cnam.fr/Jargon/
The European Jargon File searchable indeces.

http://www.wins.uva.nl/~mes/jargon/
The European Jargon File searchable indeces.

Appendix A

Projects, Groups, Events, Philosophers, News, and Predecessors in Avatar Cyberspace

Ⓣhis appendix is your guide to what's going on in and around avatar cyberspace. All the projects, groups, and events listed here are open to your participation, so feel free to visit the Web sites and join right in! Find more news, interviews and history on the subject of virtual worlds on the book companion Web site at http://www.digitalspace.com/avatars.

Projects in Avatar Cyberspace

Starbright Pediatric Network and Starbright World
Sherwood Forest Town: A virtual village on the Internet
CyberPhysical events
The VOCE
Avatar Teleport at the Digital Be-In
Connective Intelligence: TheU Virtual University Experiment in Florence, Italy
Mark Pesce's WebEarth
Van Gogh TV's Worlds Within
Avvywood: Avatars and the traditional media

Groups in Avatar Cyberspace

The Contact Consortium
The VRML Consortium
Living Worlds Standards Group
Open Community Standards Group

Events in Avatar Cyberspace

Earth to Avatars and the Annual Avatars Conferences
The Virtual Humans Conference
The annual VRML Symposium
SIGGRAPH
CHI
Cyberconf
Ars Electronica
Doors of Perception

Philosophers of Avatar Cyberspace

An interview with Mark Pesce, the Father of VRML
Some thoughts from De Digital Stad pioneer, Rob van der Haar
Clifford Stoll, an alternative voice
The Author's own writings and projects

Discussion and News about Avatar Cyberspace

The Contact Consortium events, mailing lists and, special interest groups
The VRML mailing list at Wired
VRML Consortium working group lists
The Vworlds-biz mailing list

Predecessors to Avatar Cyberspace

The WELL: Where virtual vommunity all began
SolSys Sim: First MUD for learning and living
De Digitale Stad: Prototypical webworld virtual community
Habitat: The first avatars

Projects in Avatar Cyberspace

Starbright Pediatric Network and Starbright World

In 1995, Worlds Incorporated, Sprint, UB Networks, Tandem, and Intel teamed up with Steven Spielberg's Starbright Foundation to create an avatar virtual world for kids confined to hospitals. The worlds came online at five pediatric hospitals in the United States in late 1995.

The many worlds of Starbright link seriously ill children from their hospital beds into an interactive community and a virtual-reality playspace. Children have requested their own avatars (designed by professional animators at Amblin entertainment). In Starbright, kids can play, explore, and verbally and visually communicate with each other through avatars and voice or live video. Through the avatar virtual world, they can build a community of their peers and offer each other support. It is hoped that Starbright will be

Avatars in Starbright World

effective in reducing the isolation and fear of hospital confinement, reduce dependence on some medications, and extend and improve the quality of the lives of some of these chronically ill children. These children are trapped by their condition within hospital technology. Avatar worlds give them some freedom and hope. Starbright world is an early and a stellar example of the power of avatars for good in the world. See Starbright World at **http://www.starbright.org/projects/world/index.html.**

Sherwood Forest Town: A virtual village on the Internet

Sherwood Forest Community was an experiment in virtual community building and culture in the first constructivist cyberspace environment: AlphaWorld. AlphaWorld is the public cityscape in the Active Worlds environment. Sherwood was built and populated by members of the Contact Consortium, an organization dedicated to studying, promoting, and enriching Internet-based virtual worlds as a new space for human contact and culture. Consortium members include individuals working at home, specialists in industry, researchers from universities, and the staffs of companies and government institutions. Consortium members have years of experience in designing and running MUDs, MOOs, and in computer graphics world building skills which were applied to the Sherwood Forest Community Project.

The purpose of Sherwood was to design a very natural, attractive setting with woodlands, flowers and flowing water and then attract a community of users to build a village community in that space. A unique feature of Active Worlds is that it allows users all over the Internet with nothing more than a Windows PC and a modem connection to navigate and build in a large virtual space while interacting with others.

Using this capability, Sherwood community planners recruited builders from some of the 100,000 registered citizens of AlphaWorld.

Why did we pick the theme of Sherwood Forest? Apart from the attractive fable of Robin Hood (which supplied some imaginative roles), it turns out that the Luddite movement against technology began in the Sherwood Forest region of Britain. We felt that if there was a rebellion against life in this new virtual worlds technology it might as well happen inside a virtual Sherwood Forest!

A meeting in Sherwood Old Town.

Towne charter

Every community needs some sort of charter, constitution, or set of rules, whether formal or informal. Sherwood's charter was designed to support the following goal:

To create a viable community within this new medium of human interaction and to observe how this community is built, and how it can grow and function.

The spirit of our community underlying the charter

- To learn how to work together in a new reality

- To interact with consideration for others

- To cherish individual creative independence while meeting the community needs

- To create a thing of beauty and function worthy of revisiting

- To have a way cool time

Basic community charter rules

Be considerate to others and their land and property as you would wish them to be unto you.

(Ye olde) towne services mandated by the charter

- The towne will provide you with newsworthy communication, administration, zoning, and dispute management

- The towne will maintain your mailboxes and deliver your post to others in the community and beyond

- The towne will water the flowers and keep the grass trimmed

- The townesfolk can give you building instruction

- The towne may condemn unused or misused sites

- The towne will clean up trash and provide recycling of objects and reclamation of land

- The towne will publish a free newspaper: the Sherwood Towne Crier

- The towne will tow illegally parked cars

Sherwood Timeline

Sherwood citizen co-creator and psychotherapist, Steve Lankton, builds Therapies 'R' Us clinic to treat people with addiction to virtual worlds.

When it went online in March of 1996, the Sherwood Forest community experiment was fun and very lively and deemed successful based on the richness of the experience and unexpected spontaneous occurances. Over 60 individuals participated, ranging from 9-year-old children to a professional architect and database designer. The following timeline should give you an idea of the phases and events which characterized this experiment:

August 1995: Consortium invited to enter AlphaWorld beta program.

January 1996: Forest and "ancient aqueduct" boundary defining town wall placed into the world.

February 1996: Web site built; community recruitment begins.

March 24, 1996: First big collaborative build day happens; the talking circle is used to hold an all avatar town meeting. Anthropologist makes first attempt to conduct ethnographic interviews in the town.

May 1996: Second build day fills out incorporated area of town; Therapies R Us clinic is built; a dispute over the style of Bazaar built by teenaged citizens arises. Landscape architect goes to work on site.

June 1996: Prototype virtual university is built in New Town during live exercises by students of Sophia-Antipolis University while at the MediArtech conference in Florence. This event was sponsored by the McLuhan Program of the University of Toronto. Sherwood is avacast between Italy and France and telecast to Italian media. Later that month, the third build day completes Old Town incorporated area and plans are made to build New Town unincorporated areas where freeform building is allowed.

July 13, 1996: A digital singles mixer and summer party gathering is held in Laurel's Herb Farm together with a large real-world party in Boulder Creek, California. The first-ever poetry reading was held in Sherwood Redwood Grove (the first eviction of an AlphaWorld citizen occurred during this event). Over 100 avatars participated in the event over an 11-hour period. Read about the event at: **http://www.ccon.org/events/mixup1.html**.

Late July, 1996: Vandals struck unprotected west side properties outside the town walls. A protracted effort to get the vandalized areas cleared begins. Proof must be provided to the AlphaWorld city managers that this was not a creative act. Call boxes to the AlphaWorld Police Department and Help Patrols are considered for installation at Sherwood for rapid reporting of vandalism and avabuse (verbal harrassment of community members by outsiders).

August 1996: More lots inside the New Town area are assigned and building continues. TheU virtual university, a separate virtual world, is created and a teleport transporter system between TheU and Sherwood is put into place.

Fall 1996: A teleport directly linked to Sherwood is placed at Ground Zero in AlphaWorld. The resulting high traffic encourages vandalism and unplanned seizure of neighbor's land by unknown persons. Areas around Sherwood main gate are filled with teleports to other areas in AlphaWorld. This is likened to the development of low caliber commercial motel zones around Disneyland in the 1950s.

March 1997: Attendees at ACM CHI 97 in Atlanta carry out collaborative building in the New Town area of Sherwood. Sherwood celebrates one year anniversary. Future of the site and the community is debated and a new land manager is sought.

July 1997: Sherwood is awarded an honorable mention by Ars Electronica, and is published in the Ars 1997 conference book.

August 1997: The frontage road at Sherwood main gate is hacked and a booby trap teleporter is installed there, firing citizens' avatars far from the site as soon as they arrive. An application is made to have the booby trap excised.

Sherwood goes on, and a new round of building and land management is planned. A request to make a duplicate of the town is filed with the city powers.

Come visit Sherwood

Find the home of Sherwood Forest Town on the Contact Consortium home page at **http://www.ccon.org/events/sherwood.html**. Visit the Sherwood Forest Community on the Internet by downloading and installing the Active Worlds Browser from **http://www.activeworlds.com**, entering AlphaWorld, and then teleporting to the coordinates: **105.4N 188.8E** (turn around after you land to see the main gate). Note that you can also set up your web browser to teleport directly into various parts of Sherwood by clicking on teleports found throughout the Sherwood Forest Town Web pages.

CyberPhysical events

One of the most powerful and fun uses of avatar worlds is to mix virtual with physical events. Imagine a party where on the walls are projected life-sized avatars you can walk up to and talk or dance with. Imagine a room in your home where you can walk in and be surrounded by virtual landscapes full of people and spaces you can visit. Ray Bradbury wrote a short story in his classic Illustrated Man over forty years ago about just such a room. Star Trek fans are familiar with the Holodeck featured aboard the Enterprise in The Next Generation series. This may become a reality in the Twenty-first Century as avatar virtual worlds leap off the small screens of our computers and surround us, becoming an indispensible tool of communication and community.

The projects I describe below all mix the physical with the virtual, producing their own kind of magic. They all involve projecting avatar realms out to a larger group of people. This kind of thing has been termed avacasting or cyberphysical events.

The VOCE

VOCE 3 World Song January 9 1997   'Hello San Francisco' scene

Avtars in Onlive TravelerVOCE 3 at the Digital Be-In.

Phil Harrington, working with Paul Godwin, Kevin George, and others produced one of the first cyberphysical events called VOCE, which means voice in Italian. Beginning at the 1996 SIGGRAPH conference in New Orleans, and continuing at the Earth to Avatars 1996 conference and the Ninth Annual Digital Be-In in San Francisco in January 1997. Phil Harrington is an Irish singer striving for a spiritual and cultural revolution by getting the world to sing. He teaches a technique of "releasing your voice in order to explore your inner self."

VOCE participants singing into a microphone in a virtual world at Earth to Avatars 1996.

The first incantations of VOCE used Onlive's Traveler to allow groups of VOCE participants to place their voice into a Traveler world where others are there to sing with you. Visit VOCE at **http://www.voce.com/**.

Avatar Teleport at the Digital Be-In and Digital Mixer

The Be-In is an annual event celebrating digital culture. Usually held in the city of San Francisco, it showcases some of the latest in digital pop culture and has featured speakers such as Timothy Leary, R.U. Sirius, and other Bay Area visionaries. As with the third VOCE, the 1997 Be-In also featured an Avatar Teleport. At the Teleport, Be-In partygoers could walk up to workstations and enter virtual worlds where they would find virtual partygoers. This Avatar Teleport was based on several earlier teleports tried in 1996, most notably the July 13, 1996 Digital Mixer which was a large-scale singles party hosted in three virtual worlds by a professional matchmaker (Wendy Sue Noah, then of Match.com). See the Be-In Avatar Teleport at **http://www.be-in.com/9/home/**, and the first-ever Digital Mixer at **http://www.ccon.org/events/mixup1.html**.

Connective Intelligence: TheU Virtual University Experiment in Florence, Italy

In late May of 1996, Derrick de Kerckhove, director of the Marshall McLuhan Program of the University of Toronto hosted another in his series of "Connective Intelligence" events. These were a series of workshops over five days held deep within the Lower Fortress in the heart of the exquisite Italian city of Florence. As a part of the program of MediARTech, Italy's first large web/multimedia show, de Kerckhove used his formidable connections, language and cultural skills to assemble a group of facilitators and students and pull together a remarkable experience for all involved.

The Lower Fortress in Florence, Italy— birthplace of TheU Virtual University project.

I was fortunate enough to participate in this event with Mark Pesce. My job was to host two teams of students, one Italian and one largely French. The goal was to take students on a kind of digital odyssey and bring some of the culture of their region to the world through digital media and the Internet. The Italian team chose Pinnochio, and headed off to the Tuscan village where the author of this fable lived. They modeled Pinnochio and scanned the mosaics of the town square, producing a 3D model into which they could place the wooden boy.

TheU Virtual University student team.

The second team was comprised of undergraduates from the European American University (EAU) at Sophia-Antipolis, near Nice, and a participant from the Netherlands. The vision of this team was to create a virtual university in 3D with avatars which would allow students to obtain "just in time" education. Their vision was that you could walk down 3D corridors and the interests you expressed in your profile would craft learning spaces on the fly. In this university, human and agent avatars would be there to assist in specific learning on topics such as using multimedia tools.

After hours of discussion and sketching, we decided to try and build a test campus and have it ready for a spacebridge demonstration within two days. Using the AlphaWorld environment of Active Worlds, the students constructed a beautiful

Demonstrating TheU on a live Spacebridge between Florence and Nice, France.

glass complex including a greeting area and library full of web-linked 3D terminals. This later came to be called TheU Virtual University and is an ongoing project of the Contact Consortium and these students. Visit TheU Virtual University project at **http://www.ccon.org/theU/index.html**.

On the day of the presentation, two large projection systems with sound and video were hooked up so that the audience in Florence, and in an auditorium at the EAU in Nice, could watch the demonstration of the virtual university and the team that built it explaining their vision. We could see the faculty members in France while they could see avatars representing students in both their university and in Florence within the virtual campus.

Later on that same day I presented a demonstration on a huge screen in an old hall in the Fortress where we demonstrated Sherwood Forest and TheU to the Italian press. By prior arrangement, several participants in the Sherwood experiment showed up and even said some words in Italian (through the Master of Ceremonies reading their text) to the audience. All in all this was an exhilarating experience but pointed out the difficulties that lie ahead for the avatar medium: it was difficult to communicate to observers what we were doing, exacerbated by the challenge of a language barrier.

Mark Pesce wrote a fine review of the Florence experience called And a Child Shall Lead Them: Getting an Education in the Virtual University at **http://www5.zdnet.com/ zdwebcat/content/megasource/vrml/pesce/child.html**. Find the home page of the McLuhan program home page at the University of Toronto at **http://www.fis.utoronto.ca/mcluhan/**.

Mark Pesce's WebEarth

Have you ever wanted to see the Earth from space? With WebEarth you can rotate a model of earth with the real current weather superimposed. Conceived and designed by Mark Pesce with help from John Walker and others, WebEarth is a first glimpse of how virtual worlds could be used as a tool for better planetary stewardship. In Mark Pesce's words:

> *"WebEarth builds a VRML model of Gaia (the living Earth) from space. Drawing from composite satellite photos created by John Walker, WebEarth employs a set of server-side scripts which build the model and maintain the current image database. Thanks to Neal Stephenson for the inspiration, ART+COM for proving it could be done, and Lou Stern for asking me if it can update itself automatically (it does, every 60 minutes)."*

Visit WebEarth at **http://tcc.iz.net/we/**.

Van Gogh TV's Worlds Within

Worlds Within was built by Van Gogh TeleVision (VGTV), an Austrian-German joint venture that was established in 1986 as a research and development center for interactive media. For the past ten years VGTV has developed and installed experimental prototypes in order to find out how new interactive media affects the way people communicate and what changes this will cause in our society. When I was living in Europe in the early 1990s, I remember seeing a fascinating project by VGTV: a satellite TV network where people in Scotland could be singing while other people in Italy played the guitar. All of this was fed through the satellite and mixed in real time. VGTV's network was one of the first large scale public shared virtual spaces.

Sometimes the programs would be rather dull, but other times they were magic. The key thing was that they were produced by ordinary people at home. If there is anything that characterizes the power and future of virtual worlds it is this fact: like VGTV, the content is made collectively by thousands of ordinary people, not by a large studio creating something, putting it "in a can" and pushing it out to a mass audience.

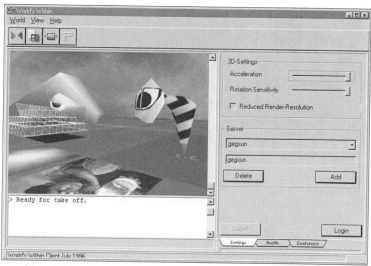

Worlds Within during the 1996 Olympic Arts Festival.

As recognition of their work, VGTV (together with Ponton European Media Art Lab) was invited by the 1996 Olympic Arts Festival to develop and host a virtual world called "Worlds Within" at the Centennial Olympic Games held in Atlanta in July 1996. The preceding figure shows a typical scene inside Worlds Within in July 1996. Other avatars (in this case, a bug) float over 3D scenes. You could build, chat, stream in music, images or video and generally do the avatar thing. Find out more about VGTV and Worlds Within at **http://www.vgtv.com/**.

Avvywood: Avatars and the Traditional Media

It would seem that a major driving factor behind the development of virtual worlds will be Hollywood and traditional media. Of course, decades of immersion in TV and film have provided most of humanity an escape into a sort of virtual world. Recently, there have been some attempts to combine television and virtual worlds, as we will see in The Mirror project below.

Case Study in Inhabited TV: The Mirror

This project was called The Mirror—reflections on Inhabited TV, and was a joint effort by British Telecom, working with Sony Corporation (they used Sony's Community Place Browser), Illuminations, and the British Broadcasting Corporation. This was perhaps the very first time that a prime time TV series was

The 1996 world cup final as experienced in the Memory world.

mirrored with live experiences in a virtual world. The figure below shows a scene from the Memory world, where viewers donned avatars to view and share commentary on the 1996 World Cup (of soccer) final match. The match is being beamed an image at a time onto a screen inside the virtual world.

The BT team that put this project together shares a vision I have had for years, that of making our favorite films, books, and TV media inhabitable. In fact, the Contact Consortium, an organization I co-founded, was formed back in early 1995 in a conversation with science fiction writer Larry Niven. After talking with Larry for some time about the possibilities of virtual worlds, he turned to me and said "you mean I could go into a virtual version of one of the worlds from my novels, like Ringworld, completely incognito and talk to fans who are role playing there?" He was fascinated by this possibility. We were excited by the prospects of the combination of text-based MUD communities and great 3D virtual worlds with avatars. We didn't have to wait long, as Worlds Chat came on-line the following month and launched us all into the era of avatar cyberspace.

This excerpt from a paper by Graham Walker will give you an idea of the grander vision for inhabited media. Find the full paper at **http://vb.labs.bt.com/msss/IBTE_Mirror/index.htm**.

"Imagine combining the proven pulling power of professional broadcast television with the enduring appeal of audience chat and participation, and you have a vision of 'Inhabited TV.' The producer defines a sophisticated audio-visual framework, but it is the audience interaction and participation which brings it to life. Professional content mixes with social conversation in a rich graphical environment. A community develops around celebrity characters, staged events and unscripted encounters.

The Mirror was an early experiment in Inhabited TV, which involved 2,000 viewers of the BBC2 multimedia magazine series 'The Net.' A research project created by BT, the BBC, Sony Corporation, and Illuminations, The Mirror comprised six multi-user on-line worlds which reflected the broadcast material. The worlds were launched on January 13 with the broadcast of the first program, and closed after seven weeks with an 'End of the World' party. In this paper we expand on the background to the Inhabited TV vision and discuss some of the experiences, data, and anecdotes from The Mirror."

You can find excellent papers and statistical documentation detailing how the Mirror experiment turned out by visiting the site put together by Tim Regan, Graham Walker, Charanjit Sidhu, Jason Morphett, Marco Fauth, Paul Rea, and others at **http://vb.labs.bt.com/SharedSpaces/**. See the actual Mirror home page that was used by the public during the experiment at **http://vb.labs.bt.com/msss/the_mirror/index.html**.

Groups in Avatar Cyberspace

The Contact Consortium

The Contact Consortium is a forum for contact, culture, and community in digital space. The Consortium was formed in early 1995 by me with an anthropologist, Jim Funaro, and a media executive and science fiction writer, Keith Ferrell. The Consortium is focused on the human experience in visual virtual environments. The Consortium hosts many events and an annual conference called Earth to Avatars. Consortium Special Interest Groups (SIGs) have been formed for topics as varied as virtual architecture, women entering avatar virtual environments (WEAVE), digital biota, psychology of avatar virtual worlds, and the anthropology of virtual communities. The Consortium has engaged in other large-scale projects in avatar virtual worlds including Sherwood Forest Town (described in the chapter on AlphaWorld and earlier in this appendix) and TheU Virtual University (described more in the section "Connective Intelligence: TheU Virtual University Experiment in Florence, Italy," earlier in this appendix).

Visit the Contact Consortium at: **http://www.ccon.org**. Consortium membership is open to companies, universities, individuals, and there is even a category for students.

VRML Consortium

The VRML Consortium is a newly formed non-profit organization designed to make VRML into a key infrastructure of the Internet. The VRML Consortium replaces the VAG (VRML Architecture Group) and features over 40 member companies and several dozen working groups. The VRML Consortium is the source for VRML, visit it at **http://www.vrml.org**.

Living Worlds Standards Group

Living Worlds is a complementary standards project to Universal Avatars. Living Worlds focuses on what is communicated between avatars and the world (or between users in-avatar). They feel that defining a standard "protocol" or language will enable richer and more compatible worlds while not restricting all the ways that avatars will be implemented. For example, Living Worlds would define a set of objects to describe gesture (e.g., wave, bow, angry hand movement) and then let each maker of an avatar world implement their own designs for these gestures. If Living Worlds is widely adopted, I could wave to you from my virtual world and you could shout back "come over" from yours.

In their own words:

> "The charter of the LW group is to distill their experience with avatar-based interaction in VRML 1.0 into a proposed standard for distributed object interaction in VRML 2.0. In its startup phase, work has concentrated on three questions:
>
> 1. What new conceptual components (if any) will a distributed VRML architecture require?
>
> 2. Between which components are standard interfaces needed?
>
> 3. How can we achieve an optimal mix of standardization (to ensure interoperability) and openness (to leave room for innovation)?"

Visit Living Worlds at **http://www.livingworlds.com/**.

Open Community Standards Group

Open Community is a proposed open standard for avatar virtual worlds consisting of extensions to Java and VRML 2.0, and is designed to integrate with the Universal Avatars and Living Worlds specifications. The proposal is a combined effort of MERL (Mitsubishi Electric Research Lab) and members of the Universal Avatars development team. It is based on the Spline (Scalable Platform for Large Interactive Networked Environments) software architecture developed by MERL.

Open Community worlds will allow users to make changes to their environment while it is running (just like what is possible in AlphaWorld now). Open Community will be infinitely extensible as it will allow changes to the world to be made through a Java programming interface.

Visit Open Community at **http://atlantic.merl.com/opencom/**.

Events in Avatar Cyberspace

Can't get enough of the virtual worlds medium? Want to meet the people who created it and continue to build it? Then come to a physical gathering and meet your community! There are many of these events throughout the year. Chances are your favorite virtual world has its own form of local citizen's gatherings. Users of WorldsAway, Virtual Places, Deuxieme Monde, and Black Sun Passport have held regular real-world get togethers. Check your favorite worlds' home pages for news of these events. If you have the time and budget, you might want to consider some of the following international conferences. I am lucky enough to be able to go to most of them every year and I hope to see you there some time!

Earth to Avatars and the Annual Avatars Conferences

Earth to Avatars, held in October of 1996 in San Francisco, was the first conference about avatars. Visionary speeches, demonstrations, panels and parties brought the avatar community together for the first time. Many of the avatar standards efforts, such as Universal Avatars and Living Worlds (described in this appendix) were first fully presented at Earth to Avatars. There were even avatar cyberspace constitution talks (does someone have the right to take and wear your avatar?). For a review of Earth to Avatars, take a look at: **http://www.ccon.org/events/conf96.html**.

Mark Meadows presenting at Earth to Avatars 1996 with digital street in the background.

If you really get hooked on avatar living, you might consider coming in person to another annual Avatars conference such as Avatars 97 or Avatars 98. You will meet me there as I created this conference and will be around helping organize it for some more years! See the Contact Consortium home page at **http://www.ccon.org** for this and other avatar events throughout the year.

The Virtual Humans Conference

The world's first conference focusing exclusively on virtual humans in virtual reality worlds was organized by VR News and held in Southern California in June of 1996. Humanoid technologies, or virtual humans, are digital representations of the human form used in military, industrial, and medical training and are increasingly appearing in motion pictures as both stars and digital extras. While not strictly avatars, virtual humans represent an important crossover to industrial applications and character animation. See the 1997 Virtual Humans Conference at **http://www.vrnews.com/vh2.html**.

The Annual VRML Symposia

The VRML community comes together once per year to help move VRML forward as a standard for representing 3D cyberspace. This event is sponsored by the VRML Consortium, its members, and working groups. Papers, courses, demos, speeches, a super demo SIG (special interest group showing cool VRML demos), and great late-night conversations highlight this event. For details on any upcoming VRML symposium (usually held in late February), see the VRML Consortium's home page at **http://www.vrml.org**.

SIGGRAPH

This is a large annual conference for computer graphics professionals sponsored by the Association for Computing Machinery. Tens of thousands of people crowd the large exhibit hall to see the latest FX (special effects) wizardry. Courses, panels, and papers from some of the finest minds in the business make this one event not to miss. See **http://www.siggraph.org** for details about SIGGRAPH.

CHI

Another special interest group of the ACM, CHI focuses its conference on computer human interface. Smaller than SIGGRAPH, this conference concentrates on user interface, agents, devices, and on virtual communities and distance learning. See **http://www.acm.org/sigchi/** for more about CHI and its local chapters.

Cyberconf

This is an annual gathering of the digerati organized by Sandy Stone of U.T. Austin. Expect the cutting edge at this event, which is officially called the International Conference on Cyberspace and started in the early 1990s, before most of us knew what cyberspace meant. Read about Cyberconf at **http://www.cyberconf.org/**.

Ars Electronica

Ars Electronica is a mainstay event in the arts and technology. Held annually at the Ars Electronica center in Linz, Austria, it is a cultural crossroads for both European and global wired culture. In 1997, Sherwood Forest Town, the Contact Consortium's virtual village in AlphaWorld, won an honorable mention, the first recognition of an Internet avatar virtual environment at Ars. Learn more about Ars at **http://www.aec.at**.

Doors of Perception

The Doors of Perception is a cyber-edge event held in the Netherlands each November. Some of the original concepts for cyberspace were fashioned at this as early as the 1990s. It is hosted by the Netherlands Design Institute, which has its Doors home page at **http://www.design-inst.nl/act.html**.

Philosophers of Avatar Cyberspace

An Interview with Mark Pesce, the Father of VRML

Mark Pesce is an Internet visionary and co-creator of VRML. What started as a vision of 3D information on the Internet has blossomed into the reality of a true cyberspace under his guidance. Mark created WebEarth, which creates a fully-interactive real-time VRML model of the planet from space, viewable on the desktop. He is also the author of several books, including VRML: Browsing and Building Cyberspace. Visit Mark's visionary home page at **http://www.hyperreal.com/~mpesce**. See the full conversation with Mark in the "Interviews" section on the book companion Web site. I asked Mark what motivated him to bring VRML to the world. His response follows:

> *"I am a radical ecologist. As I say on the first page of my book, Cyberspace is the preeminent environment for planetary management, it is the way that our children will tend the planet, because it gives them a reach that we did not have for our parents. I can stop you from polluting if I can see you doing it in Cyberspace, dammit! Which our parents could not do. PCBs get dumped into the environment because we cannot watch. This is interesting because on one side this is the panoptic mechanism of Jeremy Bentham which is a mechanism of totalitarianism. On the other side it is also a mechanism for tending. Our job lies in finding the balance."*

Some thoughts from De Digital Stad pioneer, Rob van der Haar

Rob van der Haar is an Interaction Designer from the Netherlands. After being involved in many pioneering virtual community projects, he was part of the team that redesigned and implemented the Web interface of de Digitale Stad (the Digital City of Amsterdam), one of the first and most successful visual virtual communities (see our section on it in this appendix). When I met him he was working on the Electronic Communities project of Philips Research in England. His full interview is featured in the "Interviews" section on the book companion Web site. What follows are his final thoughts.

> *"What I sometimes want to happen is that we get rid of all this technology and just live more in the real world. The other theory I have is from the War of the Worlds, where aliens come to this earth and their technology is so advanced that they don't have their bodies anymore; they just are this brain inside a machine. If these things continue, that might actually happen. We won't need our physical space anymore and will just end up as a brain inside a machine."*

Clifford Stoll, an alternative voice

Clifford Stoll is an Astronomer and award winning author of such books as Cuckoo's Egg and Silicon Snake Oil. Clifford questions all of us as to why we forsake our real, vital communities of place for an escape into the virtual. In an early interview for the book on August 13, 1996, Clifford paints a picture we should all consider before stepping into digital space:

"Avataring in a virtual world is a wonderfully addictive drug. I logged in for an hour once a few months ago and it was fun. But ask yourself, is it a substitute for a real community? Many people say it augments reality. I feel that for the people who invest so many hours online building avatars it becomes their reality. You only have a finite number of hours in a day, you can spend them watching TV for four hours, doing email or avataring or you could spend them with friends. There is an opportunity cost to everything you do and the net has a very high opportunity cost. Perhaps the net can convince you that you are doing something when you are not. Will we all be wandering around our communities with big, glassy eyes, not meeting each other?"

The author's own writings and projects

You've heard enough from me in this book, so I won't include much here except a few web links. Most of my philosophy on the topic of avatar cyberspace is contained in the Preface, Introduction, and Digi's Diary sections found in most chapters. My current projects, recent essays, and interviews can be all reached through my company home page at **http://www.digitalspace.com/**. If you really want to know about Bruce Damer as a person, and not just as his avatar, check out my own personal home page at **http://www.damer.com**.

Discussion and News about Avatar Cyberspace

You can find great news about avatars and their world on the companion book Web site and at sites all over the Internet. Be sure to check out the following mailing lists and threaded web discussions.

The Contact Consortium events, mailing lists, and special interest groups

The Contact Consortium is described earlier in this appendix. Through its home page **http://www.ccon.org** you can sign up for many special interest groups (SIGs), some of which have their own mailing lists. The Consortium maintains a mailing list for those interested in news and updates about avatars and virtual worlds, including the annual Avatars conference. You can sign up for this by visiting **http://www .ccon.org/conf97/list.html**.

SIGGRAPH threaded discussions on avatars and their worlds

In cooperation with SIGGRAPH, the Consortium is operating threaded Web-based discussions about avatars. To join the discussions, click on the "Join Online Discussion Now" link at **http://www.ccon.org/sig97/index.htm**.

The VRML mailing list at Wired

To get signed up on the most technical mailing list about VRML, nodes and all, send mail to www-vrml-request@vrml.org with text "subscribe" in the body. For instructions, send e-mail to www-vrml-request@vrml.org with text "info" in the message body.

VRML Consortium working group lists

Working groups on the VRML Consortium home page (**http://www.vrml.org**) often have open mailing lists. The VRML Humanoid and the Living Worlds Avatar Standards working groups are ones to watch for.

The Vworlds-biz mailing list

Vworlds-biz is a list that deals with the topic of Virtual Worlds (from text worlds to avatars) as a Business. Discussions on vworlds-biz are not limited to commercial uses; nonprofit and free worlds are also discussed. Detailed technical and philosophical threads are not encouraged. The vworlds-biz homepage and list signup instructions are at Maddog's Studio **http://maddog.com/**. If you have problems you can contact Frank Crowell at **frankc@maddog.com**.

Predecessors to Avatar Cyberspace

For a great set of references to where virtual community came from, see Michael Powers' book listed in our Bibliography. I have also included historical material in "An Advanced Course at Avatar University" on the companion Web site for this book.

Four examples of key historical virtual communities are covered below, each providing an important foundation stone for the medium we now call avatar cyberspace.

The WELL: Where virtual community began

Back in the late 1980s, the WELL (which stands for Whole Earth 'Lectronic Link) was created in Sausalito California. The WELL was a text based dial-up conferencing system designed for thinking people. Teen BBSs (Bulletin Board Systems) and student UseNet conferences had been going for years, but the WELL was designed to craft and carefully moderate intelligent forums. The WELL went on to go through several transformations and was perhaps the most well documented (if you excuse the pun) and influential virtual community of all time. Books such as Howard Rheingold's The Virtual Community: Homesteading on the Electronic Frontier listed in our Bibliography detail the experience of the WELL. I recommend checking out the Netiquette guide in the "Advanced Course at Avatar University" on the book companion Web site for excellent materials written by community managers at the WELL. You can also check out the WELL on the Web, including a complete community host manual and extensive historical material which can be found at http://www.well.com/.

NAU SolSySim: First MUD for learning and living

Reed Riner, professor of anthropology at Northern Arizona University in Flagstaff, initiated an extraordinary experiment back in the spring of 1990. Reed had been working since 1981 with Jim Funaro and Joel Hagen who are all part of a forward looking group of anthropologists, space scientists, artists, and fiction writers called CONTACT, Cultures of the Imagination. This group sought, among other things, to define a practical role for anthropology in the future. Reed and others initiated a project which would tie students together across multiple campuses in a text-based virtual society. He called it the NAU SolSySim. In the simulation, students conceive, design, and realize by role-playing distinct human communities housed in Martian cities, space colonies, and moon bases in a future Solar System-wide human civilization. Reed goes on to give us more insight into the NAU SolSySim process:

"Thanks to two students in that first year, John P. Jopsy Crane and John Theisen, we started building our model community in the MUD concurrently with the design and organizational activities going on in the classroom. This concurrency has been one of the distinctive features of the experience for all the participating classes. In the fourth year we moved out of Jopsy's DragonMUD, the oldest continuous MUD of its kind in the Net, into our own clone of that program.

The negotiated scenario is another feature unique to NAU SolSySim. It's derived from the two scenario-building Bateson Projects done at the CONTACT IV and VII conferences (named in honor of the great thinker, Gregory Bateson). Negotiation of the events in the time line begins immediately both within each group and among the several groupsÑand gets canonized by members of the plausibility police in a conference session at the CONTACT conference (the first week in March). After this, the students have to live out the consequences implicit in the scenario that they have negotiated among themselves."

A key component of SolSys is that the teams have no substantial knowledge of the others' plans and designs before going live in the MUD. There are also experts on-line acting as plausibility police to make sure the students' actions do not stray into unscientific territory. SolSys teams create virtual economies, political intrigues, conflict, and collaboration. Students become absorbed in SolSys and gain much more than the course credits it offers; they learn from direct, if virtual, experience how to manage human affairs.

More of these "social simulation for learning" environments need to be a part of education in the future. Avatar virtual worlds show great potential in this regard and I hope they can live up to the promise and practice of SolSySim. For more information about this unique experiment in networked learning, see Reed's SolSys page at **http://www.nau.edu/anthro/solsys**. As a footnote, the Contact Consortium and my involvement in the whole avatar cyberspace movement spring directly from CONTACT and its SolSys Sim and Epona world building projects.

De Digitale Stad: The prototypical webworld virtual community

A project called De Digitale Stad (the Digital City in Dutch) was initiated in Amsterdam way back in 1993 and 1994. In that project, which was truly pioneering for its time, people created whole neighborhoods in a graphical interface on computers connected by modems. People even had avatars, and could place those avatars in homes in virtual neighborhoods. In 1995, De Digitale Stad moved to the World Wide Web and can now be found at **http://www.dds.nl/** (note that this site is mostly in Dutch). This project could be considered the first Webworld, a virtual world constructed by its citizens using Web pages. Virtual Places and its Webtown both owe allegiance to De Digitale Stad.

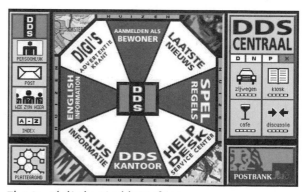

The De Digitale Stad interface.

The preceding figure shows the Web interface to De Digitale Stad as it is today. Entry points to post offices, neighborhoods, town squares, cafes, and all other city services can be accessed here. See our interview with Rob van der Haar, who worked on De Digitale Stad, earlier in this appendix.

Habitat: The first avatars

Typical view of Habitat in action.

Habitat was the very first networked virtual world in which there were people represented as avatars and who were able to communicate and form a 'virtual community'. It started out running on Commodore 64 computers way back in 1985. A typical scene from Habitat can be seen in the adjacent figure.

Rather than me trying to describe the extensive and fascinating history of Habitat, I will let Chip Morningstar and Randy Farmer (the lead creators of Habitat) tell the story. The following was excerpted from the introduction of their The Lessons of LucasFilm's Habitat, first presented at The First Annual International Conference on Cyberspace in 1990 and published in Cyberspace: First Steps listed in our Bibliography. The complete paper can be found online at **http://www.communities.com/company/papers/lessons.html**.

"Lucasfilm's Habitat was created by Lucasfilm Games, a division of LucasArts Entertainment Company, in association with Quantum Computer Services, Inc. It was arguably one of the first attempts to create a very large scale commercial multi-user virtual environment. A far cry from many laboratory research efforts based on sophisticated interface hardware and tens of thousands of dollars per user of dedicated compute power, Habitat is built on top of an ordinary commercial online service and uses an inexpensive — some would say "toy"— home computer to support user interaction. In spite of these somewhat plebeian underpinnings, Habitat is ambitious in its scope. The system we developed can support a population of thousands of users in a single shared Cyberspace. Habitat presents its users with a real-time animated view into an online simulated world in which users can communicate, play games, go on adventures, fall in love, get married, get divorced, start businesses, found religions, wage wars, protest against them, and experiment with self-government.

The Habitat project proved to be a rich source of insights into the nitty-gritty reality of actually implementing a serious, commercially viable Cyberspace environment. Our experiences developing the Habitat system, and managing the virtual world that resulted, offer a number of interesting and important lessons for prospective Cyberspace architects. The purpose of this paper is to discuss some of these lessons. We hope that the next generation of builders of virtual worlds can benefit from our experiences and (especially) from our mistakes.

The essential lesson that we have abstracted from our experiences with Habitat is that a Cyberspace is defined more by the interactions among the actors within it than by the technology with which it is implemented. While we find much of the work presently being done on elaborate interface technologies — DataGloves, head-mounted displays, special-purpose rendering engines, and so on — both exciting and promising, the almost mystical euphoria that currently seems to surround all this hardware is, in our opinion, both excessive and somewhat misplaced. We can't help having a nagging sense that it's all a bit of a distraction from the really pressing issues. At the core of our vision is the idea that Cyberspace is necessarily a multiple-participant environment. It seems to us that the things that are important to the inhabitants of such an environment are the capabilities available to them, the characteristics of the other people they encounter there, and the ways these various participants can affect one another. Beyond a foundation set of communications capabilities, the technology used to present this environment to its participants, while sexy and interesting, is a peripheral concern."

It is important to note that Chip coined the term avatar in 1985 and that the WorldsAway virtual environment described in a chapter earlier in this book is a direct descendant of Habitat, as is Fujitsu's Habitat II.

The original Habitat ran for six years in Japan and the US, but it is no longer online. Plenty of excellent history has been assembled by Farmer, Morningstar, and others at Electric Communities. I recommend checking out the complete Lessons of LucasFilm's Habitat and other links on the Electric Communities White Papers at **http://www.communities.com/company/papers/index.html** including:

- The Habitat Anecdotes by F. Randall Farmer at **http://www.communities.com/company/papers/anecdotes.html**

- Social Dimensions of Habitat Citizenry by F. Randall Farmer at **http://www.communities.com/company/papers/citizenry.html**

- Oracle Layza's Tales as retold by F. Randall Farmer, Tomoko Tsuchiya (AKA "Oracle Layza") collected stories from life in Japan Habitat over the years 1989-1990 at **http://www.communities.com/company/papers/layza.html**

Appendix B
General Questions and Answers

Have some questions? You'll find answers to your general questions in the section, "Q & A for the Non-Techie." If your questions are technical in nature, you might find answers in the section, "Q & A for the Techie."

If you have technical queries about a particular virtual world, your best source is the FAQs (Frequently Asked Questions) for each world on the companion book Web site at **http://www.digitalspace.com/avatars**. Just click on the link for the world you are interested in and the FAQ for that world will display its World Guide pages.

Q & A for the Non-Techie

In this section, I cover the most commonly asked questions about worlds and the answers to those questions.

Runnning worlds

What happens to my world software if my Internet connection is lost?

You might be able to just reconnect and keep working, but chances are you will have to close your virtual world program, get reconnected, and then re-enter your world.

Can I run a world at the same time as my other Internet software?

Yes, I often check e-mail, Web surf, and run a virtual world, all on my one modem connection. Having Windows 95 is a big help for this as it has multitasking, which makes running several things at once easy and safe (one will not crash the other so easily).

Can I run more than one world at the same time?

Yes, I often run a couple of worlds at once. If you run a voice-enabled world like Onlive Traveler, you might find that it takes up almost all of your modem capacity. Text chat worlds are pretty efficient. Sometimes running two worlds with sound can cause conflicts (one of them may have no sound if the other has "grabbed" the sound card resources).

What happens to my avatar, conversation, or building if my world crashes?

If your world software crashes, your avatar may disappear from the world and nobody will be able to talk to you until you log back in. Sometimes avatars are left hanging there (these are sometimes called cadavatars). If you were building in Active Worlds, everything you placed down will be there when you come back.

Troubleshooting

The places I built in a world are gone or look different, what is happening?

If you have been building in an Active Worlds world and have been disconnected from the server (in what is called a soft disconnect), the last few objects you placed down may not be there when you reconnect and visit your site. Sometimes when you re-enter an area, objects may have to be reloaded; wait a while and the familiar scene will return. Other worlds may completely change if you have not logged in for a while. Hosts of worlds are always trying to come up with better designs to keep people coming back.

My world seems to be running very slowly, what can I do?

You may have problems with your Internet connection (you may be connecting at lower speeds than your modem can support), so I would check that first. Other causes of slow worlds may be that you have too many programs going at once. Close the other programs and try your world again. One of the most important factors in how fast a world will run is how much memory your computer has. If you have only 16MB of RAM, say, on a Windows 95 system, I highly recommend upgrading to 32MB of RAMÑit will make a world of difference. One last tip: if you size the window where the world is displayed so it is smaller, you will notice that it displays faster.

My world is displaying, but I cannot move the mouse or get to other applications, what is the solution?

Your system may have crashed. If the mouse freezes, and you are running Windows 95, press the Control, Alt, and Del keys simultaneously (just once) and you will get a list box called Close Program. If you see a program listed which has the phrase "not responding" after it, select that program and press the End Task button. This program may be causing you the problem. If you do not get the Close Program list box, you will have to restart your computer. Press the reset button or turn your computer off and on again.

My world won't start anymore, what could be the problem?

Some files may have become corrupted. I would remove the world from your hard disk (by using an uninstaller, which may have been provided, or by deleting the folder) and then re-installing the original world software. Make sure you make a note of any user name or passwords you might have set up before you delete your world software.

A world I'm using from the CD tells me it is out of date, what should I do?

Your CD may be several months older than the worlds posted on the Internet. Go to the home page of the company that provides the world (see the chapter or link on the CD interface) and look for news about new versions and how to get them.

Are there better ways of doing things?

I am having trouble navigating with the mouse, is there a better way to get around?

Yes, switch to using the cursor keys (arrow keys) on your keyboard. Most worlds support these and they are a much better way to get around.

I am having trouble talking to people in the world with text chat, is there a better way to communicate?

Some users of worlds prefer to run a separate text chat program on the side while seeing their avatars in the world. You could investigate programs like ICQ from Mirabilis, Powwow from Tribal Voice, or Netmeeting from Microsoft.

How do I keep current on the people and events in worlds?

I met someone in a world but I can't find them again, what can I do?

This is a common problem. I would ask other people if they know that person, and try to leave a message or add them to your friends list, if the world supports that. If they are in your friends list, as soon as they enter the world, you will be notified. You might also try posting messages to newsgroups or mailing lists supported by the makers of the world or by users.

I am always being attacked by someone in a world, what are my options?

Try these steps in order: try to talk them out of it, ask for help from others, run away or log out and come back in as a different nickname, or report them to the makers of the world or community managers.

How do I find out more about current activities in my favorite worlds?

Look at the home page of the company that provides the world or check out the hundreds of links to pages built by citizens of the world. Many of these are listed on the companion Web site for this book. Users often build Web Rings, groups of linked web pages all about the world.

Building your own avatar or world?

How do I submit my own home grown avatar into the world?

Each world has different abilities to take your own custom designed avatars. Check the chapter, "Building Your Own World, Designing Your Own Avatar."

I want to build my own world environment, is this possible?

Same thing as the previous question, it all depends on the world.

How do I take a picture of someone in the world?

That's easy: if you are on a Windows PC, press the Print Screen (sometimes called PrtScr) key to capture the screen. Then you can start a paint program or even word processor and select Edit and then Paste to retrieve the captured screen. If you are on a Macintosh, press Command-Shift-3.

Can I build my own Web site newspaper about my world?

Absolutely, thousands of users have done so. After you build your Web site, contact me through the book companion Web site and I will take a look and possibly link your page in. You can also try to get your page linked to other users' pages or Web Rings or even to the home page of the company providing the world.

As a parent, what issues should I know about?

What are the benefits to my children in using these worlds?

The benefits to your children can be enormous. Through these worlds, they can engage in a great deal of communication with people from all over the world and try their hand at creating their own spaces or associations of users. If your children are interested in gaming, I would steer them away from the "twitch" shoot-'em-up games and into the more sociable and creative adventure of simulation worlds.

What do I have to worry about concerning my kids' activities in these worlds?

First and foremost, I would recommend that you make sure that your children are balanced in the use of this new medium. While avatar play can be a good substitute for passive TV watching, it is not as rich an activity as playing outside with other kids. Second I would keep a watchful eye at the worlds and conversations your children are having. If you or your child are getting uncomfortable using a particular world, avoid problem areas or users or even switch to another world. Virtual worlds are a slice of humanity.

How do I wean my children or myself out of too much life in a virtual world?

Well, this is a tough one. Discipline for your children; self evaluation for you. On the other hand, maybe this is your medium for self expression and creative exploration? Moderation in all things as the (ancient) Greeks used to say.

How will running a world affect my on-line bills?

If you are on a flat monthly rate service (and use of your world is covered by this) you should not incur any extra charges for using a virtual world. You should also check your phone line rates; if you are being billed for calls by the minute by the phone company, this could become expensive. Try to get flat rate service for your phone and on-line service, or exercise caution. You could also run an egg timer or set a time of day when your children can be avatar-ing.

Will running a world give my computer a virus or cause problems with my computer?

In two years of avatar life, no virtual world has terminally crashed my computer (other than freezing the system requiring a reboot) or introduced a virus. This could happen to you, but you are more likely to get a virus through attachments to your e-mail than using a virtual world. When you install and delete virtual worlds, however, they leave behind plenty of files. To solve this problem, you might investigate some programs which clean your hard disk of unused files. Some of these files can hang around and cause problems but I have not had too many problems in my experience.

Questions for the makers of worlds

I am running a computer that does not support a world I want, what do I do?

Chances are the maker of the world either decided not to support your computer or is working on a version for it. Check their home page for the latest information.

I have a problem or suggestion I would like to report to the maker of the world, how do I reach them?

In the chapters on each world, I sometimes list an e-mail address or reporting page on the Web you can use to contact the makers of the world. You can also usually find this by visiting the Web site of the maker of the world. Please don't contact me concerning this, I can't do anything about them and I already get a huge amount of e-mail!

How do I uninstall a virtual world or other software?

Most virtual world programs come with an un-installer program. In Windows 95 you can usually un-install software by clicking on Add/Remove programs in the Control Panel, selecting the Install/Uninstall tab, and then double-clicking on the name of the program you want to remove. You can sometimes remove software by deleting the folder it was installed in, but you must be careful because this may not delete all the files or may delete others you still want. Check everything in a folder before you delete it.

Q&A for Techies

Firewalls and proxies

Firewalls are restrictions to Internet access that are placed by the system administrators for larger networks, often inside companies, schools, or government agencies. If you are using an on-line service or dialing in to an ISP from home, you won't have to worry about firewall issues. If you are trying to use a virtual world from your workplace or school, you might have to worry about firewalls.

How do you know if there is a firewall present? If you run a virtual world but cannot see anyone else there or you can see them but not hear or communicate with them, you may well be behind a firewall. Virtual worlds often need a clear path for TCP and might also be required to receive and send data known as UDP packets traveling on certain ports. Firewalls may block this type of data or restrict the use of certain ports.

One solution to this is to find a way to dial out to an external Internet service provider, bypassing the firewall restriction (if you can obtain permission from your system administrator to do this). Another option is to ask your system administrator to allow access through the firewall for your application. A third option is to set up a proxy server, a kind of agent to handle the communications for your application. Not all virtual worlds support proxy servers, however. All in all, handling firewalls can be a complex process, determining which data, ports, and permissions must be set up. Many companies opt to acquire their own virtual world server and bring it behind their firewall, isolating it from the general Internet, or set up a special outside dial-up account.

Setting up your on-line service to connect directly with the Internet

On-line services like America Online, CompuServe, MSN, or Prodigy can be used as pipelines to the Internet. This means that you can get Internet access for "true" Internet applications like some of the virtual worlds software described in this book using one of these services. This can be a tricky operation and I recommend you contact your on-line service for help. I have provided some notes (for Windows and Macintosh users) which may guide you but they may be out of date by the time you read this. The benefit of getting your on-line service to support "packet communication" from the Internet to your virtual world is that you would not have to sign up for a direct Internet account with an Internet Service Provider and save money by using your existing on-line service.

Windows users

To use a virtual world through an on-line service, that service must support direct Internet access through the 32-bit Winsock, which stands for Windows Sockets. Winsock is a standard interface for Microsoft Windows applications and the Internet. Winsocks allow communication between Web browsers, e-mail clients, IRC clients, or any other Winsock applications and the TCP/IP stackÑthe program that talks to the Internet.

Connecting from America Online (AOL)

1. Make sure you are using America Online (AOL) for Windows version 2.5 or later.

2. Go to keyword "winsock." Follow the instructions. The download takes about a minute. Make sure you back up existing winsock software before you install AOL's version.

3. Sign off AOL, restart Windows, and log on to AOL again. You'll now have TCP/IP access over your normal AOL connection.

4. Wait until the America Online Main Menu appears, and switch to an Internet application running outside AOL, such as a Web browser or a virtual world to test the connection.

5. Note that AOL for Windows 95 users should be able to use the Internet automatically through AOL.

Connecting from CompuServe

1. Click on the Go icon and type "PPP" to get to CompuServe's Internet area.

2. Select Download Net Launcher for Windows; it is a 1.2MB download.

3. Install it and follow the instructions; it will create a new program group that includes the CompuServe Internet Dialer.

4. Click on Dial and you will connect to your normal CompuServe number with TCP/IP access.

5. Once you are connected, run your Web browser or virtual world to test and see if you are getting communications through the Internet.

Connecting from MSN (The Microsoft Network)

1. On the MSN Sign In screen, click on the Settings button.

2. Click the Access Numbers button; a dialogue box will appear.

3. In the Service Type field, select Internet and the Microsoft Network.

4. In the Primary and Backup fields, select full access phone numbers for your area, click Change, and select OK.

5. Click OK in the Connections Settings dialogue to accept the changes.

6. Restart MSN, sign in, and then run your Web browser or virtual world to see if you are getting communications through the Internet.

Prodigy users

Prodigy now offers the Prodigy Internet service, full Prodigy options and real Internet access. I recommend you consider switching to this service.

If after configuring your online service you still get no web pages coming up or communication with the Internet for your virtual world, you may have to look for further instructions through the Online service or join a technical support discussion and ask for help.

Macintosh users

Many of the on-line services for the Macintosh do not support this kind of "pass through" Internet access. Check your on-line services for help in this area as this may have changed. CompuServe users on the Macintosh can set this up. They should select Go and then PPP and select and read the Macintosh Internet Connection which will help you set up CompuServe for general Internet access.

Downloading and installing a Zip program

If you are running a Windows PC, you will find that many programs and other resources on the Internet are compressed using the popular ZIP format. This makes them much smaller to download. You can get free programs to uncompress these files once they are on your hard disk. I recommend WinZip (download an evaluation version from **http://www.winzip.com/**) or PKUNZIP (download from **http://www.pkware.com/**, the two leaders in handling ZIP files.

Downloading and installing Win32S

Win32S is a 32-bit subsystem for Windows 3.1 or 3.11 users and is required by many virtual worlds running on that platform. You can get Win32S by visiting Microsoft's home page at **http://www.microsoft.com/**.

If virtual worlds "take over" your file types

Common file types like .wrl (a VRML file) can be "taken over" by virtual worlds software or any other programs. You might find that when you double-click on a file of type .wrl, for example, a different program will start than the one you would expect. If you want to run your original VRML program, you could still do it by starting that program and loading the file inside the program, or dragging and dropping that file onto the icon for that program on your desktop. If you would like to "take back control" of your file types and what programs get started when you launch files in Windows 95, you should open any folder, select View, then Options and click on the File Types tab. This will bring up a list box you can use to manage which programs get started for each file type.

Changing your screen colors or resolution

Some virtual worlds run in various color modes. This can be confusing, but it is easy to switch screen colors. If you are in Windows 95, Windows 3.1, or the Macintosh, go to your Control Panel and select the icon called Display. This will bring up dialogue boxes to allow you to set settings like the color palette and display area or resolution. You may have to switch between 256 colors and High Color (16 bits per pixel) or True Color (24 or 32 bits per pixel). In the same interface, you can change screen display areas from VGA (640 by 480 pixels) and higher settings like 1024 by 768 pixels. On the Macintosh, these numbers may be different. Once you save these display settings, you may have to reboot your computer for them to take effect.

Index